William J. Fay

William J. Fay

AMERICAN CATHOLIC BIBLICAL SCHOLARSHIP

American Catholic Biblical Scholarship:

A History from the Early Republic to Vatican II

GERALD P. FOGARTY, S.J.

Foreword by Roland E. Murphy, O. Carm.

1817

Harper & Row, Publishers, San Francisco

New York, Cambridge, Philadelphia, St. Louis
London, Singapore, Sydney, Tokyo

Imprimi potest

James A. Devereux, S.J.
Praepos. Prov. Marylandiae

Nihil obstat

Raymond E. Brown, S.S.
Censor deputatus

Joseph A. Fitzmyer, S.J.
Censor deputatus

Imprimatur

Reverend Monsignor Francis A. Lacey
Vicar General, Archdiocese of San Francisco

Library of Congress Cataloging-in-Publication Data

Fogarty, Gerald P.
American Catholic biblical scholarship.

1. Bible—Criticism, interpretation, etc.—United States—History. 2. Catholic Church—United States—Doctrines—History.   I. Title.
BS500.F64   1989   220'.0973   88-45693
ISBN 0-06-062666-6

89 90 91 92 93 HC 10 9 8 7 6 5 4 3 2 1

To
James Hennesey, S.J.
Priest, Mentor, and Friend

Contents

Foreword to the Confessional Perspectives Series

The study of the Bible is shaped by divergent forces. On the one hand, Judaism and Christianity, the communities that understand the Bible as Holy Writ, find warrants within the Bible for study and reflection. The oft-cited instruction from Moses to Joshua recalls this tradition. "This book of the law shall not depart out of your mouth, but you shall meditate on it day and night, that you may be careful to do according to all that is written in it; for then you shall make your way prosperous, and then you shall have good success" (Joshua 1:8, RSV).

On the other hand, these communities that hold the Bible as authoritative were challenged from outside. The Bible records earlier challenges from foreigners and "pagans" confronting those inside the faith. Questions raised for the communities of faith, whether as recorded in the Bible or as presented later, have led them to search out their traditions and the scriptures. Outsiders not only questioned the bearers of "the book" but began to create their own relationship with the Bible. Individuals during the Enlightenment used the Bible to illustrate what *not* to do and believe. Critical biblical scholarship from the early nineteenth century to the present day has been understood as both friend and foe of the communities of faith.

The Society of Biblical Literature (SBL) commissioned this *Confessional Perspectives* series in order to examine the Bible within diverse religious communities. This particular volume on Roman Catholic scholarship has been supervised and edited jointly with the Catholic Biblical Association of America (CBA). Both the SBL and CBA take pride in having cooperated to bring this volume to readers. This book symbolizes the cooperation found among scholarly organizations, who find the interpretation of the Bible central to their mission. This series gives careful attention to the benefits and tensions between confessional perspectives and the outsiders' views. The studies highlight the perplexing dilemmas encountered when an object, the Bible, common to diverse groups, yields such an array of responses.

The religious and intellectual life of North America forms the background for these volumes. This social-geographical focus stems from the SBL's interest in coming to terms with the Bible in the region where the society began in 1880. The interest is not grounded in chauvinism or imperialism but in a spirit of discovery. Although it might seem surprising, very few studies on American biblical scholarship or the role of the Bible in the North America setting have emerged. The centenary celebrations of the society are yielding diverse publication series on every aspect of the Bible in North America: *Biblical Scholarship in North America, The Bible in American Culture, The Bible and Its Modern Interpreters* (all published by the Society of Biblical Literature and available through Scholars Press) and this series on *Confessional Perspectives*.

Although the Bible emerged from a world distant in time and ethos, it has no rival as a founding document that shapes life in North America. The religious communities that brought it to this shore could not have known the enormous impact it would have on them or their institutions, thought, customs, and practices. The confluence of old and new, familiar and strange, sparked creative ideas in the New World.

These books on "the book" in confessional perspective come at an important time. North American biblical scholarship plays an increasingly influential role in the intellectual communities of the world. Not only have the religious communities of the Bible journeyed over the globe, but critical biblical scholarship extends into Japan and other Eastern countries. Religion is discussed in the media and in the private conversations of many. The knowledge that Judaism and Christianity are not the only religions with books saved texts become increasingly familiar even in the West. Buddhism and Hinduism, just to mention two religious traditions, have key texts. Contributions to the understanding of the confessional perspective surrounding one book helps us to understand other religions, our own confessional perspectives, and the impact of a book on a people.

Kent Harold Richards

Foreword

ROLAND E. MURPHY, O. CARM.

It has been often stated that we must learn our history so that we will not repeat the mistakes that have been made in the past. Father Fogarty's history of the scholarly efforts of American Catholics in the field of Sacred Scripture provides all with an opportunity to learn. As the reader will see, this survey is a frank portrayal of the disputes and frictions that arose in the journey of the Catholic biblical movement to maturity.

Fogarty's vast coverage, which begins with John Carroll, enables us to see in better perspective the accomplishments that were eventually achieved in the twentieth century, despite the inauspicious history of the first half of that century. There can be no doubt about the giant step forward that came from the modest meeting of Catholic biblical scholars in 1937, when the Catholic Biblical Association of America (CBA) was founded. The CBA created an indispensable esprit de corps among the professors of Scripture throughout many seminaries and universities in the United States and also Canada. Better training and a growing awareness of the theological significance of the Bible for our times ensured a scholarly turn to the work of the CBA. The calibre of the studies published under its aegis continues to command attention throughout the world. There is no longer the former dependence upon European scholarship (whether Catholic or non-Catholic). Rather, there is a mutual dialogue with all scholars, from any area, who are willing to listen.

In retrospect, the history of the sad incompetence in biblical studies in the first half of this century, chronicled in this work, seems almost incredible now. Although he had in mind the European scene, the words of Karl Rahner capture the situation: "Between the two world wars there was perhaps no major breakthrough toward a truly new and modern theology. But there was a fundamental breakthrough to a more open Catholic and thoroughly Catholic way of thinking, which departed from traditional neoscholasticism but was still part of the Church's patrimony. In the years before World War I we passed through a period of what is called integralism and a still somewhat rigid neoscholasticism. But if you look at the period after World War I . . . then you see already a completely different atmosphere in thought. No longer were people afraid to be censored by Rome at any moment. This then developed into a particular, new theology."[1]

In the United States this development was perhaps a generation later, for it was a neoscholastic mind-set that created most of the objections to the development of Catholic biblical scholarship in the 1950s. Even now in certain quarters there remains the difficulty of a very narrow theological perspective on theological development, an inability to countenance theological pluriformity. In the light of current difficulties, it seems clear that biblical study is no longer the delicate area it once was.

Father Fogarty has noted the stress and strain that arose concerning the popularization of biblical scholarship, and the issue of launching a periodical destined for the laity. One may gratefully acknowledge that this is a dead issue now. Why? Because the best popularizers have come from the scholars who remain on top of their material. The familiar "summer Bible institutes" had their origins in the need for scholars to defend the modern historical-critical approach (already urged in the *Divino Afflante Spiritu* of 1943). They succeeded not only in this, but in generating an intense interest in biblical study. A characteristic sign of this is the difference in topics and levels of sophistication between the first institutes and those currently in vogue. A biblically literate public has been created, and their appetite has increased.

With his characteristic acumen and ability to interpret history, Father Fogarty has catalogued a development in biblical study that is truly astonishing in its rapidity and solidity. All the warts appear, but the modest, even impoverished, beginnings have led to accomplishments that all can enjoy in this ecumenical age. We need only to learn from our history.

Preface

Over the past few years, several people have asked me why I was writing a book on American Catholic biblical scholarship. They queried whether, in fact, Catholic biblical scholarship had any history. I hope that this book helps answer some of those questions.

Sacred Scripture is of course central to all Christian traditions. But for the Roman Catholic, American or otherwise, it is a book or set of writings within the Church. To understand the development of biblical scholarship, therefore, is also to understand the development of theology and the relationship between the findings of scholarship and the authority of the magisterium. This study focuses on American Catholic biblical scholarship, but that cannot be isolated from other areas of theology or from other developments within the universal Catholic Church.

In the nineteenth century, biblical scholarship became problematic for the Christian community in general and the Catholic Church in particular. The emergence of history as a discipline of its own and of historical criticism of the Bible was a challenge to the accepted Catholic theology. The historical critics, investigating the sacred text according to their new methods, seemed to jeopardize the uniqueness of the text as the inspired word of God. In the minds of many Catholic theologians, the new method was simply another form of rationalism, which held that reason alone enabled human nature to attain its end. Moreover, rationalism was not merely a philosophical system. It found expression in the nineteenth-century liberal state that sought to limit the functions of the Church. In the Church's conflict with rationalism, it upheld the absolute need for grace and denigrated nature alone. It, therefore, condemned Americanism. Americanism began as a movement in the United States with certain churchmen who argued for the advantage to the Church of the American separation of Church and State, who praised religious liberty as an inalienable right, and who used nontechnical theological language to speak of natural virtues. Exported to Europe, Americanism seemed to be yet another example of rationalism.

Most historians have argued that Americanism and Modernism were two totally distinct movements. Yet, there was a close link if one looks at the theological reaction to each movement. Many Americanists in the United States were sympathetic to the biblical movement. Several European biblical scholars saw a relation between their field and Americanism. The opponents to each movement, furthermore, were frequently the same people. The Church had condemned Americanism in 1899. In 1907, it condemned Modernism with the result that some of the leading Catholic exegetes were silenced. The condemnation had perhaps more effect in the United States than in Europe, for American Catholic biblical scholarship was not only in its infancy but it was also largely derivative from Europe. At the Catholic University of America, Father Henry Poels, a Dutchman, was forced to resign. At St. Joseph's Seminary for the Archdiocese of New York, Father Francis Gigot, S.S., a Frenchman, first withdrew from the Sulpicians and then ceased to write altogether on biblical criticism. The openness to new scholarly methods—often bordering on naïvete—that characterized the bishops who founded the Catholic University in 1889 gave way to a closed-mindedness where a particular kind of dogmatic theology reigned supreme.

Only when the Church was freed from its battle with rationalism and from some of the Church vs. State conflicts of the nineteenth and early twentieth centuries could it then reconsider its opposition to biblical criticism. The turning point in its odyssey toward Vatican II was Pius XII's encyclical *Divino Afflante Spiritu* in 1943. But another decade would pass before American Catholic scholars began to absorb the new thrust in Catholic biblical scholarship. Even then, however, they would face charges of Modernism— charges that were laid to rest only with Vatican II's constitution on divine revelation, *Dei Verbum,* a document that must be seen in light of the council's declaration on religious liberty.

In preparing my manuscript for publication, I have profited from the wisdom and criticism of several people. For reading the entire manuscript, I am exceedingly grateful to Raymond E. Brown, S.S., Auburn Distinguished Professor of Biblical Studies at

Union Theological Seminary, Joseph A. Fitzmyer, S.J., professor emeritus of Biblical Studies at the Catholic University of America, James Hennesey, S.J., former professor of theology at Boston College, and Roland E. Murphy, O.Carm., G. W. Ivey Professor Emeritus of Old Testament at the Duke University Divinity School. For reading and commenting on the last five chapters, I want to thank the Most Reverend John F. Whealon, Archbishop of Hartford, the Reverend Monsignor Myles Bourke, pastor of Corpus Christi Church in New York, and David Stanley, S.J. and Roderick MacKenzie, S.J., of Regis College in Toronto. While I tried to incorporate all their suggestions into the final version, I alone am responsible for what is either inelegant or inaccurate.

In the course of my research, I used a number of archives in the United States and Rome. In the process, I established many new friendships and renewed several old ones. Everyone who has had occasion to use the Archives of the Archdiocese of Baltimore knows that Sister Felicitas Powers, R.S.M., recently retired as the archdiocesan archivist, is the historian's ideal. Not only did she welcome me to her well-organized collection, but also kept tabs on my work, so she could send me documents that she subsequently discovered. In nearby Catonsville, Maryland, Father John W. Bowen, S.S., vied with her for hospitality to researchers at his excellent Sulpician Archives. The two of them were frequently as much my research assistants as the custodians of their own collections.

At the Catholic University of America, Dr. Anthony Zito, the archivist, and his assistant, Sister Anne Crowley, S.N.D., were extremely helpful and generous with their time. Also at the Catholic University, Father Joseph Jensen, O.S.B., secretary of the Catholic Biblical Association, opened the files of the association. He and his assistant, Maria A. Nazarczuk, graciously made room for me in their office for several weeks. Father Milton Ballor, C.PP.S., the archivist of the Congregation of the Precious Blood, made special arrangements for me to come to the archives at Carthagena, Ohio, over a weekend. Archbishop Edwin Vincent O'Hara's papers from the archives of the Diocese of Kansas City are on microfilm at the Catholic University of America. On several occasions, however, I needed copies of the original documents in Kansas City. For so expeditiously and willingly obtaining these for me, I am grateful to Father Timothy Dolan, who was then completing his excellent dissertation on O'Hara and who now is the secretary at the apostolic nunciature in Washington. At the Woodstock Theological Center Library, located at Georgetown University, I want to thank Brother Thomas A. Marshall, S.J., the former librarian, and Father Eugene Rooney, S.J., and his assistant, Catherine Briefs, for their excellent service.

At present, the Vatican Archives are available up to the end of the pontificate of Benedict XV in 1922. Many of the documents, however, have not been processed, so I was able to use only the papers of the Apostolic Delegation to the United States. For assisting me in my research in Rome on this and other occasions, I want to express my gratitude to Father Josef Metzler, O.M.I., the prefect of the archives, and the Reverend Monsignor Charles Burns, assistant archivist.

Several people granted me interviews to assist me in understanding the development of biblical scholarship in the United States. The late Bishop John J. Dougherty of Seton Hall University and the Reverend Monsignors Matthew Stapleton and Francis Rossiter, both of the Archdiocese of Boston, provided me with their insights into the association's early years. Archbishop Whealon encouraged me to investigate the significance of Edward Siegman, C.PP.S., his role as editor of the *Catholic Biblical Quarterly,* and his conflict with Archbishop Egidio Vagnozzi, the apostolic delegate to the American hierarchy. As I note in the text, Archbishop Whealon also provided me with his own correspondence with Archbishop Vagnozzi on the biblical question in the 1960s. Father John L. McKenzie set aside several days in the summer of 1983 to provide me with an understanding of the conflicts of the 1950s and 1960s. To all of these and to the late George W. MacRae, S.J., I am exceedingly grateful.

1. The Bible in American Catholic Life from John Carroll to Francis P. Kenrick

In the early years of the American republic, the Catholic community in the United States had neither the numbers nor the resources for undertaking serious scholarship. Its leaders were primarily concerned with the pastoral care of their flock, a task that became all the greater with the immigration of the nineteenth century. Yet, even in the first years after the American Revolution, the tiny American church had to address itself to some of the perennial problems that confronted and continue to confront Catholic biblical scholars: the relationship between the authority of Scripture and of the Church, between Scripture and tradition; the proper interpretation of Scripture; and the means to attain that interpretation. In 1784, John Carroll, recently named superior of the American mission, was compelled to address these problems in response to published charges from Charles Wharton. Like Carroll, Wharton had been a Jesuit until Clement XIV suppressed the order in 1773. Unlike Carroll, however, Wharton had left the Catholic Church to become an Anglican.

To justify his conversion, Wharton published a pamphlet, addressed to his former Catholic congregation in England. He argued against certain Catholic doctrines on the grounds that they were not contained in Scripture. Carroll countered by demanding with what right did Wharton

assume as a principle, that God communicated nothing more to his church, than is contained in his written word? He knows, that we have always asserted, that the *whole* word of God, unwritten, as well as written, is the christian's rule of faith. It was incumbent then on him, before he discarded this rule, to prove either, that no more was revealed, than is written; or that revealed doctrines derive their claim to our belief, not from God's infallible testimony, but from their being reduced to writing. He has not attempted this; and I will venture to say, he would have attempted it in vain, even with the assistance of his Chillingworth. Happy indeed it is for mankind, that no efforts to this purpose can succeed; for if the catholic rule of faith could be proved unsafe, what security have we for the authenticity, the genuineness, the incorruptibility of Scripture itself: How do we know, but by the tradition that is, by the living doctrine of the catholic church, which are the true and genuine gospels? . . . The testimony therefore of the catholic church, certified in the tradition of all ages, is the ground, upon which we and others admit the divine authority of holy writ.[1]

Carroll saw Scripture and tradition closely intertwined. He made this clear in his response to Wharton's charge that Catholics resorted to unwritten tradition. "And, pray, what is the tradition, to which we recur," stated Carroll,

but *the word of God* delivered down to us by the testimony of the fathers, and in the public doctrine of the catholic church: Does not the Chaplain himself receive the *written* word of God from the same testimony and tradition? Why is it less to be depended on in witnessing the unwritten word of God, than in delivering down, and separating the true and genuine books of Scripture from those, which are false or corrupted? He demands with St. Cyprian, *whence we have our tradition?* We answer, from the apostles, from their successors, from the attestation of christians spread throughout the world; and St. Augustin proves our right to assign this origin; because, says he, "what the universal church holds and was not instituted in a council, but was always maintained, is most reasonably concluded to be derived from apostolical institution."[2]

Carroll thus saw tradition as something closer to the living testimony to the meaning of Scripture than a separate content. He would have been at home with the Second Vatican Council's statement that "the apostolic preaching, which is expressed in a special way in the inspired books, was to be preserved in a continuous line of succession until the end of time."[3] Carroll was not, however, an original theologian, but was merely reflecting the theology and apologetics of his age. As his pastoral obligations increased and he was elected the first Bishop of Baltimore in 1789, he did not again turn his pen to trying to explain the relationship between Scripture and tradition. His concern about the Bible was more on a practical level.

Shortly before becoming bishop, Carroll responded to a request from Matthew Carey, a Catholic publisher in Philadelphia, to publish an edition of the Douay Bible. Carroll presumed that Carey intended to publish the "Doway Bible, agreeable to the corrections made in it by the late Bishop [Richard] Challoner [Vicar Apostolic of the London District]. He was particularly anxious to see "it in the hands of our people, instead of those translations, which they purchase in stores & from Booksellers in the Country. . . ." On the other hand, since he was not sanguine about the financial support the Catholic population would give the undertaking, he recommended that Carey publish the Old and New Testaments in separate volumes, so that the people could at least purchase the latter.[4] Carroll promoted subscriptions to Carey's venture "from the altar," but he lamented that the Catholics "in many parts of Maryland . . . have been so long used to receive, as presents from their Clergy, the Religious books, they wanted, that they have no idea of purchasing any."[5] For several months, Carroll continued to encourage Carey to publish the Douay Bible and to lament the poor response to his own requests for subscriptions. In 1790, Carey published the first Catholic Bible in the United States. It was based on Challoner's second edition of the entire Bible issued in 1763–1764. In 1805, he published another version, based this time on the Dublin "fifth edition" of Challoner, slightly revised and published under the auspices of Archbishop John Troy of Dublin.[6]

Carroll focused his interest in Scripture almost entirely on providing a Catholic Bible for his people and protecting them against the Protestant King James or Authorized Version. In 1808, he became the first Archbishop of Baltimore and two years later met with the suffragan bishops of the newly established dioceses. They decreed that "*the Douay* Bible is to be literally followed and copied, whenever any part of the Holy Scripture is inserted in any prayer-book, or book of devotion & no private or other translation is to be made use of in those books."[7] Neither Carroll nor his suffragans displayed any reservations about the Douay Bible itself. For the next century and a half, Challoner's revision of the Douay Bible would be the one in almost exclusive use in the American church. Only in 1941, was it replaced by the Confraternity of Christian Doctrine's revision of the New Testament. This use of the Douay

Bible was directly connected with what Carroll and others thought the Church taught about the use of the Vulgate as the base for vernacular translations.

In 1546, the Council of Trent adopted as its own the list of the canonical books contained in the decree of the Council of Florence in 1442 for reunion with the Jacobites. Trent added to Florence's canon the statement that, "if anyone does not accept all these books in their entirety, with all their parts, as they are being read in the Catholic Church and are contained in the ancient Latin Vulgate edition, as sacred and canonical, and knowingly and deliberately rejects the aforesaid traditions, *anathema sit.*"[8] The council thus definitively accepted as inspired some of those books of the Old Testament found only in the Septuagint, but not in the Hebrew Bible. For Catholics, this ended a thousand-year-old debate on the canon. St. Jerome himself had held that only the books in the Hebrew Bible were to be considered canonical and inspired. During the Reformation, not only Protestant but also many Catholic theologians adhered to the same position.[9]

The Council of Trent also decreed that "the old vulgate edition, which has been proven by its long use of so many centuries in the church, is to be held as authentic in public readings, lectures, preaching, and expositions, and that no one should on any pretext whatsoever dare or presume to reject it." No one, furthermore, was to interpret Scripture in a sense contrary to that taught by the Church and no edition of the Vulgate or sections of it could be published without episcopal approval. Finally, the council called for a definitive edition to be made under Roman supervision.[10] In regard to the Vulgate, Trent was legislating only for the Latin Church. In declaring that version to be "authentic," the council was stating, against the Reformers' charges, that it was free from dogmatic error, not that it did not differ from the Hebrew and Greek versions. In calling for the Vulgate to be used in theological explanations and public readings and preaching, the council said nothing about Scripture in the original languages. Nor did it address the issue of translations into the vernacular for, on that point, the council fathers were divided.[11]

The matter of vernacular translations was left to postconciliar legislation. On March 24, 1564, Pius IV published rules for the newly established *Index librorum prohibitorum.* In these, the pope warned against those vernacular translations that were "indiscriminately circulated" and declared that "in this matter the judgment of the bishop or inquisitor must be sought, who on the advice of the pastor or the confessor may permit the reading of a Bible translated into the vernacular by Catholic authors."[12] Still, the Church had not decreed that vernacular translations were to be made from the Vulgate.

In the English-speaking church, however, vernacular translations from the Vulgate took on doctrinal significance. In 1582, English Catholic exiles in Rheims published a translation of the New Testament from an edition of the Vulgate. In the meantime, in accordance with the decrees of Trent, work proceeded on providing an authoritative edition of the Vulgate. In 1590, an edition of the Vulgate was published under the auspices of Sixtus V (the Sixtine Edition). Filled with errors, it was withdrawn from circulation and, from 1592 to 1598, the Clementine (or Sixto-Clementine) edition replaced it. Although the task of editing an authoritative version of the Vulgate would continue into the twentieth century, it was a translation of the Sixto-Clementine edition of the Old Testament that Catholic exiles published at Douay College between 1606 and 1610.[13] The Douay Bible, as the entire translation became familiarly known, initially had an impact beyond English Catholic circles. The English style of the Rheims New Testament influenced the King James version (1611), translated from the original languages.[14]

The general superiority of the King James Version, particularly in English style, however, gradually led Catholics to become increasingly defensive of their own translation and to misinterpret Trent's legislation as demanding vernacular translations from the Vulgate. Two aspects of Trent's legislation became intertwined—the canonicity of the deuterocanonical books of the Old Testament, not found in the Hebrew Bible, and the authenticity of the Vulgate. In the English-speaking Catholic world, therefore, the Douay Bible took on doctrinal authority, which translations from the Vulgate did not have in other languages. This confusion would last among English-speaking Catholics, with few exceptions, until well into the twentieth century.[15]

Yet, the Douay Bible itself underwent a series of revisions, the most famous of which was that of Challoner. His first revision of the New Testament appeared in 1749 and his fifth in 1772. He published his first revision of the Old Testament in 1750 and his second in 1763.[16] In 1757, while Challoner was still working on his revision, the Congregation of the Index in Rome amended its rules of 1564 pertaining to vernacular translations. The amendment stated that all vernacular translations were to be accompanied "with notes drawn from the holy fathers of the Church, or from learned Catholics."[17] Challoner conformed with this regulation in his subsequent revisions of the Douay Bible, though his version underwent a series of subsequent revisions. It was Challoner's edition with notes to which Carroll referred in encouraging Carey to publish a Bible for American Catholics and which he and his suffragans called to be used by American Catholics.

Within a few years, however, the prescription of the Douay Bible had to be modified as immigration changed the shape of the American church. In addition to various editions of the Douay Bible, there were also American publications of Catholic translations of the Bible in French, Spanish, Portugese, and German.[18] Immigration not only created an ethnically pluralistic American church; it also produced American nativism, which shaped the next Catholic reflection on the Bible and its role in Catholic life. Protestants interpreted the Catholic prohibition of private interpretation of the Bible as a prohibition of private reading of Scripture. They also saw Catholic attempts to allow Catholic children in public schools to read the Douay Bible as an effort to remove the Bible from the schools altogether.[19]

When the bishops assembled for the First Provincial Council of Baltimore in 1829, their legislation on Scripture reflected the increased anti-Catholicism in American society. In their pastoral letter, they warned the laity

against the indiscriminate use of unauthorized versions, for unfortunately many of those which are placed in your reach are extremely erroneous and defective. The Douay translation of the Vulgate of the Old Testament, together with the Remish translation of the New Testament are our best English versions; but as some printers have undertaken in these States, by their own authority, without our sanction, to print and publish editions which have not been submitted to our examination, we cannot hold ourselves responsible for the correctness of such copies.[20]

The council also decreed that the "bishops see to it that, in the future, all editions of the Douay Version of both the New and Old Testament be made as free as possible from error, according to the best exemplar designated by them." After the council, the decrees had to receive the approval of the Congregation of Propaganda, the office of the Roman Curia, which supervised missionary countries. Into the American decree, the congregation inserted a clause taken from the 1757 amendment to Pius IV's 1564 rules for the Index in regard to vernacular translations of the Bible, that all editions of the Douay version were to be accompanied "with notes drawn from the holy fathers of the Church, or from learned Catholics."[21] At this juncture, the bishops were still only concerned with providing their people with an authentic English version of Scripture. Propaganda was also intent that any edition used have scholarly notes, written by Catholics—basically the type of edition that Challoner had made.

There were, however, problems pertaining to the Bible, other than those relating to the Douay version. What was the relationship between Scripture and tradition? Carroll had attempted to answer this question in his response to Wharton. In 1833, at the Second Provincial Council, the bishops gave a more nuanced and provocative answer. In their pastoral letter this time, they wrote: "We know not that it is the word of God, except by the testimony of that cloud of holy witnesses which the Saviour vouchsafed to establish as our guide through this desert over which we journey towards our permanent abode." The bishops avoided using the term "tradition," but argued that there was need for testimony not only for what constituted the word of God but also for its interpretation. Here, they deviated somewhat from Carroll's phrase, "unwritten tradition," and began to reflect on their own concept of the role which bishops played in tradition. As they put it:

Thus the recorded testimony of those ancient and venerable witnesses, who in every nation and every age, proclaimed in the name of the Catholic Church, and with its approbation, the interpretation of the Holy Bible, whether they were assembled in their councils or dispersed over the surface of the Christian world, is an harmonious collection of pure light, which sheds upon the inspired page the mild lustre which renders it pleasing to the eye, grateful to the understanding, and consoling to the heart.[22]

John England, Bishop of Charleston, wrote the pastoral, but he reflected the theology of Francis P. Kenrick. Irish-born, like England, Kenrick was a theologian at the First Provincial Council and then coadjutor Bishop of Philadelphia, and was widely regarded as the leading theologian among the bishops. His *Theologia Dogmatica,* the first edition of which appeared in 1839, reveals the orientation of his thought. He divided his first volume into three treatises: revelation, the Church, and the word of God. In his third treatise, he tried to provide a norm for the rule of faith:

A full and adequate rule of faith within the Christian economy must necessarily be referred to the time of Christ and the Apostles, and then suit the condition of men through all ages: but the Scripture of the New Testament, as a rule of faith, cannot be referred to the age of Christ, nor to the beginning of the apostolic preaching: for it is evident that many years elapsed before anything was consigned to writing. The apostolic writings are not known to have been collected together until the second century; and some were not recognized by some churches for another four centuries.

There were, moreover, various texts and versions of Scripture in use in different churches.[23]

Kenrick's sources for his treatise were the Fathers, Catholic and Protestant writers in England, several nineteenth-century German Catholic theologians, with only a rare reference to St. Thomas Aquinas or other Scholastics. In introducing the notion of "tradition," he strongly recommended that his readers consult Johann Adam Möhler's *Symbolik.* Kenrick wrote:

We have demonstrated that the written word cannot be the basis for a perfect and unique rule of faith; for it needs both a witness and an interpreter. What then is that certain basis which Christ established, in order that men could attain revealed truths? It is, as we have proven, the harmonious preaching of the Apostolic ministry, public and solemn doctrine. Moreover, since inspiration and revelation lay claim not to individuals, nor even to the gathering of the Pastors, but is only a type of assistance, by which they can once for all preserve the faith handed down to the saints, therefore the rule which they follow in the very act of teaching is *tradition,* that is the very doctrine of their predecessors, the very faith of the whole Church, derived all the way from the Apostolic age.[24]

Kenrick was well aware that "tradition" could mean "some sort of vague rumor celebrated in the memory of some people," but, for him, it had a much more active sense. The *"tradition,* which is the rule of our faith," he wrote, "is contained in the greatest part in Scripture, and celebrated back through the ages in the monuments and documents of Christian antiquity, and the custom and public worship of the Christian faithful throughout the world." Not only was much of tradition "contained in the Scriptures, which we know to have been written under the divine outpouring," but, if "the basis of tradition is removed, the whole structure of revelation would seem to fall into ruins" and some would even be led to "impugn the inspiration of Scripture."[25]

In expounding what he meant by inspiration, Kenrick was straightforward and centered primarily on the acceptance of the books as inspired rather than on how inspiration operated on the writer. Trent, he acknowledged, had stated that all the books and all the parts of the Old and New Testaments were to be accepted as holy and canonical, but there was a wide range of Catholic opinions about inspiration, among which he mentioned dictation and the theory that the thoughts were divinely dictated while the choice of words was left to the writers. With debates raging outside the Church on the meaning of inspiration, Kenrick asserted that "with the Church as witness and teacher, Catholics hold the inspiration of Scriptures." Even those who denied the authority of the Church were forced to admit that the "certitude of the inspiration of all the books, can scarcely, or not even scarcely, be found without the authority of the teaching Church; for in Scripture itself, many things occur, which can seem unharmonious, ridiculous, and contradictory, even to him who recognizes in some of its parts the sublime and some form of celestial quality."[26]

Kenrick affirmed the "authority of the Church in testifying to the inspiration of the Scripture." But this affirmation did not detract either from the "internal" arguments the Church drew from Scripture,

that is, the prophecies it contains, the miracles it narrates, the sublimity of things, the marvelous agreement of all the books for the glory of God and the salvation of men, and the obvious harmony in events, at least in the extraordinary ones; or from external arguments, from the consensus of the peoples, not even excluding the very sects that disagree among themselves, from the preservation of the Scriptures, and from other things of this nature: for these all retain their force, but to them is added, nevertheless, the unconquered strength of the Church in its testimony and judgment.[27]

Scripture and the living authority of the Church, then, were inextricably linked to preserve revelation.

Kenrick avoided consideration of any particular theory of inspiration, but he did treat of its extent. In answering the objection that science seemed to deny what was contained in Scripture, he argued:

The Scriptures, by divine counsel, are written down, in order that, learned in what pertains to salvation, we might know the works and benefits of God toward men, and the obligations which we ought to assume. In regard to physical things, the sacred writers used the accepted modes of speaking; somewhat popular phrases, borrowed from the appearance of things, but to which another meaning was connected, were even accustomed to be used by them; wherefore the Copernicans, equally with others, speak of the motion of the sun in familiar speech. It does not matter to inspiration whether they wrote by what reason the world revolves: for God could impel them that they narrate many things for our usefulness, without his teaching them about those things little attaining to salvation. Moreover, no less does it remain certain that they have spoken of the true order of things.[28]

Kenrick, then, anticipated some of the later theories that inspiration did not extend to *obiter dicta* in Scripture. In that regard, he came close to the teaching of the Second Vatican Council that God spoke "through men in human fashion" and that "the exegete must look for that meaning which the sacred writer, in a determined situation and given the circumstances of his time and culture, intended to express and did in fact express, through the medium of a contemporary form."[29] Kenrick, however, did not sufficiently distinguish between inspiration and revelation. But he did assert that Scripture did not always have to be interpreted literally—a theme to which he would address himself in his translation of the Bible.

Tradition, then, became something living, even prior to the writing of Scripture. The norm for the proper interpretation of Scripture was the consensus of the Fathers. There was nothing new in this appeal to the consensus of the Fathers, but the concept shaped Kenrick's approach to the continuing teaching authority in the Church. The Church of the Apostles and of the Fathers continued to be under divine guidance in such a manner that one or even many bishops could fall into error, but "infallibility" or "the privilege of inerrancy" continued to reside "in the body of the bishops, under the presidency of the Roman Pontiff."[30] In short, just as the consensus of the Fathers was the norm for the interpretation of Scripture, the consensus of the bishops, in unity with the pope, was the norm for the teaching of the Church. Kenrick would later make an interesting application of this approach to the acceptance of scientific data.

Kenrick's attitude toward the authenticity of the scriptural books was conservative. He accepted that Moses was the author of the Pentateuch on the basis of Jewish tradition, the testimony of the "author" of the books, and the testimony of writers of other nations. He likewise argued that the books of the New Testament were written by those to whom they were attributed on the grounds of the constant Christian tradition from the apostolic age, the internal notes of authenticity, the host of Christian confessions, and the difficulty of perpetrating fraud. While citing numerous Protestant criticisms, he defended the Catholic use of the Vulgate and of the vernacular translations made from it.[31] His sensitivity to Protestant criticism, much of which he acknowledged as having a point, would lead him to a much more ambitious undertaking in regard to the Bible.

In 1846, *Brownson's Quarterly Review* published a lengthy review essay of two recent translations of the Gospels. The first had appeared in London in 1836 and the translator was simply designated "a Catholic." Later on, it became known that he was John Lingard. The second was a republication of a translation by George Campbell, principal of Marischal College, Aberdeen, Scotland. The reviewer was later identified as Kenrick.[32] He recalled Carroll's meeting with his suffragans and the First Provincial Council's decree on the Douay Bible, but noted that there was no "accurate edition." He argued that vernacular translations were always subject to "improvement, which the changeableness of living languages might render necessary." In Italy, Spain, and France, the vernacular versions had been revised; yet, the "Douay version . . . [seemed to] enjoy a more exclusive authority." He then traced the history of the Vulgate on which the vernacular versions were based up to the Council of Trent's declaring it "authentic." This, he said, made it

an authoritative standard, to which appeal could be safely made in all religious investigations. It was not declared faultless; but, as it had been in general use for more than a thousand years, it was pronounced a faithful guide, on which full reliance might be placed in all that regards faith, and morals, and historic truth.

The reviewer then asserted that Campbell and other recent critics had shown the relative accuracy of the Vulgate in comparison with the Greek text.[33]

If the reviewer was, indeed, Kenrick, he was to undergo a considerable change in attitude toward Lingard's translation. Lingard had rendered *metanoeo* as "repent," rather than the Douay translation "do penance." For the reviewer, "our faith does not depend on the manner in which this term may be translated; but we should hesitate to alter the received version, whilst we know that in its Scriptural application and ecclesiastical [usage] the term implies all that we mean by the words 'do penance.'. ." He was also "startled" that "the writer seems familiar with the German Biblicists, and, although untainted with the impiety of the Rationalistic school, we fear that he may have adopted some views not altogether sound." As an example, he said that "a Catholic" had written that John 20 "looks very like the conclusion of the Gospel, and it is not improbable, that, when the Evangelist wrote it, he intended it as such."[34] The reviewer had, at least, indicated the problems with the Douay Bible, though expressing greater sympathy with Campbell's translation than Lingard's.

Whether Kenrick was the author of the reviews or not, he now undertook the task of making his own revision of the Douay Bible. It was the most ambitious scriptural task in the American church up to that time. From the time of Carroll, Challoner's revision had been simply accepted as normative, and defense of the Douay had become all the more imperative in the face of nativist attacks. From Carroll to Kenrick, the bishops simply accepted that an English translation from the Bible had to be from the Vulgate. They were pastorally concerned with placing an accurate translation in the hands of their people. Yet, in their theological expositions, whether in Carroll's answer to Wharton or in Kenrick's *Theologia Dogmatica,* and in their pastoral letters, they took a stance toward the relationship between Scripture and the Church, which would die out during the rest of the century. Their reliance on the Fathers of the Church, rather than the Scholastics, and their strong sense that the "college of bishops" united with the pope was the locus for the interpretation of Scripture would give way to the revival of Thomism and strong Roman centralization of authority.

There were other developments, however, that occurred even during Carroll's episcopate and that would necessitate a reevaluation of the way in which Christians, in general, and Catholics, in particular, treated the historicity of the Bible. Archeology and geology would revolutionize the approach to the study of Scripture. In 1798, for example, Napoleon's scientific expedition to the Nile Valley discovered the Rosetta Stone. By 1822, it had been deciphered and published. The scholarly world now had a guide to understanding Egyptian hieroglyphics. It was the beginning of a quest to place the Bible within the context of other ancient, Near Eastern languages and cultures.[35] Other discoveries followed. In 1835, Henry C. Rawlinson, an adventurous British official in the Middle East, climbed up to the Rock of Behistun, and made copies and impressions of an inscription written in three languages: Old Persian, Elamite, and Akkadian. He subsequently deciphered the Persian part, which provided the key to the other languages. The cuneiform code had now been broken.[36]

Scientific discoveries in other fields were also beginning to influence the understanding of Scripture. Early in 1806, Anthony Garnier, S.S., former professor at St. Mary's Seminary in Baltimore, wrote Carroll that some German professors were denying the inspiration of the sacred books and were seeking natural explanations for the miracles of Jesus Christ. Geology and history, he continued, were challenging the Mosaic narrative of creation and the deluge.[37]

For the moment, however, American Catholics in the early nineteenth century had taken little, if any, notice of these developments. It was left for Kenrick, a generation later, to attempt to place his revision of the Bible within the larger context of these scientific advances.

2. Kenrick's Translation of the Bible

While the American bishops were intent on providing a Catholic version of the Bible in English for their people, they also acknowledged the limitations of both the original Douay Bible and Challoner's revision. Francis P. Kenrick took upon himself the task of updating the language of the Douay and, initially, of defending the value of the Vulgate against Protestant critics. Originally, he began the revision of Genesis with the assistance of his brother, Peter R. Kenrick, vicar general of Philadelphia before his appointment as coadjutor Bishop of St. Louis. In September, 1843, Francis wrote Peter to chide him for not continuing the work, for, "if, therefore, you are not willing to undertake the work, the faithful will be left without it." By this point, Kenrick was beginning to move away from the conservative stance, expounded in his *Theologia Dogmatica,* and to recognize some of the difficulties in studying Scripture. He had become fascinated with the theory proposed by J. G. Eichhorn (1752–1827), who suggested that Moses had used preexisting writings in composing the Pentateuch.[1] While Eichhorn still held to the Mosaic authorship, he had developed the earlier work of Jean Astruc, a French physician, to distinguish two separate documents in the Pentateuch. In the rapidly progressing field of biblical criticism, Kenrick could not, in retrospect, be considered to be advanced. But Kenrick's sympathy for Eichhorn at this juncture indicated that he was at least open to some of the new developments. His recognition of the problems regarding the composition of the Pentateuch might explain why, though it was the first section he began, he did not publish it until 1860.

Kenrick began his revision while he was Bishop of Philadelphia (1842–1851) and completed it after he became Archbishop of Baltimore (1851–1863). It was paradoxical that, even as he was beginning his work on the Bible, he became embroiled in a dispute about the use of the Bible in public schools. Early in 1843, he had obtained permission from the Philadelphia school board to allow children to read any version of the Bible approved by their parents. Nativists construed this as the bishop's attempt to remove the Bible from the public schools altogether. Tension built up between nativists and Irish immigrants and led to rioting during two periods in 1844, May 6–9 and July 5–7. Two Catholic churches were burned and several people were killed. A grand jury, appointed to investigate the May rioting, reported that it was due to "the efforts of a portion of the community to exclude the Bible from our Public Schools."[2] Kenrick made no allusion to nativism, however, either in his work on the Bible or in his correspondence with his brother Peter—conducted, as befitted two prelates, in very formal Latin.

Kenrick's version appeared in six volumes, published between 1849 and 1860. The first to appear was *The Four Gospels,* translated from the Vulgate, "and diligently compared with the original Greek text." In an introductory letter to the hierarchy, he stated that he was not intending to replace the "received version" and that his "annotations . . . are for the most part selected from the holy Fathers, although occasionally I have availed myself of the researches of modern writers, unhappily estranged from Catholic communion." This irenic tone carried through his prefaces to the various books and his citations of the King James Bible. But his main thrust was to vindicate the Vulgate. He acknowledged the critical work on the Greek text, done by J. J. Griesbach and J. M. Schott [Scholz?] in Germany and George Campbell and S. T. Bloomfield in Britain, but cited them to specify the judgment of John Kitto that "the Vulgate of the New Testament generally agrees with the oldest manuscripts of the Italic, and is one of the best critical helps towards restoring the true text of the Greek." He also acknowledged his indebtedness to the translation from the Greek by John Lingard, an English Catholic priest.[3] In notes, he indicated where the Greek text and the King James translation deviated from the Vulgate.

The Gospels were only the beginning of Kenrick's work, in which he showed his general sympathy with the King James Bible. But, at times, he did reveal his preoccupation with preserving Catholic doctrine. Thus, he found it necessary to add a note to Mt

1:23: "Behold a virgin will be with child and will bring forth a son.
. . ." The note read:

> The Hebrew term strictly means a virgin, one who is concealed in the retirement of her father's house, and is unknown to man. It is only by *catechresis* that it could be applied to a young female after sexual intercourse. The same may be said of the corresponding Greek and Latin terms.[4]

Kenrick's rendering of the verse and his note would continue to bring praise from conservative Catholics as late as 1952.[5]

Kenrick was ambivalent in regard to certain aspects of historical criticism then developing. On the one hand, he made no allusion to the synoptic problem and accepted the authenticity of each of the Gospels. On the other hand, he did alert his readers that some scholars had challenged the authenticity of the last twelve verses of Mark. His choice of words, however, sometimes drew upon himself Catholic criticism. Where the Vulgate of Mt 3:2, had *"poenitentiam agite"*, for example, he translated it as "repent" and added a note that he was trying to bring out the notion of the need for a change of heart, rather than the exercise of the virtue of penance. Such deviation from the accepted language was too much for Ignatius Reynolds, Bishop of Charleston. As Kenrick told his brother, Reynolds found "fault seriously with my new version of the Bible; and in particular blames my use of the expression in some instances 'to repent,' instead of the accepted term, 'to do penance.' " Reynolds urged him to abandon the entire project, but was "not unfavorable to the design for a corrected version, to be made by the cooperation of three Bishops, one in England, one in Ireland, and one in this country." Kenrick would only "marvel at the vehemence" with which Reynolds attacked "the 'Repent' Version."[6] Reynolds had made a relatively minor criticism, but it illustrated the importance with which people would treat any change in the familiar language of an older translation.

Some of the published reviews of Kenrick were somewhat confusing. Nicholas Wiseman, rector of the English College and a specialist in oriental languages, had earlier given a generally favorable review to Lingard's translation, but he expressed harsh criticism of it in his private notes.[7] Shortly before being named Archbishop of Westminster and a cardinal in 1850, Wiseman also reviewed Kenrick's version in the *Dublin Review*. As he had done with Lingard, he placed a succinct review of Kenrick's version within a much longer essay on biblical piety.

Wiseman praised Kenrick for vindicating the Vulgate and for his English style. But Wiseman's tone was far more polemical than Kenrick's. "When we consider the scorn cast by the reformers upon the vulgate," Wiseman wrote, "and their recurrence, in consequence, to the Greek, as the only accurate standard, we cannot but rejoice at the silent triumph which truth has at length gained over clamorous error." With an eye possibly peeled toward Lingard, he noted that Protestants had been among those who vindicated the Vulgate; yet, the educated, including some Catholics, persisted in their prejudice that the Greek text was preferable. "Now Bishop Kenrick," he continued, "has taken the simplest mode of removing it [that prejudice]. He shows, in a few words, that where the Anglican version agrees with the Greek, but differs from the Latin, the best modern Protestant critics give preference to the latter." Where Kenrick had been irenic toward certain Protestant critics, Wiseman's reaction was quite different. The field of Scripture scholarship, said Wiseman,

belongs exclusively to Catholics, and . . . they alone can properly occupy it. After all the boasted researches of the moderns, what has been done? What are the commentaries of Kuinoel, Rosenmüller, Campbell, or Bloomfield? Sapless, heartless, devotionless, merely critical and philological notes, which help one not a step to taste and relish the sweetness of the divine narrative, or to learn its true lessons. There is in them neither breadth of view nor depth of penetration; they walk you over the surface, and, if anything, deaden the perception of those inner and hidden treasures, those rich mines which lie beneath the letter.[8]

Some of Wiseman's "sapless, heartless, devotionless" critics were, of course, the same ones Kenrick had cited favorably. Both men wished to defend the Vulgate, but each would take different approaches and see Protestant scholarship in a different light. Wiseman saw his church besieged by its enemies; Kenrick saw his in relation to others. Wiseman wrote a second essay, which purported to be a continuation of his review of Kenrick's work, but which, in fact, made no mention of it.[9]

Wiseman's faint praise of Kenrick's work may, in fact, have been a veiled warning to the American for his positive assessment of Protestant advances. The differences between the two men and their approaches may explain why, within a few years, Wiseman would not respond to the suggestion of having Kenrick and John Henry Newman collaborate on a joint translation from the Vulgate. Kenrick himself seems to have been confused by "the critique of Wiseman" and asked his brother's opinion.[10]

In the United States, however, Kenrick received favorable reviews. Orestes Brownson, the American philosopher and convert to Catholicism, who was usually sparing in his compliments, commented that "it is, under any point of view, the most important contribution to the branch of Catholic literature to which it pertains, that has recently, or to our knowledge ever, been made in the English language,—although we are bound to add, that this is by no means saying as much as some might imagine." He added: "If the learned doctors and scholars so numerous among us, would each be half as industrious in some department . . . as the learned Bishop of Philadelphia is in the several departments he cultivates, we should soon rise to literary independence, and be able to collect an English library not unadapted to the wants and tastes of a cultivated Catholic family."[11]

Even before he received the reviews of his translation of the Gospels, however, Kenrick was at work on the rest of the New Testament. For the Acts of the Apostles, he acknowledged the assistance of Augustine F. Hewitt, a convert and, later, one of the original Paulists.[12] In 1851, he published *The Acts of the Apostles, the Epistles of St. Paul, the Catholic Epistles, and the Apocalypse.* In his introduction, he noted that, in accordance with some suggestions, "I have adhered more closely to the Rhemish translation" than he had in translating the Gospels. He then proceeded to defend his use of "repent" in his Gospel translations as the more accurate translation of the Greek *metanoeo,* which had been rendered in some Latin editions as *poenitemini.* This, he noted, had been the way in which Lingard translated the word. Similarly, he defended his translation of Jn 2:4 as "Woman, what has thou to do with me?" as preferable to the Rhemish rendition of "What is to Me and to thee?" "Strictly literal," this may have been, but Kenrick found it "scarcely intelligible."[13] It would become characteristic for Kenrick to use the prefaces of later volumes to respond to the critics of previous ones. Moreover, while translating from the Vulgate, he did revert to the Greek, whenever that reading seemed preferable.

He was also aware that the information he provided in notes may have caused some unease:

> The freedom with which I have quoted Protestant and Rationalistic authors may seem scarcely consistent with the Rules of the Index, which require that the annotations should be taken from the fathers, or from Catholic divines. The attentive reader will, however, observe, that in all matters of doctrine and moral instructions I draw from the purest fountains of orthodox faith, and that I avail myself of the testimonies of those who are outside the pale of the Church, only by way of acknowledgment on their part, or in matters purely critical, in which they have brought their stores of erudition and their natural acuteness of mind to the vindication of the sacred text. I have felt the more free to make such references, because in this work I have chiefly had in view the instruction of students in theology; cherishing the hope of being enabled hereafter to publish the whole New Testament in a more popular form for the general edification of the faithful.

While still basically conservative, he also alerted his "students in theology" to some of the critical problems. While defending, for example, the Pauline authorship of Hebrews, he gave all the arguments against it.[14]

In the meantime, the American Catholic church continued to expand. In 1850, new archdioceses were established—in 1846, Peter Kenrick had already become the first Archbishop of St. Louis. In 1851, the same year he published the rest of the New Testament, Francis Kenrick was transferred to the metropolitan see of Baltimore. The next year, he presided, as apostolic delegate, over the First Plenary Council of Baltimore, a national council with all the new archbishops and their suffragan bishops. While the council passed no new legislation about Scripture, it did declare that all the legislation of previous provincial councils, including the statements on Scripture, applied to the entire American church. Despite his increased episcopal responsibilities, Francis Kenrick continued work on his translation. In 1857, he published *The Psalms, Books of Wisdom, and Canticle of Canticles.* Perhaps to assuage the reservations of Wiseman, he dedicated the volume to the cardinal. In presenting the Psalms, he gave the enumeration according to both the Hebrew original and Vulgate translation. But in rendering Ps 22 of the Vulgate, he may have been consciously avoiding the King James Version. Instead of saying "the Lord is my shepherd," he retained the Douay rendition: "the Lord ruleth me." In a note, he added that the Lord ruled "as a shepherd."[15]

In 1858, the bishops of the Province of Baltimore held their ninth Provincial Council, a legislative assembly of the Archbishop of Baltimore and his suffragan bishops. After Kenrick was asked to absent himself, the senior suffragan, Bishop Michael O'Connor of Pittsburgh, presided over a special session. Praising Kenrick's version, the bishops proposed that, once it was completed, it be adopted for common use in the United States. They had heard, however, that the English bishops had entrusted a new translation to John Henry Newman. They, therefore, proposed that Newman and Kenrick collaborate, so that "a single version would be prepared, which could be brought into use in both England and these states." The bishops at the council delegated John McGill of Richmond, Patrick Lynch of Charleston, and Augustine Verot of Florida to seek the English hierarchy's cooperation.[16] Though Reynolds had earlier expressed his reservations about Kenrick's version, the majority of the bishops of the Province of Baltimore now desired that it be the basis for a common version.

The information the Americans had about Newman possibly doing a translation was correct. In 1856, at the second synod of Westminster, the English bishops had decided to entrust him with a new translation from the Vulgate. Cardinal Wiseman waited two years, however, to notify Newman officially, but he made no mention of expenses for the undertaking and merely specified that Newman was to own the copyright. When Newman received Bishop Lynch's notification of the American decision, his reply indicated his ambiguity. Kenrick, he wrote, was "a man so immeasurably superior to me, in station, in services to the Church, in theological knowledge, in reputation, in qualifications for the work, and in careful preparation for it, (who moreover has actually given to the world complete and ready for the use of the faithful, so great a portion of it); but on the other hand I am pledged to the Bishops of England by duty, by gratitude, and by my word."[17] In addition to Newman's hesitancy to abandon the English project, the English bishops never responded to the American request for a joint effort. Though Newman never undertook his own translation, he did have further comments on Kenrick's work, but that was some years in the offing.

Kenrick himself had some reflections on the suggestion of his fellow bishops. The bishops preferred his version to the Douay, he told his brother, and Newman had written him "that he wished to use it as the basis of his own version." He then added the information that, in a recent issue of the *Dublin Review,* there was as essay on English translations, with "no notice of my version."[18] The omission of Kenrick's work may well have been a sign of Wiseman's displeasure.

In 1859, Kenrick published *The Book of Job, and the Prophets.* He noted that he continued "the revision of the Douay version . . . to remove the slight blemishes that originated in an overscrupulous adherence to the letter of the Vulgate, which has not characterized in the same degree the Catholic translators of other nations, although equally deferential to its authority." While seeking "a vindication" of the Vulgate, he noted "the Hebrew manuscripts and ancient versions which support its readings, and . . . pointed to the source of apparent discrepancies. . . ." As with his earlier work, he continued to show awareness of some new biblical criticism, but he also seemed to think it necessary to defend himself. "The closeness with which I press upon the footsteps of [Ernest Frederic] Rosenmüller," he wrote,

and of other learned critics and interpreters not of the Catholic communion, should not startle the devout reader, who naturally expects the guidance of the Fathers of the Church in the exposition of the Sacred Scriptures. Divine Providence has drawn this advantage from the boldness with which some moderns have examined them, that their historical truth has been established, their sublimity admired, and the excellence of their moral standard acknowledged by men not influenced by reverential feelings.[19]

In some ways, this was the weakest of Kenrick's works. Nevertheless, while he accepted Isaiah, for example, as the work of one author, he did note that some critics argued against it. He translated Is 7:14 as "Behold, the virgin shall conceive, and bear a son."

In a note, however, he explained that St. Jerome argued that it referred to "a maiden as yet retired in her father's house, and unknown to man," but he added the information that Wilhelm Gesenius "and others insist that it means a marriageable girl, which, however, does not imply that she is not a virgin."[20]

Brownson took the opportunity of reviewing the volume to offer some reflections on the Douay. The original Douay Version, he said, was done "by men exiled from their native land . . . more in the habit of expressing their thoughts and feelings in foreign idioms than in their native tongue." This resulted in a version "by no means pleasant to English taste, or intelligible to the ordinary Englishman, acquainted with no language but his own." Bishop Challoner, though "a holy man," in his revision, had "done all that mortal man could do to render it spiritless, tame, and feeble." Kenrick was "repairing much of the literary mischief he did, but he has not repaired it all." Brownson had a bolder suggestion. He was aware that Newman was supposed to do a translation. He recommended that, "if the habits, associations, and prejudices of the existing generation of English-speaking Catholics be not insuperable, we would urge the learned divine and consummate English scholar to take the version made by order of King James, as the basis of his proposed version, instead of adopting the Douay, or making an entirely new translation." He acknowledged that the King James Version had errors, resulting either from the text on which it was based or from mistranslation, but these, he thought, could be corrected against the Vulgate, which Trent had declared to be authoritative. Were all such corrections of the King James Version made, he continued,

we shall have probably, the best representation of the Holy Scriptures in our mother tongue that we can ever hope to obtain. What we propose is, not that we adopt the Protestant version bodily, but simply that it be made the basis of an amended version, and departed from only for some reason,—doctrinal, philological, scientific, or critical reason of some sort. There is nothing in the decree of the Council of Trent, that requires our English translations to be made from the Vulgate, or that in matters not involving doctrine, that even requires us to follow it, providing Biblical criticism, the testimony of recensions and manuscripts, &c., authorize a different reading; and a translation made directly from the original tongues into English will always be fresher, and represent the sense with its delicate shades, far better than a translation made from them through the Latin.

Brownson seems to have been alone among American Catholics in recognizing that Trent had not required that vernacular translations be made from Vulgate. It was his hope that, were his suggestion adopted, "it would prepare the way for introducing a common version, or the use of the same version by both Catholics and Protestants."[21]

Kenrick felt he could not follow Brownson's advice, since, as he wrote his brother, "the Holy See holds the [Latin] Vulgate to be the norm for translations into the vernacular." He feared he would be thought too "daring," if he followed the King James version and the original text on which it was based, rather than the Vulgate. Yet, he had difficulties with the Vulgate translation of the Pentateuch, on which he was then working. "In the whole of the Pentateuch," he observed,

the translator has turned the text with much freedom, omitting repetitions, substituting pronouns for nouns, abbreviating the text, and sometimes amplifying it. If I set forth all the peculiarities of the text as they are, and follow closely the way of the Protestant translation, it will appear that I am betraying the cause which I have undertaken to vindicate, that is, the integrity of the Vulgate.

He concluded by reporting that Brownson thought Newman should "do the work, with hardly any consideration of the Vulgate."[22]

In 1860, Kenrick published the Pentateuch, the section of the Bible on which he had begun work over twenty years earlier. In 1843, he had told his brother about his fascination with the theory of Eichhorn that Moses had compiled the Pentateuch from preexisting sources. When he finally completed his work, he was more reserved. Asserting that "rationalists" like Eichhorn had not yet proven their point, he came out more strongly for the Mosaic authorship of the entire corpus, "although," he added, "the supposition that Moses availed himself of such records is not irreconcilable with the authority, or even the inspiration of the work . . ."[23]

In dealing with the problems of translation, Kenrick was bolder. He quoted Alexander Geddes as saying: "The chief study of the

English translators was to give a strictly literal version, at the expense of almost every other consideration, whilst the author of the Vulgate endeavored to render his originals equivalently into such Latin as was current in his age." For that reason, Geddes preferred the Vulgate over the King James for being "smooth, easy, and intelligible." Having paid his respects to the Vulgate, Kenrick then moved on to express his own view of the King James Version:

For my own part, where no doctrinal bias betrays itself, I have no disposition to detract from its literary excellence, especially as regards its close adherence to the text. In revising the Douay translation I have constantly had in view the Hebrew original, which, however, I did not always feel at liberty to render closely, when it would imply a departure from the Vulgate, since this is the standard of all vernacular versions for general use, according to the settled usage of the Holy See. In endeavoring to express the meaning of the text without abandoning the Vulgate, I may occasionally have used terms in a sense somewhat forced. In cases when the Vulgate offers a reading different from the actual Hebrew, it is quite probable that it may be derived from some manuscript of high antiquity; but when the Latin interpreter manifestly had the same reading as that which is now received, although he rendered it somewhat freely, I think it desirable that the English translation should approach as nearly as possible to the original. I have conformed in many instances to the received appellations of objects, the mode of spelling certain names of more frequent recurrence, and have otherwise deferred to usage, although of Protestant origin, feeling that, in things indifferent, conformity is desirable, and that every approach to uniformity in the rendering of the inspired word, without sacrifice of principle, or violation of disciplinary rule, is a gain to the common cause of Christianity.[24]

In short, though Kenrick still sought to vindicate the Vulgate and advertised his work as "A Revised Edition of the Douay Version," he was beginning to display serious reservations about the Vulgate.

Kenrick also consciously alerted his readers to scientific developments in the nineteenth century, which might force a new approach to Scripture. Though making no allusion to evolution—Charles Darwin's *Origin of Species* had been published in 1859—he did discuss the geological arguments for giving an older date to the world than the Genesis account would imply. He expressed a norm for determining the relationship between science and the Bible, which was analogous to his use of the consensus of the Fathers as the basis for the proper interpretation of the Scripture. "We feel bound to respect the judgment of the learned," he wrote, "when they agree so decidedly in declaring the results of their investigations." Disagreement among the learned, however, would "detract much from the weight which they might otherwise have, and our veneration for the sacred text does not allow us hastily to abandon its letter, or absolutely to embrace what does not appear to harmonize with it."[25]

Kenrick further reminded his readers that the "science of geology was unknown to the ancients [and] the Mosaic narrative was not understood by all the Fathers of the Church as implying the creation of the universe in six days." The "diversity of views" among the Fathers, he continued, "shows that on this point the tradition of the Church was not absolute and dogmatical, so that if, with the progress of science, it become manifest, that a vast succession of ages can alone account for the structure of the earth . . . such indefinite periods may be admitted, without departing in any respect from the authoritative teachings of antiquity." He took an economic approach to the historicity of the scriptural account of creation. He insisted that all that had been "divinely revealed" in Genesis was "the origin of all things from the creative act of God, and the creation of man, as stated by the inspired author."[26]

Kenrick applied the same principles to the discoveries of astronomy about the relationship between the sun and moon, which differed from the Genesis account. "It was worthy of Him [God] to teach us, through Moses," Kenrick wrote, "necessary truth connected with practical duties, whilst He withholds from us knowledge which might gratify our curiosity and flatter our pride. It detracts nothing from the claims of Moses to inspiration that he did not communicate, or perhaps know, matters of science." He concluded by paraphrasing the recommendation of Augustine "not to insist tenaciously on interpreting Scripture in such a way as to place it in opposition to the discoveries of science, lest mistaking our own views for its divine dictates, we put a stumbling-block in the way of the learned."[27]

Peter Kenrick thought that his brother should have expanded his introductions and that his treatment of geology "presents some hesitation."[28] Francis, though cautious, was a man unafraid of the scientific developments of his age and their relation to Scripture. His theological method, relying so heavily on the Fathers, enabled him to take a more economic view of what constituted revelation and the nature of inspiration.

Brownson was, in general, pleased with Kenrick's work, though he wished he had taken "more liberty . . . with the Douay version." He also recognized that Kenrick had been criticized for imitating the King James Version and for citing Protestant authors in his notes. About the former criticism, he felt that it was "a mere question of English, in which the Catholic scholar is not necessarily superior to the Protestant." After all, he noted, "St. Jerome, when he studied Hebrew, took Jews for his masters." In regard to Kenrick's citing of Protestant authors, he said:

Cicero was a heathen, but Cicero was a tolerable master of Latin. It is not easy for us to understand why a Protestant may not be as good a grammarian, and as good a philologist as a Catholic, or why their heresy need hinder them from learning geography, the natural and civil history, or the natural productions of the Holy Land.[29]

In Brownson's mind, intolerance of error was not to be construed as bigotry and narrow-mindedness and it was "not necessary that we should deny all common sense and common honesty, in the natural order, to those who remain out of the Church." Just as the Church preserved the Greco-Roman culture, the work of "pagans and idolators," so the "Biblical scholar" should be allowed "full liberty to borrow light, and take facts wherever he finds them." Kenrick, he concluded, had "in no instance abused his liberty as a scholar" and he hoped that his version would become the standard one in general use among Catholics, though he feared that booksellers may have already invested too much in other editions of the Douay Bible. He especially urged the adoption of Kenrick's text, since Newman's version had been indefinitely postponed.[30] The mercurial Brownson had given Kenrick high praise indeed, but his own openness toward Newman at this point was only a passing phase of his intellectual journey. Despite Brownson's encomium, Kenrick's version would not become the standard American one, for reasons to be seen.

Later in 1860, Kenrick completed his work with the publication of the historical books, including the deuterocanonical books. He dedicated it to the American hierarchy. In a "General Introduction," he summarized all the work he had done since he published his version of the Gospels. He now was more forthright about his attitude toward the Vulgate. Schott's critical Greek New Testament, he asserted, supported the Vulgate. But the relation of the Vulgate to the Old Testament text presented numerous difficulties and, "in the historical books, it scarcely has the advantage." He had particularly preferred the "Protestant version" for the Pentateuch, the Psalms, and even the Prophets, where the Vulgate was a more literal translation of the Hebrew text. He ended his introduction with a plea to all his readers, but especially seminarians and priests. "The critical study of the Scriptures," he wrote,

is well worthy the attention of our ecclesiastical institutions. It is calculated to attract young men of intelligence and research, and to attach them to the study of the Oriental languages. It prepares them to defend successfully the authenticity and integrity of the Divine writings. It diminishes and takes away the ground of controversy, and prepares the Catholic clergy for meeting those who are without with great advantage.[31]

To urge the study of oriental languages in American "ecclesiastical institutions" was a noble sentiment, but one that would not be realized for several generations.

In his treatment of the various books, Kenrick's approach was again irenic. While retaining the Vulgate designation of the Four Books of Kings, he also used the Protestant terms for the first two as the "Books of Samuel." He likewise preferred "Chronicles" to "Paralipomenon." He placed the deuterocanonical works at the end of his book. From St. Louis, Peter Kenrick congratulated his brother on the completion of his work, but he strongly advised against a new publication of the entire version. He preferred that a totally new translation be made either from the Vulgate or from the original languages. In his mind, there had already been sufficient revision of the Douay version, "but the Douay version itself has already ceased to be pleasing."[32] This was but the first instance of Peter Kenrick's opposition to the further dissemination of his brother's work.

Francis Kenrick never did publish a complete edition of his revision of the English Bible, but he did issue a new edition of the entire New Testament. In making his revisions, he gave his manuscript to George Allen, professor of Latin and Greek at the University of Pennsylvania, a convert and former Episcopal priest, and to Levy Silliman Ives, a convert and former Episcopal bishop of North Carolina.[33] In the meantime, he had received the further advice from Brownson that he make greater use of the King James Version in order to produce a common edition for both Catholics and Protestants. This advice, Kenrick rejected, because "the protestant version can hardly be made the basis for a Catholic translation, which, following the discipline that prevails, ought to conform to the Vulgate."[34]

Francis Kenrick had problems other than seeming to follow the King James Version. He also faced criticism, if not an outright charge of heresy, from members of the hierarchy. In 1858, Martin John Spalding, Bishop of Louisville, challenged his note on *baptizo*, which Kenrick had interpreted to mean immersion. Spalding wished him to omit the note altogether, since "the Baptists out here have been exulting over it too much."[35] As Kenrick was completing his new edition, Spalding again wrote him. While encouraging the new edition for "general use," he recommended that, if it were to receive the approval of the hierarchy, it would "be well for you to communicate to them . . . the changes you prepare to make . . . and the modification, if any, of the notes, so as to make them more popular, & perhaps more conformable to the Rules of the Index."[36] Kenrick agreed to make some alterations in the note about baptism, but he refused to "dissemble its primary meaning, and the fact that immersion of some kind was the original and ordinary mode of Baptism." In regard to Spalding's veiled charge of heterodoxy, Kenrick replied that he was "desirous to conform strictly to the Rules of the Index and Roman usage. My constant reference to the text and to critics may appear bold, but [Dom Augustin] Calmet [1672–1757] and other Catholic writers have led the way."[37]

In 1862, Kenrick published a complete New Testament with some minor changes in the notes.[38] While Spalding hesitantly adopted it for his diocese, he still thought Kenrick was too gentle and that "the Church, though so mild, has not been in the habit of letting off so gently heretics who wrest the scriptures with evidently perverse intention."[39] Kenrick and Spalding represented two different approaches to theology and apologetics. The former believed in taking the positive insights of Protestant scholars and showing their compatibility with Catholicism. He had displayed this irenicism even when dealing with the nativists in Philadelphia. The American-born Spalding was closer in mentality to Wiseman. In upholding the truth of Catholicism, it was imperative to give the enemy no quarter.

Kenrick had, in the meantime, requested John Gilmary Shea, a layman, who was the first serious historian of American Catholicism, to write Newman about the joint translation, proposed by the bishops of the Baltimore province. Newman congratulated Kenrick on completing his work and attempted to explain Wiseman's failure to respond. "I did not know," Newman wrote,

what I find by your letter, that your Grace had been in some suspense as to the intention of the English bishops with respect to it. For myself, as you seem to wish me to speak on the subject, I can only say, that I have been in the same suspense myself, and know nothing beyond the facts of the Bishop of Charlestown's [sic] letter. The Cardinal's many anxieties and engagements, and his late and present indisposition, doubtless are the cause of a silence, which I am sorry you have felt to be an inconvenience.[40]

Newman later told John E. D. Dalberg, Lord Acton, that he had never actually seen Kenrick's version, though he had ordered it from his bookseller. "From what I have heard said," he wrote, "I suppose he will have done a good work, in breaking down many narrow traditions as to translation. He has been accused of going too near the Protestant version, and has defended himself." Like Peter Kenrick, however, Newman recognized the difficulties in translating from the Vulgate. Kenrick's "translation will at least be a platform," he thought, "and in that light an important gain necessarily, considering his position, his theological knowledge, etc etc." But he believed there was need for "another platform" and asked Acton whether German critics had done "a dissertation on the Latin of the Vulgate, and a history of the change of the Latin tongue, in point both of structure and style, between Cicero and (say) St. Augustine." Such study on the Latin language, he argued, was "a necessary preliminary to a *translation* from the Vulgate."[41]

Newman's praise of Kenrick, especially in a letter to Acton, a close friend, indicates the esteem with which the archbishop was regarded in the English-speaking world.

That Kenrick's translation did not become the standard one, at least in the United States, was due to a series of factors. He died in 1863. In 1866, the bishops of the United States assembled for the Second Plenary Council. Presiding over the council was Martin J. Spalding, who had succeeded Kenrick as Archbishop of Baltimore. The bishops appointed a committee to choose an English version of the Bible. Speaking for the committee, Archbishop John Baptist Purcell of Cincinnati recommended that Kenrick's version be adopted, after it had been revised, with the addition of Bishop Challoner's notes. The minutes of the council record that Archbishop Peter Kenrick "vehemently opposed" the suggestion. After considerable debate, the bishops then voted to drop their decree specifying a particular English version of the Bible. In their decrees concerning Scripture, they simply repeated what the Council of Trent had legislated about Scripture and tradition and about private interpretation of Scripture. In regard to English versions, they adopted verbatim the vague decree of the First Provincial Council in 1829 stating that the Douay was to be used.[42] In retrospect, it is difficult to determine whether Peter Kenrick opposed the republication of his brother's work in its entirety or only in a truncated version, without the critical notes. Archbishop Spalding later thought that Francis Kenrick originally intended his work for students—by implication, then, a version, without the notes, could be published for the general public.[43]

In approving the decrees of the council, the Congregation of Propaganda acknowledged the validity of the council's suppressing its decree specifying a particular version. It felt, however, that, since there was still danger that Catholics would use the Protestant version, the bishops should determine on a particular version. In communicating the congregation's decision, Cardinal Alessandro Barnabò, the prefect, suggested that Spalding would be acting in accord with the Ninth Provincial Council which had, of course, proposed the joint Kenrick-Newman edition, if he began an emendation of the Douay version, after consulting theologians and biblical scholars and comparing the various editions of the Douay, "as well as other English versions, if any exist besides the Douay."

Such a new edition, concluded the cardinal, would gain the approval of other bishops and could then be proposed in another plenary council "for the common use of the faithful to the exclusion of other versions."[44] Barnabò directly alluded to the council of 1858. Kenrick, moreover, had sent copies of his version to Propaganda. The cardinal, therefore, may have been urging that the American bishops seriously consider adopting Kenrick's work. For the time being, however, the cardinal's letter provoked no attempt to produce a standard American Catholic version of the Bible. But it did provide an impetus in the 1930s, as will be seen, for an American Catholic translation of the New Testament from the Vulgate.

Within a few years of the Second Plenary Council, the American bishops had their first experience of an ecumenical council. The First Vatican Council represented a new shift in theology, subtle at first, but increasingly apparent as the century came to a close. For the moment, however, the Americans took little cognizance of these new theological directions. They were more concerned with the debate over papal infallibility. In that debate, Peter Kenrick took his place among those who opposed the definition. For him, papal infallibility was only a theological opinion and could not be elevated to the level of a doctrine even by a council. Both he and his American opponents, particularly Spalding of Baltimore, appealed to his brother's work, *The Primacy of the Apostolic See*. But in his use of Scripture to support his argument, he reflected Francis's affinity for the Fathers. It was "a rule for interpreting the scriptures," he said, "that they were not to be interpreted contrary to the unanimous consensus of the Fathers." Since such unanimity was relatively rare, one should follow the interpretation of the greatest number. This principle he then applied to Mt 16:18: "You are Peter and upon this rock I will build my church." Only seventeen Fathers interpreted this to mean that Christ would build His church on Peter, while forty-four Fathers understood the rock to be "the faith, which Peter confessed."[45] Peter Kenrick would be one of the last bishops to submit to the definition of papal infallibility after the council. Quite clearly the theological reasoning, which the two Kenricks used, belonged to an age different from the one then emerging. That new age may have contributed to the failure to have Francis Kenrick's Bible reprinted.

In 1884, the American bishops assembled for the Third, and last, Plenary Council of Baltimore. Again, they discussed the need for a common Bible, particularly in light of Cardinal Barnabò's letter after the Second Plenary Council. Many bishops praised Kenrick's "version" and urged that it be reprinted. Peter Kenrick responded that his brother had not produced "a version properly speaking, but a new edition of the Douay version." When one bishop proposed that this edition be reprinted with all its notes, Kenrick replied that he would renounce his ownership of the copyright, if there were no legal problems.[46] But here ended the discussion of either reprinting Kenrick's work or of selecting a particular English version of the Bible for the American church. In their pastoral letter, the bishops urged every family to have "a correct version" of the Bible. "Among other versions," they recommended "the Douay, . . . which was suitably annotated by the learned Bishop Challoner, by Canon Haydock, and especially by the late Archbishop Kenrick."[47]

One of the bishops present for the discussion of adopting Kenrick's Bible was Archbishop Michael Heiss of Milwaukee, who had himself written on the New Testament. In 1863, as rector of the Salesianum, the seminary for Milwaukee, he had published *The Four Gospels: Examined and Vindicated on Catholic Principles.* While he cited Kenrick, however, Heiss was not open to any of the new criticism. German Protestant scriptural theologians had undermined the doctrine of inspiration, he said, because they started with the premise "that Scripture *alone* is the infallible authority for man on earth," but they failed to realize that "to prove the divine inspiration of Scripture without *another infallible* authority, is impossible." Proponents of "this new science" demanded that the Scripture be interpreted in accordance with modern philosophy. As an example, he cited J. G. Eichhorn, with whom Kenrick had been impressed—at least in his private letters to his brother. Heiss announced that the purpose of his work was "to oppose this baneful criticism, without troubling the reader with all the details of its evaporations." "Only once," he said, was he "tempted to adopt such a modern theory," and that was in regard to postulating a "primitive gospel" as the common basis for the Synoptics. He had considered this "harmless," but then "considering that such a primitive gospel is never mentioned by any of the fathers, and is rather opposed to their view on the origin of these three gospels, we gave it up."[48]

Heiss was, by and large, true to his word. He argued strenuously from tradition for the authorship of the four Gospels and rejected that any of the Synoptics relied on any other. To prove the historical value of the four Gospels, he constructed a harmonized account of them. On the issue of inspiration, however, he came close to Kenrick. Asking how the early Christians determined which books were inspired, he answered, "only read what St. Irenaeus and Tertullian say: they refer to the testimony of ecclesiastical authority." But in his exposition, he showed that he was imbued with a theology different from Kenrick's. To the Church, he wrote, which "by divine institution" was "the living continuation of the apostolical preaching of the gospel of Christ," was

intrusted the whole *deposit of faith,* that is all that was taught by the apostles; to her also has been promised the assistance of the Holy Ghost, to be guided in all things into truth, so that she may be capable of being the faithful guide and interpreter of the *deposit of faith,* intrusted to her care.[49]

Heiss's mention of a "deposit of faith" represented an important theological shift, which as will be seen, was further emphasized at the First Vatican Council.

Heiss had made no attempt to hide his prejudice against the new criticism. His work was not a major piece of scholarship, but it was representative of the type of reflection on the Scripture that would become increasingly common in the last decades of the century. His approach to New Testament criticism also indicated that on the eve of the First Vatican Council, there was theological tension within the American church—a tension that would become more apparent as the biblical question and other issues drew more of the Church's attention.

Throughout the nineteenth century, the American bishops had sought to provide an orthodox and readable English version of the Bible for American Catholics. Kenrick's version was, by far, the most ambitious undertaking of the century. But he was a theologian and not an expert in biblical scholarship, which was then just in its infancy among Catholics. Nevertheless, his notes at least introduced his readers to the problems being raised by the biblical critics, and his theology was one open to new developments. Already in his lifetime, however, he was thought to be too "daring." Both Wiseman and Spalding criticized him for being too benevolently disposed toward Protestant critics. He differed from them in his approach to apologetics. But he also differed from the new theology—the Thomistic revival, which Leo XIII had encouraged in his encyclical *Aeterni Patris* in 1878—which was then taking shape in the Catholic Church at large.

amen The Thomistic revival was, however, not a return so much to Thomas as to a particular school of Thomistic commentators. These theologians were unable to grapple with the development of doctrine or historical criticism. Francis Kenrick's theology was based, not on the Scholastics, but on the Fathers; it was open to development. The shift in theology may have conditioned the failure of the American bishops to approve his version of the Bible for common use. There would be no further attempts to provide an American Catholic translation until the late 1930s and Kenrick's version was virtually forgotten in the American church.[50] The last official mention of it was at the Third Plenary Council. But that council also took important actions toward creating an American Catholic intellectual life, including the development of a progressive approach to the study of Scripture.

3. The Emergence of Criticism in the American Church: 1885-1897

The Third Plenary Council, *18 8 4* which made the last official mention of Kenrick's version, represented a turning point in the intellectual history of the American church. Unlike all the other national councils, it had been summoned by Rome, in part to test the loyalty of the American bishops, so many of whom had opposed the definition of papal infallibility at the First Vatican Council. The Americans, as was noted, had been exposed in Rome to a new type of theology, which, in turn, shaped a new ecclesiology. Johann Baptist Franzelin, S.J., professor of dogma at the Gregorian University, was symbolic of the new trend.

NEW THEOLOGICAL ORIENTATIONS

Prominent as a theologian at the First Vatican Council, Franzelin had earlier opposed Newman's notion of consulting the faithful on matters of doctrine.[1] At the council, Franzelin had a key influence on the constitution on faith, which had decreed that the Church held the books of Scripture, "to be sacred and canonical, not because, having been carefully composed by mere human industry, they were afterwards approved by her authority, not merely because they contain revelation, with no admixture of error, but because, having been written by the inspiration of the Holy Spirit, they have God for their author, and have been delivered as such to the Church herself."[2] This was a shift from Kenrick's emphasis on the acceptance and use of the books by the Church and represented the Church's growing concern with preserving the doctrine of inspiration against the increasing incursions of rationalism.

The Catholic discussion of inspiration at the council took place in the context of the questions raised by historical critics of the

Scripture. The phrase "God is the author of Scripture" had in the past been subjected to a variety of interpretations, such as "God is the authority or cause of Scripture." St. Thomas Aquinas himself had not dealt specifically with inspiration. He had, however, written about prophecy. From the Thomistic treatment of one type of scriptural book, nineteenth-century Catholic theologians attempted to construct theories of inspiration in general.[3] Franzelin made what was to become the dominant contribution to the discussion.

Simply put, Franzelin began with the time-honored statement that "God is the author of Scripture," but then he attributed to God everything that is known of a human author. From this, he derived a theory of "content inspiration." Inspiration was the charism that enlightened and stimulated the mind of the human author to write down only those truths that God wished to communicate to the Church. This constituted the "formal word" or element of Scripture. Inspiration was distinguished from "assistance" which extended to the "material words," by which the human instrument conveyed the inspired truths.[4] Before the end of the century the Catholic biblical world would become embroiled over the meaning of "God as author," as the starting point for the discussion of inspiration.

Franzelin also played a role in formulating the council's treatment of tradition in its relation to Scripture. Kenrick had emphasized tradition as the process of preserving the correct interpretation of Scripture. The council declared that "all those things are to be believed with divine and Catholic faith which are contained in the word of God, written or handed down (verbo Dei scripto vel tradito), and which the Church, either by a solemn judgment, or by her ordinary and universal magisterium, proposes for belief as having been divinely revealed." The "doctrine of faith," the council continued, "is like a divine deposit handed on (tradita) to the Spouse of Christ, to be faithfully guarded and infallibly declared."[5]

Reflecting so much of Franzelin's thought, the council's formulation thus represented a move away from tradition as a process to tradition as content. But by "Spouse of Christ," as Yves Congar, O.P., noted, "the council understands here above all the magisterium, especially that of the Roman Pontiff."[6] Pius IX himself had encouraged the identity between tradition and the papal magisterium with his unfortunate, but well attested, statement "La Tradizione son'io."[7] The council, moreover, truncated the Tridentine formulation of the relationship between Scripture and tradition to imply that they were two separate sources.[8] This new theology of tradition, to which Franzelin had so significantly contributed would greatly alter the Church's understanding of previous magisterial pronouncements on Scripture. Pius IX recognized his achievements in 1876 by naming him a cardinal.

But it was not only Franzelin's theology that would influence the American church. In 1883, the Holy See convoked the Third Plenary Council and summoned all the archbishops or their representatives to Rome for a series of meetings with Propaganda. Franzelin was designated as the *ponente* to draw up for Propaganda the agenda for the forthcoming plenary council of the American bishops. Sprinkled throughout his *ponenza* were references to the need to increase Roman centralization of the Americans.[9] Among the decrees that the Americans passed at the council was one to establish a "seminarium principale" or Catholic University. It was to be the intellectual center for the American church, particularly for the graduate training of the diocesan clergy. When the council had concluded its work in December 1884, the decrees were sent to Rome for approval. Franzelin was again appointed the *ponente* to examine the conciliar legislation. Bishop John Moore of St. Augustine, one of the American procurators of the council, reported an audience he had had with Leo XIII, in which he summed up his reaction to Franzelin. The cardinal, he said, "has a hard head, he is full of speculative theology, abstract principles, and scholastic distinctions...."[10] Though there is no record of Franzelin's opposition to the establishment of the Catholic University of America, as such, its subsequent location in Washington antagonized his American Jesuit colleagues, who already had their own institution, Georgetown University, in that city.

Franzelin's brand of "speculative theology" found expression in the American Jesuits' theological center of Woodstock College, outside of Baltimore. It included among its first faculty in 1869 several Italian refugees from the *risorgimento.* Its first dean of studies, Camillo Mazzella, had been a leader in the Italian Thomistic revival. In 1879, Leo XIII summoned him to Rome to take up the chair vacated by Franzelin and to implement Thomism in the Gregorian University. Seven years later, upon the death of Franzelin, he was named a cardinal and subsequently became prefect of the Congregation of the Index.[11] Much of Mazzella and other Jesuits' theological orientation was shaped by their own political experience of having been expelled from their own countries and of seeing papal temporal power wrested away by the Kingdom of Italy. Even after the time of Mazzella and the original Italian founders, however, Woodstock remained a bastion of reaction. One of the principal objects of its opposition was the Catholic University of America.

THE FOUNDING OF THE CATHOLIC UNIVERSITY OF AMERICA

As the first trustees of the university met for preliminary discussion about the selection of a faculty, they illustrated how dependent the American church was on Europe and how naive they were about the nature of a university. In January 1885, for example, the trustees "decided that the Professor of Scripture be a German." They specified neither his field nor training, but only the nationality of the man they had in mind. But it is significant that they were turning to the nation, where progressive Scripture scholarship was then developing. At the same meeting, they also voted that the "most suitable" candidate for rector would be Father John B. Hogan, S.S., then president of St. John's Seminary, Brighton, Massachusetts, and former professor at St. Sulpice, Issy, France. Hogan would not become the rector, but he did become president of the Sulpician College at the university and would develop into an apologist for the new historical method of biblical criticism. For professor of science, the trustees thought St. George Mivart was "desirable."[12] Mivart would soon draw attention to his theories, as he moved beyond the sphere of science into biblical theology. Within a few years, he had several articles on the Index of Forbidden Books and would later be excommunicated.

The university never offered Mivart a post, but several years later, Archbishop John Ireland of St. Paul wrote Bishop John Keane, the first rector of the university, that "I do not forgive you for the loss of Mivart. Don't be afraid of good sound liberalism. Confidence in self, & the support of the American people will carry us always through." Ireland also offered some interesting advice for a member of the teaching body of the Catholic Church. "You must educate your professors," he told Keane, "& then hold on to them—making bishops only of those who are not worth keeping as professors."[13] Ireland's remark was characteristic. Not a scholar himself, he was open to the new trends in Europe. This was a mentality he shared with other liberal leaders, who supported the Catholic University, John Keane, Cardinal James Gibbons, the Archbishop of Baltimore and chancellor of the university, and Denis J. O'Connell, rector of the American College in Rome. In 1890, Ireland was gathering a faculty for his own seminary in St. Paul. From Rome, O'Connell remarked, "if you could only get [Alfred] Loisy of Paris for Scripture. He is the best Biblical scholar in the church."[14] Gibbons, too, shared in this naive enthusiasm for new scholarship. In *The Catholic World,* he had highly recommended *Criteri Teologici* by Canon Salvatore di Bartolo of Palermo. Di Bartolo had limited biblical inspiration only to matters of faith and morals and related areas.[15] The work was placed on the Index of Forbidden Books in 1891. The liberals displayed their naïvete from the very beginning of their cherished institution of the Catholic University.

When Keane sought his faculty, he was not successful in obtaining a German as professor of Scripture. But the first professor actually appointed was Henry Hyvernat. He had studied under Fulcran Vigouroux, S.S., at Issy, where he was a classmate of Marie-Joseph Lagrange, who later entered the Dominicans and became one of the foremost Catholic exegetes. Hyvernat then taught oriental languages and biblical archeology at the Apollinare in Rome, where Keane met him.[16] The university's first professors of dogma and scholastic philosophy represented a different cast of mind. Joseph Schroeder, professor of dogma, was from Cologne and Joseph Pohle, professor of scholastic philosophy, was from Fulda. Both were representative of the type of Scholasticism, which would prove to be incapable of dealing with questions of historical criticism. Early in 1891, Schroeder displayed his mentality by publishing three articles on "theological minimizing" in the *American Ecclesiastical Review.* The object of his attack was di Bartolo. His first concern was the Italian's argument that the Church could not define that papal temporal power was a dogma of faith. He then attacked di Bartolo's notion of inspiration in limiting it only to matters of faith and morals.[17] Father Charles Grannan, however, an alumnus of the American College in Rome and also a professor of dogma, would gradually shift over to being positive in his assessment of the newly developing field of criticism.

Intellectual life in the United States, both Catholic and Protestant, was then in ferment. At Union Theological Seminary in New York, Charles Augustus Briggs was transferred from the chair of biblical languages to a newly established chair of biblical theology. His inaugural lecture accusing Protestants of "bibliolatry" resulted in his being tried for heresy in the Presbyterian church, and being dismissed from the ministry. Union Theological then became independent of the Presbyterian church and Briggs was later ordained in the Episcopal church.[18] The controversy flowed over into Catholic circles. From Woodstock came the first of numerous diatribes against biblical criticism from the pen of Anthony J. Maas, S.J.

ANTHONY J. MAAS, S.J.

Born in Westphalia, Maas taught Scripture at Woodstock, later became rector and then provincial superior of the Maryland-New York Province. He was among the first Americans to enter the lists of the biblical field since Kenrick, but, in his hands, many of Kenrick's and others' claims about the Church in relation to Scripture took on new meaning. He attacked Briggs for making no provision in his theories for the role of some authority to determine revealed doctrine and asserted the superiority of oral tradition to Scripture. In Maas's mind, Briggs had ignored the question of inspiration and its relation to inerrancy—a constant theme in Maas's writings. When Briggs stated that neither the Scripture nor the creeds claimed inerrancy in matters not related to faith, Maas replied, "if the writers of the canonical books compose their works under the in-breathing of the Holy Ghost and under his special guidance, as the Scripture testifies, they must also be granted the privilege of writing inerrantly." If this were not the case, the Holy Spirit would be responsible for the errors. Where Briggs spoke of the need to compare the different "theologies" of each book, Maas countered that there was development from one book to another, but not different doctrines.[19] Maas thus set the tone for his treatment of biblical criticism—and that tone would become dominant in American Catholicism.

Maas had already indicated the orientation of his thought in his *Life of Jesus Christ according to the Gospel History,* first published in 1891, with the *imprimatur* of Archbishop Michael Augustine Corrigan of New York and the approbation of Cardinal James Gibbons of Baltimore. He intended his work "for readers who have neither the leisure nor opportunity to consult many Commentaries and works on ancient history." He, therefore, had "endeavored to mark off clearly historical facts and dogmas of faith from human conjecture and pious belief." He pointed out that his "text is entirely framed out of the words of the gospels, in such a manner that nothing is omitted and nothing added." When confronted with "different opinions" about "important historical or doctrinal difficulties of the text," he emphasized the "more probable explanations" and rejected "the untenable ones." "Though it may seem less dignified to state controverted points as such, than authoritatively to determine them," he found it "more useful" to pursue the former approach and had "contented himself for the most part with assigning a greater or less probability to the various opinions." He revealed his pride in his achievement by stating that it could have as well been entitled a "gospel-commentary," as a "Life of Jesus."[20] Maas sounded as if he was more inclined to use logic than historical investigation in his study. His suggestion of a "gospel-commentary" as an alternative title for his work sounded innocuous enough, until the reader realized that Maas was trying to create one Gospel behind the four traditions.

Maas directly linked inspiration with the authorship of each Gospel. The discrepancies between the various accounts could, therefore, be easily harmonized and Maas sought to do that in a single continuous narrative, ignoring the theological nuances of each Gospel writer. Where Kenrick had used the Church's acceptance of each book as a guarantee for its inspiration, Maas used that acceptance as a guarantee of inspired authorship. The testimony of early Christian writers, Maas wrote, "clearly demonstrates that the authenticity of the four gospels was an article of belief of the Church early in the second century." In regard to the fourth Gospel, he would simply assert: "How could a spurious document find its way into the very canon of the inspired books under the claim of a Johannine authorship, when scarcely twenty years had elapsed since St. John's death, and when his disciples were still numerous and influential?"[21]

In an age when the study of Scripture was becoming specialized, Maas was a generalist and did not confine himself to the New Testament. In 1893, he published the first volume of *Christ in Type and Prophecy.* In his approach, the Old Testament had to be interpreted literally, and Church doctrine became the hermeneutical tool for the true interpretation. For example, to interpret Gn 3:15, he appealed to the tradition of "the Fathers of the Church" who "unanimously speak of Eve as the type of the Blessed Virgin." Maas found this tradition reenforced by "the view of the Church expressed clearly in her liturgy, the common reading of her authentic Latin version of the Bible, and the Papal bull 'Ineffabilis Deus,' in which the dogma of the Immaculate Conception is taught *ex cathedra.*" While Kenrick had been sympathetic toward critics such as Rosenmüller, Maas dismissed those critics, who would make the story "mere myth." His argument was ingenious. "For if all is mere myth," he asked, "why have all the nations of antiquity developed mythologies which are identical rather than similar? And if it be said that the critical analysis of the Pentateuch suggests the mythical character of the Mosaic story, we point to the fact that this is incompatible with the Mosaic origin of the Pentateuch."[22]

Maas carried his typology to absurdity. In an article of the same year, "Adam's Rib—Allegory or History," he wrote that "no intelligent student of Holy Writ can fail to recognize" that the account of male and female in Plato's Symposium was "the distorted record of a tradition which had lost its original likeness in being coupled with the extravagant myths of pagan superstition." How much richer than "the flippant cynicism of the philosopher," he thought, was the "sober earnestness of the inspired writer."[23] Though commentators such as Origen and Cajetan had considered the story an allegory, Maas believed it essential to take it as historical or else the relationship between type and antitype would be jeopardized. Paul, Augustine, Jerome, Bernard, and Thomas had all agreed in seeing that Eve being fashioned from the rib of Adam was the type of the Church being fashioned from the side of Christ.[24]

In 1891, Maas had already given an indication of how he would harmonize the Gospels. Four years later, he illustrated the theological premises, underlying his work, in his treatment of the synoptic problem in the *American Ecclesiastical Review*. From the patristic testimony, it was obvious to him that the synoptic Gospels were "the records of the catechetical instructions of the Apostles." These instructions, in turn, "were based on that of St. Peter, but were developed according to the needs of the catechumens." He reached his conclusion from "the two facts of St. Peter's residence in the three principal primitive churches in Jerusalem, Antioch, and Rome, and of St. Peter's primacy in the apostolic college." "Even St. Paul," he continued, "though he had not lived so long under the influence of St. Peter as the other Apostles, follows the same method of preaching as the Prince of the Apostles." Maas reached this conclusion by comparing Paul's "discourses in Pisidia, at Athens, and before Festus and Agrippa, with those of St. Peter before Jewish audiences and the Gentile Cornelius."[25]

In his commentary on Matthew in 1898, Maas followed a similar line of thought, but he made it more syllogistic. It was clear to him that in Mt 16:18 Peter was the "rock," which provided the Church with "stability, firmness, and unity." Since these qualities, as necessary for the Church as for any society, were "supplied by the ruling authority, it follows that the rock must be the seat of authority in the Church; and since the foundation must remain as long as the building, the rock on which the Church is built must persevere as long the Church is to last." Answering the objections of those who rejected this interpretation, he stated—without any analysis of the appropriate texts—that "the expressions of St. Paul about the apostolate and his behavior toward St. Peter do not contradict the solemn declaration of Peter's primacy."[26]

From the retrospect of almost a century, it is difficult to determine whether Maas was seriously trying to understand Scripture or was more intent on proving Petrine primacy as a bulwark of papal primacy. The Roman question—the status of the pope within the Eternal City—and the *Kulturkampf*—Bismarck's attempt to subjugate the Church to the Prussian State—seems to have influenced his approach to Scripture more than knowledge of the historical method then being brought to bear on the synoptic problem. The musings of the Woodstock Jesuit might have been forgotten, had his theological premises not become more common among conservative interpreters of Leo XIII's encyclical on the biblical question.

PROVIDENTISSIMUS DEUS AND BIBLICAL CRITICISM

In 1893, Leo XIII issued *Providentissimus Deus*. He placed his teaching about biblical studies in reaction to the "rationalists," who denied inspiration. Professors of Scripture, he said, were to use the Vulgate, which Trent had declared to be the "authentic" version, but were to use the Hebrew and Greek, whenever there was any ambiguity. He encouraged more advanced students and seminarians, however, to learn the oriental languages in which the Scripture had originally been written. He praised "the art of criticism," by which he meant "lower criticism," the verification of the text. But he warned that "there has arisen, to the great detriment of religion, an inept method, dignified by the name of 'higher criticism,' which pretends to judge of the origin, integrity, and authority of each book from internal indications alone."[27] History and historical criticism were clearly going to be problematic for Catholic exegetes.

In regard to apparent contradictions between the Scripture and science, Leo noted that the sacred writers "did not seek to penetrate the secrets of nature, but rather described and dealt with things in more or less figurative language, or in terms which were commonly used at the time, and which in many instances are daily used at this day, even by the most eminent men of science." In the words of Thomas, continued the pope, the writers "went by what sensibly appeared." Immediately after treating the natural sciences, the pope declared that "the principles here laid down will apply to cognate sciences, and especially to history."[28] It was but a logical conclusion for the liberal exegetes to develop what they termed "historical appearances." But, as will be seen, they would meet serious opposition to this approach in the early twentieth century.

It was Leo's treatment of inerrancy and inspiration, however, which caused future controversy. "It is absolutely wrong and forbidden," he stated, "either to narrow inspiration to certain parts only of Holy Scripture or to admit that the sacred writer has erred." He was particularly harsh on those who wished to limit inspiration only to matters of faith and morals. Since God is the author of Scripture, inspiration and error were incompatible, "for all the books which the Church receives as sacred and canonical are written wholly and entirely, with all their parts, at the dictation of the Holy Spirit; and so far is it from being possible that any error can coexist with inspiration, that inspiration not only is essentially incompatible with error, but excludes and rejects it as absolutely and necessarily as it is impossible that God Himself, the supreme Truth can utter that which is not true." After quoting the First Vatican Council on Scripture, the pope then considered the nature of inspiration itself:

Hence, the fact that it was men whom the Holy Spirit took up as his instruments for writing does not mean that it was these inspired instruments—but not the primary author—who might have made an error. For, by supernatural power, He so moved and impelled them to write—He so assisted them when writing—that the things which He ordered, and those only, they, first, rightly understood, then willed faithfully to write down, and finally expressed in apt words and with infallible truth. Otherwise, it could not be said that He was the Author of the entire Scripture.[29]

The formulation of the theology of inspiration was familiar to those who knew Franzelin's thought. Cardinal Mazzella had drafted that part of the encyclical and incorporated into it Franzelin's theory.[30]

The response from American Jesuits was predictable. Maas's colleague at Woodstock, James Conroy, S.J., summarized the encyclical, but concentrated most of his energies on chastising the "higher critics." He claimed to be making a distinction between revelation and inspiration, but then proceeded to confuse them. Everything "contained in the Scriptures," he wrote, "is an object of faith," even such statements as "Abraham begat Isaac," which could have been known without revelation. "Many parts—nay, most parts—of the Scriptures," he continued, "can be the word of God only by inspiration, since they are not direct revelations of God. Hence, it must be concluded that such parts of the Scriptures are inspired." If there were scientific or historical inconsistencies in the Scripture, these had to be due, he said citing Augustine, to the failure of a copyist or translator or of the reader's ability to understand. In this way, Conroy could dismiss all forms of "higher criticism" which he feared "was fast gaining popularity with individuals, if not with schools, in the United States."[31]

He likewise rejoiced that Leo had called for Scripture professors to draw from the Vulgate, but, in his exposition, he came dangerously close to making the Vulgate the inspired version. Theologians "of the age," he said, had hoped that Leo might alter the traditional stance toward the Vulgate, which "had been declared to be authentic by the Council of Trent." "From this declaration, according to the common opinion of theologians, it follows that the Latin Vulgate is a faithful rendering of the original Scriptures—at least as far as dogmatic texts are concerned—so that no dogma contained in the original text is substantially changed or modified, or not sufficiently expressed, in this version." It was only logical for Leo to reinforce the teaching of Trent, he concluded, because "the Vulgate version was from the very beginning in constant use in the Church, to whose infallible keeping the Scriptures, as well as the unwritten traditions, have been entrusted."[32] It mattered not to Conroy that the Vulgate had not, in fact, been in use "from the very beginning."

Maas was surprisingly restrained in his treatment of the encyclical. It was "a disciplinary measure" and not "a dogmatic pronouncement," he noted; yet, it implied "certain dogmatic truths and even asserts them plainly (the inerrancy of the Bible, e.g.)." The principal focus of his article, however, was to argue that the encyclical did not espouse "verbal inspiration," but spoke of "the inspired authors" writing "under the dictation of the Holy Ghost, because they received from Him, mediately or immediately, all the truths they recorded, but not because the Holy Ghost supplied the outward expression of those truths." While not specifying the particular action of inspiration on the human writers, the encyclical reinforced the teaching of Trent and Vatican I on the inerrancy of Scripture and "the Catholic notion of inspiration (which is convertible with principal authorship)." By repudiating those authors who limited inspiration only to matters of faith and morals, the pope had ruled out the theories, "with certain qualifications," of "Newman, Mivart, Lenormant, Loisy, di Bartolo, Semeria, Savi, Rohling, Drey, Kuhn, Aberle, Schanz." Leo's quotation of Thomas Aquinas that the sacred writers "went by what sensibly appeared," in matters of nature, prompted Maas to remark that God had accommodated Himself "to man's way of thinking and expressing thought," which "may be extended without scruple or difficulty so far as men are accustomed to regard such relative expressions as contained within the limits of truthfulness."[33] Yet, Maas could not apply the same norms to the historical truthfulness of the Scriptures. It was this inability and his rejection of "verbal inspiration" that would bring him into conflict with more liberal exegetes and, ultimately, cause him to harden his position. As the question unfolded in the United States, Maas would make further appeal to the authority of the encyclical and would come to dominate the discussion on biblical criticism, especially after the turn of the century. But in the 1890s, his was not the only voice in the American church.

AMERICAN CATHOLIC LIBERALS AND THE BIBLICAL QUESTION

Even while Maas and his Jesuit colleagues were preparing to mount their attack on biblical scholarship, the American Catholic liberals were engaged in widening their contact with European scholars. After *Providentissimus Deus,* Loisy had been forced to resign from the Institut Catholique of Paris. On July 10, 1894, he sent Denis O'Connell a copy of the last number of his *Enseignement Biblique,* "printed," he said, "at the moment when the injustice of the times has obliged my review to die. This will complete that collection, and not leave my commentary on the synoptic gospels suspended in the middle of a sentence."[34]

A few months later, Loisy again wrote O'Connell, who had earlier recommended to Loisy, John A. Zahm, C.S.C., professor of science at the University of Notre Dame. Loisy was now introducing O'Connell to Baron Friedrich von Hügel, "an excellent man, who is at the same time both a philosopher and an exegete." Von Hügel was going to seek O'Connell's "advice and assistance in a delicate work he is pursuing." Turning to *Providentissimus Deus,* Loisy feared that a bad interpretation of it would be "a stumbling block" to some Anglicans seeking reunion with the Catholic Church. His own "adventures," he noted, had "begun with a commentary on that encyclical." For himself, he had "no intention of publishing anything of importance on matters of exegesis for several years," nor did he "believe it opportune to resume publication of my review." In the meantime, he planned on working "peacefully," and would leave "the ideas I put into circulation the time to make their way." "I will follow myself," he concluded, "the same advice I have given: the best way to resolve the biblical question is to study the Bible. It was not bad advice, for it has since then been given in the encyclical, under a different form."[35] Loisy and O'Connell shared more than interest in biblical studies. Zahm, a Holy Cross Father, taught science at the University of Notre Dame and was already developing his theory about the compatibility of evolution and Church teaching. Von Hügel, an English layman, was interested in the biblical question and became something of an exegete in his own right. Introduced by Loisy, he and O'Connell formed a strong friendship in Rome. In 1895, O'Connell would have something more in common with Loisy, for Leo XIII demanded his resignation as rector of the American College.[36]

CHARLES GRANNAN: A CAUTIOUS CRITIC

While O'Connell was moving into European intellectual circles, back at the Catholic University of America, Father Charles Grannan made his first hesitant sally into the biblical field in 1894. In the *American Catholic Quarterly Review*, he tried to explain to his readers the nature of "Higher Criticism." For him, the failure to use "the sane critical investigations to which all literature and all history have been subjected" betrayed "a want of faith in God's word." Lower criticism, he noted, showed that "we may contend that St. John wrote the first Epistle ascribed to him, and yet deny that he wrote the famous 'Comma Joanneum.' " Some "advanced critics," he acknowledged, "reject most external evidence, and depend almost exclusively on internal evidence, which is subjective and mostly fanciful and capricious." He believed, however, that "ultra conservative critics rely almost entirely on external evidence." It was possible that "both [schools of critics] are wrong."[37]

Grannan, however, was still a neophyte in the unfolding discipline of biblical criticism. "Destructive criticism," he said, tended to undermine the divine authority of Scripture, but higher criticism had done "good work when it discredited the once prevalent belief in the *verbal* inspiration of Scripture, according to which every word, every syllable, every letter, every punctuation mark, and every vowel point was said to have been revealed to the sacred penman while in a trance or ecstasy, during which he committed all to writing as mechanically as a type-writer."[38] Such a careless use of the term "verbal inspiration" would win Grannan a sharp rebuke from Father Joseph Bruneau, S.S., but, at this point, he was simply trying to explain to a broad Catholic audience the issues involved in higher criticism.

"Though first cultivated by Catholics," Grannan argued, "Biblical Criticism, especially in its most objectionable features, is now intimately bound up with Rationalism." The difficulty arose when critics like Wellhausen went beyond the evidence or drew apodictic conclusions from the lack of evidence. As an example, Grannan noted:

On the pedestal of a monument erected to the memory of Thomas Jefferson, at Monticello, in Virginia, there is this inscription: "Thos. Jefferson, Author of the Declaration of Independence, of the Statute for Religious Liberty and Founder of the University of Virginia." And yet, strange as it may appear, not so much as one word about his having been President of the United States.

Grannan feared that some "higher critic" in the future would conclude that "Thomas Jefferson, President . . . , was quite a different man from Thomas Jefferson, Framer of the Declaration of Independence." He was not opposed to legitimate higher criticism, but only to the form it took when its practitioners ignored the possibility of the supernatural and adapted "the general principles of Atheistic and Deistic evolution" to account for "the origin of the Christian religion." Such an approach was "rationalistic philosophy" rather than higher criticism. He made his own the statement of William Sanday of Oxford that true higher criticism "makes no assumptions of a philosophical or theological character, and certainly none which interferes with a full belief in the real objective inspiration of the books to which it is applied."[39]

For Grannan at this stage, the problem was not with higher criticism, but with some of the higher critics. "No real Pope," he said, "was ever so loud as they in proclaiming the dogma of their own infallibility."[40] Grannan made no claim to be an original scholar, but his sympathy with higher criticism developed rapidly. In 1895, *The Catholic University Bulletin* was founded as a scholarly journal. In an article in the first issue, Grannan noted that three ecumenical councils had said that Scripture was "inspired because

'God is its author'; beyond this general indication we are left much to ourselves in the discussion of this very interesting subject." For himself, he openly embraced "the critical history of the origin of the sacred books." Yet, he continued to see Gn 3:15 as the "proto-evangelium," from which "we can trace throughout the entire Old Testament the gradual development of this idea; we can everywhere see the image of a marvelous man, a most singular man, gentle yet awful, near yet distant as the unseen God.''[41] In the classroom, however, Grannan seems to have been more liberal and he contributed, indirectly, to the removal of the university's first rector, Bishop John J. Keane.

In 1893, Grannan assigned Father William Russell a thesis for defense in a licentiate examination. It read: "While the Council of Trent does not admit any difference in point of canonicity, it does not expressly condemn the opinion held by Jerome and the Greek fathers that there is a distinction of authority between the Protocanonical and the Deuterocanonical books of the Old Testament." Monsignor Joseph Schroeder immediately remonstrated with Russell, unsuccessfully, that the thesis had been taken from a work of Loisy, still on the faculty of the Institut Catholique in Paris. He then brought the matter before the faculty, where he found his only ally to be Joseph Pohle. Two years later, he had occasion to meet with Archbishop Francesco Satolli, who had become the first apostolic delegate in 1893. Satolli asked him for any theses, used at the university, pertaining to Scripture. In June, Schroeder wrote an account of the whole affair for Satolli and enclosed a thesis to be defended that year. The new thesis read: "Though the Decree of Trent declared all the books of Scripture to be equally sacred and canonical, still the Council did not expressly condemn the opinion of Jerome and many of the Greek fathers, who admitted a difference of authority between the protocanonical and deuterocanonical books of the Old Testament." Schroeder's letter was placed in the file pertaining to Keane's dismissal as rector, in 1896.[42]

PROGRESSIVE BIBLICAL SCHOLARSHIP IN THE UNITED STATES

While Grannan was gradually developing into a more liberal biblical theologian, the *American Ecclesiastical Review* had not yet definitively become the bastion of reaction. Alfred Loisy, whom Schroeder had seen fit to criticize as early as 1893 and who had then been dismissed from the Institut Catholique, contributed four articles between 1896 and 1898: "The Scriptural Account of the Disciples of Emmaus," "Vobiscum Sum," "The Transfiguration of Our Lord," and "Gethsemane."[43] None of these, however, were indicative of his more controversial work. But there were also American voices, similar to the European liberals. Shortly after Maas introduced the readers of the *Review* to his ingenious solutions to biblical criticism, Joseph Bruneau, S.S., struck a different chord.

JOSEPH BRUNEAU, S.S.

Bruneau, professor of Scripture at St. Joseph's Seminary, Dunwoodie, New York, outlined the new theories of inspiration then being developed in Europe. Bruneau chose as his starting point a refutation of Brook Herford's Dudlein Lecture at Harvard in 1895. Herford had asserted that, in order to show that Catholics reverenced the Bible as much as Protestants, the Council of Trent had decreed "absolute verbal inspiration." Bruneau first noted that many Catholic scholars in Europe as well as Maas and Grannan in the United States had repudiated "verbal inspiration" as antiquated. He then chided them for being unaware of some of the newer theories of "verbal inspiration," which did not make the sacred writer, in Grannan's term, "a typewriter." To illustrate his point, Bruneau analyzed the work of a number of scholars, some of whom would not endear him to Roman authorities. Giovanni Semeria, an Italian Barnabite, held that the Bible was "a multiple production, like the construction of a house," in which it was not necessary that "the architect" had "fashioned the bricks." Semeria concluded that the relationship between God, as author, and the words used was that "God, the primary author of Scripture, *allowed* the writer to choose the words; but He *did not make him choose them;* otherwise we would find no imperfection at all."[44]

Bruneau acknowledged that Semeria had failed to show the manner in which the words could be said to be inspired. Here he thought Hermann Schell had solved the problem in his *Dogmatik*. Schell had said:

Inspiration does not formally signify a shifting in the relations between the divine and human causality to the disadvantage of the latter, but a heightening both of the divine influence and spontaneous activity. Materially it extends as far as the human authorship, including the *will,* the plan of *thought,* and the execution or *words;* for these three activities are not only synchronous, but conditional, and influence each other mutually, so that no one or no two of them would suffice as the sole vehicle of Inspiration. In all limiting schemes the spontaneous share of the sacred writer falls short of the origination which we find in other writers, whilst God on His part cannot be said fully to speak to us.[45]

Schell seemed to imply that all of Scripture was not revelation and this would be a crucial question in the years to come. He would, moreover, become associated with the liberal bishops who supported the Catholic University.

Bruneau was still more favorable toward his former professor, "the prominent biblical scholar Abbé Loisy," who had attempted to clarify some of the points raised by Semeria. In what Bruneau styled Loisy's "unfortunately discontinued magazine *L'Enseignement Biblique,* the exegete stated: *"I admit verbal inspiration. . . .* I could never understand how the Sacred Books were inspired as to the substance and not as to form; how, the ideas being furnished to the sacred writer by inspiration, he had only to cast about for words."[46] Loisy's statement was sufficiently vague, but what he opposed seemed to be a paraphrase, if not a parody, of Franzelin's theory of inspiration.

In Loisy's mind, "the ancient tradition down to Suarez" had been "favorable to verbal inspiration." The modern problem arose when, "for the Vulgate the same inspiration was desired as for the original texts of Scripture; once verbal inspiration is done away with, a version may be as divine as the primitive book." Those who rejected verbal inspiration, he continued, hoped to account for "individuality of style." For Loisy, this was absurd, "as if this individuality did not pertain as well to the thought as to the style! As if grace overthrew nature!" While proponents of verbal inspiration had "often confounded inspiration with revelation," he argued "that the upholders of limited inspiration have fallen into the same confusion." Both were in danger of looking "upon the inspired writers as simply automatons, and their writings as simply the mechanical results of their pens, without any trouble of thought on the part of the authors."[47]

Bruneau next summarized an earlier article of Loisy on the history of the dogma of inspiration. Loisy held that the human and divine elements in the Bible were "so intimately connected that they constitute a work in which it is impossible to distinguish what is due exclusively to human agency from what is exclusively divine." Acknowledging his dependence on Peter Dausch, he argued that "the inspired book is all of it the work of God, but it is at the same time no less the work of man." To attempt to dichotomize the book and make "God . . . the author of the ideas and man the author of the words" or anything similar would engage in what Dausch called *"vivisection."* For Loisy,

both God and man have (but in a widely different manner) a right to be called authors of the Bible in its entirety—of its ideas and words—substance and form, religious truths and historical or cosmological data. Neither ancient tradition, properly interpreted, nor reason, sanction the divisions which modern writers under the influence of polemical bias, have tried to effect in the Bible. The composition of the Sacred Books has been a supernatural work which the divine concursus has penetrated through and through so that not a wit of it can be said to be due exclusively to God or man.[48]

By being thus so favorably disposed toward Loisy, Bruneau was treading on dangerous ground, for it was clear that the French exegete was repudiating Franzelin.

Bruneau was trying to have his readers realize that it was essential to distinguish between revelation and inspiration. Here he relied upon another of his former professors in Paris, Eugène Lévesque, S.S., who defined inspiration as an active "help to convey truth . . . not given to know, to receive, but to transmit." "In revelation," however, "the mind is passive, so that it may receive a manifestation of truth." By drawing such a distinction, Bruneau believed that "verbal inspiration" did not mean "a *revelation* of each word," for this would mean that "God would not be the principal, but the exclusive author of Scripture." For Bruneau, inspiration did "not require revelation" and yet implied "more than Revelation." Revelation would mean only that "the sacred writers *received* divine thoughts." With inspiration, "the manifestation of truth is a motion from God, which directs the writer to express what God wants, and nothing more; but nothing less."[49]

To develop the distinction between inspiration and revelation, Bruneau introduced the readers of the *American Ecclesiastical Review* to the theory of Marie-Joseph Lagrange O.P. The Dominican exegete argued that nonverbal inspiration was "an administrative compromise . . . , but not at all a theological distinction." It was a theory "created by men who, wrongly, imagining inspiration to be a mechanical pressure, attempted to resolve some difficulties in referring to the writer *at least* the choice of words." This made the writer first totally passive in receiving revelation and then totally active in choosing the words to communicate the revelation. Such a theory, said Lagrange, would *"deny the inspiration of thoughts, when not necessarily revealed."* "Modern studies," he thought, would reestablish "some ancient systems on a more scientific basis." In that process, not only would apologetics not suffer, but it "will feel more comfortable in the large edifices of traditional theology than in the modern halls, hastily built up, as a provisional refuge by Cardinal Franzelin."[50] Bruneau's favorable report of Lagrange's attack on Franzelin placed him in the camp of those against whom the Jesuits and other conservatives would soon be reacting.

While showing his sympathy for new theories of verbal inspiration, Bruneau acknowledged his ignorance of how the "psychological, supernatural action" influenced the sacred writer and "how God can act upon an instrument such as man, who by his nature is free, so that everything in Scripture comes from God, everything from man." He was only eager to point out to his readers that "exegetists of undoubted authority in the biblical world" did not reject verbal inspiration, which they did "not conceive . . . as distorted by some modern theologians under Protestant influences; but as espoused by the solemn and authorized voice of Catholic Tradition." Harking back to the theological sources of Kenrick, he found it "gratifying to see that the most recent opinion turns out to be but the teaching of the Fathers." He further raised the question, however, of the relationship between theology and biblical studies. While a professor of Scripture should also be a theologian, he argued that it was within the spirit of *Providentissimus Deus* "to say that in questions of Biblical theology, only those authors should be taken into serious account who have made a deep and thorough study of the traditional doctrine of the Church together with the criticism of the Sacred Books."[51]

Bruneau was not an original scholar, but he was the first on the American scene to report on the development in European scholarship. By mentioning Maas by name and by criticizing Franzelin indirectly, he showed the liberal orientation of his sympathies. For the moment, these were all open issues, about which the Catholic world debated freely. He would return to the *Ecclesiastical Review* several more times before the century ended and would again display his liberal tendencies. As will be seen, however, by that time, the question of inspiration had become associated, if not intertwined, with other questions dividing the American church.

CHARLES GRANNAN ON INSPIRATION

In the meantime, Grannan reentered the discussion in 1897 with a far more mature grasp of the topic of inspiration. In *The Catholic University Bulletin,* he asserted that, since the Reformation, Protestants and some Catholics had so stressed a "mechanical" theory of inspiration, that they omitted the "conscious and voluntary activity of the writers whom the Holy Ghost employed." At the opposite extreme to this mechanical theory was the "natural" one, which held that "inspiration is nothing more than the higher development of that natural insight into truth which all men possess in some degree; that it is an order of intelligence which, in morals and in religion, naturally results in the production of sacred books of the same sort as the Bible. . . ." Grannan wished to avoid both extremes and noted that, although God could have written the Bible Himself, "he preferred to write it with the cooperation of a human intellect, and with the consent of a human will, and with the resources of a human memory. He preferred to instruct and save men by the instrumentality of men. He preferred to use human instruments, so as to make the Bible a human book, and to give to it all the peculiarities which characterize the works of man."[52] By referring to the "instrumentality of men" for both instruction and salvation, he thus began to relate the question of inspiration to Christology. He would make this yet more explicit.

Without precisely stating the types of criticism, to which, as "works of men," the books of Scripture could be subjected, Grannan argued that "the same Scripture, which claims to be the word of God, claims, also, to be word of man." Nor did he explicate any particular theory of inspiration. Instead, he contented himself with a description of how the Bible could be both fully human and fully divine. "In the composition of every book of the Bible," he wrote,

two agencies were at work, God and man, and thus divine operation and human cooperation went hand in hand throughout. The Bible is the joint production of God and man. It is all *from* God, its first cause, and all *through* man its channel, and all *by* man, so was more than a lifeless channel. The primary cause or author of the Book is God; the instrumental cause or writer is man. Consequently, the Bible is never to be regarded as merely human, nor as merely divine, nor as partly human and partly divine, but as all human and all divine.[53]

Grannan was thus coming close to the theory of Loisy.

For Grannan, there was an "analogy between the divine and human in the Bible and the divine and human in Jesus Christ." While the union of the two natures in Christ was "hypostatical or personal," however, the union of the two elements in the Bible was "merely verbal." As a result, the Incarnate Word of God was worshipped, but the written word or Bible was not. There were passages in the Gospels, he said, in which "we see the weakness of His Humanity" and others in which "we see evidence of His divinity." The same was true for the Scripture, for

the written word of God in its source or first principle, that is, when spoken by the mouth of God in heaven, is perfect. But as soon as the divine thought externalizes itself in language, clothes itself in human speech, and incarnates itself, so to speak, on the written page, it partakes of the many imperfections common to human language, "sin alone excepted"; that is, to the exclusion of error.

In treating the issue of error in Scripture, Grannan was at his weakest in attempting to link freedom from error with holiness. Too many Christians, he said, had emphasized "the divine element, not too much, but too exclusively." While they sought to avoid the pitfall that, "if the Bible is all human, it is all fallible," they forgot "that, in Scripture, the human is so strengthened by grace, and so modified by the divine with which it is united and vivified that it cannot err." Only in the Incarnate Word was humanity perfectly sanctified and sinless, but, in Scripture, it was necessary to distinguish inspiration from sanctification, for "the writers of Scripture, though 'holy men of God,' may not have been absolutely sinless; yet they committed no error in what they wrote."[54] Grannan, unfortunately, failed to indicate the areas in which the Scripture writers "committed no error."

Grannan was one of the few Americans grappling with the issue of inspiration. At this point, his contribution to the discussion was twofold. First, he related the significance of the Incarnation to the human authorship of Scripture. Just as it was "much better . . . for us that our redemption was worked out for us by the man-God," he wrote, so too "the human element in Scripture has had its share in making Holy Writ more loved and better understood than ever it would have been if written by angelic pens and in the language of the angels." Second, he drew the parallel between the "mental, moral and physical development" of Jesus in the New Testament and the "growth in the truth revealed in Holy Writ" from the Old Testament to the New. But he had failed to explain the nature and extent of inspiration and the meaning of biblical inerrancy. He only vaguely asserted that "the written Word" could not be "perfectly human, unless it shared in the imperfections of human language and in the limitations of human thought."[55]

Grannan would return to his topic a year later. By 1897, however, he was the most progressive American Catholic thinker in the biblical field. His thought had noticeably developed from suspicion of historical criticism to open espousal. He had introduced his readers to the useful analogy between the human and divine natures in Christ and the human and divine elements in Scripture. In this, he was ahead of his time. But he was not alone. Bruneau and other Sulpicians were publicly sympathetic with the new European trends. But their orientation ran them afoul of Jesuits, both in the United States and Europe. They and the liberals had also suffered defeat in the forced resignation of O'Connell from the American College and of Keane from the Catholic University. Their attitude toward historical criticism of the Bible, moreover, had now become intertwined with other issues, not least among which was the emerging movement known as Americanism. What was needed was a catalyst to bring together European and American thinkers on these various issues.

4. Americanism and the Biblical Question: The Convergence of Ideas

By 1897, the American church was divided into liberal and conservative camps. The liberals, led by John Ireland, wished to take an aggressive stance toward American culture. They had called for cooperation between Church and State in providing education and supported the nascent labor movement in the United States. Without intending it, they had also alienated European conservatives, who saw them surrendering to the State, notably in the field of education, the rights that the European church was desperately trying to preserve. In the United States, they had won the antagonism of Archbishop Michael Augustine Corrigan of New York, German-American Catholics, and the Jesuits. The liberals had made the Catholic University their intellectual citadel and could count on the support of the Sulpicians. But they faced an increasingly organized opposition, which, for the time being, centered only on Americanism.

AMERICANISM AND THE BIBLICAL QUESTION AT THE FRIBOURG CONGRESS

Earlier in the year, Walter Elliott's *Life of Father Hecker* had been translated into French. With a preface by the Abbé Félix Klein of the Institut Catholique, *La Vie du Père Hecker* transformed Hecker from a deeply spiritual priest, seeking to mediate Catholicism to Protestant America, into the ideal priest of the future, who based his spirituality on the interior direction of the Holy Spirit, rather than the exterior authority of the Church, and who promoted the active virtues, which produced the saints of the modern age, rather than the passive virtues, which produced monks and hermits.[1]

Controversy soon arose in France, not so much from a faulty translation of the biography of the founder of the Paulists, as from the inability to interpret one culture to another. The argument over what was now known as "Americanism" flowed over into the biblical question. The first step toward the intertwining of the two issues occurred at Fribourg, Switzerland.

For some time, Grannan and other liberal members of the Catholic University faculty had sought to rid themselves of Monsignor Joseph Schroeder, whom they knew to have been partly responsible for Keane's forced resignation. They also wished to gain the assistance of European scholars in showing that Schroeder did not represent the only approach to Catholic theology. In this, they had the support of liberal members of the hierarchy. At the same time, the Americanists sought to clarify the meaning of the distinctive tradition of the American church in the midst of the European debate over Hecker. Denis O'Connell was designated to be their spokesman. In August 1897, O'Connell, Zahm, Grannan and Edward A. Pace, a university colleague, traveled to Fribourg, Switzerland, to attend the Fourth International Catholic Scientific Congress. It was a gathering of virtually everyone with new ideas in the Church and provided a personal link between Americanism and the biblical question. O'Connell read a paper entitled "A New Idea in the Life of Father Hecker." It argued for the value to the Church of the American separation of Church and State, which flowed from Anglo-American Common Law. Zahm, then the Roman procurator for the American Holy Cross Fathers, spoke on evolution and dogma. Marie-Joseph Lagrange, O.P. presided over the section devoted to biblical studies and delivered a discourse on the historical criticism of the Pentateuch. Baron Friedrich von Hügel sent a paper, read for him by Semeria, on the sources of the Hexateuch. Maurice Blondel, according to von Hügel, was also to be present, but there is no record that he actually spoke.[2]

At first glance, the ideas presented at the Fribourg congress seem disparate. Yet, there was an interlocking consistency—at least in the minds of the conservatives. To speak, as O'Connell had, of the separation of Church and State and religious liberty seemed to surrender the very rights the Church in Europe was seeking to defend from the usurpations of the European liberal State; it appeared to be an American form of the rationalism which the European Church was trying to combat. To show the compatibility of evolution with the Church's doctrine, as Zahm had asserted, seemed to endanger the notion of God as Creator. Von Hügel's and Lagrange's acknowledgement that the Old Testament, as it exists, was the product of several sources raised the question of who was the inspired author. Blondel's notion of philosophical personalism appeared nothing more than subjectivism and individualism. For the Fribourg progressives, the heart of the issue was the potentiality of human reason under grace or inspiration. For their opponents, the emphasis on human reason was the very basis of all the problems the European church confronted.

After the congress, O'Connell and Zahm paid a visit to Hermann Schell in Würzburg, as they sought to broaden the international base of their program of Americanism.[3] Encouraged by European support for their theological orientation, the American opponents of Schroeder succeeded in having him removed from the faculty of the Catholic University, despite the support offered him by Cardinal Andreas Steinhuber, S.J.[4] Back in Rome, O'Connell continued to internationalize Americanism. Early in 1897, his apartment had been dubbed "Liberty Hall" and became the meeting place for the "Club" or "Lodge." Its members included, besides O'Connell and Zahm, Louis Duchesne, the church historian, von Hügel, David Fleming, O.F.M., an English consultor to the Holy Office, and, on occasion, Giovanni Genocchi, an Italian biblical scholar.[5] Every Tuesday, they gathered for dinner and conversation.

LAGRANGE AND THE PENTATEUCH

As Americanism was entering its international phase, *The Catholic University Bulletin* directly entered the European fray of the biblical question. It published a summary of Lagrange's paper, done by von Hügel—the only English version of the work.[6] O'Connell also arranged for the *Bulletin* to publish the full text of von Hügel's paper.[7] Lagrange noted that source-criticism of the Pentateuch had originated with a Catholic, Jean Astruc. He then traced "the growth of Pentateuchal criticism outside the Church, resulting in the present practical unanimity as to the existence and general character and extension of the four great documents of the Elohist *(E)*, the Jahvist *(J)*, Deuteronomy *(D)*, and the Priestly Code *(P)*." He emphasized, however, that the "first beginnings" of that type of criticism occurred with the work of Richard Simon, the seventeenth-century French oratorian.[8]

Lagrange arranged his treatment under five questions. First, he rejected any "theory of Canonicity and Inspiration" which held that the sacred books were "always composed once for all" without subsequent "remodellings." All that the dogma of inspiration required, he argued, was "the inspiration of the final redactor," but this did "not necessarily demand the inspiration of the documents employed by him." He concluded that "we are, then, not obliged to attribute to the primitive author the final redaction of a Biblical book."[9] In other words, Lagrange did not link inspiration with the original authorship.

Second, Lagrange treated the "evolution of the Law." All "semblance of contradiction" in the Pentateuch would be removed, he maintained, if one recognized that there was a "primitive Mosaic legislation," compiled partly from "existing customs," and "that the laws of the Priestly Code are its normal conclusion."[10]

Third, Lagrange treated the Bible's internal evidence for the Mosaic authorship of the Pentateuch. He asserted that phrases, such as "God said to Moses" or "Moses wrote," were too vague to designate Mosaic authorship in the strict sense. While Deuteronomy was, indeed, attributed to Moses, it may well have been "entirely pseudepigraphical." Yet, this should cause no difficulty for its being inspired, for "the wisdom of Solomon seems to prove that a pseudepigraphical book can well be an inspired one." Lagrange had also treated the question of the New Testament testimony of Jesus and concluded:

the authority of our Lord ought not to be involved. The writer is not of those who limit His knowledge, even as man. But the proposition: "Moses wrote this law," remains substantially true, even if it cannot be applied to the complete redaction of the law; Our Lord came to bring back hearts to God, not to treat of literary problems; and, as to the one difficult passage (John V, 45, 47), the real antithesis is here between the *written* book of the law (known to all the world under the name of Moses) and the *spoken* words of Our Lord; the literary question as to the composition of the Pentateuch is not even raised.[11]

Lagrange's fourth topic was the "tradition" that Moses was the author of the Pentateuch. Here Lagrange drew a distinction: "We get, first, a double modality: Moses is the legislator of Israel, Mosaism is at the bottom of the whole history of the people of God—there is the *historical* tradition; Moses was the redactor of the Pentateuch which we possess; there is the *literary* tradition." Those who defended the Mosaic authorship had failed to make this distinction. Yet, the attribution of the account of Moses' death to Joshua and the assumption of subsequent glosses on the text were already examples of the "beginning of internal criticism," against which the defenders of the Mosaic authorship contended. Moreover, it was difficult to determine the precise authorship of a complete book; councils and theologians, for example, had attributed to Dionysius the Areopagite works that no contemporary scholar would allow to him. Finally, there was no way to "find a witness to the literary fact of the total composition." Lagrange illustrated his point by analogy with the Lord's Prayer. "We generally admit," he wrote,

that the words of Our Lord have been in a certain measure, transformed by the primitive oral teaching of the Church; we have in the Gospels two forms of the *Pater Noster,* and do not hold ourselves bound to maintain that Jesus Christ pronounced them both; why then should we believe that Moses wrote both forms of the Decalogue?[12]

In this context, Lagrange approached the relationship between canonicity and authorship. "Whilst pronouncing on Canonicity," he wrote, the Council of Trent had "avoided deciding the question of Authorship." He argued that the council's reference to the "Pentateuch of Moses" was a "disciplinary rule," which "cannot be extended beyond what is practised [*sic*] with regard to the Epistle to the Hebrews, the origin of which was actually discussed in the council." He granted that he was asking "something more for the Pentateuch, yet this will ever remain the Pentateuch of Moses, if that great man laid the foundations of its legislation."[13] The binding force of Trent's statement, as will be seen, became controversial in the United States, for some prominent theologians argued that the council had indeed made a declaration about the authorship of the Pentateuch. As Kenrick had done in the United States a generation earlier, Lagrange thus linked inspiration with canonicity rather than authorship. This was his fifth and final question.

In treating "the Historical Value of the Pentateuch," Lagrange acknowledged that he was dealing with a crucial issue. But the question was whether Mosaic authorship safeguarded the "historical character" of the facts narrated. If one granted that Moses used preexisting sources, then the date of the final redaction was less important than the "existence of written sources" prior to Moses. Within this framework, Lagrange argued for the advantage of the four-source theory of the composition of the Pentateuch. If the Elohist, Yahwist, and Priestly Code had each used the preceding document, then there were "three witnesses instead of one" to "the veracity of the history of Israel." Though each may have had a different interpretation of the history, the final redactor insured "the correctness of our judgment, by putting the various narratives into parallel for us." The situation, for him, was not unlike that of the synoptic Gospels, which made it impossible to "force them into absolutely the same mold"; yet "their agreement on essential points" provided "the best criterion for the veracity of the general account."[14]

Lagrange was anxious to avoid a literal interpretation of the Bible. For him, "the Primitive History (of the first chapters of Genesis)" and "the idealized History (of the Priestly Code)" presented "historical subject matter, taught by means of accidental forms which the author does not give as true in themselves, but as a formula more or less precise of the truth." To justify his position, he appealed to the Fathers. They had distinguished between "inspired prophecy" and "inspired history" and thus interpreted Ezekiel in a spiritual sense and the description of the Tabernacle as pertaining to Christ. They had also treated the Pentateuch as essentially a book of law, for which history was but a framework. Lagrange then attempted to explain the type of truth that one could expect to find in Scripture. "God has not," he wrote,

with regard to such and such like historical and chronological details, chosen to instruct us, to teach us things that do not concern salvation. But He has not, for all that, led us into error, although He has sanctioned the use of historical processes so foreign to our habits; all the harm comes from ourselves, who prefer Jewish literalness to the instinct of the Fathers, who rose higher.[15]

Kenrick would have been at home with Lagrange's analysis, which would, as will be seen, provide the basis for Henry Poels's subsequent argument for the new biblical method. But for the journal of the Catholic University to publish large excerpts of Lagrange's paper drew further Roman attention to the American liberals.

Bruneau praised both von Hügel's and Lagrange's papers in the *American Ecclesiastical Review*. Reviewing Lagrange, he admitted that the new critics did not totally agree on their analysis of the Pentateuch, but, in his mind, they had reached "a very substantial unanimity . . . on the main features of the case." But, beyond the criticism of the Pentateuch, he realized there lay the broader questions of "the nature of inspiration, the relations between inspiration and authorship, the kind of truth which belongs to Biblical statements, etc."[16] In a subsequent issue of the *Review*, he acknowledged that von Hügel's paper on the Hexateuch indicated the high probability that there were, indeed, four sources to the books. For Bruneau, it was a good example that not all critics were rationalists. "Among Catholics," he said, "we have Abbé Loisy a rare combination of caution and courage, competence and charm, one, too, equally at home in the philological and historical niceties and in the philosophy and theology of these increasingly important questions." Bruneau went on to praise Loisy's application of higher criticism to the story of the flood, as a compilation of the Elohist and Yahwist sources; it seemed plausible to Bruneau that the Jews had borrowed from a Chaldean narrative.[17]

With the publication of the articles by Lagrange and von Hügel, *The Catholic University Bulletin* had become a principal vehicle in the English-speaking world for the dissemination of the new biblical scholarship. In the same number of the *Bulletin* in which Lagrange's article appeared, Grannan published "The Human Element in Scripture." He seemed to have benefited from his Fribourg exposure to Lagrange. His article sought to articulate some of the "limitations of human thought." The Scripture writers, he argued, utilized existing secular literary works which they "copied out into scriptures under the influence of Inspiration." Reflecting the influence of European exegetes, he stated that "the thoughts expressed in Scripture . . . were written with the assistance of a human intellect, and with the consent of a human will, and with the resources of a human memory, and were colored by the creative faculties of the human imaginatian [*sic*]." Before arguing for any theory of inspiration, he said, it was necessary to recognize that "historical criticism has placed the books of the Bible on a level with the most reliable of human documents."[18] He was now clearly in the camp of the progressives, but he had still not indicated what he meant by inspiration or its compatibility with error.

Unfortunately for the progressives, the question of the human authorship of Scripture began to become intertwined with the question of human initiative in the Americanist movement. By drawing the analogy between the human and divine elements in Scripture and the human and divine natures in Christ, Grannan and his sympathizers were raising questions not only about the role of human reason in writing the Scriptures but also about Christology. At the same time, the Americanists were asserting the advantage to the Church of American religious liberty and were praising human initiative, under the direction of the Holy Spirit. To the conservatives, this appeared to be, if not Pelagianism, a denial of the need for external authority. The intertwining of the two separate movements—Americanism and biblical criticism—provided the context within which American Catholic biblical scholarship next developed.

REACTIONS AGAINST AMERICANISM

The period after the Fribourg congress represented a turning point for the American liberals. From March 3 to April 9, 1898, a series of articles appeared in *La Vérité*, entitled "L'Americanisme Mystique" and signed "Martel." The author was Father Charles Maignen of the Society of the Brothers of St. Vincent de Paul, who had already gained notoriety for his opposition to Leo XIII's plea for French Catholics to support the Third Republic. Hecker, he argued, had so emphasized the interior guidance of the Holy Spirit that he denigrated the external authority of the Church. The Paulist, furthermore, had praised "active virtues," appropriate for republicans, over "passive virtues," more suited for monarchists. The American, Maignen asserted, had also watered down doctrine in order to gain converts and had relegated religious vows to the Middle Ages. Gibbons, Keane, Ireland, and O'Connell, each in his own way, had illustrated their dependence on Hecker's legacy and were trying to carry their campaign from the New World to the Old.[19]

Other European conservatives soon entered the fray. In 1898, Alphonse J. Delattre, S.J., professor of Hebrew at the Jesuit scholasticate at Louvain contributed his *Catholicisme américain* accusing the Americanists of individualism and Gallicanism. In opposition to Hecker's and O'Connell's praise of the Anglo-American common law, he argued that the Church had experienced its golden age, when it had lived under the Roman Law.[20] As will be seen, both Maignen and Delattre were later also active in the campaign against biblical scholars.

Unfortunately, the war of words between the two worlds escalated into a shooting war. The Spanish-American War provided the context within which European Catholics feared the possibility that American ideas would be imposed on Europe, not through persuasion, but through force of arms—a fear which Ireland and O'Connell did nothing to assuage. *La Vérité* had announced that Maignen would soon publish his articles in book form. Due to the influence of the Sulpicians, Cardinal François-Marie Richard of Paris refused to grant the book his *imprimatur*. Maignen then obtained a Roman publisher and received the *imprimatur* from Alberto Lepidi, O.P., Master of the Sacred Palace. The American liberals all protested, to no avail, the apparent Vatican approval of Maignen's *Le Père Hecker: est-il un Saint?*[21]

AMERICANISM AND BIBLICAL CRITICISM: THE ROMAN INVESTIGATIONS OF 1898

During the summer of 1898, Leo XIII appointed a commission to investigate Americanism. Some of the American liberals began to suspect the link in the conservative mind between Americanism and the biblical question. Grannan wrote O'Connell:

I hear everywhere that Dr. Schell has an immense number of supporters, but most of them talk but little. Are there not bishops enough in America to prevent the condemnation of Americanism, American and even European? What are they good for? But I forget: it is enough to reflect what most of them were, before they became bishops, to know that they are good for nothing.
I hope our Bulletin will not come in for any share of the censure passed on the "Revue Biblique." It will soon be impossible to write anything at all on S. Scripture. In the last few days I have been reviewing a pamphlet written by [illegible] Profs who left Freiburg in der Schweiz. It is interesting, all the worse so as it gives all the documents in the case. The Dominicans are made to play a very sorry role in it.[22]

In Rome, awaiting the outcome of the investigation of Americanism, O'Connell narrated for Ireland the complex issues then being examined. He had just had several conversations with Lepidi and felt that he had successfully explained to him the distinction between the Americanism held in the United States and in Europe. He felt quite sure that Mazzella, Satolli, and Salvatore Brandi, S.J., editor of *Civiltà cattolica,* were being consulted on Americanism, since it was the English life of Hecker, which was being quoted to him. But he noted

a perfect feeling of spite & madness is running wild here just now. They are really acting & talking like men that have lost their senses. The poor old Pope is trying to find a cool place to sit down in and care for his health, and the others, like powers long kept confined, are now rushing like [illegible] lions for their prey, before the Pope dies. It is the pent up madness of 10 years that is breaking out. This is their "hour." Another party of them is engaged in preparing a decree against Evolution, soon to appear, and some wanted a condemnation of "La Revue Biblique." Rev. Dr. [Salvatore] Minocchi, a prominent Hebrew scholar at Florence and translator of many of the books from the Hebrew, received one morning without any intimation or explanation an order to write nothing more on Scripture. Genocchi is trying to arrange his case.

He concluded his description of this flurry of activity by noting that "Duchesne says he always observed that the H. Office is worse during the months of June & July."[23] At the same time, O'Connell's friend, Genocchi, the Italian exegete, reported to Umberto Fracassini, also a Scripture scholar and superior of the Seminary of Perugia, that some people in Rome were beginning to consider "critico-biblical studies as an apparent part of dangerous Americanism."[24]

The references that Grannan and O'Connell had made to the *Revue biblique* concerned Lagrange's denunciation in Rome by Archbishop Piavi, O.F.M., Latin Patriarch of Jerusalem. The Franciscan had accused Lagrange the previous April of embracing "German rationalism" in the address he had given in Fribourg and which had been published in the *Revue.* Though Lagrange's superiors supported him, they did, shortly thereafter, recommend that he publish a proposed commentary on Genesis in a series of articles, rather than in a book.[25] Biblical scholarship and Americanism at least had in common that they were both under investigation at the same time by the same people. But there were other questions under investigation.

The issue of evolution, to which O'Connell had also alluded, had a direct effect upon the Americans. In September 1898, the Congregation of the Index had condemned John Zahm's *Evolution and Dogma*. The issue became complicated, because Zahm had just been named provincial superior of the Congregation of the Holy Cross in the United States. Roman authorities postponed publication of the decree of condemnation, until they could consult with Zahm's superior general, Gilbert Français. When Français arrived in Rome, he welcomed the assistance of Denis O'Connell, but wrote Zahm that it was his association with O'Connell and the Americanists that had created the problem. The issue was finally settled when the Congregation of the Index decided not to publish its decree, on condition that Zahm withdraw all copies of his book from sale.[26] The threads of several seemingly independent intellectual movements were now being woven together by the conservative theologians.

In the meantime, during the fall of 1898, Grannan reported that the university faculty was in low spirits. Gibbons, Ireland, and Keane seemed unable or unwilling to do anything to combat the attack on Americanism. "Really it is a pitiable sight," he said, "to see this great Party as helpless as babies, as cowardly as a flock of sheep, numerous, but without a leader. Not one of the 'Big Ghree [sic]' has any of the necessary qualities for leadership, if you except one of them, & even he has not the necessary persistency." Grannan did not specify which of the "Big Three" he had in mind, but he most probably meant Gibbons. If the liberal American bishops were loathe to combat the attack on Americanism in 1898, a few years later, none of them would make any effort to defend Scripture scholarship. For the moment, Grannan was pleased to announce that he had forty-eight students enrolled in his course on Scripture—more than double the size of the next largest class at the university.[27]

Testem Benevolentiae

Though Grannan and O'Connell had both made allusions to the Roman mentality in examining both Americanism and the biblical question, neither seems to have seen any direct relationship. On January 22, 1899, Leo XIII issued his apostolic letter *Testem Benevolentiae*. The letter condemned the notion "that, in order to bring over to Catholic doctrine those who dissent from it, the Church ought to adapt herself somewhat to our advanced civilization, and, relaxing her ancient rigor, show some indulgence to modern popular theories and methods." The pope was concerned that this notion was applied "not only with regard to the rule of life, but also to the doctrines in which the *deposit of faith* is contained." Those who supported such a notion would attempt "to pass over certain heads of doctrines, as if of lesser moment, or to so soften them that they may not have the same meaning which the Church has invariably held."[28]

The letter went on to reprove those who urged "that a certain liberty ought to be introduced into the Church, so that, limiting the exercise and vigilance of its powers, each one of the faithful may act more freely in pursuance of his own natural bent and capacity." Such people, it said, wished "to imitate that liberty which, though quite recently introduced, is now the law and foundation of almost every civil community." Such an approach would deny the right of the Church "to guard the minds of Catholics from the dangers of the present times." Such times showed the need for "this office of teaching [more] than ever before," when "liberty" was confused with "license"—"the passion for saying and reviling everything; the habit of thinking and of expressing everything in print."[29]

Leo then questioned some of Hecker's apparent teaching, namely on the role of the Holy Spirit within the individual Christian's life. The letter condemned those who held that "all external guidance is rejected as superfluous, nay even as somewhat of a disadvantage." This was, of course, a caricature of Hecker's theory, but it was clear that the pope's fear was that the theory would jeopardize the role of the Church as the guarantor of the Holy Spirit. On the one hand, he reproached those who seemed to imply that previous ages had "received a lesser outpouring of the Holy Spirit." On the other hand, he acknowledged, with the Second Council of Orange, that the illumination of the Holy Spirit was essential for one to accept the saving truth of the Gospel.[30]

The citation of the Second Council of Orange served as a warning against Pelagianism, of which Americanism might be a new expression. It was "hard to see," said Leo, "if we do away with all external guidance . . . , what purpose the more abundant influence of the Holy Ghost, which they make so much of, is to serve." Those who spoke of this abundance of the Spirit seemed also to "extol beyond measure the natural virtues as more in accordance with the ways and requirements of the present day, and consider it an advantage to be richly endowed with them, because they make a man more ready and more strenuous in action." This seemed to imply that "nature . . . , with grace added to it," was "weaker than when left to its own strength." "Rare," indeed, was "the man who really possesses the habit of these natural virtues." Only with "some divine help" could one observe "the whole natural law." "If we do not wish to lose sight of the eternal blessedness to which God in His goodness has destined us," Leo concluded, "of what use are the natural virtues unless the gift and strength of divine grace be added?"[31]

In short, the letter rebuked those who extolled human nature without grace. Grace and the external guidance of the Church were necessary for human nature to attain its end. In the Church's combat with rationalism, grace had become rare, and it was necessary to remind her members of original sin. But how did this relate to the biblical question? According to the prevailing theology, the new exegetes could not apply mere natural criticism to the sacred books, for this would imply that Scripture was a natural work. To preserve the inspiration of Scripture, the exegete had to acknowledge that the mind of the human author was supernaturally elevated to such an extent that a book of the Bible was a unique form of literature and could not be subjected to comparisons with other ancient Near Eastern literatures or to any other form of higher criticism, for the Scripture had God as its author. Inspiration had to be restricted to an author, whose name was known by tradition. To accept the possibility that the books of Scripture went through a series of redactions or to argue that several sources were put together to form a given book could mean that inspiration, like grace for the Americanists, would not be rare.

FIRST REACTIONS AGAINST BIBLICAL CRITICISM

At the time, few of the progressives either in Europe or in the United States probably saw any connection between the condemnation of Americanism and the growing opposition against the biblical exegetes. Yet, the reactions to both movements continued

to run parallel to each other. In November 1898, Lucien Mé-
chineau, S.J., professor of Scripture at the Gregorian University,
published an article accusing Lagrange of going over "to the camp
of our adversaries." Later that month, Leo issued a letter to the
Minister General of the Franciscans, warning them of the dangers
of some modern tendencies in the study of Scripture. Lagrange
was convinced that the pope had actually intended the letter for
the Dominicans. Finally, on January 28, within a week of *Testem
Benevolentiae*, Father Frühwirth, O.P., the Master General, wrote
Lagrange, warning him of the letter addressed to the Franciscans.
He also ordered that every article to be published in the *Revue
biblique* be first submitted to Rome to be read by censors, whom
he would choose.[32]

BIBLICAL SCHOLARSHIP IN THE UNITED STATES

For the moment, the American conservatives seem to have taken
little notice of the biblical question, but had focused only on
Americanism. Bruneau continued to teach in Corrigan's seminary.
In addition to his reports on biblical studies in the *American Ecclesiastical Review*, he made his own original contribution to the
discussion of the higher criticism of the New Testament.

JOSEPH BRUNEAU'S *Harmony of the Gospels*

In the summer of 1897, Bruneau completed his *Harmony of the
Gospels*. Published with Corrigan's *imprimatur* and dedicated to his
students at Dunwoodie, the book arranged the synoptic gospels in
parallel columns. In his preface, Bruneau stated that, "although it
would have been outside his plan and province to treat the 'Synoptic question,' the writer dares to say that some of the notes, as well
as the disposition of the paragraphs might throw some light on the
critical study of the composition of the Gospel, or the solution of
the synoptic problem." He also noted that he had not "intentionally ignored" any of the synopses of the gospels then current, but
one such work, which he had ignored, was Maas's *Life of Jesus Christ*.
The conclusion of Bruneau's preface illustrated his sympathies. "I
am especially indebted," he wrote, "to the lessons and works of my
former professors: MM. Fillion, Vigouroux, Martin, and Loisy. It

is a pleasant duty to acknowledge that all that may be good in this little publication is more theirs than mine."[33]

Bruneau sprinkled his text with numerous references, principally to Lagrange and Loisy. In his footnote to Mt 1:1–17 and Lk 3:23–38, for example, he cited both exegetes for his argument about the different genealogies. "The solution that St Luke gives the genealogy of Mary," he wrote,

whilst St Matthew gives that of Joseph has no foundation at all in Tradition (XIVth cent.) and seems evidently against the wording of Luke. Moreover it is Joseph's descent which is of importance. The Evangelists intended to show that Jesus was the heir of David; now they thought that his title of legal son of Joseph was enough to give him a right to the Davidical throne, and prove the fulfilment of the prophecies. It does not follow, as the Rationalists claim they did not believe in the virginal birth of Jesus; since everything in their narrative supposes this miracle. Both pedigrees refer to Joseph, but both being incomplete, different names are given by Matt. and Luke who considered the details of the names rather as an accessory question, since there is so much of an artificial arrangement, especially in the list of Matt. (14+14+14).

It would be many years later before American Catholic scholars again resumed this interpretation. But Bruneau was less scholarly in his lame attempt to reconcile the visit of the Magi in Matthew with the presentation in Luke.[34]

JOHN B. HOGAN, S.S.

Bruneau was but one of several Sulpicians promoting the new approach to the study of Scripture. At the Catholic University, John B. Hogan, S.S., former professor of dogma and moral theology at Issy and president of the Divinity College from 1889 to 1894, began, in 1891, to publish a series of articles in the *American Ecclesiastical Review* on "Clerical Studies." His first article had, in fact, appeared in the same number of the *Review* with the third of Schroeder's articles against di Bartolo. Named president of St. John's Seminary in Brighton, Massachusetts in 1894, he continued the series and published it in book form in 1898. His proposals for seminary education were decidedly historical and he lamented that since the Middle Ages the Bible had "ceased to be at the centre of clerical studies, and this was the direct result of the new movement which gave birth to scholastic theology." The Bible, he continued, was replaced with "logical argument" and "it gradually gave way to the *Sentences* and to Aristotle." Though the great Scholastics had all written commentaries on the Scripture, he acknowledged, their successors ceased to make the Bible the focal point of their theology.[35] While couching his exposition in a simple narration of facts, Hogan was, of course, attacking the Scholasticism that Leo had sought to revive.

The Renaissance and Reformation, he noted, had brought a renewal of biblical studies, but it was the achievement of the nineteenth century to apply scientific criticism to the Bible. Not only were scholars studying it in the original languages; they were also recognizing that, while inspired, it bore a "human imprint." Archeology had opened new vistas and the discovery of the Rosetta Stone had unlocked the mysteries of ancient Near Eastern languages. New manuscripts were being discovered and existing ones subjected to the new forms of literary criticism. For Hogan, it was an exciting period, but, he regretted, non-Catholic scholars were doing most of the work. Catholics could well rejoice in this achievement, he continued, because

for the devout reader of the Bible there are no difficulties, no problems. Questions of origin, of authorship, of textual criticism, have no existence. The human element of the scriptures vanishes, as it were, laying bare the divine, and setting the reader, like Moses on the mountain, in the dread presence of God Himself.

The truly devout, however, would have to study the Bible scientifically, for "edification must ultimately rest on truth."[36]

Hogan was well aware that he was proposing a general program of seminary study that did not accord with the accepted norms. He may, therefore, have been shrewd, rather than naive, in making no distinction between liberal and conservative exegetes. While acknowledging, for instance, that there were no good concordances for the English Catholic Bible, he recommended those for the Protestant Authorized Version, based on the original languages. While Protestants, he noted, may have produced more commentaries, because of their reliance on Scripture alone, he wrote that Maas's recent commentary on Matthew "opens among ourselves a series full of promise." Maas would hardly have been happy to find himself linked with a number of non-Catholic German com-

mentators or to read Hogan's assessment that "scarce anything
can be found [in them] opposed to Catholic orthodoxy." For more
advanced students of the Bible, he recommended the *"Revue Biblique* (quarterly), which is gradually assuming a position of authority among scholars, and the *Revue d'Histoire et de Littérature Religieuse*
(bimensal), containing articles of the greatest value." Disingenu-
ously, he neglected to note that the latter journal was edited by
Loisy.[37]

Hogan was daring in his approach to the interpretation of
Scripture. The literal interpretation, he said, led to defensiveness
against the new sciences of astronomy, geology, and evolution.
Those who adhered to this interpretation had forgotten the principle "that God in the Bible accommodates Himself to the minds of
men, and follows the laws of their language; that other meanings
besides the literal had, at all times been admitted in certain cases,
and might be admitted in many more when circumstances required
it." In the American church, he was thus reminding his readers of
one of Kenrick's principles. Granted that, by stating that the Bible
was "the word of God," Leo had repudiated those who argued that
the Bible contained only religious and moral truth, he argued that
the pope had "helped to lighten" the task of exegetes

in particular by pointing to the circumstances that the language of the
Bible is popular, not technical, and by accepting all the consequences
which follow from such a fact. Nor have they been slow to avail themselves
of such a concession. More freely than ever before do we find them
admitting in the inspired pages loose and inexact statements, side by side
with what is strictly accurate; figurative language of all kinds, metaphors,
hyperboles, rhetorical amplifications, facts veiled in poetic forms, seeming
narratives which are only allegories or parables, all the ordinary modes
of human speech, in a word, and all the literary peculiarities of Eastern
peoples.

For Hogan, "the fundamental position is this: THAT INSPIRA-
TION DOES NOT CHANGE THE ESTABLISHED LITERARY
HABITS OF A PEOPLE OR OF A WRITER; that, consequently,
what is considered no departure from truth in an ordinary book,
should not be viewed otherwise because the book is inspired."
"Literary habits of a people" accounted for the "substantial accuracy," though "not exactness of detail," in the different accounts
of the Resurrection in the Synoptics and in John.[38]

Were these new methodologies challenging the inspiration of the Bible? Hogan believed that biblical scholars had freedom within Leo's guidelines. Some might, indeed, judge as "extreme" the questioning of the story of creation or the deluge, the date and authorship of the books of the Old and even New Testaments. The Mosaic authorship of the Pentateuch, he continued, had been "almost universally rejected by the highest Biblical authorities, and even by many of the most 'orthodox' Protestant teachers," and was "being gradually questioned among Catholic scholars." While these positions had failed to win "the approval of all," "they are openly assumed; they are favored by some of our ablest Catholic scholars; they have been one of the salient features of the last Catholic Congress in Fribourg; and our best-known organs, in England, in France, in Germany, ventilate them freely."[39] How, then, were Catholics to reconcile these new assertions with the doctrine of inspiration?

The whole contemporary debate over inspiration, Hogan believed, resulted from two different methodologies, that of the theologians and that of the biblical scholars. He admitted that either side could go to extremes, but he thought the controversy had arisen from the fact that, while inspiration was "an article of faith, . . . what is implied thereby has never been defined, nor, perhaps, can it be defined, except by approximation." His sympathies clearly lay with the biblical scholars, for, "because of all the work that has been done on the Bible in recent times, with results which are no longer seriously questioned, theologians have to acknowledge, however reluctantly, that henceforth much less can be built on the Bible than has been done in the past." For Protestants, this might cause "dismay," he concluded, but Catholics could "contemplate it with perfect equanimity. Their faith is based, not on the Bible, but on the Church."[40]

Hogan may have intentionally skirted the issues raised by the debate over inspiration by emphasizing the role of the Church. But his general approach found a sympathetic reader in St. George Mivart, once considered for a professorship at the Catholic University. Mivart quoted Hogan extensively in an article he wrote in January 1900—the last one before his death. Mivart saw the condemnation of Americanism, the case against John Zahm, and the movement against biblical scholars as expressions of intolerance and the triumph, which he predicted would be temporary, of

"Curialism." The party of intolerance, he said, was "represented by the *Civiltà Cattolica*, the late Louis Veuillot and the Canon Delassus and Abbé Maignen of the present day, and their allies—notably some pious anti-Dreyfusards."[41] He argued that much of what had been previously believed was now contested and discarded. For his argument, he used Hogan's assertion that modern scholarship showed that "indiscriminate trust" could no longer be placed in the Fathers, that theologians could no longer rely as much on the Bible, and that the sacred writings could no longer be used for the study of science.[42] As examples of beliefs that might be dying out, he used the bodily resurrection of Christ and the Virgin Birth.[43] Mivart's article was admittedly offensive and the work of a bitter man. It brought about his excommunication.[44]

In April, Hogan learned that he too might be under investigation. As he wrote Denis O'Connell,

Somebody in Rome—your successor [William H. O'Connell, then rector of the American College] I believe—has sent word here that people connected with the Index are looking after my "Clerical Studies"—in connection with poor Mivart's quotation from them. In one sense I should be very glad that some of these people would read the book—if they know English enough to do so—it would perhaps broaden them a bit.[45]

A year later, Hogan was dead and there was no further mention of his being under investigation. But a French translation of his book, with certain important omissions, won a favorable review from Loisy, who later remarked, Rome "condemns in me what it approves in M. Hogan."[46] It also greatly influenced Eudoxe Irénée Mignot, Archbishop of Albi, in his *Lettres sur les études ecclésiastiques.* Mignot was one of the few French prelates to defend Loisy.[47]

Americanism and biblical scholarship were, of course, separate movements. But there were essential similarities, both in the theologies, which underlay each, and in the close, and sometimes complex, personal relationships, that existed between proponents of either issue. Many of the opponents of Americanism later entered the lists against the biblical scholars. Charles Maignen, for example, became a distinguished member of the "Sodalitium Pianum," which engaged in a witch hunt against suspected Modernists.[48] Delattre, as will be seen, was one of the first to attack Lagrange in Jerusalem and Henry Poels in Washington. The condemnation of Americanism, however, had an even more direct effect on the development of American Catholic biblical scholarship. It created an environment of theological reaction and of intellectual slumber. The sympathy of Bruneau and Hogan for the new exegetes would be kept alive among a number of Sulpicians. But the old leaders of Americanism, who had been sympathetic with the biblical scholars, would turn into the repressors of scholarship. None symbolized this more than Denis O'Connell. In November 1897, he had arranged for Charles Briggs to meet von Hügel.[49] It was for the two scholars the beginning of a long friendship, which, as will be seen, would lead to both of them criticizing Rome's attitude toward biblical scholarship. But, as rector of the Catholic University, O'Connell would show no signs of his previous liberalism and would be personally responsible for the conservative reorientation of the university, as he guided it through the Modernist crisis.

5. American Prelude to Modernism: The Catholic University and Henry Poels

The condemnation of Americanism brought about the retrenchment of American Catholic intellectual life, but, at the turn of the
century, biblical scholars took no note of the complex interrela-
tionship between the condemned movement and their own endeavor. In the United States, the progressive theologians among
the Sulpicians and the professors at the Catholic University continued to write on the biblical question. The Jesuits, particularly
at Woodstock College in Maryland, began an increasingly strident
attack on the new exegesis and virtually provided a mirror image
of what their confreres were doing in Europe, particularly in
Rome. Roman authority and Roman theology became synonymous with Catholic orthodoxy, whether it was in the Romanization
of the hierarchy that followed upon the condemnation of Americanism,[1] or in the type of theology that gradually came to dominate not only Jesuit schools but also those that imitated them. The
new century dawned, however, with little clue to the events that
would unfold during the first decade. For the time being, the
Sulpicians, particularly at Dunwoodie, continued their progressive
scholarship. The Catholic University of America was the locus for
the first battle for the Bible in American Catholicism.

THEOLOGY IN THE UNITED STATES IN THE EARLY TWENTIETH CENTURY

By 1903, Denis O'Connell had returned to the good graces of
Roman officials, especially Cardinal Francesco Satolli, the first
apostolic delegate to the American hierarchy and later the prefect
of the Congregation for Seminaries and Universities. With the

strong support of Charles Grannan and other liberals at the university, O'Connell assumed the rectorship of the university. Archbishop Ireland and other leaders in the Americanist movement saw his appointment as the triumph of Americanism. O'Connell, however, determined to rid himself of any taint of heresy, gradually alienated those faculty members who had been instrumental in his appointment. Conflicts of personalities and of ideologies became intertwined, as the American Catholic church lost its openness toward biblical developments.[2]

There is no better indicator of the initial openness of the American church toward biblical scholarship than the response of the *American Ecclesiastical Review* to the condemnation of five of Alfred Loisy's books by the Congregation of the Index in 1903. The author of the response was probably Herman Heuser, the editor. He praised Loisy as an apologist, on the grounds that "to oppose mere tradition against scientific investigation is like combatting a man who confronts you with a pistol by means of a stout stick." Heuser feared that, because Cardinal Andreas Steinhuber, S.J., was prefect of the Index, those unsympathetic with the Church would say "Rome has allowed itself once more to come under the spell of the Jesuits as in so many other cases." He wished to avoid the extremes of both those who decried any use of criticism and those who challenged the validity of the Church's actions. In his mind, the Church condemned Loisy, "because his statements not only lack sufficiently convincing proofs, though he himself may have an instinctive certainty regarding them, but because they are an injury to the children of her household."[3]

ANTHONY J. MAAS'S REPORTS IN THE *AMERICAN ECCLESIASTICAL REVIEW*

While Heuser may have appeared relatively open to the critical method, he directly contributed to the shift in the American Catholic theological mentality. In 1900, he asked Anthony Maas to be the exclusive writer for the *Review*'s "Recent Bible Study" column—the column to which Bruneau had previously contributed. Heuser further suggested that Maas write anonymously, because, he later recalled, "otherwise there was likelihood that controversies would be stirred up, owing to differences of opinion regarding the extent of Biblical inspiration and kindred topics of Exegesis, among representatives of scholastic groups who claimed for them superior merit of patristic tradition."[4]

Heuser could not have made a poorer choice. Maas's bias against historical criticism was already well known from his earlier contributions to the *Ecclesiastical Review.* During his years of absence from the *Review,* he had continued to write against biblical criticism, primarily in the *Messenger of the Sacred Heart.* [5] Maas and several of his Jesuit successors at Woodstock created a caricature of biblical criticism and sought to assure that several generations of the American Catholic clergy were kept ignorant of the biblical movement.

Maas's conservative reports on biblical scholarship reflected the Roman buildup against exegetes, the initial phase of which was the condemnation of Loisy. In 1904, Alphonse J. Delattre, S.J., one of the first to enter the lists against Americanism, published his *Autour de la question biblique.* His primary target was Lagrange's *Méthode historique.* But the secondary object of his sally was a man of greater significance to the American church, the young Dutch scholar, Henry Poels, who had published a brochure entitled *Critiek en Traditie, of De Bijbel voor de Roomschen.* Delattre took Poels to task for arguing that, while there could be material errors in the Scriptures, they were not formal ones as long as the sacred writer incorporated them "without making them the object of critical judgments." Where Poels argued that Jerome recognized that there were "insoluble difficulties" and even contradictions in Scripture, Delattre countered that Poels's position would make the writer of Scripture a true author and not a mere copyist. For Poels, "the defenders of so-called tradition" ran counter to Jerome's "great freedom" in speaking of "the history contained in the biblical books." For Delattre, "the real defenders of tradition" had Jerome as their "most glorious ancestor," who had set forth as a creed that the Scripture was to be interpreted literally.[6] In the writers Delattre cited, he went well beyond even the conservatism of *Providentissimus Deus.* Yet, in the meantime, he was appointed professor of Scripture at the Gregorian University in Rome. Ignorant of this new appointment, Lagrange felt compelled to answer Delattre in a pamphlet which the Master General of the Dominicans ordered to be circulated only privately.[7]

Back in the United States, Maas enthusiastically reviewed Delattre's book and took the opportunity to warn his readers against the "new exegesis." His words dripping with sarcasm, he described the new school, whose

leader, Father Lagrange, describes the Catholic exegesis practised [*sic*] from the fourteenth to the nineteenth century as *un exercice en chambre* with little history and less philology. The countless folios written by the illustrious commentators of the last centuries may be allowed to rest in their dust with impunity. A gap of exegetical barrenness separates St. Thomas from Father Lagrange. . . . What is worse, M. Blondel discovers philosophical loopholes in the New Exegesis.[8]

The school, he admitted, had a strong defender in Eudoxe Irénée Mignot, Archbishop of Albi, but he commended the answer given Mignot by Charles Maignen—a name familiar to Americans as the author of *Père Hecker: est'il un saint?* While he granted that *Providentissimus Deus* left open whether "the inspired historian 'went by what sensibly appeared,'" he thought Delattre had sufficiently disparaged the new exegetes' appeal to Jerome for their precedent. Such an appeal, he noted, had been made by Harnack and others, but "Jerome's opinion on the Canon of the Old Testament, and on other points of Catholic teaching is not considered decisive; why then make him the highest arbiter in the present question?"[9]

After such a strong attack on Lagrange, Maas's treatment of his fellow Jesuit, Franz von Hummelauer, was informative, though noncommittal. Von Hummelauer, who had advanced considerably in his opinions since Bruneau had reported of him, held many of the same positions as Lagrange. He had three principles for explaining the role of the exegete. First, he should consider the literary form of the sacred writings, in terms of which "the Book of Genesis presents the form of national tradition or folk-lore, while the Book of Ruth may be considered as a form of family tradition." Second, he should consider the "human side of inspiration." In Maas's account, von Hummelauer merely "supposes the well-known principle that by merely quoting a source we do not become responsible for the objective truthfulness of the same. A quotation is true if it faithfully reproduces the original text." Maas seemed to be uneasy with the German Jesuit's presentation, but still he reported it without comment. Von Hummelauer's third principle was the "human authorship of the inspired books." Paraphrasing his German colleague, Maas noted that, aside from a few fundamental facts, such as that each book had both a divine and human author and that Paul was the author of "nearly all of the fourteen . . . epistles," "the Church has no authentic tradition as to the authorship, the composition, and the history of the inspired books." Von Hummelauer believed, in Maas's words, that the solution of such questions "belongs to literary criticism rather than to theology. It is, therefore, as independent of the authority of the Fathers as are other scientific problems." In words surprisingly reminiscent of Grannan's, Maas concluded his essay: "The incarnate word of God became like unto men in all things excepting sin; similarly, the inspired word of God became like human writings in all things excepting error."[10] In retrospect, it is difficult to determine if Maas was noncommittal toward von Hummelauer's views simply because he did not wish to criticize a fellow Jesuit. It would be the type of "error," which could exist in Scripture, however, which settled Maas firmly in the mold of the conservatives. In future articles, he continued to reflect the attacks of Delattre on Lagrange—attacks for which he had the authorization of the General of the Society of Jesus.

Letter of Louis Martin, S.J., to the Society of Jesus

On November 4, 1904, less than a month after Maas's relatively open article appeared, Louis Martin, S.J., issued a letter to all provincial superiors of the Society of Jesus. He reminded them that, in accordance with the Constitutions of the order, written by Ignatius Loyola, Jesuits were to join the study of Scripture with a firm foundation in scholastic theology. This provision had particular relevance in the present age when the "impiousness" of D. Strauss, who "had attempted to destroy the foundations of all revealed religion," had been replaced by "another way, to attain the same end, namely the historical method." Unfortunately, said Martin, this new method had even infected Catholic scholars, who argued that the battle against "the new attacks of the impious and rationalists" required the use of "new arms and a new method." Such efforts were "vain and futile," for "the true doctrine of inspiration, the common understanding of Catholic doctors, and even the sound laws of logic are destroyed. For it generally happens that, after rejecting the serious study of the holy Fathers, or, what is worse, after explaining them according to whatever was agreeable to the rationalists, those opinions are attributed to the holy Doctors, which they would not even dream of." Each provincial was to warn his subjects of the dangers of this new method.[11] Lagrange had no doubt that Martin had him in mind, for the general had referred to the "historical method," the term used by *Civiltà cattolica* in referring to Delattre's attack on Lagrange.[12] For the biblical question in the United States, Martin's letter provided Maas with any encouragement he may have needed to attack the new exegetes. But now he no longer had to look for enemies across the ocean. He had a target much closer to home.

THE APPOINTMENT OF HENRY POELS TO THE CATHOLIC UNIVERSITY OF AMERICA

In 1904, the Catholic University appointed Henry Poels as professor of Old Testament. In 1897, he had completed his doctorate in theology at Louvain under Albin van Hoonacker. In his dissertation, entitled *L'Histoire du Sanctuaire de l'Arche,* he argued that the Mosaic law in its present literary form contained laws from a later period and reflected "developments and new applications of the old Mosaic principles to the changed historical, political and social conditions of the Hebrew tribes."[13] Though he was a diocesan priest, he then taught at the scholasticate of the Missionaries of the Sacred Heart in Antwerp, where he wrote a series of articles on the Mosaic authorship of the Pentateuch for *De Katholiek.* In one of them, he criticized J. P. van Kasteren, S.J., for his inability to see the significance of the historical method. In 1899, Bishop Casper J. M. Bottemanne of Haarlem delated him to the Holy Office for his liberal teaching. The consultor assigned to the case judged that Poels's teaching placed him among the "rationalists" and that he should not teach seminarians, but Cardinal Lucido Parocchi, secretary of the Holy Office, refused to transmit the response to Bottemanne. Loisy commented at the time that he believed Poels's heresy had "consisted principally in abusing a Jesuit," "the greatest of crimes" and an "unforgivable sin."[14]

On August 30, 1901, Leo XIII appointed a committee to prepare for the establishment of the Pontifical Biblical Commission. Poels and Grannan were both appointed to this preparatory commission, but Lagrange was excluded because of his advanced ideas.[15] As Poels told David Fleming, O.F.M., another consultor of the commission, his appointment was "a rehabilitation." On October 30, 1902, Leo issued his apostolic letter *Vigilantiae* formally establishing the Biblical Commission. This time, Lagrange was listed among the consultors, together with Poels and Grannan.[16]

In the summer of 1903, Grannan, then in Europe, telegraphed Poels to meet him in Brussels to discuss his taking the post of professor of Old Testament at the Catholic University. At the same time, Poels had been offered a position in Rome by David Fleming, then the secretary of the Biblical Commission, and had also been offered a seat in the Dutch parliament. Shortly after Poels's meeting with Grannan, Denis O'Connell, the rector of the university, wrote Poels asking him to meet him in Louvain. O'Connell told him that he intended to submit his name to the board of trustees for the chair in Old Testament. Poels's only condition was that he be given a rank commensurate with his qualifications. Unbeknownst to Poels, he was walking into a heated controversy. By that point, only six months after assuming office, O'Connell had managed to alienate Grannan and his other former supporters. In February 1904, Poels received a letter of appointment from O'Connell in the name of the trustees. In May, he received a second letter of appointment from the senate of the university, signed by Grannan. He subsequently learned that, at a meeting of the faculty senate, O'Connell refused to answer whether Poels had been appointed. The senate, then, voted to appoint him as an assistant professor for a term of one year. This appointment, subject to reversal by the trustees, was, of course, not according to the conditions Poels had laid down.[17]

Shortly after the senate action, Poels received a cable from O'Connell asking whether it was true his name was omitted from the consultors of the Biblical Commission. Poels initially thought that, because of his decision to go to Washington, he had been omitted as a consultor from Holland. He immediately requested information from Fleming, who replied that whoever was responsible for such a rumor was guilty of a "deliberate calumny." Poels forwarded Fleming's letter to O'Connell, who acknowledged it "with joy." Subsequently, Poels learned from O'Connell that the apostolic delegate, Archbishop Diomede Falconio, had asked whether the rector "had taken sufficient precautions, in selecting me for the chair of Old Testament." In September 1904, Poels received a visit in Holland from Grannan, who gave him some vague warnings about the need to be cautious in Washington. The two of them sailed together and arrived, late in September, in Washington, where Poels found that O'Connell was absent and had made no arrangements for him to live in Caldwell Hall, the residence for priest-faculty members. Temporarily, he took up residence, ironically, in the room formerly occupied by Schroeder. When O'Connell returned, he greeted him coldly and told him to be wary of Grannan, who had been responsible for informing the delegate that Poels held advanced views of the Old Testament. Poels expressed his disbelief and then refused to say whether Grannan had spoken against O'Connell while they were traveling together to the United States.[18]

Poels had had a bad introduction to the Catholic University and it became worse when he learned that the original appointment he had received from O'Connell was at the rank of associate professor, a rank higher than that voted by the faculty senate. In March 1905, he petitioned the dean and faculty for promotion, who, without notifying O'Connell, unanimously recommended Poels for associate professor. He also found that, while O'Connell's original letter of appointment was as associate professor, the salary was for an assistant professor. As he later recalled it, "during the struggle between the Rector and the Faculties and Senate, I stuck to my books."[19]

POELS ON HISTORY AND INSPIRATION

In January 1905, Poels published the first of three articles in *The Catholic University Bulletin* on "History and Inspiration." Just as the Church faced Hellenistic philosophy at the beginning of the third century, he reasoned, it confronted literary and historical criticism at the beginning of the twentieth. He praised the work of the Fathers and acknowledged that "the wall built by the giants of the Middle Ages, will weather the storms of time . . . , but they did not and could not make a bridge between Christianity and modern science." The theological crisis of his day, Poels believed, had arisen because of the study of history "according to new and truly scientific methods." He admitted that the "enemies of Christianity" may well have acclaimed the new methods, but, for him, "truly scientific criticism *can be nothing else* than an apology for truth; and every apology for truth is, of course, an apology for Christianity itself."[20]

Poels's treatment of inspiration reflected his affinity with Lagrange. "The whole Bible is inspired, in all its parts, in all its sentences, and even in its *obiter dicta,*" he wrote, but biblical statements "must needs be true only in that sense in which God and the inspired author wished it to be understood." Error existed only where there was "a *judgment* or affirmation." It was the role of the critic to determine the sense affirmed by the author. It was on this point that Poels set himself at odds with his theological opponents. To determine the true sense "intended and expressed by the sacred writer," it was "not sufficient . . . merely to examine the words and grammatical construction of single sentences. We must also consider the *context;* not only the immediate context, but at the same time—what theologians frequently seem to forget— the more *remote* context, that is to say, *the literary character of the whole book.*"[21]

To illustrate his position, Poels drew the distinction between the "author" and "the man . . . as he is the representative of his generation." As an example outside the biblical field, he chose St. Thomas Aquinas who reflected the common opinion of his age in citing the works of Dionysius as though they were written by a contemporary of Christ's. Thomas also accepted the scientific opinions of his age and relied on the Vulgate, which "all scholars agree . . . is not a correct rendering of the original text." Poels then applied to the Bible the distinction between "author" and the "man" as representative of his age—a distinction he argued was derived from Jerome. Where Scripture called St. Joseph "the *father* of Christ and the Virgin Mary the *wife* of St Joseph," Jerome had commented that, aside from Joseph, Mary, and Elizabeth and perhaps a few others, *"all considered Jesus to be the Son of Joseph.* And so far was this the case *that even the Evangelists, expressing the opinion of the people,* which *is the true law of history* . . . , called him the *father* of the Saviour. . . .*"* To Delattre's argument that Jerome adhered to the literal interpretation of Scripture as history, Poels countered by pointing out that Jerome did "not admit the strictly historical sense of some biblical texts, and that *for this reason* he recurs, either to 'the true law of history,' or to a spiritual sense." On the basis of Jerome's "law of history," Poels concluded that "we do not see any reason, why we should admit that generally they [the inspired authors] knew more than the contemporaries about profane things, which God did not reveal to them."[22] In other words, like Lagrange and others, Poels was adapting to history what *Providentissimus Deus* had said about "sensible appearances" in regard to science.

Poels made it clear that "in regard to biblical *history,* it must be stated first of all, that wherever a positive religious doctrine supposes necessarily the truth of an historical fact, this historical fact becomes *per se* a 'dogmatic fact,' and belongs thus to the *religious* teaching of Holy Scripture." To distinguish between the author and the representative of a generation, between a "dogmatic fact" and a mere manner of speaking, Poels argued, was no more difficult than it was for any other "ancient Semitic book of history." In explaining the process of making that distinction, he threw down the gauntlet to conservative theologians. Any difficulties that might arise from the application of his theory, he asserted, were derived from the difficulties of the biblical narratives themselves. "The only way for theologians to resolve the difficulties," he continued,

is to become critics and to study the character of ancient historiography. We are confronted with literary *facts.* No theory can change them. But we have to explain them in such a way, that these facts do not imply errors on the part of the inspired authors. As soon as we know the *facts,* that is to say, the literary character of the narratives, the application of our principles offers no longer any difficulty. If the opinions of some theologians do not agree with those *facts,* critics have no right to change the facts, but theologians have to change their opinions.[23]

Poels had not only presented his own view of the relationship between theology and the new criticism, he had also singled out Delattre. This would bring him to Maas's attention.

Poels went on to develop his position in his subsequent article on "The Fathers of the Church." Like Hogan, Bruneau, and Grannan, he argued that Christ "did not found His Church upon dead writings but upon living teaching," the transmission of which was entrusted to "official teachers." While revelation had been entrusted only to the authors of Scripture, it was clear that there had been "an *'evolution'* of Christian doctrine" from the first to the twentieth century. Here too, Poels foresaw conflict with theologians. While there could be no valid evolution or development of doctrine that was not "a branch of the tree of Christ . . . , for the theologians, who study the principles, branch and bud are one; while historians compare the tree in its maturity to the mere sapling."[24] The development of doctrine was another point of disagreement with the type of theology that Poels and his contemporaries were confronting.

Just as in Scripture he distinguished between the author and the man of his age, Poels now drew the distinction between the Fathers as "witnesses of the Church" and "as scholars of their day." Inasmuch as the Fathers sought to acquire "knowledge of the biblical teaching on 'faith and morals,'" they were "scientific," but they had no knowledge of the twentieth-century science of literary and historical studies. Instead, they simply accepted the views of history common in their age. When confronted with difficulties about a particular passage of Scripture, they therefore resorted to a spiritual interpretation. In his own age, Poels chided a certain "class of 'prudent' Catholics" for adhering to the historical character of every passage of Scripture. "If there should be a clash between true historical science and a theological school," he stated, "the responsibility for the dishonor and for the far-reaching consequences of such a condition of affairs, would fall upon this theological school."[25]

Poels was worried that this theological mentality made Catholic laymen in universities incapable of reconciling their faith with the findings of the natural sciences and history. "Catholic scholars," he asserted, "ought to be more 'prudent' than, in our opinion, Father Delattre was in writing his *Autour de la question biblique.*"[26] Poels was simply trying to defend the validity of the new historical method and explain that it was not against the Church's tradition of the living word of God, but he had drawn upon himself the antagonism of conservative Jesuits.

Poels's difficulty with theologians like Delattre was that they considered all scriptural texts to be alike, whereas the critic had to ask about the type of literature with which he was dealing. Inspiration illuminated the mind and strengthened the will, but it did not annihilate the "ordinary man," subject to the limitations of the knowledge of his day. Matthew could, therefore, mistakenly cite Jeremiah, when he meant Zechariah and Mark could confuse Malachi with Isaiah, but both evangelists accurately reported a religious truth. Jerome, said Poels, had acknowledged their error and, while his appeal to a spiritual sense in some cases might not satisfy a contemporary critic, he did at least go beyond "the letter."[27]

While his contemporary Catholics would not follow the Fathers in appealing to a spiritual sense of Scripture, Poels feared they might have gone to "the opposite extreme," under the influence of "the ideas of Protestantism, worshipping the dead letter of the Bible." If the Fathers were too free in their interpretation, they had the example of the New Testament itself, which made "accommodations" of the Old Testament. Within Catholicism, however, this presented little danger, "since the interpretation itself was controlled by the living teaching and divine authority of the Spouse of the Holy Ghost." Like Hogan, Gigot, and, even earlier, Kenrick, Poels argued for the Church as the safeguard of the proper interpretation of Scripture. The Church's battle with Protestantism, he believed, had shaped its approach to the biblical question. During the Reformation, "Catholics, of course, had to avoid even the appearance of esteeming the Bible less than Protestants did." Later on, however, "Catholics and orthodox Protestants were alarmed by the complete ruin of Christian faith among those Protestants who did not not keep to the 'letter.' " But for the Church, "the critical study of biblical history teaches us that we must once more take up our old Catholic tradition, provided that we avoid in the interpretation of the Word of God that exaggeration of the secret and spiritual sense, which spoiled the work of some of the greatest of our ancient scholars."[28]

Poels had yet another fear of the influence of Protestantism on Catholicism. In reaction against the Protestant stress on individualism, "there seems to be among some Catholics a strained and quite unnatural fear of the *individual,* who might go his own way in scientific questions of theology, and who examines by himself, without any scruples, the divine Scriptures." Yet, he argued, the Fathers had no hesitation of asserting that the sacred authors did not, at times, intend to affirm the historical sense of Scripture. While biblical studies declined in the middle ages, and "the time of the *'Catenae'* had come," St. Thomas and the great Scholastics remained proponents of the rights of the individual and of the scientific method. Through the work of individuals, said Poels, science advanced and, within science, no "single scientific argument" could be "possible when the individual must appeal to others."[29]

Poels was clearly making a plea for freedom of intellectual inquiry. Yet, perhaps with Loisy in mind, he spoke of the "humility," which was "one of the characteristics of truly learned men," and of the necessity of "the most learned man, when confronted with the higher authority of the Church . . . to bow his head." Within a few years, he would be required to apply those words to himself. For the time being, however, he was merely endeavoring to "present the true state of affairs in some of those little Catholic worlds, which their inhabitants identify with the one, saving Catholic Church." To expand those "little Catholic worlds," he urged the return to the Fathers, who did not have that "kind of sickly apprehension of that freedom and 'individualism,' which in matters of science is a question of to be or not to be." Promising his readers a future article on St. Jerome's appreciation of a "self conscious 'individual,' " he concluded that, in Scripture studies, "the killing of personal initiative would become especially dangerous if, some time, the tendency of those theologians should prevail, who underwent the influence of the Protestant worshipping of the 'letter.' "[30]

Poels had echoed many of the pleas of Hogan, Grannan, and Bruneau. In his treatment of the role of the individual, however, he had trod onto the same dangerous ground that proved to be the undoing of the Americanists. Like the Americanists, he had an optimistic view of human nature and saw individual initiative held in check by humility and obedience to the Church. He may have been correct in seeing his conservative opponents too much influenced by Protestant "worshipping of the letter." But there were other influences closer to more recent Catholic theological development. As was seen, the First Vatican Council spoke of "tradition" as "a divine deposit entrusted to the Spouse of Christ," the Church.[31] As Yves Congar has noted, however, "by 'Church' the council means here above all the magisterium, especially that of the Roman Pontiff."[32] The council further defined that the pope, when he spoke "ex cathedra" on matters of faith and morals "enjoyed that infallibility with which the divine Redeemer wished to endow His Church in defining doctrine about faith or morals," and that such statements were "irreformable of themselves."[33] The council thus paved the way for some theologians to see in every papal statement an expression of the infallible magisterium. By the end of the nineteenth century, some theologians and bishops had concluded that both the "letter" of Scripture and the "letter" of magisterial pronouncements had to be preserved. Far more was involved, therefore, than what Poels feared was a Catholic imitation of Protestantism. It would be fully a year before Poels completed his articles on "History and Inspiration," but, by that time, he had drawn a direct attack from Maas.

MAAS'S ATTACKS ON POELS

In the June issue of the *American Ecclesiastical Review,* Maas took the offensive against both Lagrange and Poels. Unfortunately, the Jesuit archival sources are no longer extant, but it is highly probable that Maas was in correspondence with Delattre or other Jesuits in Europe. Even if Maas was not in direct correspondence, he hardly needed any further justification for his attacks than the letter of Martin to the Society of Jesus against the historical method. In his *Méthode historique,* Lagrange had argued that the nature of ancient Near Eastern literature made it impossible to subject it to Aristotelian logic and that, according to his theory of verbal inspiration, everything was inspired, but not everything was revealed. Maas now subjected Lagrange's theory to the very type of syllogistic logic that the French Dominican said could not be applied to the study of the Scriptures. Lagrange had stated: "God teaches whatever is taught in the Bible, but he does not teach anything more than what is taught by the sacred writer, and the latter teaches only what he intends to teach." Maas challenged Lagrange's use of the term "teach" and his assertion that everything in the Bible was inspired but not everything was revealed. In Maas's mind, Lagrange's method could neither determine when God was teaching nor solve the historical and scientific problems. The Jesuit argued that there was no justification in claiming

that the writer did not intend to say what is actually said in the passage, and this merely in order to get rid of extrinsic difficulties. Recent apologists appear to sin in this respect when they solve scientific and historical difficulties by maintaining that God did not intend to teach science or history in the scriptures, or that the sacred writers did not intend to write science or history in the modern critical acceptance of the word.[34]

Maas's assertion on the relationship between the Bible and science, of course, was more restrictive than *Providentissimus Deus*.

Maas had presented virtually a caricature of the way in which theologians regarded history. The question of historical appearances and "implicit citations," he said, had been definitively settled by the decision of the Biblical Commission in February, 1905. He noted that the decision required that his fellow Jesuit, Franz von Hummelauer, abandon his liberal tendencies, but he saved his real invective for "the poison that certain readers might gather out of Dr. H. A. Poels' two articles." Though Poels might not agree with the commission's decision, Maas patronizingly concluded: "If Dr. Poels does not quarrel with the Biblical Commission, we will not quarrel with him."[35]

For the next year, Maas carried on a long and tedious debate with Thomas á Kempis Reilly, O.P., an American then studying at the École biblique in Jerusalem, who attempted to show how Maas misinterpreted and mistranslated Lagrange. The exchange was a prime example of the inability of the prevailing theological school, represented by Maas, to hear what the historical critics were saying.[36]

POELS ON JEROME AND INSPIRATION

Onto the American scene, which had now become charged with the acrimonious debate over inspiration, Poels introduced his third and final article, which concentrated on Jerome as a biblical commentator. Unlike the Scholastics, who sought to take a consistent, ordered approach to the entire corpus of Catholic teaching, Jerome was a translator and commentator. Unlike many of his contemporaries, said Poels, Jerome sometimes held that it was the Hebrew Bible, not the Septuagint, which was the inspired version. At other times, however, Jerome followed the tradition of "Irenaeus, Justin, Epiphanius, Augustine, and his other contemporaries who maintained the inspired character of the Version followed by the Church." Jerome had, Poels argued, contradicted himself in attributing inspiration both to the Hebrew Bible and the Greek translation, but he kept urging that, instead of being concerned with "words and syllables," the believer should seek "merely 'the sense' of the inspired writings."[37]

In seeking "the sense" of the Scripture, Poels asserted, Jerome had frequently resorted to numerology or to the secret meaning of names. In these and other instances, Jerome showed himself "a child of his time." In recounting history, Jerome likewise reflected the manner of his age and "no one wishes to go back to Jerome," Poels continued, "in order to be taught historical criticism." Jerome and other contemporary commentators made no distinction between types of history and frequently they appealed to a spiritual sense of the Scripture. Yet he did provide a model for "modern Catholic critics in their study of biblical history." As Jerome sought to defend the "Hebraica veritas," he frequently pointed out to his opponents the irrefutable contradictions between New Testament quotations from the Old Testament and the Hebrew Old Testament itself. "Since his opponents agreed that the Apostles were inspired," Poels stated, "Jerome was entitled to conclude that such 'contradictions' were not *real* contradictions, involving an error on the part of the New Testament writers."[38]

Poels now returned to Jerome's "law of history," introduced in his previous article. The biblical writers, Poels said, had no intention of writing history in the modern sense. Here he found himself in combat with the theologians, whom he had earlier reproached. The German Jesuit, Christian Pesch, S.J., professor of theology at Ditton Hall, England, and Valkenburg, the Netherlands, had attacked him, inaccurately, for saying the question of inspiration was to be solved by historians and critics, but not by theologians. Poels countered by charging that Pesch had failed to consider the nature of biblical history, the understanding of which required knowledge of not only theology but also history and literature.[39] In Poels's analysis, "*biblical* historians" had to be understood, not as "mere *witnesses* of the events narrated," but as "the inspired *judges* and *interpreters* of the past." They were far more than "popular" historians, but were "prophetical" and "political" ones, whose

narrative of the past is primarily the author's *interpretation* of the events related; it is the author's *judgment* passed on the acts and life of a person or a people: not merely a series of impartial statements of fact. This higher kind of "prophetical" or "political" history is, practically, the interpretation of the lower kind, whether "scientific" or "popular." As far as the *form* is concerned, every history is evidently a narrative. But the aim and object of prophetical and political historians is quite different from that of a story-teller.[40]

Taking into consideration the Biblical Commission's decree ruling out "implicit citations," Poels continued to assert "that historians relate and describe the past, which itself has disappeared, according to what is left of it in sources and traditions, or what we may call its 'historical appearances.'" "Popular historians" made no effort scientifically to examine the reality behind these appearances, but they implicitly affirmed "the strictly historical reality of every detail related by tradition and mentioned in their books." Here Poels attempted to explain the type of affirmation the historian was making. "Prophetical and political historians," he wrote,

must be regarded as implicitly affirming the truth of the traditions related in their books, *in as far as the truth of their interpretation of the objective past, such as they have the intention to give, depends upon the truth of the tradition, which they actually are interpreting.*
When we hold that an author intends to write or interpret history, we implicitly admit that the author, as such, would be mistaken if he did not write or interpret history, but fiction. When, further, we maintain that the historian's interpretation of the past is true, we implicitly admit that the testimonies adduced by him afford a true image of the real past. However, we insist and we repeat, that image must needs be true only in as far as the truth of the interpretation of historical reality depends upon the truth of the image. In a book which interprets popular history, this image is given according to tradition, without any guarantee, on the part of the writer, of such details as do not compromise the truth of the interpretation which he intends to give of the real past.[41]

In a sometimes tedious way, Poels was attempting to convey the notion that literary images might convey more truth than scientific history, for they expressed the spirit behind the events rather than merely narrated them.

Poels recognized that he and his fellow exegetes had to defend their critical method. In his defense, however, he may have drawn unnecessary attention to himself. He recommended, for example, an article by Adolf von Harnack on "legends as sources of history," to illustrate the difference between the history of facts and events and the history of the interpretation of facts and events. The Old Testament prophets, said Poels, "*judged* the events occurring in their days." The history they produced "was not a lifeless photograph," but a "living factor of the highest importance in the history of the development of the present into the future." Their "history" became a "power" within the history of Israel. For Poels, such history was far more worthy "of divine inspiration" than "the mere accurate report of witnesses." "The work of a photographer may satisfy curiosity," he said, "but it does not influence the real history of living and toiling mankind."[42]

For a generation steeped in higher criticism, Poels's exposition of the nature of biblical history is overly detailed and wearisome. For many of his contemporaries, however, the new historical criticism was a threat to Catholic doctrine. Poels took no notice of the Maas-Reilly debate over Lagrange then raging in the *American Ecclesiastical Review,* but he did defend Lagrange against an attack in *Études.* Regarding the Biblical Commission's decision on "implicit citations," he commented "that there is a great difference between asserting that an author interprets 'traditional' history, and saying that the history, written by the author, is false!"[43]

In many ways, Poels represented Lagrange in America. With the great Dominican, he was on the defensive. He promised, in future articles, to examine each of the historical books of the Old Testament separately and to show that Jerome's "law of history," properly understood, did "not come into conflict with the inspired character of the Bible." He wanted, first of all, to examine "Jerome's 'Credo scripturaire'," the phrase that Delattre had used to argue for the literal interpretation of Scripture.[44] Poels, however, was to do no more writing. The buildup against Modernism would soon claim him as one of its most tragic victims.

6. Modernism and Poels's Dismissal from The Catholic University

Henry Poels was the only Catholic biblical scholar in the United States who fell under official Church censure and was forced to leave his teaching post. He became controversial because he held the position, common to most progressive Catholic scholars of the day, that the Pentateuch was a composition of several sources put together after the time of Moses. Unfortunately, that position now met opposition.

THE MOSAIC AUTHORSHIP OF THE PENTATEUCH

On June 27, 1906, the Biblical Commission issued its response stating that Moses was "substantially" the author of the Pentateuch.[1] This seemed to sound the death knell for the new critics. Sometime either that year or early the next, Marie-Joseph Lagrange, O.P., expressed his concern to Henry Hyvernat, his former classmate at Issy and then professor of Semitic languages at the Catholic University. The problem, Lagrange thought, was that Rome was so fearful that the development of dogma meant its alteration that it believed "the remedy to the situation is the bloc of Fr. Delattre." He urged that, if Hyvernat had any "zeal for the good of the Church," he make it known that the "bloc" stood for little and that far from extinguishing any "conflagration," it was actually setting "part of the fire." The issue, said the exegete, was "to sustain the entire dogmatic structure with little freedom in the criticism of history." Lagrange was worried that "we who wish to work for the good are counterbalanced by the imprimaturs of those who do not care for it."[2]

Lagrange was not alone in his assessment of the influence of Delattre. Von Hügel saw the Jesuit symbolizing the mentality behind the Biblical Commission's decision on the Mosaic authorship of the Pentateuch. Writing to his friend Charles Augustus Briggs of Union Theological Seminary in New York, he said he had been informed

that this decision and the appointment at the Roman Gregorian University of that thoroughly reactionary and obscurantist Pere Mechineau, S.J. in succession to that already, one would have thought, sufficiently Philistine Pere Delattre, S.J. who was given that Professorship of Scripture held by that fine, candid, critically competent scholar, Padre Enrico Gismondi, S.J. (whom I have the honour to call my friend) are intended as attempts to impose this kind of toothless blind apologetic upon us as *scholarly* and by the authority of *scholars.* [3]

Von Hügel also suggested that he and Briggs collaborate on a critique of the commission's decision. As will be seen, this took the form of an exchange of open letters between himself and Briggs in September 1906, and was published as *The Papal Commission and the Pentateuch.* [4] Maas had already accused Briggs of denying inspiration in 1891; now he ignored von Hügel altogether and concentrated his attacks only on Briggs.[5] The following year, an anonymous reviewer in *The Catholic University Bulletin,* usually friendly to the new exegetes, took issue with both Briggs and von Hügel. The Baron, said the review, "takes for granted" that, if "the so-called historical method," were "applied to the Pentateuch," it "will surely disprove its Mosaic origin."[6] The Catholic University was clearly beginning to go through a new reactionary phase in regard to the biblical question, though O'Connell, the rector, did make some attempts during this period to have Lagrange lecture at the university.[7] There were still other indications of the shift in attitude of the *University Bulletin* and its editor, Thomas J. Shahan. Around the time of the negative review of the Briggs-von Hügel book, Poels submitted the reviews of two books. In regard to a book by Alphons Schulz, Poels was "noncommittal" and simply acknowledged that "the author's conclusion is evidently incompatible with the strict Mosaic origin of the whole Pentateuch. . . . But, in his opinion, the recent decision of the Biblical Commission on the subject leaves Catholic scholars perfectly free." In reviewing a book by C. Telch, however, Poels acknowledged the author's "bona fides," but argued that "good faith alone is not enough to justify the writing of a book in which leading Catholic scholars and pious priests are accused of heresy." Though Poels's reviews were already in galley form, Shahan ordered them withdrawn.[8] The university, however, simply mirrored the reaction of the American church to Modernism.

On July 3, 1907, the Holy Office issued *Lamentabili*, a list of condemned propositions of the Modernists. Among the propositions was that inspiration did not so extend to the entire Scripture in such a way as to preserve each of its parts from any error.[9] On September 8, Pius X issued *Pascendi Dominici Gregis*, condemning what the pope saw as the unified heresy of Modernism. In the context of historical criticism, the pope condemned those who would apply this method to the study of Scripture, for the critics dismembered and partitioned the Scripture with "the result" that

the Scriptures can no longer be attributed to the authors whose names they bear. The modernists have no hesitation in affirming commonly that these books, and especially the Pentateuch and the first three Gospels, have been gradually formed by additions to a primitive brief narration—by interpolations of theological or allegorical interpretation, by transitions, by joining different passages together. This means, briefly, that in the sacred books we must admit a vital evolution, springing from and corresponding with the evolution of faith. The traces of this evolution, they tell us, are so visible in the books that one might almost write a history of them. Indeed, this history they do actually write, and with such an easy security that one might believe them to have with their own eyes seen the writers at work through the ages amplifying the sacred books. To aid them in this they call to their assistance that branch of criticism which they call textual, and labor to show that such a fact or such a phrase is not in its right place, and adducing other arguments of the same kind. They seem, in fact, to have constructed for themselves certain types of narration and discourses, upon which they base their decision as to whether a thing is out of place or not. Judge if you can how men with such a system are fitted for practicing this kind of criticism. To hear them talk about their works on the sacred books, in which they have been able to discover so much that is defective, one would imagine that before them nobody ever glanced through the pages of Scripture, whereas the truth is that a whole multitude of doctors, infinitely superior to them in genius, in erudition, in sanctity, have sifted the sacred books in every way, and so far from finding imperfections in them, have thanked God more and more the deeper they have gone into them for His divine bounty in having vouchsafed to speak thus to men. Unfortunately, these great doctors did not enjoy the same aids to study that are possessed by the modernists for their guide and rule—a philosophy borrowed from the negation of God, and a criterion which consists of themselves.[10]

Coupled with the Biblical Commission's decision of the Mosaic authorship of the Pentateuch, the encyclical virtually destroyed Catholic use of the historical method in biblical studies. The question remains as to how the Catholic Church could have found itself caught up with having to equate inspiration of the sacred books with knowledge of their authors. The answer may have been, as Poels had earlier suggested, that many Catholic theologians had spent so long combating Protestantism that they had adopted some of its principles. But the answer may also have been much closer to home in the new type of Catholic theology that was then prevailing. The First Vatican Council, as was noted above, saw tradition as a deposit entrusted to the magisterium. By the early twentieth century, the new theologians were so intent on preserving revelation against the rationalist incursion that they thought it equally imperative to defend the divine origin of both Scripture and magisterial statements. In defining the canon of Scripture, the Council of Trent had referred to the "five [books] of Moses."[11] Some theologians now saw Trent's description of the Pentateuch, in accordance with the Judeo-Christian tradition of referring it to Moses, as a conciliar definition that Moses was, in fact, the author. This at least seemed to be the line of reasoning of Fulcran Vigouroux, S.S., the first secretary of the Biblical Commission.

In his five-volume work, *Les livres saints et la critique rationaliste*, Vigouroux had addressed this issue in 1890. "The Christian tradition," he wrote, "has always unanimously attributed the composition of the Pentateuch to Moses." Citing the "Fathers, the doctors, the interpreters and the Catholic commentators," who had never deviated from this tradition, he added: "and the Council of Trent has been a faithful echo of the belief of the Church in naming Moses as the author of the first five books of the Bible, in the Canon of Scriptures." For Vigouroux, the tradition of the Church, which Trent had reinforced, could not have been otherwise, for "the Church itself has received this belief from the synagogue. It is in effect certain that, in the era of Our Savior, the Jews attributed the Pentateuch to Moses." As proof, Vigouroux had only to cite the six passages where Christ spoke of Moses.[12] In short, to deny the Mosaic authorship of the Pentateuch would be to impugn not only the tradition of the Church, including the Council of Trent, but also the words of Christ Himself. As will be seen in the next chapter, however, this was precisely the position which Francis Gigot, S.S., was trying to refute and his attempts to explain the tradition of the Church in a new way would create a painful situation for the American Sulpicians.

For the time being, however, the most immediate effect of the encyclical on the Catholic University of America was the response of Cardinal Gibbons, in the name of the bishops, thanking the pope for the encyclical and announcing the establishment of a "committee of vigilance."[13] It was ultimately not so much *Pascendi*, however, as the Biblical Commission's decision on the Mosaic authorship of the Pentateuch that now caused Poels's problems.

POELS UNDER ATTACK

Poels had already drawn Roman attention to the university's approach to biblical studies. In 1907, Delattre published *Le Criterium à l'usage de la nouvelle exégèse biblique.* He was principally responding to Lagrange's answer to his earlier *Autour de la question biblique,* but he reserved some of his venom for Poels, whose reproach for "lack of prudence" he found "very gratifying," coming as it did from a scholar who denied that the Scripture writers and the classical historians, like Thucydides and Herodotus, were writing true history.[14] The Jesuit clearly had no idea of history, which had come to the fore as a scientific discipline in the nineteenth century. History and theology, as both Hogan and Poels had reminded their readers, used different approaches to the truth. Within the theological worldview of the early twentieth century, conflict between them became inevitable. Poels became one of the few American casualties.

Though Poels himself did not seem to be aware of it, he had become the object of suspicion at the university by the spring of 1907, six months before Delattre published *Le Criterium.* At the meeting of the university trustees in April 1907, O'Connell stated that Poels was not being recommended for promotion to full professor, because of doubts concerning his agreement with the response of the Biblical Commission. Poels's case was to be investigated by a special committee which would report to the trustees at the next meeting in the fall. By that time, however, Poels's situation had become intertwined with that of Grannan, with whom O'Connell continued to feud. The trustees asked O'Connell's opinion about Grannan, who also seemed to be teaching contrary to the Biblical Commission. They had before them a resolution demanding Grannan's resignation, but, when O'Connell refused to make any comment, by a majority vote, they rescinded it.[15]

POELS AND PIUS X

Poels, still a consultor to the Biblical Commission, was, in fact, perplexed at the commission's decree on the Mosaic authorship of the Pentateuch. He had originally planned to teach a course on "Hebrew Institutions, as seen in Law and History" in the academic year 1906–1907. He had, however, substituted a course "on the present state of the so-called Biblical Question," without reference to the Pentateuch. To assuage his conscience on the matter, he went to Rome in the summer of 1907. He first saw Cardinal Satolli, prefect of the Congregation for Seminaries and Universities, and asked him "If I would still be within the limit of the Decisions, if I maintained that, generally speaking, the institutions, mentioned in the Pentateuch, were of Mosaic origin, although the documents in which these institutions are described, and in their present literary form, did not all actually come from the pen of Moses." Satolli told him that he had to consult the Biblical Commission itself. Poels next had an audience with Pius X and, because he was not fluent in Italian, took with him as interpreter Giovanni Genocchi, also a consultor to the commission. Having explained his problem to the pope, as he later reported, he had the following exchange:

His Holiness realized the difficulty of my position. Natural law, he said, forbade me to go against my convictions, while due regard for authority precluded all opposition to the pronouncements of the Cardinals of the Biblical Commission. He at first suggested that I should teach some other branch, such as New Testament or Dogmatic Theology. But Fr. Genocchi explained to him that University Professors are, or, at least, are supposed to be, specialists; and that therefore, such a change was impracticable. His Holiness finally said that I should follow the advice of Fr. Genocchi and of Fr. Janssens, Secretary of the Biblical Commission.[16]

After the audience, Poels had the impression that the pope had indeed expected him to teach another field, but Genocchi denied this and both he and Janssens urged him not to resign from the university. Poels asked only that Genocchi inform the pope of the advice given him. Back in the United States, Poels failed to hear from Genocchi and then wrote Janssens to see the pope and inform him of the advice he and Genocchi had given. Only in May 1908, did Janssens reply with the assurance that the pope had approved of the advice, since Poels in his "lectures . . . did not contravene the decisions of the Cardinals of the Biblical Commission, and showed respect to authority."[17] In the meantime, Poels had said nothing to anyone at the university about his audience with the pope. At their meeting in November 1907, however, the trustees examined Poels's case. Since his appointment as associate professor did not expire until January 1909, they unanimously voted to do nothing to change his status.[18]

At this point, the story became more complicated than a contemporary soap opera. During the summer of 1908, first Grannan and then O'Connell also had audiences with Pius X. In Grannan's audience, he apparently did not discuss the biblical question at all. In O'Connell's interview, however, he told the pontiff he was having a problem with a professor of Scripture, who was "exercising a very bad influence on the students." Presuming he meant Poels, the pope said he had ordered the professor to resign. A short time later, O'Connell confronted Grannan with the assertion that he knew that the pope had ordered him to resign. When Grannan denied that he had discussed the Pentateuch during his audience, O'Connell then went to Genocchi, who the pope had said was present for the audience with the "professor." O'Connell then learned that the pope was thinking of Poels and not Grannan, but he feared bringing the case of mistaken identity to the pope's attention. Back in the United States, O'Connell informed Poels late in September that he was not to resume his lectures at the university until he had previously arrived at an understanding with Cardinal Gibbons, the chancellor.[19]

THE CASE AGAINST POELS

Poels attempted, unsuccessfully, to have O'Connell read the letter he had received from Janssens the previous May. He then met with Gibbons, to whom he read Janssens's letter. The cardinal acknowledged that Poels had a valid case, but said that he would have to consult O'Connell. O'Connell, in turn, said that the matter would have to wait until the meeting of the board of trustees in November. Poels then cabled Janssens, who replied, in an ambiguous cable, that "steps" were being taken in Rome. On the basis of this cable, Gibbons instructed Poels to begin his classes and said that the board would consider the matter at its November meeting.[20] Gibbons, however, was careful to obtain the apostolic delegation's approval of his action.[21]

At their November meeting, the trustees spent most of their time discussing a report of a special committee appointed to investigate establishing a school of biblical science. O'Connell stated that nothing had been done about the new school because of his problems with Grannan and the uncertainty about Poels.[22] Gibbons did, however, submit to Pius X his first annual report of the committee of vigilance established to safeguard Catholic orthodoxy. The cardinal noted that the committee had only one "doubt" and that was "about the mind of the Rev. Doctor Henry Poels toward certain decrees of the Biblical Commission, although from other aspects it is known that his scriptural knowledge is excellent and that he adheres to the most correct principles in both theology and philosophy." On behalf of the hierarchy, Gibbons was submitting this doubt to the pope.[23] About this action, Poels seems not to have been informed.

In the meantime, O'Connell became auxiliary bishop of San Francisco in December and Thomas J. Shahan was named the new rector of the university. Only as the trustees prepared for their meeting in the spring of 1909 did Gibbons inform the secretary of the board, Bishop Camillus Maes of Covington, that the Poels case would have to be settled. At the same time, the cardinal also filed with the trustees his report of the committee of vigilance with his remark about Poels. Maes, who became a supporter of Poels, instructed the exegete to draw up a written defense of his position for the trustees. The trustees then passed a motion "exonerating him of the charges and accepting his answer as satisfactory. He remains in his position as Professor of Old Testament."[24]

Thus, the case seemed to be settled, when Pius X again entered the scene. In July 1909, Shahan had an audience with the pope, who expressed indignation that Poels was still at the university.

Pius wrote out for Shahan his own recollection of his conversation with Poels. It was opportune, said the pope,

that Monsignor Shahan, the new rector of the University, know how things went between the Holy Father and the aforesaid Professor. In the Autumn of 1907, the Rev. Dr. Poels accompanied by Father Genocchi was received in audience by the Holy Father, and Professor Poels with the greatest candor said that in connection with the studies made by him and in accordance with the opinion of the most learned critics, he could not accept the decisions published by the Biblical Commission on the Mosaic authorship of the Pentateuch, and then he asked what step he ought to take.

After admiring and praising the loyal frankness of Poels, the Holy Father declared that, if he were firm in these ideas of his, he could no longer continue in that chair, because he could not teach his students that of which he was not convinced, and, on the other hand, would most seriously fail in his duty by teaching what was not in conformity with the magisterium of the Church. Since it appeared that this decision mortified him, the Holy Father turned to Father Genocchi and said: Does it appear to you that this sentence is too severe? And Father Genocchi replied: the response is logical and just. And with this, the audience was concluded without the Holy Father advising him (as is natural) to consult anyone else.

This same response the Holy Father would also give to Dr. Poels today, as long as he persisted in that persuasion, without assuming any responsibility for anything anyone else might have said or written, regardless of his position of authority.[25]

Pius X's account, of course, totally disagreed with Poels's.

Shortly after Shahan's meeting with the pope, Cardinal Raffaele Merry del Val, the Secretary of State, wrote to Cardinal Gibbons to inform him that the pope was going to demand that Poels swear, in a written statement, that he accepted and would "faithfully teach the doctrines and conclusions given by the Pontifical Biblical Commission." If Poels could not swear to the statement, he had to resign his position. On August 1, Gibbons passed on this information to Shahan with the request that the rector write to Poels. Since the pope himself was to draw up the formula for Poels's oath, Gibbons did not yet know its content, but promised to send it to Poels as soon as possible, "for his consideration and signature, if he can see his way to sign it." "In the meantime," concluded the cardinal, "there is of course no use in his appearing at the University, before the terms of His Holiness have been complied with."[26]

Shahan immediately cabled Poels, then vacationing in Europe, to await a letter from him before returning to Washington. A few days later, Poels received the letter. Describing his audience with Pius and the pope's account of his audience with Poels so different from Poels's own, Shahan declared that

> I scarcely need call your attention to the gravity of this discrepancy between the facts of your audience as related by the Pope and as they are put down in your statement. Nor can I undertake to say what will be the attitude of the Board of Trustees when at their November meeting the Pope's account of your audience with him is placed before them, as the Holy Father has commanded me to do.

In other words, Shahan was accusing Poels of lying. He concluded his letter by quoting from Merry del Val's letter to Gibbons requiring that Poels sign a sworn statement that he would abide by the decisions of the Biblical Commission. Finally, he told Poels to remain in Europe until Gibbons had forwarded to him the formula drawn up by the pope.[27]

Poels immediately cabled Gibbons for the oath to which he was to swear. On September 8, he received it. It read:

> Ego, Enricus Poels, spondeo, voveo ac juro super sancta Dei Evangelia me sincere accepturum et fideliter traditurum omnes doctrinas ac conclusiones quas hucusque promulgavit aut de futuro promulgabit Commissio Biblica Pontificia. In cujus fidem manu mea subscripsi.

On the same day, Poels received another letter from Shahan. The rector stated that, since the pope had given such a different account of his conversation with Poels, it would be better for Poels to resign, especially after the trustees realized that the pope had ordered him to resign in 1907. Even if Poels were to take the required oath, Shahan believed it imprudent for him to continue teaching.[28]

Immediately upon receiving the oath and Shahan's letter, Poels left for Rome, where he met with Merry del Val on September 11. He expressed his willingness to accept any papal command, but, as he put it, "I did care, and cared very much, for my honor as a man and as a priest." When the cardinal asked him about the oath, he replied:

I could sign this formula, I told him, if the words "sincere accepturum et fideliter traditurum" could be understood in this sense: that I, not only externally, but also internally and "sincerely," recognized the high authority of the Pontifical Biblical Commission; that, therefore, also *in foro interno*, I attributed to all its decisions, either given in the past or to be given in the future, all the authority which Catholic theology teaches to be due to the Decisions issued by this high ecclesiastical tribunal; that, in the future as well as in the past, I always would "faithfully" teach the Decisions given, if the words "fideliter traditurum" were intended to signify: that I was expected "faithfully" to communicate to my students the Decisions given, and, moreover, not only not to criticize those Decisions in my lectures, but, on the contrary, to put stress on the authority of the Pontifical Biblical Commission, which issued them, and on the great need of ecclesiastical authority in this modern world of scepticism and modernism. However, His Eminence the Cardinal Secretary of State was not satisfied with this interpretation of the formula. He said that I had to testify under oath that I admitted *in foro interno* the truth of all those Decisions. My signing of the formula would be understood to mean, first of all, a solemn affirmation of my personal belief—in conscience—that Moses was the author of the Pentateuch. Furthermore, he declared I had to teach the Decisions of the Biblical Commission as being part of my personal teaching. It was not sufficient that I should merely communicate these Decisions to my students, in the way just indicated.[29]

In vain, did Poels plead that to sign the oath in this sense was a violation of his conscience and had not been required of other professors. When he brought up Janssens's letter, Merry del Val simply denied its truth and accused Poels of not obeying the pope's command to resign his position.[30]

On September 12, without notifying Poels, Merry del Val cabled Gibbons that Poels was not to be allowed to teach before the trustees of the university met again in November. On the same day, Poels met in Rome with Cardinal José Vives y Tuto, O.F.M. Cap., prefect of the Congregation of Religious and a member of the Biblical Commission. The Spanish Franciscan was one of three cardinals who enjoyed the complete confidence of the pope—the others were Merry del Val and Gaetano de Lai, secretary of the Consistorial Congregation. He represented the most conservative reaction against Modernism.[31] It is, therefore, surprising that he assured Poels that he would try to correct the mistake. Then, Poels discovered another unlikely supporter. "By mere chance," he met Leopold Fonck, S.J., rector of the Biblical Institute, who, as Poels noted, had been extremely critical of his scholarship and orientation. Fonck had, in fact, been engaged for some time with a battle against Lagrange, whose École biblique, he thought, had a "deadly spirit" that should be destroyed.[32] Fonck accepted Poels's story and the corroborating testimony of Janssens's letter. He promised that he himself would intervene with the pope for Poels. But first, he wished to consult Merry del Val. In the meantime, Fonck took Poels to Cardinal Rampolla, then president of the Biblical Commission. The cardinal said, however, that, since the case had not been formally brought before the commission, it had to be settled by the pope and secretary of state. On September 17, Fonck finally had a long interview with Merry del Val, after which Cardinal Vives y Tuto also spoke with the cardinal. At this point, Poels was brought in to Merry del Val, who now said he believed there had been a misunderstanding, but he hesitated to bring it before the pope who was "quite nervous about it." Instead, Fonck would speak to the pope and would communicate the result to Poels, who was advised not to seek an audience himself.[33]

Fonck immediately saw the pope and explained to him the initial confusion between Grannan and Poels, adding his own testimony about Poels's "character and scholarship." Pius X accepted Fonck's intervention and authorized him to write Poels. The important points in Fonck's letter were:

2. In order to safeguard your honor and your good name, the Holy Father declared that tomorrow morning he would order the Cardinal Secretary of State to announce to Cardinal Gibbons, either by cablegram or letter, *ut hoc anno nihil innovetur.* The Holy Father in this connection also repeatedly declared that he would not have it said to the Cardinal Archbishop that a condition had been laid on you requiring you to resign during the year.

3. The Holy Father will leave everything further to you personally. He told me expressly that you must leave at once in order to commence your lectures in Washington for the new school year.

4. Also in regard to the points of doctrine which occasioned the difficulties, I expressed to the Holy Father my conviction that, among the adher-

ents of the broader tendency in Exegesis, you are certainly on the right side and belong to the most conservative representatives of these opinions. The Holy Father received this statement with joy.

5. At the conclusion of the audience, after many other things were spoken of, the Holy Father repeated again, of his own initiative, that he charged me to convey to you his love and blessing and that to-morrow he would inform Cardinal Gibbons through the Cardinal Secretary of State as above described.

I send you this short report in order that you may find some consolation in it. During the year we will see what God's will is. I will for my part be gladly ready, where I can, to defend you, in order that you may continue to use and exercise your strength and talents in the service of God and His holy Church for the good cause. I confidently trust that the love of our Divine Saviour will turn to the best also this heavy trial, and rejoice on my side that through this I have become better acquainted with you.[34]

Fonck's information may have been accurate in terms of his understanding with Pius X, but Merry del Val seemed to have a different understanding. On September 18, the secretary of state cabled Gibbons to await a letter before taking any action in regard to Poels.[35] In the letter that he sent the next day, Merry del Val explained that he now realized that "the serious misrepresentation of the Holy Father's intentions and directions was not due to" Poels. Had Poels "not been misled," the cardinal continued, "he would have long since acted in accordance with His Holiness's instructions." As a result, Merry del Val thought

it would not be fair to act abruptly now and cast a stigma upon his honour as a priest. As however his intellectual position remains the same and the reason for the Holy Father's original directions still holds good, His Holiness suggests the following settlement, viz: that Prof. Poels should be allowed to resume his teaching under two conditions. First, that he shall abstain from any teaching not in complete conformity with the doctrine and guidance of the Holy See; and secondly, that during the course of the academic year he shall make arrangements to definitely quit the University. Prof. Poels has expressed his willingness to accept this course of actions and is anxious to show that he sincerely submits to the Holy Father's authority.[36]

Merry del Val's condition that Poels resign at the end of the academic year was, of course, contrary to what Fonck had told Poels.

On October 6, Poels arrived back in Washington where he found a chilly reception. Shahan told him that Merry del Val insisted that he resign during the coming academic year. Poels then received confirmation from Gibbons personally that Merry del Val had imposed that condition. Poels again wrote Fonck, who prevailed upon Merry del Val to cable Gibbons. The cable cryptically stated: "Sincerity of Dr Poels explanation being fully recognized by holy Father J [sic] beg your eminence to keep my last letter entirely private and absolutely prevent all publicity."[37] Poels interpreted the cable to mean that Gibbons was to ignore the previous demand that he resign.[38]

POELS'S DISMISSAL FROM THE CATHOLIC UNIVERSITY

On November 17, Poels presented his case personally to the university trustees, who had at hand all the information on the events that had transpired since Shahan's audience with the pope the previous summer. After his presentation, Archbishop Patrick Ryan of Philadelphia asked him if he could sign the oath, sent by the pope the previous July. Gibbons repeated Ryan's question. Poels explained that the point of his entire visit with Merry del Val and of the subsequent letters from Fonck and the cardinal was that he not be obliged to take the oath, except according to his interpretation, which would not make him dishonest. After his explanation, Ryan stated "that settles it." Gibbons, too, demanded that Poels sign the oath. Only Bishop Matthew Harkins of Providence spoke in Poels's support.[39]

When Poels had left the room, Maes introduced the following resolution: "In view of the explanation made by the Rev. Dr. Poels, considering that he has been permitted to teach since the beginning of the scholastic year and that there is some misunderstanding in the case, His Eminence having graciously promised to write again to Rome, Resolved that the Rev. Dr. Poels be allowed to continue to teach until a final answer is received from Rome." The trustees unanimously adopted the resolution and instructed Maes to inform Poels.[40] Poels was convinced that his dismissal from the university was imminent, but then received Maes's letter stating that there would be no change in his status until Gibbons had heard from Merry del Val.[41]

Two days after Poels's appearance before the trustees, Gibbons wrote Merry del Val. The cardinal told of Poels's narration of his audiences in Rome the previous summer and of the letter from Fonck, "which, as far as we could judge, was of a purely private character." He then said the trustees, "in obedience to the order of the Holy Father," asked Poels to take the oath. When Poels refused, "unless permitted to add his own interpretation of the said oath," the cardinal continued:

we decided that we could not longer with a safe conscience retain Doctor Poels as Professor of Sacred Scripture, being mindful in particular of the recent utterances of the Holy See concerning the teaching of professors in ecclesiastical seminaries. We did not, however, decide to dismiss him at once, but to lay before the Holy See the following considerations that incline us to wait until next June, the end of our scholastic year. First, the danger of public scandal arising from the sudden cessation of his teaching. Second, because at such short notice it would be difficult to find a suitable professor for this Chair of the Old Testament. Third, to avoid the stigma that an immediate removal would put upon this professor.
As the Trustees by this action have endeavored to comply with the wishes of the Holy Father so far as they have been known, I earnestly hope that His Holiness will give his approval to this decision and thus put an end to a situation which, if continued, would prove detrimental both to the University and to the cause of religion.[42]

Gibbons's letter was not in accord with the trustees' resolution, which had merely stated that Poels was to be allowed to continue teaching, "until a final answer is received from Rome." The cardinal's attitude, moreover, was rather different from what it had been a year before, when it did not seem to matter that there would be a "sudden cessation" of Poels's teaching. His third point, concerning the stigma attached to Poels, may have been due to Maes's influence. Whatever the interpretation, both in Poels's account and in Gibbons's own letter to Merry del Val, the cardinal totally ignored the significance of Poels's conversations with Merry del Val and Fonck's interventions; he acted as if nothing had happened to alter the pope's original command of July. Finally, Gibbons never communicated the contents of his letter and the precise decision of the trustees to Poels.

Shortly after Gibbons wrote Merry del Val, he suggested that Archbishop Ryan write the pope requesting that Poels remain until the end of the academic year. Ryan replied that he had already written Merry del Val, but not the pope. He added:

On reflection, I think it will be safer for the university that the Dr. should leave at Christmas. "He has a grievance," which he is certain to ventilate before professors and some favorite student friends. He openly refused to comply with the conditions laid down by the Pope, & this is already known by many outside the university. Under these conditions I feel I could not ask the Pope's permission to retain him. I tried to lay both sides of the question before Cardinal Merry del Val, but as I proceeded I felt there was only one side to it. I mean from the standpoint of the good of the university whose interests are entrusted to our care. Things have changed since our conversation.[43]

In short, Ryan simply disregarded Poels's arguments about preserving his integrity, and wanted his immediate removal from the university. On this point, however, he was not to have his way.

In the meantime, Archbishop Diomede Falconio, the apostolic delegate, had also reported the trustees' action to Merry del Val. For the delegate, regardless of what had happened in Rome, it was simply a matter of knowing "whether or not Prof. Poels intends to accept the decisions of the Biblical Commission and to adhere to them in his teaching of Sacred Scripture." Gibbons and the trustees, he concluded, could come to no other resolution than to terminate Poels's relationship with the university.[44]

On December 8, 1909, Merry del Val responded to Gibbons's letter. The pope "commended and approved everything" that Gibbons and the university trustees had done in regard to Poels, "so that, after the professor refused to subscribe to the decisions of the Biblical Commission, Your Eminence and the other aforementioned prelates decided that that professor should be dismissed from his teaching position next June." The secretary of state warned, however, that "until that time, it will be necessary that his teaching be closely and fittingly watched, so that his students do not learn anything detrimental."[45]

In the meantime, Poels seems to have been unaware of Gibbons's correspondence with Merry del Val, for he had again written Fonck, who assured him that Gibbons was "not pushed by Rome" and that Poels was "*not* obliged to believe in conscience 'that Moses is the author of the Pentateuch in its present literary form.' " Though Fonck may have thought that his letter settled the matter, he, too, seems to have been ignorant of Merry del Val's response to Gibbons. For the next few months, Poels continued to write Fonck and explain his position. In the United States, his only defenders among the bishops were Maes and Harkins. As he told Maes in February 1910, "I hope you will pardon me when I say that, in my opinion, his Eminence Card. Gibbons and Rector Shahan are not looking for truth and for justice, but merely try to please the Cardinal Secretary of State; even if I have to be wronged." Maes had suggested that Poels bring his case before the Investigating Committee, which would meet at the university in March, but, in Poels's mind, this would be simply another occasion for humiliation.[46]

Shortly afterwards, Poels thought he had at least the psychological support of Father Charles Aiken, Dean of the Faculty of Theology and professor of apologetics. According to Poels, Aiken told him on March 7 that he had asked the advice of the faculty in regard to the rejection of Poels for promotion to full professor the previous year. He suggested that the faculty "express a vote of sympathy" to be forwarded to the Investigating Committee. The faculty, however, decided to take no action, lest "the ire of Rome would come down on the whole Faculty." Aiken further stated that Grannan had voiced his opinion that "the matter was of too serious a character to be touched in any way by the Faculty." Poels thought that his readers, who recalled that it was the charge O'Connell originally brought against Grannan that caused Poels's problem, would "understand why this attitude of Dr. Grannan deserves a special mention."[47] Aiken, however, later emphatically denied this account and asked Falconio to forward his "explanation to the authorities in Rome," lest "they should be led to think that I had been helping him in the imprudent stand he has taken."[48]

In view of Gibbons's request that Merry del Val approve the decision that the trustees had made to dismiss Poels, Fonck informed Poels that there was nothing more he could do. Poels's final act in his defense was a long letter to Bishop Maes on March 21. He accepted the fact that he was to be dismissed, but he saw this in terms of Gibbons simply acting out of face-saving diplomacy. "If I myself am not found willing to offer my resignation," he wrote,

the board merely states that my services are no longer wanted. Of course the Cardinal knows perfectly well that in the present circumstances this failure to reappoint me will be practically—and will generally be understood to be—a regular discharge and a public disapproval by the Board of either my action toward Rome or of my teaching in the past. But "diplomacy" does not seem to take into account trifles of this kind. The Cardinal holds that, by this diplomatic move, he will, without any diffiulty [sic], make an end to this long and entangled case, which for two years has been annoying him and his two friends, Mgr. O'Connell and Mgr. Shahan. Besides, as he sees things, this decision will show to Rome his willingness to check and to repress in America anything that might in the least suggest the idea of Modernism, or doubtful orthodoxy, on the part of any American priest."[49]

It was a rather devastating critique of the only cardinal in the American church. Poels further promised Maes that he felt duty-bound to print the entire account of his case, for distribution to the trustees, in order to vindicate his honor.

Poels intended his "Vindication of My Honor" for private circulation. He sent it only to a few colleagues in Europe, in addition to the university trustees. Though it was available in a number of American archives, it was published only in 1982 by Frans Neirynck of Louvain who had the copy Poels had sent to A. van Hoonacker.[50] Poels's brochure narrated all the complicated details of his case, complete with copies of all the correspondence he could obtain. It also provided information that he thought shaped the case against him. Recalling the tension between O'Connell and Grannan, as well as other members of the faculty, he wrote: "I soon realized that especially for a foreigner the wisest part was to keep away from those internal quarrels; of which, from the day when I arrived in this country, I was a witness full of disillusionment and of disgust."[51] His characterizations of some of the principals involved in his case, though unflattering, unfortunately bear up under scrutiny. "In Monsignor O'Connell," he said, "the love of truth was not highly developed." He had, in fact, told O'Connell to his face "that you deliberately do not speak the truth."[52]

He could more readily understand the attitude of Merry del Val toward him, for he was sure the cardinal was aware of Delattre's attacks. "In the works published by the opponents of the New Catholic School of Biblical Exegesis," Poels wrote,

my name is frequently mentioned as one of the first among those of the leaders of this school. The well-known book by Fr. Delattre, *"Autour de la question biblique,"* certainly did not dispose towards me very favorably the adherents of the so-called Conservative School, who probably had never read my studies—published in Dutch—with which Fr. Delattre was finding fault. In his titanic struggle against Modernism, and other things which His Eminence thinks are connected with it, the Cardinal Secretary of State is generally well informed, by a host of friends, about everything going on in the field of Catholic Biblical studies. I therefore have good reasons to suppose that my name—as being one of the only three that had been singled out by Fr. Delattre among those of all the Catholic Scripturists living in the present day—had been mentioned to Cardinal Merry del Val before I ever went to see the Holy Father.

Merry del Val, thought Poels, believed that much of the "sad condition of the Catholic Church" was due to priests abandoning "the teachings of the Fathers and of the great mediaeval schoolmen" in preference to "modern historical science and certain currents of modern thought." In view of the cardinal's sense of duty to rid the Church of such priests and of the information he had received about him, Poels concluded that no one could "find fault with him for proceeding against me. But at present the Cardinal Secretary of State is convinced that I am not at all such a dangerous person as he for a long time thought I was."[53]

Merry del Val had been brought to change his opinion through the influence of Fonck, whom Poels termed "my great and noble friend," whose "action will be estimated by the readers at its full value, when they know we belong to opposing schools, that we had written against one another, and had never seen one another's face before I met him last summer in Rome, by mere chance, and then told him how my priestly honor was at stake."[54]

As for the hierarchy, Poels had different reactions. He felt that he would have fared better in the hands of Falconio, rather than Gibbons, even though the delegate honestly believed that the decisions of the Biblical Commission were true. Of the American bishops, Poels could praise only Maes and Harkins, who, he hoped, "will never have to feel ashamed in him, whose cause they have so boldly defended, not because they saw in it the cause of some personal friend, but because they believed it to be a cause of justice."[55] Maes's support of Poels was, in fact, surprising, for in 1902 the bishop had demanded that one of his priests, Father Thomas McGrady, retract statements he had made in praise of Ernst Renan, Charles Darwin, and several other radical thinkers. A strong advocate of socialism, McGrady had had no problem with Maes for his social views, but he refused to abide by the bishop's demands and left the priesthood.[56] Harkins's support was more interesting. He had been named in first place on the *terna* for Coadjutor Archbishop of Boston in 1904. In a letter-writing campaign that led to the appointment of William Henry O'Connell to the post, Harkins was accused of espousing "the Americanist spirit" and of allowing his diocesan newspaper to laud "Higher Criticism."[57]

Poels's pamphlet was distributed to the university trustees shortly before their meeting on April 6, 1910. At that meeting, Gibbons communicated Merry del Val's letter to the trustees. To avoid opening the case, the cardinal "deprecated all discussion." The trustees unanimously voted that, since Poels's contract with the university had, in fact, expired in January 1909, and he had been allowed to continue teaching past that date only at the sufferance of the trustees, he was to be informed that his relationship with the university was to be severed in June.[58]

On April 10, Falconio communicated the trustees' decision to Merry del Val. He also enclosed a copy of Poels's pamphlet. Though Poels thought he would have been treated more fairly by Falconio than by Gibbons, he may have been unpleasantly surprised to read the delegate's words about him. The pamphlet in itself, wrote Falconio, was "more than sufficient to bring the board to free itself of such a professor." His own opinion was that

in regard to the unlimited freedom of thought that is in vogue in these states, we have need, more than elsewhere, of professors who are sincerely and profoundly orthodox; otherwise, there is much to be feared in regard to the education of our young ecclesiastics. Your Eminence will pardon me if I say: Dr. Poels, thanks to the actions of his friends, disgracefully, has been tolerated far too long to the serious detriment of this university.[59]

Unfortunately, Falconio did not specify which "friends" of Poels he had in mind.

In Merry del Val's response to Falconio, he disputed Poels's account of his conversation with the cardinal in September of 1909. Poels had said that Merry del Val interpreted the oath to mean that he had to admit *"in foro interno* the truth of all those Decisions." "The truth on the contrary," Merry del Val told Falconio,

is that I said to Dr. Poels in this regard, that if he was not first intimately persuaded and convinced of the decisions of the Biblical Commission, he would not be able to teach according to their norms, because neither could his teaching be faithful, nor could he sincerely guarantee the orthodoxy of that teaching.

Poels, it will be recalled, had promised that he would never teach contrary to the decisions of the Biblical Commission, but he objected to being compelled to swear that in conscience he believed those decisions to be true. For Merry del Val, this was insufficient. To be an orthodox teacher, one had not only to be externally loyal to the Church; one also had to be convinced even that the decisions of the Biblical Commission were true. Merry del Val concluded his letter by remarking that he agreed with Falconio that "after this experience, in the future, professors nominated" were going to be "truly and totally orthodox."[60]

AN INTERLUDE: THE ATTEMPT TO HIRE JOSEPH DAVID AT THE CATHOLIC UNIVERSITY.

Had the Catholic University administration known Merry del Val's sentiments on assuring orthodoxy there, it might have proceeded more cautiously. At the same trustees' meeting in April when they dismissed Poels from the faculty, they also voted to appoint Joseph David associate professor of New Testament. David was a priest of the diocese of Grenoble in France and was then the chaplain of St. Louis des Français in Rome. Shahan nominated him because he knew Coptic and had the strong recommendation of Henry Hyvernat.[61] No sooner had the trustees' action reached Rome, however, than Merry del Val cabled Falconio in code on June 10 that such an appointment "would not be received with pleasure by the Holy See."[62] Falconio immediately conferred with Shahan, who assured him that any "promise" made to David would be withdrawn on the grounds that the priest did not yet have the doctorate. The rector further informed the delegate that David had been recommended by a "person" about whose "complete orthodoxy" there could not be "the least doubt." He avoided identifying Hyvernat, but said that the same "person" had testified "not only about David's ability but also about his trustworthiness in doctrine, especially because of the fact that he had obtained the Licentiate [in Scripture] from the Biblical Commission."[63]

Two years later, Merry del Val again warned Falconio's successor, Archbishop Giovanni Bonzano, about David, who, said the cardinal, was closely tied to the author of a series of articles, published in *Italie,* "against the persons attached to the Holy See and its directives, and particularly against myself." The priest, he continued, was "frequently the inspiration of the articles, if not the reporter." Merry del Val had been further informed that David was in correspondence with Hyvernat about succeeding him as professor of Semitic languages. Bonzano was to call the attention of Cardinal Gibbons and Shahan to this information and put them on guard "against the danger . . . of any similar succession."[64] After consulting Shahan, Bonzano assured Merry del Val that David was not under consideration for a post at the university.[65] This ended any attempt to hire David at the university. The suspicion cast on the university because of this little episode, however, made Shahan and university officials all the more cautious.

In December 1912, Merry del Val wrote Shahan commending his administration of the university. He noted that

considering the hold the University has already taken in the Great Republic of the West, and the well merited confidence it is inspiring in the minds of both lay and ecclesiastical aspirants to higher education and culture, I have no doubt that its influence on the spread of the Catholic Faith, of Catholic principles and ideals throughout the country will be of the utmost moment and of immense benefit.[66]

Shahan was delighted. Sending a copy to Bonzano, he said he would disseminate it throughout the country, for "it will do much good, exhibiting as it does the earnest good-will of the Holy See towards the University."[67] Perhaps Merry del Val's letter was totally unrelated to the David affair, but it was under that heading that Bonzano filed it.

The Catholic University's negotiation with David was only an interlude, but it illustrated the sensitivities of Roman and university officials to anything even faintly smacking of lack of orthodoxy. It was the Poels case that was the tragedy; and it serves as an indication of how much the American church was in retreat after the condemnation of Americanism. The Catholic University of America, previously the citadel of the liberals, now lapsed into a dogmatic lethargy of safe theology. The American church was safer perhaps than even Rome, for Poels was retained as a consultor of the Biblical Commission until his death in 1948—he was consistently listed in the *Gerarchia Cattolica* and later the *Annuario Pontificio* as "professor emeritus" of the Catholic University of America. After leaving the university he returned to Holland, where he was a pioneer in Catholic social action and was named a monsignor in 1916.[68]

Curiously, throughout the entire affair, Poels had not run into difficulty with either the Holy Office or the Biblical Commission directly. Rampolla, as secretary of the Holy Office and president of the commission, obviously was not in command of the battle against Modernism. Satolli, too, the prefect of the Congregation for Seminaries and Universities, was not involved in the controversy. Pius X himself and Merry del Val, the Secretary of State, were the principal Roman actors. In fact, more recent scholarship indicates that the pope himself was personally responsible for much of the witch hunt against suspected Modernists, and that Merry del Val was frequently accused of being too diplomatic. In the Poels case, however, it is impossible to assess whether the pope or Merry del Val bore the greater responsibility for the outcome. What is clear is that the Roman Curia was divided in its attitudes toward biblical scholarship. The positive response that Poels received from Rampolla indicates the tension existing between the Holy Office and the Secretariat of State. Rampolla had been Secretary of State under Leo XIII and his election as pope in 1903 was precluded only by the veto cast against him by Cardinal Jan Puzyna Kozielsko of Krakow in the name of the Austrian emperor. The Rampolla school would return to power in 1914 with the election as Benedict XV of Giacomo della Chiesa, who had been substitute Secretary of State under Rampolla. Under Benedict, there would be a thaw in the anti-Modernist freeze—his first encyclical, *Ad Beatissimi,* was a strong denunciation of "integrism" as the ardent anti-Modernist crusade was known.[69] But that was still some years in the future and before then the campaign against Modernism took yet other victims, especially the progressive Sulpicians and other priests at the New York archdiocesan seminary at Dunwoodie.

7. Francis Gigot, the Dunwoodie Sulpicians, and *The New York Review*

The Poels case was the most dramatic example of personal tragedy and scholarly retrenchment in the wake of Modernism, but the Catholic University was not the only institution that underwent change because of the biblical question. Farther to the north at the seminary for the Archdiocese of New York at Dunwoodie, the Sulpicians continued to carry the torch of progressive scholarship, already lit by Bruneau and Hogan. Curiously, though Corrigan was conservative on the question of Americanism and frequently opposed Gibbons for accepting the advice of the Sulpicians, he accepted their innovative program in his seminary. Edward R. Dyer, S.S., was the president of the seminary until 1902. Under him, the seminary entered into an arrangement to allow seminarians to take courses at Columbia University and at Union Theological Seminary and to have a limited exchange of faculty, as least as lecturers.[1] In 1902, Corrigan died and was succeeded by the more moderate Archbishop John Farley. The same year, Dyer became vicar general of the American Sulpicians and was replaced as president of the seminary by James Driscoll, S.S. In 1905, Driscoll, with Farley's encouragement, began publication of the *New York Review*, the most ambitious scholarly undertaking in the American Catholic church up to that point. It also added to the tension that already existed between the Dunwoodie Sulpicians and their superiors, particularly in France. That tension had first surfaced in regard to the writings of Francis E. Gigot, S.S. on Scripture. After he joined the Dunwoodie faculty in 1904, however, his contest with his French superiors became intertwined with the *Review*.

FRANCIS GIGOT AND THE BIBLICAL QUESTION

Albert Houtin, who had written the first history of Americanism, also wrote one of the first histories of Modernism. He remarked that, while the Sulpicians in France were trying to preserve their students from any taint of Loisy's influence, "they were citing him with honor in their seminaries in the United States."[2] Houtin may have been exaggerating, but, as was seen above, Bruneau cited Loisy favorably, and Loisy found Hogan sympathetic to his thought. But of all the Sulpicians in the United States, the most distinguished biblical scholar was Francis E. Gigot, S.S.

Gigot had been professor of Scripture at St. John's Seminary, Brighton, Massachusetts from 1885 to 1899 and had begun his most important writing while Hogan was the rector there. In 1899, Gigot was transferred to St. Mary's Seminary in Baltimore. But for some time he had been chafing at the growing conservatism of the Sulpicians under Jules Joseph Lebas, S.S., elected superior general in 1901. He had first drawn Lebas's attention when he was suspected of publishing an article, entitled *"L'avenir de la théologie biblique,"* in *Annales de philosophie chrétienne,* the journal edited by Maurice Blondel.[3] The article had been simply signed "A Sulpician," but Lebas discovered that the author was "one of our priests . . . in America."[4] Driscoll, however, later reported that "the strenuous hunt for the author of the famous article . . . was given up, because not having struck the right trail, it was finally concluded that Fr. Hogan wrote it."[5] Hogan had, of course, died in 1901.

In 1900, Gigot in Baltimore had published his *General Introduction to the Study of the Holy Scriptures.* Since the publisher was in New York, however, the book had Corrigan's *imprimatur* and Hogan's *nihil obstat.* Like Hogan, Gigot emphasized that Catholics had less to fear from modern criticism than Protestants, for "Catholics built their faith primarily on the teaching of a living Church, whereas Protestants rest their whole belief on the written word of God."[6] Implicit in his argument was that tradition was not so much content, as the process of handing on the living faith.

Despite the animadversions of *Providentissimus Deus* in 1893, Gigot reacted positively to the theories on inspiration of Cardinal John Henry Newman, Canon Salvatore di Bartolo, and Maurice d'Hulst, rector of the Institut Catholique in Paris. All had limited inspiration to matters of faith and morals, and had not applied it to science or history. He acknowledged, however, that there were others, like Franzelin and Mazzella, who treated the question "from the safe harbor of dogmatic theology," as the Tübingen theologian, Peter Dausch, had noted. It was because of such disagreement over inspiration, said Gigot, that Leo XIII had issued his encyclical, which effectively supported the conservative views. The papal pronouncement had made Catholic scholars more cautious, he continued, but there was still no unanimity about precisely what inspiration meant.[7]

Gigot's *General Introduction* was a relatively safe work, in which he took no definitive position on the question of inspiration. But he intended the book as the first in a three-volume study of Scripture. In 1901, he published his *Special Introduction to the Study of the Old Testament: Part I. The Historical Books.* This also had Corrigan's *imprimatur*, but the *nihil obstat* came from James F. Driscoll, S.S., then the rector of St. Austin's College, the residence for Sulpician students in Washington, where Gigot resided while teaching at St. Mary's Seminary. Gigot made it obvious that his sympathies lay with those scholars who held that the Pentateuch was not written by Moses, but was a compilation from at least four sources.[8] In regard to the Jewish and Christian tradition of attributing the Pentateuch to Moses, he added that it had no "theological binding force," since there was "no positive decision declaring it an article of Catholic belief." "It is true," he continued,

that, in their enumeration of the sacred books, the Fathers of Trent speak of "the five books of Moses, . . . Josue," and that they speak thus without misgivings as regards the authorship therein implied. But it is none the less true that, as clearly appears from the whole tenor of the discussions of the Council and from the very wording of their definition, they intended to, and did actually, settle only the question of the *sacred* and *canonical* character of the books enumerated.[9]

Gigot thus followed Lagrange's opinion on this point, but also placed himself in opposition to Vigouroux.[10]

Gigot's work received favorable reviews and was widely adopted as a textbook in American diocesan seminaries. Yet, it also received some negative or at least ambiguous comment. Anthony Maas took note of it in the context of reporting on an article by

Reginald Walsh, O.P., in the *Irish Ecclesiastical Review* and on a review of it in the same journal. Summarizing Walsh's article, Maas recalled that Eichhorn had "developed Jean Astruc's Document-Hypothesis." Maas appended a note, however, that, while Gigot and others had portrayed Astruc as a "devout Catholic," one writer had pointed out that the French physician had left his wife and grown children to become the "paramour of the most notorious woman in Paris," and it was during his nineteen years of unfaithfulness that he had produced his "writings on the Bible." Maas then moved on to consider a relatively favorable review of Gigot's work in the Irish journal, but drew attention to the reviewer's taking "exception to the way in which Fr. Gigot appeals to Mivart, Leroy, and Loisy as exponents of Catholic opinion," all of whom had been formally rebuked by ecclesiastical authority or even excommunicated.[11] Maas had not drawn his own conclusions about the value of Gigot's book for use in seminaries, and, as will be seen, at one point seemed even to favor its adoption. But he set a tone for later American Catholic writers of denigrating the historical approach to the Bible of such men as Astruc by casting them as sexually immoral. For the time being, nevertheless, Maas did not make Gigot the object of the full attack of his venom.

As Gigot was preparing the second volume of his work, however, he ran into difficulties with his superiors in France, who were reacting both to hostility from the French government and to the increased Roman opposition to biblical criticism. Early in 1902, Lebas sent a circular letter to all Sulpicians reminding them that they were required by rule to have all their writings approved by censors appointed by the general. He also requested copies of Gigot's *General Introduction to the Study of Scripture* and part one of his *Special Introduction* "for examination," as Driscoll reported, "par les hommes compétents que nous avons auprès nous." Driscoll feared what Lebas meant by "competent men" and told Dyer, the vicar general, that Gigot was "already casting about to see where he can find a place when asked to resign as a member of the Society [of St. Sulpice]." Driscoll, moreover, felt that since he himself had given the *nihil obstat* to "the most compromising of Fr. Gigot's books," his own fate was tied to that of the exegete.[12] After consulting Daniel E. Maher, S.S., president of the seminary at Brighton about Driscoll's letter, Dyer responded that "the censorial developments are very grave," but warned Driscoll of the need for caution. It may well have been, he continued, that "the non-compliance with rule may be one of the strong points against Father Gigot, but he should not be the only one to bear the brunt of this."[13]

During the next year, Gigot's situation became more grave. In the fall of 1902, Leo XIII announced that he would appoint a Biblical Commission. "The idea is certainly excellent," wrote Driscoll, *"provided the right men are put on the board."* But he shuddered "at the idea of such a commission being made up of men like Satolli, Mazzella, etc. (I know of course, that the latter is dead (Deo gratias [crossed out]. I mean requiescat in pace), but there are plenty like him left)." He heard that there would be representatives from various nations on the commission and thought "it would be most desirable to have America represented by Fr. Gigot. There is no other except Maas, from whom the Lord deliver us!" In the meantime, he sought to have Alphonse Magnien, S.S., Cardinal Gibbons's theological adviser, see whether the cardinal and Archbishop John Ireland could use their influence to have Gigot appointed.[14] Gigot, of course, was not chosen, but, instead, Charles Grannan of the Catholic University was named the American representative. Gigot was increasingly falling under a cloud and still had not received permission to publish the second volume of his *Special Introduction.*

On December 13, 1902, Gigot wrote Lebas to explain his position. Less than two weeks later, Lebas replied that Gigot's works had been "examined with the greatest care and with perfect impartiality." Unfortunately, however, the examiners had judged that "Fr. Gigot, in his Special Introduction . . . accepts some theories and opinions which are not in conformity with the *common teaching* of Catholics, which is all the more grave since his work is intended for seminarians." The general then enclosed a list of some of the passages that the examiners found objectionable. Lebas, moreover, rejected Gigot's argument that his books were written for America, for they were now becoming known in France and the Society bore the "responsibility before the public and before the Holy See for the doctrines taught on the other side of the ocean." He, therefore, instructed Gigot not to publish a second edition of his work without making the revisions, which the examiners had noted, and not to publish the second part of the *Special Introduction* without following the norms of censorship which he had earlier communicated.[15] Gigot immediately forwarded a copy of Lebas's letter to Dyer, his American superior. Lebas had "written within the briefest delay after the reception of my long document," Gigot declared, and "the decision is just what might be expected from our Superior General and his consultors."[16]

During the next few months, Dyer sought to work out a compromise. He forwarded a copy of Lebas's letter to Maher, president of St. John's Seminary in Brighton, who thought "that with good will, prudence and some diplomacy, professors may be able to keep sufficiently within the lines and yet give useful courses." But Maher added his own opinion on the meaning of the "common teaching" of the Church. "We are in a period of transition," he told Dyer,

and the ideas that the examiners of Fr. Gigot's book take exception to, are gaining ground amongst Catholic scholars, and before many years will be taught without opposition. I notice neither the examiners nor Fr. Lebas speak of these ideas as *erroneous*, but as in *opposition* with what is *up to the present the common teaching*.

His principal concern was that Gigot not leave the Society.[17] Dyer and Gigot were, in the meantime, in consultation in preparing their respective responses to Lebas's letter. Gigot even offered to omit from his second volume "every expression . . . that betrays a personal leaning towards new theories and opinions."[18]

On January 15, 1903, Gigot sent his reply to Lebas. Noting at the outset that the examiners had claimed that he used the expression "contradictory details" in treating of the first two chapters of Genesis, he pointed out that he had in fact spoken of "differences" and "divergences," words that in either English or French had connotations distinct from "contradictions." He then challenged the specific objections that the examiners had raised against particular passages of his book. To the charge that his position was in opposition to "the common teaching of Catholics," he replied that he was treating both old and new theories in the same manner in which Vigouroux had done in his *Manuel biblique*. He was, however, writing in a religiously pluralistic country, where Protestant journals circulated freely, and, therefore, felt an obligation to explain old theories while discussing the new ones. Maher and Driscoll, the censors for the first volume, had, he concluded, agreed with his apologetic purpose.[19]

Dyer's letter to Lebas was a bold defense of Gigot. The report of the examiners, he said, was "grievously unjust." The misrepresentation of Gigot's meaning as he had expressed it in the English language merely illustrated "the incompetence of the examiners." Dyer then proceeded to cite all the Catholic journals and religious orders that had given favorable notice to the book. He mentioned in particular that Herman Heuser, the editor of the *American Ecclesiastical Review* and professor of Scripture at the Philadelphia archdiocesan seminary, had written him that Maas would like to see the volume adopted in all seminaries in the country—a surprising revelation in view of the Jesuit's ambiguous report of the review of Gigot's book in the *Irish Ecclesiastical Review*. In regard to Lebas's argument that Gigot's book was dangerous to seminarians, Dyer countered that "we think that it is necessary to prepare our students for what they will encounter immediately after their departure from the seminary" and that the biblical question was being discussed in the principal journals of the country. He next told the general that he had spoken to Cardinal Gibbons, who asserted that "it would be deplorable to place an obstacle on the work of Fr. Gigot" and bring harm to the Sulpicians if their French superiors tried to determine what was best for the United States according to the special needs of France. Dyer was willing to grant that some writings might be "harmful" in France and should not receive authorization for dissemination there, but he was arguing for the "fundamental principles of St. Sulpice, to follow the direction of the bishops, in those dioceses where the society labors."

In further defense of Gigot, Dyer added a significant reflection on what he thought should be the proper approach to the "common teaching" of the Church. Gigot's two books, he noted, had caused no controversy in the United States and the American superiors, Magnien, Hogan, Rex, Driscoll, Maher, and himself had all encouraged their publication. "We believed," he continued,

that not only was there nothing dangerous in these works, but rather that there was nothing contrary to our grand rule about the teaching in our seminaries: that it is the teaching commonly received from the Church which ought to be set forth. . . . But this rule cannot mean that this common teaching is to be presented as if it had almost the value of definitions of faith, as is too frequently done. It ought to be presented with its true theological note, otherwise we fall into the error which we intend to avoid, and we do not give the doctrine of the Church. If we gave opinions their true value, if we also presented other theories, as much as possible, with their true theological note, would there be such disturbance of the spirit and even of faith, when it becomes necessary to abandon some positions held for a long time by the poorly instructed masses, even ecclesiastics, as if they were some necessary teaching of the Church? The works of Fathers Hogan, Vigouroux, Tanqueray, Guibert, etc., and the practice of the most authoritative professors, attest that at St. Sulpice, we have understood and applied this rule in the sense indicated.

Dyer concluded his letter by informing the general that Gigot had promised to remove from his second volume any expression that displayed a personal tendency in favor of the new theories.[20]

Lebas responded on February 9. He had communicated both Gigot's and Dyer's letters to his consultors, but felt that "the circumstances in France and at Rome" were so "serious from the point of view of doctrine and especially exegesis," that the consultors could not reverse their decision. Gigot had to submit the manuscript of his second volume to them prior to its publication. Lebas argued that he and his advisers knew the European situation and had "the grace of office soundly to judge the true interests of the society." That the consultors did not accept Dyer's offer to examine Gigot's work himself, he continued, was not because they thought him "deficient in knowledge or integrity," but because they were "convinced that what is happening in France and at Rome at this moment demands an extreme vigilance from us." The consultors felt that they alone had the "responsibility for the doctrinal authority of the society," and, accordingly, the sole right to judge works written by Sulpicians.[21]

Dyer was "distressed" at Lebas's reply. As he told Driscoll, he saw no point in going to Paris, for he felt his own authority had already been undermined and his representation of American affairs ignored. He only hoped that Gigot "will not break away from us. Let us stand & act together."[22] Gigot, for his part, was already looking for other positions and had been in contact with Heuser about an appointment to the faculty of St. Charles Borromeo

Seminary in Philadelphia. For the time being, he would continue to reside at St. Austin's College, as a temporary arrangement, "whether I remain in St. Sulpice or not."[23]

For over a year, Gigot was in suspense as Lebas's consultors examined his second volume. In the fall of 1904, he joined the faculty at Dunwoodie, composed of six Sulpicians and eight diocesan priests. In November, Lebas died and Pierre Henri Garriguet, S.S., was elected to succeed him. But the situation of the Sulpicians in France was desperate. As part of its program of radical laicization—20,000 members of religious orders were expelled between 1903 and 1904—the French government had ordered the bishops to replace Sulpicians with diocesan priests in their seminaries by the academic year 1905–1906. Dyer explained this to the Dunwoodie faculty upon his return from Garriguet's election, and also spoke to Gigot about the reasons for holding up the publication of his second volume.[24]

The French situation shaded the treatment of the Gigot case and increased the unrest at Dunwoodie. Early in January 1905, Gigot wrote Dyer for permission to use in class the page proofs of the section of his work already printed. He recalled that he had been allowed to do this both at Brighton and at Baltimore, before Lebas became superior general. He hoped that Dyer would be able to give the necessary permission, for "if the matter must be submitted again to Paris, I have [sic] better give it up at once. Paris, as you know, has already—at least practically—denied me the desired freedom." He concluded by asking Dyer's pardon for any "pain" he had caused him when he had asked "about the prospect for the publication of my second volume of Special Introduction to the Old Testament."[25] Dyer gave his permission for Gigot to use the page proofs of his book for class and assured him that "there was no apology needed whatever, my dear Father;—you have had a great deal to put up with, and a little too much heat is easily understood."[26]

At this point, however, Gigot's situation had become complicated by Driscoll's decision to found at Dunwoodie the *New York Review,* a project that Dyer thought would distract the faculty from their primary purpose of teaching seminarians and draw unfavorable attention to the Sulpicians.[27] Gigot, for his part, now began pushing for a solution. On February 4, he informed Dyer that

Heuser had requested him to write "a series of articles on the historic character of Genesis, etc." for the *American Ecclesiastical Review.* He wished to accept the offer, but did not want to have to send his manuscript to Paris for censorship. He was also "tired waiting for an opportunity to have" his second volume "appear." "May I therefore hope," he asked, "that it shall appear after it has been re-examined in this country without sending the proofs and MS. thereof to Paris?"[28] A short time later, he returned to the same theme. Vigouroux, he knew, was one of the examiners of his first volume of the *Special Introduction* and had stated that Gigot did "not teach the Catholic doctrine," particularly in regard to the "Authorship of the Pentateuch." Gigot believed that he had presented in his book the traditional view of the Mosaic authorship of the Pentateuch "with its proper theological value," namely that the Church had made no formal decision. In light of this criticism, he could not expect Vigouroux to approve publication of his second volume, and, therefore, urged Dyer to permit its publication without censorship in Paris.[29]

In the meantime, the London *Tablet* had published an unsigned review of the first part of Gigot's *Special Introduction.* The book was "erudite" and "useful," said the writer, but "in spite . . . of the many excellent qualities" that it possessed, "we cannot pronounce the book before us suitable as a class-book for Catholic students." The reviewer objected that

Father Gigot states the arguments for both views [traditional and more recent] but in a way which would lead one to suppose that long-standing traditions must give way before modern criticism. In treating the question of the authorship of the Hexateuch, which he terms Genesis Josue, he states, first of all, the arguments which have been constantly urged in support of the traditional view; and then proceeds to show the weakness of the separate points of evidence. When, however, we turn to his statements regarding the recent theories we find the views of their supporters given without any such criticism, as though they were settled facts; not a word is said to show that many of their arguments have been disproved, and their methods shown to be false.[30]

This review now further complicated Gigot's case.

Pressured by Gigot, Dyer appointed two American Sulpicians, John F. Fenlon, S.S., and L. F. M. Dumont, S.S., both at the

Sulpician College in Washington, as censors of his proposed articles for the *American Ecclesiastical Review.* Dyer asked Gigot to revise the second part of his *Special Introduction* in light of the criticisms of the *Tablet* review and submit it to the same two censors. The question of whether this book would still need approval from Paris was left in abeyance.[31] At this point, there was a noticeable change in the tone of Dyer's correspondence. Until late February, as vicar general, he had been supportive of Gigot's scholarship and had earlier defended him in Paris. After that date, however, he seemed to be more concerned about the future of the Sulpicians in the United States, who were in turn influenced by events in France. His attitude toward Gigot seemed to be shaped by Driscoll's increasing independence at Dunwoodie.

Driscoll continued to argue that it had been a Sulpician custom in Canada and the United States for the local superior to censor a book. He had, moreover, drawn Garriguet's criticism for founding the *New York Review.* In Dyer's opinion, Driscoll wanted to have articles for the journal censored according to his own interpretation of the Sulpician rule.[32] As late as September, however, Gigot seemed satisfied with the arrangements Dyer had made for the censorship of his second volume. He had suggested that Dyer replace Dumont with Driscoll to facilitate getting Farley's *imprimatur.* Then he had second thoughts, because he had "reflected that all things considered, Fr. Dumont's censorship would decidedly carry in Paris a weight which Fr. Driscoll's would not carry."[33] In other words, Gigot seemed reconciled to having to obtain approval from Paris to have his book published and was satisfied that Dyer had his best interests at heart. But his attitude changed during the next few months, as his case became subordinate to Dyer's concern over the *New York Review,* the first number of which had appeared in the summer of 1905.

In December 1905, Driscoll, as the superior of Dunwoodie, attended a meeting of Dyer's council in Baltimore, but he gave no indication that there was anything wrong. On January 9, 1906, however, he, Gigot, and three other Sulpicians announced to Dyer that they were withdrawing from the Society and were remaining at Dunwoodie as diocesan priests. For the next few days, Dyer sought in vain both by letter and in person to have them reconsider their decision.[34] Of the Sulpician members of the faculty, only

Bruneau stayed in the Society, but was immediately transferred to Brighton.

Relieved of the necessity of obtaining special censorship in Paris, Gigot published the second volume, his *Special Introduction to the Study of the Old Testament: Part II. Didactic and Prophetical Writings.* It had the *nihil obstat* of Driscoll, as the *censor deputatus* of the Archdiocese of New York. Despite all the revisions Gigot had made over the previous three years, it was still a relatively progressive work. He treated Isaiah 1–39 separately from Isaiah 40–66, for example, and mentioned the arguments of the higher critics in favor of separate authorship. He concluded by quoting Newman that "it does not matter whether one or two Isaias wrote the book which bears the prophet's name, the Church, without settling this point, pronounces it inspired.["]³⁵ Shortly after its publication, the Biblical Commission issued its decision on the Mosaic authorship of the Pentateuch. An anonymous reviewer in the *American Ecclesiastical Review,* probably Maas, gave the new volume relatively high praise, but drew attention to Gigot's first volume and the decision of the Biblical Commission. In the first volume, said the review, "Gigot made no secret of his leanings toward the pronounced views of those critics who question the immediate authorship of some of the historical books, notably of the Pentateuch." These "leanings" had placed Gigot "in an attitude of separation from, if not contradiction to, the views of the Abbé Vigouroux, who defends the absolute Mosaic authorship of the first five books of the Bible." This was the position taken by the Biblical Commission, and, while it was "not necessarily intended to be an infallible pronouncement of the Church," it defined "the attitude of Catholics in practical controversy." When Gigot had written his first volume, the reviewer continued, the "Catholic position had not been authoritatively defined" and, therefore, "there was no ground for criticizing the author." Once the Biblical Commission had spoken, however, it "would seem to require the revision of the chapters in Father Gigot's first volume referring to this topic, in such a manner that the student may not be biassed [*sic*] against the evidence for the Mosaic authorship."³⁶ The reviewer, whether Maas or not, seemed somewhat confused on the authority of the Biblical Commission's decisions. They were not "infallible," but they "authoritatively defined" the Catholic attitude on biblical questions.[37]

Gigot did not revise his first volume, nor did he initially give up writing. He made several significant contributions to the *New York Review*. In addition to book reviews, he published multi-part articles on "Studies in the Synoptic Gospels," "The Authorship of Isaias," "The Higher Criticism of the Bible," and "Divorce in the New Testament: An Exegetical Study"; he also wrote articles on the books of Jonas and Job and on Abraham. The reaction of his superiors to the founding of the *Review* seems to have provided the context for his final decision to withdraw from the Sulpicians, as he sought greater academic freedom. When the *Review* came to an end, however, so did his scholarly productivity, for the reaction against Modernism in the United States virtually meant the reaction against scholarship.

THE NEW YORK REVIEW

The *New York Review* was published only between 1905 and 1908. Its demise occurred in the aftermath of Pius X's encyclical *Pascendi Dominici Gregis,* issued on September 8, 1907. The official reason given for ceasing publication was the lack of financial support, but Modernism was also involved. Two separate, but interrelated, issues contributed to Roman suspicion of the *Review*—the case of Edward J. Hanna and the publication of an advertisement for George Tyrrell's books after the former Jesuit had been excommunicated.

Hanna had been a seminarian for the Diocese of Rochester at the American College in Rome, when Denis O'Connell was rector. The prize student of Francesco Satolli at the Urban College of Propaganda, he had been awarded the doctorate by acclamation in 1886. O'Connell then prevailed on Bishop McQuaid to allow him to remain in Rome as a *repetitore* at the American College. By September, Satolli was asking Hanna to substitute for him at the Urban College. Although O'Connell would have liked to retain Hanna in Rome, after only a year, McQuaid appointed him professor of theology at St. Bernard's Seminary, Rochester, New York.[38] There, Hanna drew little attention, until McQuaid demanded that his faculty publish. Between September 1905 and December 1906, he wrote for the *Review* a three-part article on "The Human Knowledge of Jesus Christ." Dealing in the first part with Scripture, he warned of the necessity of avoiding the extremes of "losing sight of" either the divine or human natures of Christ. The Church, he argued, had not definitely decided on whether there were limitations to Christ's knowledge, but the question could only be answered by a study of the Scripture, the Fathers, and later theologians. In the next part, Hanna dealt with the Scripture texts that implied limitation in Jesus' knowledge, which, he concluded, seemed consistent with His full sharing in human nature. In the final part, Hanna showed that, until Gregory the Great, the early Fathers admitted some limitation of Jesus' knowledge.[39]

Hanna's position was conservative enough by most standards of the day, but not by those then being raised in Rome. At the Urban College of Propaganda, Alexis M. Lepicier, O.M.I., professor of dogmatic theology, repudiated Hanna in his lectures as early as the spring of 1906. Otherwise, Hanna's work drew little attention. In the spring of 1907, however, Archbishop Patrick W. Riordan of San Francisco requested that the Holy See appoint a coadjutor to him and recommended that Hanna be named. McQuaid strongly supported the nomination and all seemed to be going forward, when suddenly Hanna's orthodoxy was called into question. In July, the Holy Office had issued its decree *Lamentabili,* followed in September by Pius X's *Pascendi Dominici Gregis.* In Rochester, Hanna's enemies lost no time in applying to him the charge of heresy. Father Andrew E. Breen, professor of Scripture at the seminary, wrote to a friend in Rome that Hanna was guilty of liberal tendencies and could have better entitled his article in the *Review* the "Ignorance of Christ." Breen's own competence in the biblical field was derived from his four-volume *Harmonized Exposition of the Four Gospels,* which had drawn Lagrange's attention in 1900 as the work of a man whose only resemblance to contemporary scholars was the arrangement of his material.[40] Breen's letter was passed on to Merry del Val, who requested that Cardinal Giovanni Gotti, Prefect of the Congregation of Propaganda, make inquiries about Hanna with Archbishop Diomede Falconio, the apostolic delegate to the American hierarchy. Falconio sent Gotti a copy of Hanna's work with the observations that the *Review* "seems a little suspect of Modernism" and that Lepicier had already refuted Hanna's article in class.[41]

In November, McQuaid wrote to both Gotti and Merry del Val in Hanna's defense. A month later, on the advice of both Riordan and McQuaid, Hanna also wrote Gotti to explain his position. In his explanation, he wished to distance himself from the nineteenth-century Protestant theories that the Son of God had abandoned His divine attributes in assuming human nature. "If I erred," he told the cardinal,

I erred in method, not in doctrine. Apart from us the Protestants hold a doctrine called "kenosis" which truly negates the divinity of Christ; apart from us the Protestants and some Modernists hold that Our Lord had erred especially in reference to the day of judgement. I have written these articles to defend the divinity of Our Lord against the Protestants and to affirm him free of every suspicion of error against some Modernists.[42]

While Hanna's and McQuaid's letters were crossing the Atlantic, Archbishop Farley learned that not only were Hanna's articles on the knowledge of Christ under investigation but also his article on absolution in the *Catholic Encyclopedia,* which Farley was sponsoring.[43] By January 1908, American newspapers were reporting the Roman investigation of Hanna.[44] In the meantime, the Congregation of Propaganda appointed Lepicier, who had originally criticized Hanna, to examine all of his writings. As the congregation began its deliberations, Cardinal Satolli defended his former student's writings, but requested that Hanna write a fourth article for the *Review,* upholding the traditional view of Christ's human knowledge. The article appeared in the *Review* in the spring of 1908, two years after the original articles. Both Satolli and Lepicier had read it beforehand. In it, Hanna repudiated any notion that his previous articles could be interpreted as meaning that Christ could possibly have thought or spoken any error, and he asserted that Christ always enjoyed the beatific vision.[45]

In retrospect, there seems to have been a relationship between the tendency toward a high Christology, emphasizing the divinity of Christ, and reactions against both Americanism and the biblical question. With Americanism, the Holy See feared individualism and even Pelagianism; it therefore played down human nature and made grace rare. With the biblical question, Rome rejected multiple authorship of the Pentateuch and of the Gospels, retained the traditional attribution of the books to a particular author, and limited to him the charism of inspiration. With Christology, it found it dangerous to speak of the limitations on Christ's human knowledge.

Despite Hanna's clarification, Rome still was not satisfied. In the summer, Archbishop Farley and Cardinal Gibbons both went to Rome where they had to defend the American church against Merry del Val's charges that Americanism was part of Modernism. According to some reports, Farley had a heated audience with Pius X, who also expressed strong reservations about the orthodoxy of some of the articles in the *Catholic Encyclopedia*. In the end, Hanna was rejected as coadjutor Archbishop of San Francisco on September 8, 1908—an action that made possible Gibbons's influencing Riordan to accept Denis O'Connell as auxiliary bishop.[46] In 1912, however, O'Connell grew tired of San Francisco and became Bishop of Richmond. His transfer paved the way for Hanna to be named auxiliary bishop of San Francisco and to succeed Riordan as archbishop in 1918.

In the meantime, McQuaid bristled when he learned that the accusations against Hanna had originated in Rochester. He demanded that each faculty member of the seminary sign a statement denying any responsibility for Hanna's delation to Rome. Breen refused and then submitted his resignation from the faculty. As McQuaid told Farley, "when it became known that Dr. Breen was the professor at St. Bernard's who was Dr. Hanna's accuser, he handed in his resignation which met with immediate acceptance." The bishop thought he had "shown unusual forebearance toward Breen, who is so self-conceited that he is unable to appreciate it."[47] Breen left Rochester to teach at St. Francis Seminary in Milwaukee.

Hanna's writings had drawn Rome's attention to the *New York Review*, which now fell under closer scrutiny. On December 12, 1907, Merry del Val wrote Falconio that the "modernist movement" was making inroads "among the Catholic clergy and laity" in the United States. He had in mind "the 'New York Review' which has for its center the archiepiscopal seminary of New York, and which, especially through the collaboration of known modernists, could facilitate the diffusion of dangerous teachings." One indication of this dangerous tendency of the seminary was "the fact of the familiarity of certain graduates of the aforementioned seminary, who had been sent to Rome to take their degrees at the Gregorian University and lived with the Pallotini Fathers of S. Silvestro, with a certain one of the above mentioned propagandists of Modernism." The cardinal instructed the delegate to use "great delicacy" with Archbishop Farley "to realize the necessity of removing the danger of modernist tendencies from the aforementioned review, starting with the collaboration of notorious modernists such as the priests Ernesto Buonaiuti and Nicola Turchi of Rome, and the French abbés Dimnet and Houtin and as many others as find themselves in an analogous situation."[48]

At this point, the documentary evidence becomes confusing. On December 24, Falconio drafted a reply to Merry del Val in which he said that he had drawn Farley's attention to the matter. The archbishop, he reported, had "already summoned all the professors together and given them peremptory orders to adhere to the teachings and counsels of the Holy Father" and had informed them of his resolve "not to tolerate the least divergence." Farley assured Falconio that there would be "sufficient vigilance."[49]

Although Falconio told Merry del Val on December 24, 1907, that he had already discussed the *Review* with Farley, on January 14, 1908, he wrote Farley about Merry del Val's complaints, but without revealing the source. Specifically, the delegate mentioned the Modernist writers in the *Review* and brought up the "familiarity" of the New York priests studying in Rome "with some one of the above mentioned modernists." He prefaced his paraphrase of Merry del Val's charges with one of his own. He called to Farley's attention an advertisement in the *Review* for the "Books by Rev. George Tyrrell." A close friend of von Hügel, Tyrrell had been dismissed from the Society of Jesus in 1906. In October 1907, he was excommunicated, not because of his books, but because of a series of letters he had written against *Pascendi Dominici Gregis* in the London *Times*.[50] "Such an advertisement," in Falconio's mind, "appears to be a violation of both the letter and the spirit of the recent Encyclical on modernism 'Pascendi' reproduced in the same number of the N.Y. Review!" With this in view, Falconio took "the liberty of suggesting that for the future Your Grace should see that writers who have a tendency for the condemned doctrine of modernism should not write for the Review or at least that they should first submit their communication to your approval."[51]

In Farley's response on January 23, he made no allusion to any communication from Falconio prior to the letter of January 15. He promised that henceforth everything that would appear in the *Review* would be "carefully revised by myself and the Diocesan Censors." He noted that, in accordance with *Pascendi*, he had "some time ago appointed six additional vigilantes." He then presented the history of the *Review*. It had "started on the motu proprio of the Sulpicians when they had charge of our Seminary at Dunwoodie," he stated, but then added an account different from Dyer's. "Rev. Dr. Dyer was so anxious for its success," he continued,

that he asked me for a letter which should say that I wished the Review to go on, so that his Superiors in France might not interfere with it, which letter I gave him. For this reason I have hesitated to direct the publication of the Review to cease, as I was inclined to do on receipt of your letter. If Your Excellency or the Holy See so directs I shall order the cessation of the magazine after the issue of the next number to which the subscribers are entitled who have paid up for the year.[52]

Farley then addressed each of the charges raised by Falconio. To begin with, he stated, "I feel that I owe it to you as well as to the Review to respectfully submit that in some very important points charged against the magazine the party who informed Your Eminence [*sic*] was guilty of bearing false witness." He had personally gone through the journal and found that Dimnet and Houtin had never written for it, and the other authors had written when they were still in good standing in the Church. As far as the advertisement for Tyrrell's books was concerned, it had slipped in by accident, through an oversight on the part of Father John F. Brady, the managing editor, who was then tending his dying father. Brady would publish an apology in the next issue of the *Review*.[53]

Finally, Farley turned to the charge that some of his priests were on familiar terms with a certain person with Modernist tendencies. He presumed that "the person . . . whose friendship is not desirable" was Giovanni Genocchi. Farley's priests had become acquainted with Genocchi when they had first arrived in Rome and needed an English-speaking confessor. He concluded by pointing out that he had given much thought to the places where the future professors in his seminary would study. "Some persons here suggested Innsbruck, others Freiburg, others Jerusalem," he noted, but "all these I rejected and determined on Rome, the Center of Catholicity as the place where they would imbibe at the fountain head the teachings of the Church."[54] Why Farley believed that Genocchi was suspect of Modernist sympathies is difficult to determine. Only the previous summer, Genocchi had acted as interpreter for Poels with Pius X. He continued to be a consultor of the Biblical Commission. As will be seen, however, he was also at this time informing Charles A. Briggs on Roman affairs. Merry del Val and other Roman officials may well have recognized the source of Briggs's information in his published articles on the growing reaction against biblical studies. But Farley did not know Merry del Val was the source of Falconio's charges.

Despite Farley's defense, it was clear that the *Review* was under suspicion. The last issue published was for May-June, 1908, which appeared only in September. The editors announced that they were ceasing publication because of lack of financial support, but secular and Catholic newspapers in both the United States and Italy reported that the journal had been suppressed because of its Modernistic tendencies. In September, the *Washington Post,* for example, linked the cessation of the *Review* with a series of articles by Lepicier condemning Hanna. The newspaper also reported that the *Catholic Encyclopedia* had fallen under suspicion.[55] A month later, the *Washington Times* carried a story that Farley, who had just returned from Rome, would have to resolve the conflict caused by Hanna's article on "Absolution."[56] Thomas F. Coakley, then the secretary to the rector of the North American College in Rome, reported that Pius X had in fact hurled a specially bound copy of the first volume of the *Catholic Encyclopedia* to the floor of his library.[57] Whatever reservations there were in Rome about the encyclopedia, however, no official action was taken against it. What happened to the Dunwoodie faculty was a different story.

The Dunwoodie faculty and especially the former Sulpicians, who remained there, fell under suspicion. In the summer of 1909, Farley, again in Rome, cabled back to New York that Driscoll, the president of the seminary, was to be named a pastor. The new president was Father John P. Chidwick, chaplain to the New York

City Police Department and former Navy chaplain. Gigot remained on the faculty, but never again published anything major. Francis P. Duffy, the associate editor of the *Review* and contributor of a series of notes on current theology, remained at Dunwoodie until 1912, when he became a pastor and later distinguished himself as "Fighting Father Duffy" of the Sixty-ninth New York Infantry Regiment in World War I.[58] The appearance of the *Review* had seemed to be the first breath of scholarly fresh air in the American church, but, in retrospect, its short life was actually the last gasp of a progressive theology that had been developing during the previous decade. With the demise of the *Review* and the transformation of *The Catholic University Bulletin* into more of an in-house organ, the American church was left without a scholarly publication until the 1940s.[59]

While Hanna had first drawn Roman attention to the *Review*, the Vatican may have been concerned with the Archdiocese of New York and its seminary for other reasons. Dunwoodie had had very close relations with Union Theological Seminary and particularly with Charles Augustus Briggs, then professor of what would now be called ecumenical theology. But Briggs's association with Catholic liberal thinkers extended beyond the United States. Vatican officials already knew of his published correspondence with von Hügel on the Pentateuch. They may not yet have been aware, however, of his friendship with Giovanni Genocchi, a liberal consultor to the Biblical Commission. Falconio, as was seen, had noted to Farley the suspicion that New York priests had aroused by visiting Genocchi. Genocchi was also a friend of Hanna's and had advised Riordan about the Roman suspicions about his appointment to San Francisco.[60] Briggs was now cast in the role of spokesman for his liberal Catholic friends, particularly von Hügel and Genocchi.

8. Charles Augustus Briggs: Spokesman for Catholic Exegetes

Briggs had been one of Dunwoodie's closest Protestant friends and had been actively involved in the Catholic biblical question. A biblical scholar, he had caused controversy in the Presbyterian Church in 1891 for his criticism of Protestant "Bibliolatry," the worship of the letter of the Bible. That controversy led to his being suspended from the ministry in the Presbyterian Church and to his joining the Episcopal Church. As was seen, the controversy also first brought him to the attention of Maas and other Catholic conservatives.[1]

Briggs was one of the foremost English-speaking exegetes. With Samuel R. Driver of Oxford University and Francis Brown, he edited the *Hebrew and English Lexicon*. He and Driver were also the editors of the *International Critical Commentary on the Holy Scriptures of the Old and New Testaments*. But Briggs had another interest— a burning desire to work for the reunion of Christianity and this brought him to Rome. There, he met Denis O'Connell and, through him, Baron Friedrich von Hügel and Giovanni Genocchi. The publication of Briggs's and von Hügel's views on the Biblical Commission's decision in favor of the Mosaic authorship of the Pentateuch received unfavorable reviews in the *American Ecclesiastical Review* and *The Catholic University Bulletin*—one of the early signs of the growing conservatism of the university.[2]

Briggs's published exchange with von Hügel, however, was but one of his attempts to speak for liberal Catholic exegetes. In the course of his writings, he locked horns with Archbishop John Ireland, erstwhile leader of Americanism, for Briggs saw an intimate relationship between ecclesiology and Roman decrees on the biblical question. He was important for American Catholic biblical studies, not only because of his contacts with European scholars, but also because of his published disclosures of the growing "integrist" movement.

BRIGGS AND VON HÜGEL ON THE MOSAIC AUTHORSHIP OF THE PENTATEUCH

Von Hügel had interpreted the Biblical Commission's decision in light of the conservative reaction that was transforming the Gregorian University in Rome. He feared that, if there were no protest from the scholarly world, the decision would be the first statement in a new syllabus of errors. On August 28, 1906, he therefore asked Briggs to enter the discussion. It was not merely a Catholic question, he argued, but one that pertained as well to the Protestant "Bibliolaters," a play on the word that Briggs had used in his controversial address at Union Theological Seminary, when he was transferred to the newly created chair of biblical theology in 1891. He was also asking Samuel R. Driver for his assistance, but suggested that Briggs give his opinion in the form of a letter to which he could respond. He then chided his American friend for his naïvete about Janssens. "I did not like," he remarked,

when you told me of Dom Janssens' *broad* sympathies and *warm praise* to you of Newman to tell you, there and then, that the man was once more showing how hopelessly double-faced opportunist that narrow Neo-scholastic is. Some years ago he published in the *Revue Benedictine* a general denunciation of English (Roman) Catholics, finishing up with the declaration that this was no wonder since they had been led and permeated by such hopelessly and to the end semi-Protestant minds as Newman and Manning [Edward Henry Manning, Archbishop of Westminster and later cardinal]. The man is now hard at work getting a Cardinal's Hat; and his successor [to be?] David Fleming in the resident Secretaryship to the Biblical Commission. This Decree is the first public victory there [and] means the triumph . . . of the a-prioristic medievalists.[3]

Von Hügel passed on to Briggs information he had obtained about the Biblical Commission from a friend, probably F. R. Clarke, an English scholar, who was a consultor of the commission. In preparation for the establishment of a permanent Biblical Commission, Leo XIII had appointed a committee of twelve men. "The original commission of 12," von Hügel wrote,

had fully 9 men solidly friendly to Loisy and Lagrange. Vigouroux was the only definitely old-fashioned upon it. And I know direct from one of those 12 that they deliberately rejected Janssen [sic] as an A-priorist and Neo-Scholastic, quite unfit for this kind of work. But when the com. got enlarged from 12 to 40, a considerable majority—something like 25 against 15 was given to the anti-clerical [sic] party; and it could only be a question of time that this majority should get one of its own men for secretary and a series of decisions to its liking. It has now got Janssens and this Decree, and will doubtless take care to give us others like it, if this one is well, or even simply silently received.[4]

Two weeks later, Briggs sent his initial critique of the commission's response on the Mosaic authorship. Von Hügel suggested, however, that Briggs redraft it in the form of an inquiry, to which he would then reply. He also informed Briggs that Driver was not at that time willing to make any written statement, but he was optimistic that James Knowles, editor of the *Nineteenth Century,* would publish their exchange in his journal.[5] Briggs then redrafted his critique. As von Hügel made the final revisions, he explained that he wanted to make "it clear throughout that we are busy only with the authorship of the 4 great Documents, and not with the question whether stray fragments of Mosaic sayings or writings may not be lurking here & there." He had, however, run into difficulties in finding a publisher. Knowles had retained the manuscript for over a month before rejecting it, so von Hügel submitted it to Longmans, which immediately accepted it, with permission to translate it into Italian.[6]

Von Hügel wrote the preface to the joint letters. Dated All Saints Day, 1906, it noted that they exchanged their correspondence, while each was on vacation "away from most of our books and papers." Their weeks of examination had convinced them not only of "the importance and inevitableness" of the critical positions but also of their "responsibilities and duties as Biblical Students within the Christian Church." Their purpose was to gain "the definitive, operative recognition, by Ecclesiastical Authority, of sound critical historical method, and of this method's most assured results."[7]

Dated September 4, 1906, Briggs's letter stated that he had been "surprised and dismayed" to read in the *Corriere della Sera* the commission's decision. He was especially disturbed because, while in Rome, he "had the very highest authority for the statement . . . that a reasonable amount of liberty would be given in Biblical Criticism, so long as its results did not conflict with the established dogmas of the Church." This decision, however, represented a change of policy, for

the Church has never committed itself officially to the Mosaic authorship of the Pentateuch; and to recognize that Hebrew laws and institutions were a development of a divinely guided Theocracy, rather than given all at once to Moses at the beginning of the Hebrew Commonwealth, suits the Roman Catholic position as to Christian Dogma and Institutions, better than the usual Protestant position that we must build on the New Testament alone.[8]

Briggs thus aligned himself with the way Lagrange and Gigot had analyzed the alleged binding force of the traditional attribution of the Pentateuch to Moses.

Briggs blamed the change of policy on the Scholasticism then dominant in Rome and had no hesitation in naming the perpetrators. He had read Janssens's work on dogmatic theology "with profit and admiration . . . but his treatment of the Bible is so unscholarly; and his use of the Hebrew language shows such profound ignorance, that no serious worker could deem him competent to give an opinion in matters of Hebrew Scholarship, and his name discredits at once the report of the Commission." Fulcran Vigouroux, the other secretary of the commission, stood "for an antiquated apologetic." Though Briggs recalled that Pius X had personally told him "that such decisions, even when approved by the Pope, have not the character of infallibility," he was still concerned that "his name when given to any decision, carries an authority with the faithful beyond estimation." Now he feared that "the authorities of Rome will be so blind as to put this decision in a new Syllabus," which would only bring upon the Church the abuse hurled against her by the Syllabus of Errors.[9]

Briggs then turned to a critique of the substance of the commission's decision. Since the question of the Mosaic authorship of the Pentateuch had already been settled "in the arena of Biblical scholarship," he argued, he contested the first part of the commission's decision rejecting, out of hand, that the "arguments amassed by the Critics" were sufficient to deny the Mosaic authorship. He was certain that the commission members had not seriously weighed the critical arguments from language, style, historical situation, or the biblical theology of each of the four documents. Taking on two of the leading Roman scholastic theologians, he noted that

it is safe to say that the differences in style are not merely such as distinguish the chief dogmatic authorities of modern Rome, such as [Louis] Billot and Janssen [sic], but such rather as distinguish these still living writers from the Medieval Schoolmen, Duns Scotus and Bonaventura. To my mind it would be easier to prove that Thomas Aquinas was the author of these four theological systems, than to show that the four great documents of the Pentateuch had one and the same author, Moses.[10]

Briggs turned next to the Biblical Commission's argument that both Testaments, the Jewish and Christian traditions, and "internal criticism of the text" all attested to the Mosaic authorship. The evidence of both Testaments, he declared, meant nothing more than that in the Scripture "certain laws, predictions and sayings are put in the mouth of Moses," in the same manner in which the Psalms were placed "in the mouth of David." But, he continued, the Biblical Commission would hardly want to argue that David was the author of the Psalms. Briggs was, moreover, concerned that the passages the "anti-critics" used to argue for the Mosaic authorship would in fact place "the Old Testament . . . in irreconcilable conflict with itself on the question in debate." The traditional Jewish and Christian attribution of the Pentateuch to Moses was "nothing more than the continuation of the Biblical usage of 'Moses' as the name of the Pentateuch and of the personified Law." Such attribution, he stated, "does not belong to authoritative tradition, but to unverified and unauthorized tradition."[11]

Briggs next turned to the commission's statement that Moses may have entrusted the writing of parts of the Pentateuch to other persons, who "faithfully rendered his meaning, wrote nothing contrary to his will, and omitted nothing," while Moses remained "the principal and inspired author" and may have used preexisting sources. Such a position, Briggs asserted, totally ignored the "splendid work of Biblical scholarship during the past century."

So different were the documents in language, style, and theology, he declared, that "the hands that wrote the great documents of the Pentateuch were hands that wrote many centuries after Moses, and Moses has no responsibility whatever for their work."[12] As Briggs stated it, his position tended to remove any Mosaic influence on the development of the Pentateuch.

Briggs reserved some of his sharpest, and most telling, criticism for the commission's concession that "some modifications" may have been introduced into the Pentateuch, "such as additions after the death of Moses, either inserted by an inspired author, or attached to the text as glosses or interpretations." The commission allowed that "it is lawful to investigate and judge [these modifications or glosses] according to the laws of criticism," as long as "due regard" was "paid to the judgment of the Church." Briggs thought this slight concession presented a dilemma. Either the Church recognized the "laws of criticism" or it did not. If it did, then "it must abide by the verdict of those laws."[13]

Briggs, however, was more concerned about the commission's "distinction between additions 'inserted by an inspired author' and additions 'attached to the text as glosses or interpretations,' " for this seemed

on the face of it, to imply a dangerous heresy, for which certainly the Biblical Critics of my acquaintance would refuse responsibility. For it seems clearly to assert that the glosses and interpretations attached to the text are not from inspired authors, and hence that a considerable, but undetermined, amount of the Pentateuch is not inspired. Now the chief work of Biblical Criticism at the present time is just this work of detecting the glosses and interpretations of the older documents by later hands. The number of these is constantly increasing. Hence the inevitable result of this decision of the Biblical Commission is to withdraw inspiration from a considerable portion of the Pentateuch, and to render a further very considerable portion of it of doubtful inspiration. This is certainly a more dangerous position than any that has been taken up by sober critics. The only safe position is that the Canon as it stands is an inspired book; that the inspiration of the sacred writings does not depend upon Amos and Ezra or any other known author; and that the inspiration of the glosses and additions is just as sure as the inspiration of the originals.[14]

Briggs, then, was arguing against the prevailing theology of inspiration, which would limit that charism to the original known author, for the commission's formulation implied that not all of the Pentateuch was inspired. He argued, instead, that the notion of inspiration included within it the recognition of the book by the Church.

Concluding his "letter," he asserted that he really did not believe that the "majority, or the spokesmen of that Commission . . . sincerely" desired "the application of historical method to historical subject-matters, or peace, prosperity, and reunion of Christendom," but that they preferred "direct conflict with scholarship and science," and "would plunge the Church into the gulf to save their own interests." He was, however, convinced that

the Church will not go into the gulf. It will eventually throw off its incompetent advisers; and other counsellors, more worthy, will take their place, and the movement for right method in the right place, for the union of sincere scholarship and science with deep faith, peace, and charity will go on, all the more rapidly for the temporary check and inevitable, practical demonstration of the utter fruitlessness and acute danger of such direct conflict with a huge mass of facts.[15]

Von Hügel dated his response September 29, 1906. He recalled how much time he had spent on Pentateuchal criticism and the paper he had delivered on the Hexateuch at Fribourg in 1897—a paper which, as was seen above, was published in *The Catholic University Bulletin.* Many scholars had agreed with his conclusions, he continued, and among them were Loisy, von Hummelauer, and Lagrange—it did not seem to matter to von Hügel that, by this point, several of Loisy's works had been put on the Index. Other scholars had also contributed to the progressive Catholic biblical movement: F. R. Clarke of England, van Hoonacker, Poels—whom von Hügel erroneously identified as a Belgian—Minocchi in Italy, and Gigot in the United States. He, therefore, felt justified in asserting that he and Briggs had many supporters for their position.[16]

Much in the manner of Hogan, von Hügel sought to show the relationship between personal religion and the Church. "I remain as convinced as ever," he wrote

that religion requires a social environment, an historical and institutional training-ground, vehicle, and expression, a Church; that the primary object and test of such a Church is Religion and not Science or Scholarship;

and that the Roman Catholic Church not only contains *de facto* a great mass of Christian faith, truth, and life—this much will now be conceded by all candid Protestants, and can truthfully be asserted, in various degrees and ways, by fair-minded Catholics, of other Christian bodies—but that it represents, with a unique fulness, consciousness and continuity, certain fundamental, inalienable constituents, rights and duties of complete religion. And alongside of this persists the complementary conviction that the different energizings and requirements of man's multiform nature are, at bottom, too deeply interdependent, for the whole man and religion itself not infallibly to suffer in the long run, if his instinct for Science and Scholarship is persistently and gravely thwarted or deflected; that the deepest spirit and the logic immanental to the presuppositions and final positions of Catholicism positively require a sincerely historical and thoroughly critical treatment of the history and literature of the Bible: and yet there, before me, are the facts of the Church-condemnations of critics as great and epoch-making as Richard Simon at the end of the Seventeenth Century, and Alfred Loisy at the beginning of the Twentieth, with many another trouble threatened or executed, before, between and after these two culminating points, from, say, the time of Erasmus, right down to this last July.[17]

Though the decision had "received the Papal sanction," however, von Hügel gave it a minimalist interpretation. While it should not be "criticized," except "under the pressure of serious necessity" and only by those "conversant with the complex and critical problems," still "it is not put forward as a Dogmatic Decision, but, apparently, as a simple Direction and Appeal from scholars to scholars."[18] Von Hügel was, of course, a bit too optimistic in so minimizing the authority of the decision, for it was certainly more than "a simple Direction and Appeal" for Poels, who was removed from his teaching post because he could not accept the decision in conscience.

Von Hügel was somewhat disingenuous in remarking that "I have not studied Dom Janssen's [*sic*] works; but I have no reason to think you are unfairly prejudiced against him, and certainly he is no Historical Critic, no Old Testament Scholar." The baron, of course, had very strong views on Janssens, which he had already communicated to Briggs. "Vigouroux's signature" on the decision, he continued, "is no doubt much less significant than that of his junior, resident and very active colleague; for the Abbé is now old, after doing much work according to certain preconceptions which younger, fresher minds have found to break down under the stress of the facts when fully and fairly faced."[19] In von Hügel's mind, it seems, far more dangerous than antiquated scholarship was the new scholasticism.

Von Hügel leveled three major criticisms against the Biblical Commission's decision. First, he insisted "upon the immense[,] because strictly cumulative[,] force of the argument . . . for the real existence and the widely different ages of the different documents." Only a "careful student of the Hebrew text," however, could determine the differences in "the vocabulary, style, institution, history, ethics, and theology," which "all grow and change *together.*" As one example, he pointed out the different prescriptions about sacrifice in each of the four documents.[20]

Von Hügel next picked up on one of Briggs's themes—"the unworkableness" of the commission's argument that Moses may have entrusted some of the writing to his contemporaries and then issued them in his own name. "Such a view," he argued,

gives a strangely elastic interpretation to the strict affirmation of Mosaic authorship: it insists upon Mosaic authorship, even literary authorship, and this, primarily in order thus to satisfy the great "tradition," and yet explains the authorship in a manner that cannot satisfy that "tradition" if taken as evidencing what it is here declared to prove. That tradition is rather of God dictating to Moses, than of Moses dictating to Joshua; of Moses inspired by God, not of Joshua inspired by Moses. What strictly Rabbinical Jew, what correct Mahommedan, would accept such an "Authorship" as the one suggested by the Commission?

This, said von Hügel, would make Moses similar to "a prolific modern Novelist," who farmed out part of his writings to "subordinate scribes, . . . but we cannot, surely, think of Moses doing so, in proportion as we insist upon the profound importance and the inspired, indeed revealed character of his work and message and upon their completion within his own life-time."[21]

Von Hügel had a further "insuperable difficulty" with the commission's approach. All four documents gave "characteristically varying versions of solitary interviews and dialogues between Jahveh or Elohim and Moses." How, then, "could Moses commission three other writers to chronicle, each in varying fashion and each in a manner somewhat different to his own, things experienced only by himself?"[22]

Von Hügel's final argument against the Mosaic authorship was that the "evidence . . . simply precludes the possibility of contemporary composition of those great documents." The Biblical Commission's decision, he declared, was analogous to stating that "the Anglo-Saxon King Alfred, who died in 901 A.D.," had commissioned the Magna Charta, Edward II's Articles of Reform, Thomas More's writings, and Charles I's Petition of Rights. In analyzing the possible Mosaic origin of some of the laws, however, von Hügel was less rash than Briggs. Granted that D and P contained formulations that could not possibly have gone back to the time of Moses, he stated,

It is in many cases demonstrable that those laws are considerably, sometimes immensely, older than their formulations or framework now before us, and some great central enactments doubtless go back to Moses himself. Nor do these our positions of themselves decide anything concerning the historical exactitude of this or that narrative: such an account may, in its present form, be very late, and yet may transmit important details of factual truth; another may be very early and yet be little more than a symbol or parable, the vehicle of some spiritual or moral experience and truth.[23]

In other words, the antiquity of certain laws, and even the possible Mosaic influence on them, was not in itself an indication of the early composition of the documents.

Like Briggs, von Hügel was concerned with more than a critique of the commission's decision. He also reflected on the nature of the Church. He saw "four necessities . . . working within Catholicism as such towards a final acceptance, however slow and cautious, of a consistent and sincere historico-critical method for the Bible also." "Catholicism" was, first of all, "essentially not a simple Illuminism or Fideism, but a Religion which, in its completeness, is simultaneously Historical and Institutional, Critical and Speculative, Mystical and Operative, thus calling into play the whole man and various faculties." Catholicism was, therefore, "wedded, amongst other things, to history, and hence to historic proofs and methods." There could not ultimately be one "standard of historic method and proof" for accepting "Irenaeus's testimony to the Roman Church" or the evidence of Peter's sojourn in Rome and a different standard for determining the authenticity of the Pentateuch, the writings of Jeremiah and Ezechiel, or Deutero-Isaiah. Ultimately, he continued, these documents would have to be submitted to "thorough historical investigation."[24]

Von Hügel's second observation was that "Catholicism . . . is essentially a missionary, an aggressively universalistic religion, hence inevitably a spirituality that learns as well as teaches, that gets and assimilates as well as moulds and gives." The Church, then, would finally have to accept the historical method, if it was to "retain a message for, and a hearing from, the educated West-European world, since nothing is more certain than that this cultivated non-Roman Catholic world is, in part unconsciously, often slowly yet everywhere surely, getting permeated and won by critical standards and methods."[25]

Third, von Hügel echoed the theme that Briggs had sounded in his controversial lecture on "Bibliolatry," and that Hogan and Gigot had also expressed. "Catholicism," he declared,

is essentially a "Church and Bible," not a "Bible only" religion. Its genius, history, and most elementary defence presuppose the Bible to be a complex and difficult, not a simple and easy literature; a library, not a book; a succession of literary precipitates of religion—a religion which, already lived and loved, both corporately and individually, before such registration, comes in time, and now more corporately than individually, to sort out and canonize those precipitates, as so many models and crystallizing-points for further corporate and individual religious life and love. The Church, the Community of believers, first Jewish and then Christian, produced the Bible even more than the Bible produced the Church. And hence the old war-cry of Protestantism, "the Bible and the Bible only," is ceasing, one gladly thinks, to characterize the actual religious convictions of the most historically-trained present-day Protestants. In any case such Bibliolatry is not Catholic.

Through its decision, therefore, the Biblical Commission was coming dangerously close to an "un-Catholic super-exaltation of the Bible."[26]

Finally, von Hügel argued that the Church would have to accept the historical method because "Catholicism is essentially a life and an organism that has grown and is growing." Here, however, he touched upon the development of doctrine, with which the prevailing Roman theology could not deal. Catholicism had already acknowledged such development, he argued, by accepting "the immense changes from Polygamy to Monogamy and from the *Lex Talionis* to the Law of Forgiveness, since the Church, with grand profundity and courage, refused to follow Marcion and proclaimed the Old Testament to come from the same God as the New." Such development, moreover, "of more than a simply logical, analytical order, is being more and more admitted in detail by Catholics for the much slighter changes observable in Christian Church History." It remained for scholars to trace the "intermediate steps" in the Old Testament "into the Deutero-canonical Books and even Philo," and the "lesser or different though still real growth and variety of apprehension within the New Testament itself."[27]

Von Hügel's notion of development illustrated his profound optimism about the world and human nature. For him, there was not a total dichotomy between the world and God, nature and grace. The "Lord's Person, Life, and Teaching," he declared, was unique and normative for "spiritual truth and practice." While it was legitimate to "talk of a period of Revelation followed by one of simple Assistance," nevertheless,

there will, between Christ and His Spirit and the nowhere utterly God-forsaken world into which they have come, ever be a sufficient affinity for the former to be able to penetrate, appropriate, satisfy, and measure all the goodness, truth, and spiritual hunger variously yet ever present in the world. From Moses back to prehistoric times, forward to Christ and on from Christ to the end of time, we thus get *one* great chain of slow, varying, intermittent yet true development occasioned by God in man, and moving from man towards God. And if so, then the chief difficulty raised by the critical view of the various documents disappears: for such a truly dynamic conception would englobe and spiritualize it all.[28]

In short, von Hügel's world in the present dispensation was not one totally depraved, but was permeated with the Holy Spirit, which enabled human nature to cooperate with grace and thus contribute to the development of doctrine.

Von Hügel thought that these four "necessities" or "principles" were ones on which he and Briggs could agree, but there were objections that could be raised against both of them. First of all, Briggs had stated that he did not think that the Biblical Commission was really interested in peace. Von Hügel reminded his friend that they were still in the minority among Christians, whether Catholic or Protestant. What Briggs had actually called for was the "acceptance, on the part of all these simple traditional Christians, whether Catholic or Protestant, of the conclusions of the critics," who were still "a scattered few." Von Hügel acknowledged that the majority of Protestants found a temporary affinity with the official Catholic position on the Bible. He noted the irony that conservative Protestants had "taken over much of even the non-obligatory, current mediaeval and antique Catholic teaching in the matter," and that Catholic theologians had adopted the principles of the Protestants, against whom they had been fighting. Von Hügel also suspected that Briggs might argue that perhaps Roman Catholicism, "the mother of West-European civilization," might not have sufficient life left to make "one more such mighty renovation," and that the Biblical Commission's decision was an illustration of its inability to accept the modern world and encourage scholarship.[29]

Von Hügel had three answers to these objections. First, he admitted that, with good reason, "*all* Religious Institutions without exception are at their worst in the matter of their relations with Science and Scholarship, doubtless chiefly because they exist, at bottom, as the incorporations and vehicles of requirements and realities, deeper and more immediately important and necessary than are even Science and Scholarship." Religion, then, served a human need far deeper than science. Nevertheless, von Hügel did not think it justified

for Protestant ecclesiastical bodies to throw the stone at Rome in these matters: if Rome has had Erasmus, Simon, Loisy, the others have had Colenso, Robertson-Smith, and yourself. Thus even now, Catholics have not had any solemn condemnation of Pentateuchal criticism, and the Protestant Churches have had three [i.e., Colenso, Robertson-Smith, and Briggs].[30]

Von Hügel next proposed that there had to be a mutual relationship between science and scholarship on the one hand and religion on the other. "Science and Scholarship, having for some four centuries slowly proved their formidable power, mostly as though this power were unlimited and destructive only," he declared, "are themselves now coming to discover fully their own respective essential methods, ends, levels and limitations." Science and scholarship might be "simply irresistible within these limits of their own," but they also "demonstrably presuppose and require a fuller, deeper world of reality and life than is theirs; and religion will be able to find room for these other levels of life, on the day when it has fully learnt, on its side, that it cannot henceforth attain again to its own deepest fruitfulness, unless it can and will frankly accept and encourage such autonomies within its own ampler life." It would be the task of theology in the future to "resolve the antinomies thus occasioned."

Von Hügel concluded by giving two examples of the Church's acceptance of the critical method: the Areopagite writings and the Johannine Comma. St. Thomas, he recalled, had virtually accepted the Areopagite as second in importance only to Scripture. Beginning with the fifteenth century, however, critical scholarship gradually showed it to be a work of the fifth century. On the Johannine Comma, von Hügel was on shakier ground. Though the Holy Office had declared it to be authentic in 1897, he argued, as late as 1905, a German priest, K. Küstle, wrote *Das Comma Johanneum*, a dissertation disavowing it, and the work received the *imprimatur* of the Bishop of Freiburg and was "published by the Great Papal publishers, Herder." What had happened with the Areopagite writings, once deemed so important, and with the Johannine comma, he predicted would also happen with the Pentateuch.[31] Despite von Hügel's statement, however, the Johannine comma continued to be a disputed point among Catholics, as will be seen.

The von Hügel-Briggs correspondence appeared in November 1906. By January 1907, it had been translated into Italian and published in *Rinnovamento,* a liberal Italian Catholic journal for which Maude Petre later said von Hügel was largely responsible.[32] The Italian translation provoked an immediate response from Janssens. He had a "fond memory" of their "theological conversations," he wrote Briggs, but was surprised to find specific mention of himself "in a document destined for publication." Briggs, it was true, had praised his expertise in scholastic theology, but the remarks about his limited knowledge of Hebrew, he thought, went beyond "normal courtesy." He then explained that simply because he signed the commission's decision, as the secretary, that did not give him any "special responsibility" for the decision itself. He noted also that Thomas Weikert, a consultor of the commission and friend of Briggs, had regarded the findings of Wellhausen as unfounded.[33]

Briggs responded to Janssens that he had been "called into the field by the request of Catholic Scholars whom your report had silenced." Janssens could claim all he wanted that he merely signed the decision, Briggs asserted, but "you gave your name and its authority to the Report of the Biblical Commission, which challenges Biblical Scholars the world over in their cherished convictions and forces Catholic Biblical Scholars to either silence or submission under protest." For his part, Briggs was not at all surprised that Weikert rejected Wellhausen's position, for, "if your Report had condemned the characteristic affirmation of the School of Wellhausen, you would have given little trouble to Catholics Scholars, or to me." Briggs's problem was that the decision "in fact condemns Critics without qualifications." He predicted that, with Catholic scholars silenced, "you can only excite the resentment of Protestant Scholars, and Catholic Scholars will secretly sympathize with them and help them." Such "suppression of scholarly convictions" could only be "perilous to the Church," he concluded, because it was "very dangerous to smother the fire," for "an explosion is sure to come sooner or later."[34] Briggs forwarded a copy of his letter to von Hügel.

BRIGGS AND *PASCENDI DOMINICI GREGIS*

In the meanwhile, Briggs had prepared an article for the *North American Review,* "The Real and the Ideal in the Papacy." Still optimistic about some form of a reunited Christendom under the pope, he spoke of the need for a reform of the papal office. Pius IX's Syllabus of Errors, he said, had been "an intrusion of Papal jurisdiction," beyond its competence, and had "injured the influence of the Roman Catholic Church to a very great extent and has been productive of great mischief." He was now worried that

the proposed issue of another syllabus by Pius X is a reactionary policy, which if carried out can only greatly imperil the influence of the Papacy upon the present generation. The continual inscribing on the Index of many of the best works of modern scholars, even those of devout Roman

Catholics, is resented by scholars of all faiths. The recent decisions of the Papal Commission, under the lead of incompetent divines, against the sure results of modern criticism, present clear evidence of the intolerance of modern Roman scholasticism.[35]

Briggs's writing on the need for reform of the papacy and the curia now brought him to the attention of the American Catholic hierarchy.

JOHN IRELAND AND THE BIBLICAL QUESTION

Archbishop John Ireland of St. Paul, still trying to vindicate himself after the debacle of Americanism, had now become the papal loyalist in regard to the biblical question. Yet, his approach was still balanced. In January 1907, the *North American Review* carried an article entitled "Three Years and a Half of Pius X." It was signed simply "A Catholic Priest" and stated that the papacy was condemning scholars in an effort to arrest historical criticism. In February 1907, Ireland published a rejoinder, "The Pontificate of Pius X," in the same journal. He stated that "the Catholic Church is by no means a school of slavish subjection, nor of total surrender of thought or action." "The infallibility which the Church attaches to its teachings," he continued, "is limited to formal, authoritative, so-called *ex cathedra,* declarations of matters of faith and morals," but it did not extend to "deductions from dogma by theologians, applications of it to practical life, relations established between it and science or history." While "the teaching office of the Papacy" was not "limited" to "the official and formal definition of dogma," and the pope, as "the guardian of dogma," made use of various congregations to assist him, Ireland asserted, "it is not held that Papal infallibility sheds its rays over the deliberations of the Roman 'Congregations.'" Decisions of these congregations, therefore, were not infallible, but were intended to put the scholar "on his guard, lest with the gold of truth he mingle the dross of error."[36] In this context, Ireland then addressed the question of those whose works had been put on the Index.

Among the works recently condemned was Loisy's *Autour d'un Petit Livre.* Though Ireland had earlier attempted, on Denis O'Connell's advice, to obtain Loisy for his diocesan seminary and had written the French exegete a letter of support for his *L'enseigne-*

ment biblique, now he challenged "A Catholic Priest" to read the book and tell him "what is left therein of the doctrine of the Incarnation and the Redemption, . . . of the divine origin of the Church and the Sacraments." Ireland next turned to an analysis of the Biblical Commission's response on the Mosaic authorship of the Pentateuch. "The decision," he wrote, "refuses . . . to expel altogether the authorship of Moses from the first five books of the Bible" and "lays down rules, by which glaring objections to a complete Mosaic authorship are obviated." Far from stifling scholarship, Ireland went on, the commission "opens the way to further careful study, to the clear conclusion of which it impliedly [*sic*] promises its adhesion."[37] Ireland had been careful to distinguish between the authority of the pope and the Roman congregations and to place the decision of the Biblical Commission within the context of the Church's role in safeguarding orthodoxy. In his approach, he would have been considered liberal a generation later. For the moment, he was intent on maintaining good relations with Merry del Val.[38]

In April, Ireland responded to Briggs's article, "The Real and the Ideal in the Papacy." "The treasures in the keeping of the Church are so precious," he wrote, "that extreme vigilance must be its rule. Better, by far, now and then, an excess of vigilance than, now and then, a lack of prudent care and forethought." This was precisely the issue that Ireland thought Briggs did not understand, for

in this light, the recent decision of the Scriptural Commission regarding the authorship of the Pentateuch is quite comprehensible. Perhaps the Professor is a little too confident of his own opinion, that Moses should be eliminated for good from the books that have so long borne his name. Modern criticism has yet to speak its last word in this matter. Nor were certain books recently placed on the Index so plainly innocuous as the Professor would lead us to believe: even to theologians outside the Congregation—and many of those most liberal-minded—those books were far from being free of fatal defects, especially the works of Abbé Loisy. As to whether the Syllabus which, report says, is soon to be given out by Pius X, will prove to be dangerous reactionarism [*sic*], we should wait until we have read it before giving judgment. Nor will the Syllabus of Pius IX appear to be such a dreadful "intrusion of Papal jurisdiction" as the Professor would have us believe, when, in our perusal of it, we give due weight to the circumstances determining the original pronouncement of each separate article, and gather from those circumstances its meaning and intent.[39]

It mattered not to the archbishop that his cherished Americanist movement had been condemned precisely because theologians did not "give due weight to the circumstances determining the original pronouncement" of the Syllabus of Errors. American biblical scholarship could expect no help from the bishops, even those who had once prided themselves in being "liberal."

In September, shortly before Pius X issued *Pascendi,* Briggs published his response to Ireland. Acknowledging that the archbishop had written "in the most irenic spirit," he argued that "the pathway to reunion is to constitutionalize the Papacy." Iterating a theme he would later develop, he stated that "the policy of unlimited jurisdiction and absolute submission weakens the power of the Catholic Church." He then recounted a conversation he had had with Pius X only two years before when they had been discussing "the reunion of Christendom." He had said to the pope

that, if the obstacles were to be removed, there must be freedom to investigate the difficulties. He said that all reasonable freedom of investigation should be given. If only the Pope would in some way make good his word, and guarantee Catholic scholars reasonable liberty of investigation of the great problems that divide Christendom and obstruct the unity of the Church, I am sure that a splendid array of Catholic scholars would spring up, and with the cooperation of Protestant scholars of the same spirit, the hard problems would be solved, and the unity of the Church secured. Scholarship demands liberty; it cannot thrive under a policy of suppression and absolute submission to an unlimited jurisdiction, and to immeasurable claims, which may easily be extended to cover any and every traditional opinion of scholastic philosophy, mediaeval law and patristic exegesis.[40]

Briggs had already attacked Scholasticism in his correspondence with von Hügel. Now he pointed out the other severe limitations of members of the curia. They were, he said, men of "very great ability and learning in Canon Law, in the Ceremonies of the Church, and in Scholastic Theology; but . . . sadly deficient in Biblical and Historical scholarship." Not only was the curia "disqualified to make decisions in an immense range of questions that interest the modern world," it was also "antiquated in its methods, as well as in its organization," which "have nothing whatever to do with the divine constitution of the Church."[41] Ten years earlier, Ireland might have agreed with Briggs and have even spoken in similar terms, but the era of such strong episcopal leadership had passed.[42] Briggs, for his part, would soon have occasion to develop the relationship he saw between the biblical question and ecclesiology as he worked with his liberal Catholic friends to ward off the anti-Modernist reaction.

THE BIBLICAL COMMISSION AND THE GOSPEL OF JOHN: VON HÜGEL'S REACTION.

While Briggs was engaged in his exchange with Ireland, he had continued his correspondence with von Hügel and Genocchi. On March 26, 1907, after an interruption of several months, von Hügel resumed his correspondence with Briggs. "It is no joke to be a Catholic scholar," he said; "the dominant school is, I think, less and less near to giving us that reasonable liberty without which the scholarly life in the Roman Church must either be stunted, or must drive him, who lives it, into revolt, or must keep him in a state of painful strain and conflict." He then went on to tell of those positive responses he had received to their publication. He had heard from Archbishop Mignot, Hippolyte Delehaye, S.J., who wrote in the name of the Bollandists, Dom Morin, O.S.B., "almost a confrère of Janssens," and van Hoonacker. He had also been asked to write the preface for the publication in book form of a series of articles on the Pentateuch by F. R. Clarke, a recently-deceased consultor of the Biblical Commission. This, he thought, "would constitute an effective counter-blast" to the reactionaries. Moreover, he continued, "the Bollandists are pressing me to do it."[43] It was not surprising that he should have received support from the Bollandists, for this group of Belgian Jesuits, in contrast with their contemporaries, were noted for their scientific study of history.

Being a Catholic scholar may already have been "no joke" for von Hügel, but it soon became worse. On May 29, 1907, the Biblical Commission issued its decision affirming that John the Apostle was the author of the Fourth Gospel and declaring that it was historical.[44] Von Hügel suspected that Briggs might be more tolerant of this decision, so he warned his friend that it "would simply veto any conception of the book which would make it, even only in part, a treatise and a theology and much influenced by Philonism—things already proclaimed with all possible freedom by Père Calmes in his big and small commentaries (1904, 1906), published with the *Imprimatur* of the *Magister Sacri Palatii!*" For his own part, he was convinced

that "not all the King's horses and all the king's men" will ever put the purely simply historical eye-witness-character of this Gospel "up again"; and that an at least moderately critical view, i.e. an allegorical and doctrinal pragmatism has to be frankly conceded here, unless we would keep the key to a solidly historical comprehension of the Synoptists and of the N.T. generally, forever in our pockets. Insist upon the full simple historicalness of the 4th G, and you ruin what the 3 first have got, really, of this quality.

He felt "very certain" that this decision was "but one link in the ever increasing, tightening chain that aims at smothering the simply necessary examination and discussion of these things."[45] Briggs, then in London, acknowledged that he was "not surprised that the Biblical Commission have [*sic*] taken another step, and what more likely than to determine the problem of the 4th Gospel, for which they are probably about as well prepared as for the problem of the Pentateuch."[46]

VON HÜGEL, GENOCCHI, AND BRIGGS ON *Pascendi*

In the meantime, Genocchi was keeping Briggs informed of Roman events. Despite "the highest pitch of reaction," he still enjoyed the favor of Pius X, though he had made no "mystery of my satisfaction for your's and Baron von Hügel's letters about the Biblical Commission." "There is an uncheckable movement in Italy," he continued,

which frightens the scholastic uncritical men. The Pope is afraid and trusts above all the Jesuit [*sic*] cardinal Merry del Val and Capuchin Vives, both Spaniards and great defenders of the Faith (which is an extremely good thing), but also inquisitors of the old stamps [*sic*] and modernism hunters.[47]

At this point, Genocchi accepted the conventional wisdom that Merry del Val was the *éminence grise* manipulating a pious pope through fear. It should be recalled, however, that Cardinal Vives y Tuto had defended Poels or had at least protested his being mishandled.

During the summer of 1907, Genocchi reported the increasing reaction against scholars. Umberto Fracassini had just been removed from his teaching position in the seminary at Perugia, and his "fault is only to have taught 6 years ago that the old view of the Pentateuch is untenable." In Genocchi's evaluation, Fracassini was "the most learned biblical scholar we have in Italy and quite a saintly priest: but he is a *'modernist'*." If Genocchi's account of the pope's attitude toward the biblical question is correct, however, it might explain the pontiff's *volte-face* in the Poels case:

I heard the Pope saying (I was not alone with him) that a scholar has to keep his own opinion about [the] Pentateuch, even if opposite to [the] decree of the Biblical Commission, but such a man cannot be a professor in our ecclesiastical schools. We answered freely that in such condition of things we would see only hypocrites or ignorant men in Holy Scripture keeping in peace our biblical chairs. The Pope was struck by the assertion and sighed; but not withstanding he does not think it opportune to change.[48]

Far from thinking it opportune to change, the pope issued *Pascendi Dominici Gregis* in September.

A few weeks later, von Hügel gave Briggs his evaluation of the situation. He had been prevented from meeting Briggs in Italy, because he had been engaged in "much consideration with friends and much correspondence concerning the Encyclical against 'Modernism' (barbarous word, the Civilta Cattolica's invention!)." He suggested that, if Briggs wanted to understand the "treacherous treatment of Tyrrell," he should consult " 'Corrispondenza Romana,' ostensibly non-official, documented by the Card. Sec. of State." Briggs, he thought, now had "the fullest right to be very sharp and thorough" in any treatment he might give to the encyclical. For himself, von Hügel noted:

My impressions concerning the Decree (such as I wrote them to you at the time of its appearance) have been confirmed by much subsequent reflection and discussion: the document implied throughout the dependence of historical enquiry upon scholastic methods, tests and tribunals. Most inconsistently, but in an interestingly tell-tale manner, it omits all propositions concerning the O.T., except that entirely vague, indeed, very strange one given by it. As to the encyclical—Part I is not the Pope's own work—Part II is surely most painful reading, but is, we fear, much more nearly the Pope's own handiwork—Part III is doubtless far the most important, if indeed the Pope can succeed in enforcing even one half of it. Pray note, especially the striking, in its way fanatic, "Procul, procul" exclamation, as to keeping all those tainted with "modernist" error from the sacred ministry. This sentence, indeed many before and after, are most certainly penned by the Pope himself, that saintly peasant, "questa natura aspera ed colta," as one who knows him intimately well described him to me.[49]

While von Hügel meted out a share of the blame to Merry del Val, he was gaining the insight that it was a very frightened pope behind the more extreme statements then emanating from the Vatican.

Briggs had, in the meantime, met in Paris with Paul "Sabatier and a number of liberal Catholics, whom he had gathered there to meet me." With their encouragement, as he told von Hügel, he was preparing an article on the encyclical. Reflecting the attitude of his Catholic friends toward making Scholasticism normative for interpreting all Christian doctrine, he proposed

to show (1) that the Modernism such as is described in the encyclical does not exist. It is a caricature, and simply shows that its authors have not read with any degree of attention the authors they propose to condemn. (2) The Encyclical is *uncatholic,* because it sins against the Catholic principle of *semper.* When it antagonizes Modernism with Medievalism and makes the latter the standard of doctrine, it no less antagonizes Ancient Christianity and the Christianity of Jesus Christ and his apostles, who knew nothing of the Scholastic dogma. The same may be worked out, as regards the principle of *ubique et ab omnibus.* The Papal document is one of the most *sectarian* that has ever been issued.[50]

As Briggs continued his exposition, he disclosed a certain ambiguous knowledge of Catholic doctrine. On the one hand, he made encyclicals vehicles for defining faith and morals. On the other hand, he upheld the position on the episcopacy which he had earlier expounded in his exchange with Ireland. *Pascendi* was "not a proper encyclical," he said in his third point, for

it is not a definition of faith and morals. It is not an exposition. It is really a polemic document against an imaginary enemy. It is an invective effort in the worst of tempers, altogether unchristian from its lack of charity and its fullness of hate, misrepresentations and slander. (4) The plan of organized inquisition is a violation of the fundamental principle of Canon Law, which has developed side by side with dogma in the Church and upon which the government and discipline of the Church depends. It destroys the legal right of the priests and the bishops and makes the Pope the absolute despot of the Church, with a bureaucratic administration, the most exaggerated known to history. But when the Pope undermines and destroys the Canon Law, he thereby undermines and destroys the foundation of his own authority, and deprives himself of biblical and historical support, so that the whole system will crumble when a strong, determined attack is made upon it.

As he was preparing his article, Briggs assured von Hügel "of my profound sympathy with you and other persecuted Catholic scholars."[51]

A few days later, Genocchi informed Briggs of the Roman atmosphere following the encyclical. He had just read Briggs's response to Ireland in the *North American Review,* and had arranged for a summary of it to appear in the *Giornale d'Italia,* a new Roman newspaper sympathetic to the Modernists. Socialists and other anti-Christians, he reported, could not "tolerate the successful efforts of 'modernists' removing from the Catholic Church what may make it unbearable to the world; therefore they like to have found a Pope utterly disowning that kind of Christian apology." The Vatican, however, took "great satisfaction" in "such approbations." Secrecy, spying, and repression of scholarship were, however, becoming tools for upholding orthodoxy. "There is now in the Secretary of State," Genocchi revealed, "a keen old journalist, Mgr. Humberto Benigni, the director of that 'Corrispondenza Romana.' "[52] Benigni had become the organizer or, at least, the coordinator of the *Sodalitium Pianum,* known by its code name *Sapinière,* an international group committed to rooting out all suspected Modernists. What became known as "integrism" had already begun, and more recent scholarship indicates that Pius X not only actively encouraged it but also funded the operation.[53] At this early date, Genocchi was aware of Benigni's role, but it would still take him some time to discover that Pius X was a leading actor. Of greater significance was that Genocchi passed on his knowledge of the intrigue to Briggs, through whom it would eventually become public in the United States.

A short time later, Genocchi forwarded to Briggs a copy of Ernesto Buonaiuti's *Programma dei modernisti.* By the middle of November, Briggs was finishing his article on *Pascendi.* As he told von Hügel, "the American bishops are seeking to evade it [the encyclical], as they did the one against Americanism, whether with the same success, I doubt."[54]

While Briggs was busy corresponding with his European friends and writing on Catholic Modernism, he had not neglected his contact with Dunwoodie. He had invited James Driscoll, president of the seminary at Dunwoodie, to lecture at Union Theological Seminary. In view of the growing Roman suspicion of the *New York Review* and Dunwoodie itself, and of the Hanna case, Driscoll had consulted Archbishop Farley, who thought he should decline the invitation. As Driscoll told Briggs, Farley believed that "in the present acute crisis . . . my acceptation would probably be misinterpreted and cause much annoyance to him and to myself." Driscoll had to "admit that the Archbishop's view is right" and was "dictated by simple prudence and not from any narrowness of mind on his part." "I need hardly say," he went on, "that nothing so violent and drastic as the recent curial documents has appeared on the part of the Vatican authorities since the days of the Inquisition." He compared the "crisis to nothing but a cyclone during which people must simply make for the cellar," but predicted, too optimistically, that "fortunately it is not in the nature of things that such disturbances should be of long duration."[55]

Driscoll may have exaggerated his importance in the Modernist movement, but, if his evaluation is to be trusted, he and the seminary were under close scrutiny. Farley was attempting to protect him and was sympathetic with the liberal orientation of Dunwoodie under his administration. "Now this institution," Driscoll wrote,

has for some time been looked upon by certain invidious heresy hunters in the Catholic Community, as a hotbed of Liberalism, or as it is now called, Modernism; furthermore, The New York Review edited by myself and a couple of confrères is looked upon in the same light, and it has been more than once denounced to the Roman authorities. Dr. Hanna, a professor of dogmatic theology in the Seminary of Rochester, was lately made a candidate for bishop of the Archdiocese of San Francisco, but he has been "held up" in Rome on a charge of unorthodoxy based chiefly on three articles which he wrote for our Review, and it is more than probable that he never will be promoted, at least under the present papal adminis-tration. You must have noticed also the absurdly drastic measures im-posed upon the bishops towards the end of the Encyclical; how, for instance, no person having any sympathy with the Modernists can be retained as professor in a Seminary or university. Now my sympathy with Modernism is pretty well known, as well as my intimate friendship with several of the most noted of its promoters, and so with all this you can readily understand that the Archbishop, tho' well disposed towards me and some of my views, is at present anxious lest he may be obliged to remove me from my present position and suppress the publication of the Review.

Within a few months, of course, the *Review* would cease publica-tion. While Driscoll had given a dismal description of the intellec-tual retreat of the American church, he did not seem to be aware of how drastic the situation was in such institutions as the Catholic University. He suggested that Briggs invite Denis O'Connell, re-cently named a bishop, to give the lecture.[56]

In February 1908, Briggs published "The Encyclical against Modernism." Following the basic outline he had sent to von Hügel in October, he showed that some of the propositions condemned in *Lamentabili* were taken out of context of the original writings of Modernists.[57] Using the information he had obtained from Genocchi, he noted the "recent Papal decree of excommunica-tion against the unknown authors, and all who assisted them in the composition of '*Il Programma dei Modernisti, Risposta all'Enciclica di Pio X: "Pascendi Dominici Gregis"* '; in which several representative Italian priests show very clearly that their views are represented in the Encyclical." In Briggs's mind, the encyclical had implicitly condemned John Henry Newman's notion of the development of doctrine. He concluded that "it is a thankless task in the Roman Church to be defenders of the faith. The greatest apologists have been discredited in Rome: Bellarmine, Bossuet, Möhler, Schell and now Newman."[58]

In view of the encyclical's list of Modernist errors, Briggs que-ried "What Catholic outside the Roman Curia does not desire one or more of these reforms?" Reflecting his initial observations to von Hügel, he argued that, "if the scholastic philosophy and theol-ogy of Thomas Aquinas is to be the universal norm for the Roman Catholic Church, the Roman Church thereby divests itself of Cath-olicity, for it sins against the established principles of Catholicity,

'Semper, ubique et ab omnibus.' " Briggs's point was that medieval Scholasticism thus became the norm for interpreting not only the past but the future and thus the Church used "Scholasticism" and not "Apostolicity" as "the historical test of a genuine Christianity." He did not content himself, however, with a general treatment of the limitations of scholasticism. As he had already done in his published correspondence with von Hügel, he mentioned some of the contemporary Scholastics by name. "Any one can see," he wrote, "who will study the system of the chief Roman scholastics at the present time, such as Billot and Janssen [*sic*], that, while they use the forms of St. Thomas and base themselves on his system, they really introduce into the system scholastic materials, new and old, which are not homogeneous with St. Thomas, but which make a heterogeneous system that St. Thomas himself would be the first to repudiate."[59]

Briggs felt that the encyclical was so vague that the American bishops would simply ignore it and state that Modernists "do not exist in 'our diocese.' " In treating the vigilance committees, which the encyclical required to be established in each diocese, however, he developed his idea, already expressed to von Hügel, that this in fact undermined the authority of the bishops. "The Bishops have their rights in the divine constitution of the Church as well as the Pope," he wrote,

and these rights are protected by the same Canon Law that protects the Pope's; and, unless I am greatly mistaken, these rights are infringed upon in an unprecedented manner by this arbitrary ordinance of the present Pope. All the Bishops are successors of the Apostles; the Pope is the primate of the Bishops as St. Peter was of the Apostles. The Pope no more absorbs unto himself the whole authority in the government of the Church than did St. Peter.

Briggs reminded his readers that the First Vatican Council, in defining papal primacy, had also upheld the "ordinary and immediate power of episcopal jurisdiction." The encyclical, he argued, violated this teaching, for

in this Encyclical, the Pope, without consultation with the episcopate, but solely under the advice of certain unnamed cardinals and other members of the Roman Curia, issues an ordinance requiring a "sworn report" from the Bishops as to their fidelity in enforcing his new Inquisition. If that is not an usurpation of authority and an enslavement of the episcopate, it

is difficult to imagine what could be regarded as such. If Jesus Christ and
His Apostles committed all ecclesiastical authority to the episcopate as the
successors of the Apostles, it is no longer exercised by them in the Roman
Church; but their place has been taken by a Curial body in Rome appointed by the Popes responsible only to the Popes, but without any
divine rights whatsoever.[60]

   Briggs's concern, however, extended beyond the usurpation of
episcopal power by the curia. "The General of the Jesuits," he
reminded his readers, "is called the Black Pope; more powerful
than any one in Rome but the real Pope." Yet, "none of these
orders, none of these Generals of orders, has any part in the divine
constitution of the Church, and any part they take in it is in defi-
ance of the divine rights of the episcopate."[61] Briggs would clearly
have been more at home with the theology of episcopal collegiality
at the Second Vatican Council. He would have resounded to the
stirring speech of Father Joseph Ratzinger after the first session of
that council about the significance of the establishment of episcopal conferences. These conferences, said Ratzinger, "possess as a
right a definite legislative function" and "appear as a new element
in the ecclesiastical body politic, and form a link of a quasi-synodal
kind between the individual bishops and the pope." The establishment of "conferences of bishops as a canonical factor for the first
time," he continued, "will in the end have greater significance for
the theology of the episcopate and for the universally desired
strengthening of episcopal authority than the actual schema dealing specifically with the Church," then under consideration.[62] But
Vatican II was still a half century away for Briggs, whose own hopes
for Christian unity were now being dashed on the rocks of the
anti-Modernist reaction.

THE AFTERMATH OF *PASCENDI:* INTEGRISM

Von Hügel praised Briggs's analysis of *Pascendi,* but reported that
the integrist witch-hunt was increasing. Cardinal Andrea Carlo
Ferrari, Archbishop of Milan, had to defend himself in his Lenten
pastoral letter and condemned the fanatical right wing. By prior
arrangement with Briggs, von Hügel was sending the royalties
they received for their correspondence on the Mosaic authorship
to *Nova et Vetera,* [63] an Italian journal, which acted as the organ for

Buonaiuti and George Tyrrell, and called for internal reform of the Church.[64]

Genocchi, meanwhile, continued to keep Briggs directly informed of Roman affairs. In January 1908, he reported that "several professors of H1. Scripture were dismissed in these days for their modernistic tendencies." He was himself frequently accused before the pope. One of the accusations was one that Farley had heard from Falconio. The pope had asked Genocchi, "why so many learned men, Italian and strangers, why so many university students come to me?" His popularity did "not please the Jesuits," he continued, "who know my ideas and my sincerity. They also know that several young students owe to their connexion with me their keeping to the Faith." His "unpardonable sin," he thought, was that "I do not adhere to Jesuit politics and doctrine."[65] In May 1908, however, Genocchi thought that the anti-Modernist movement had reached a climax and was beginning to decrease. Though some still wanted his removal from Rome, the pope "refused, saying that he has confidence in me and my honesty, although I am partly a modernist."[66]

A month later, Genocchi reported that the Vatican was adopting a policy of silence in regard to the "excesses of some publications." He himself thought that "Une lettre d'un pretre moderniste" and Loisy's response to *Pascendi* "were regrettable and come from irritated men."[67] When the Biblical Commission issued its decision on the unity of the Book of Isaiah, Genocchi reported that the decision was totally that of the cardinals on the commission. He had himself been attacked for his views on the book, but continued to have the pope's protection.[68] While keeping up a running commentary on Roman events and his own situation in regard to the pope, Genocchi reserved his harshest comments for the Jesuits.

Early in 1909, Genocchi reported that Pius X was defending him against attacks from Merry del Val and the Jesuits.[69] But soon the situation grew worse as the pope placed the Pontifical Biblical Institute under the exclusive direction of the Jesuits. "Instead of a Catholic high school [a *Hochschule*, or research center]," he wrote, "we will have a Jesuitical workshop, to cast minds in the mould exclusively prepared by the black Pope and Card. Merry del Val." It was also obvious to him that Leopold Fonck, S.J., would become rector, "one of the most intolerant and troublesome men I ever saw."[70] This was a departure from Leo XIII's plan in creating the institute, Genocchi continued a few days later, for both Fracassini and Poels were originally to have been appointed to its faculty. Fonck soon lived up to Genocchi's dire predictions when he pitted himself against Lagrange and the *Revue biblique*.[71] It should be recalled, however, that Fonck had defended Poels. "What a shame!" Briggs remarked to von Hügel about the Biblical Institute; "how greatly has the pope changed in his policy." He now thought "the cause of Church Unity seems dark but the brighter days may come."[72] Reporting on Tyrrell's death and Henri Bremond's suspension from the priesthood for saying prayers at the grave side, von Hügel agreed that there was no hope for Christian unity during Pius X's pontificate.[73]

In June 1909, Briggs published "Modernism Mediating the Coming Catholicism." Again, he seemed to have derived his information from Genocchi and focused his strongest criticism on the curia. There were "signs that a reaction has already begun," he said, and "some of the most distinguished prelates of Italy, France and Germany have rebuked the most offensive spies and detractors of their brethren, whom this sad controversy has brought to the front." He had even heard that the pope had "uttered words of caution." Most of all, the "public press of the world is boiling with indignation because of the arrogant dictation, and impertinent interference with their affairs, of Monsignore Benigni, the *protégé* of Cardinal Merry del Val, and his 'Corrispondenza Romana.' "[74] By this early date, therefore, Benigni's role in the integrist movement was public knowledge to American Catholics, if they were but reading Briggs's reports.

Briggs, however, was too optimistic about the Catholic church in the United States. "There is more Modernism in America than the authorities know of," he told von Hügel early in 1910.[75] If there was widespread "Modernism in America," it was being rooted out, for it was at this very point that Poels was dismissed from the Catholic University. Briggs continued to place the blame for the repression of scholarship on "the sad intolerance of the Papal Secretary of State and his associates." "I do not know of any period of history," he wrote, "or of any historic magnate who has committed so many severe blunders in so short a time as Merry del

Val."[76] Only gradually did Briggs learn that the pope himself had to bear more of the blame for Merry del Val's actions.

Throughout Genocchi's extant correspondence with Briggs, he had consistently spoken of enjoying Pius X's protection and had placed the responsibility on Merry del Val for the anti-Modernist extremes. By 1911, however, he began to change his opinion. Louis Duchesne's *Histoire ancienne de l'église* would soon be placed on the Index, he informed his American friend, and there was a definite crisis. Merry del Val and his friends said that no one could prevent the pope from speaking out, but he was growing weaker and saw Modernism everywhere. Genocchi himself could no longer speak with him.[77] Any hope for a change would have to wait for a new pontificate. Genocchi's sporadic letters reveal a scholar who gradually came to be aware that, though the pope may have been personally friendly to him, he was actually behind the anti-Modernist movement. From that point of view, they provide a first-hand account of Roman integrism. Briggs, who had been so anxious for Christian unity and who had acted as a spokesman for liberal Catholic exegetes, dedicated his *Theological Symbolics* to Genocchi in 1914.

The correspondence between Briggs and von Hügel reveals their deep concern not only for Scripture scholarship, but also for Church unity. Both held ecclesiological positions that would have to wait for several more generations to be accepted. Curiously, however, neither of them referred to the particular crises in the American Catholic church, such as the Poels case or the demise of the *New York Review* or Gigot's work. Briggs's significance for American Catholic biblical scholarship, therefore, is not his direct contact with American exegetes, but his dissemination to an American audience of information he derived from his European Catholic friends. His articles charted the development of integrism and he alerted American Catholics, if any indeed were listening, to Benigni's spy network. The "Sodalitium Pianum" consisted of only a few members, placed in positions of prominence, who used codes to communicate with themselves and with Benigni, who then published their findings in the *Correspondance de Rome*. But there were also numerous other sympathizers reporting on the suspected heterodoxy of seminary professors and even bishops.[78]

Although Benedict XV, as was already noted, put an end to the *Sodalitium Pianum*, the legacy of the anti-Modernist crusade remained. On September 1, 1910, Pius X prescribed a lengthy and detailed oath against the tenets ascribed to Modernism. It was to be taken by all clerics before their ordination to the diaconate, pastors, religious superiors, and all professors in philosophical and theological seminaries at the beginning of each academic year. In regard to Scripture, the oath stated: "I reject that method of judging and interpreting Sacred Scripture which, departing from the tradition of the Church, the analogy of faith, and the norms of the Apostolic See, embraces the misrepresentations of the rationalists and with no prudence or restraint adopts textual criticism as the one and supreme norm."[79] In itself, the oath added nothing to the campaign against the historical critics—that may explain why Briggs and his correspondents, from the available evidence, made little comment on it. But it created an atmosphere that prevailed until the Second Vatican Council.

Briggs was probably the foremost exegete in the United States. His love for Scripture had led him to seek Church unity. His criticism of the pontificate of Pius X was severe, but it never lacked respect for the authority that he thought was essential for assuring that the word of God remained alive in the Church. What he objected to was not Church authority as such, but the scholastic theological development of that authority in the early twentieth century. His articles contain his reflections on some of the leading Roman scholastic theologians, such as Louis Billot, S.J., who came to symbolize orthodox theology incapable of considering history as part of its enterprise. This theology, reinforced for the next half century by the oath against Modernism, would shape the next generation of Catholic scholars and dominate seminary education.

9. Anti-Modernism in the United States: 1910-1940

Americans, in general, and American Catholics, in particular, are notoriously ahistorical. They are prone to take the immediate past as normative for all the past. The condemnation of Modernism, following so closely on the heels of the condemnation of Americanism, caused the American church to reel away from anything that smacked of heresy. The creative scholarship of Poels and his mistreatment by the highest of Church authorities, the biblical exegesis of Gigot and his open espousal of the historical method, the *New York Review* and its mission to introduce American Catholics to the best in European scholarship—all of this was erased from the corporate memory of the American Catholic Church.

ROMANIZATION OF THE AMERICAN CATHOLIC CHURCH

The condemnation of Modernism arguably had more of an impact in the United States than in Europe, for American scholarship was still in its infancy in the early twentieth century, and, even then, it was largely derivative from Europe. What replaced it was equally derivative from Europe, but the cast of mind was totally different. Absent was the openness of men like Hogan toward the new historical method in the study of Scripture and other branches of theology. Present was the type of Thomism, against which Briggs reacted so strongly and which Louis Billot, S.J., virtually personified.

THEOLOGY AND ECCLESIOLOGY

Billot was almost a caricature of the new Thomism then rampant in Rome. In his life, he embodied all the fears of an ecclesiastical Rome reacting against rationalism and the liberal state. A Frenchman, he continued to support monarchy and repudiated republican government. A Thomist, according to his understanding of the great theologian, he proudly rejected history. He bragged that, in his twenty years of teaching, his students did not know there was such a thing as "the biblical question." Buonaiuti said of him that he was "a bony and angular figure of a theologian, lean and dry, for whom religious and Christian life had taken on the shape of an eternal syllogism."[1] A consultor to the Biblical Commission, he boldly applied Aristotelian syllogisms to every problem in Scripture—the very approach that Lagrange had shown could not be taken. Genocchi described for Fracassini, Billot's effort to defend the Johannine Comma in 1903. Relying on Franzelin's thesis that every dogmatic text derived from the Vulgate was authentic, Billot was undaunted by the objection that the text was not in the Greek codices. "If it is not there, it ought to be there," he responded; "look further, you will find it." Even the Biblical Commission could not accept Billot's syllogistic reasoning to prove the authenticity of the text. "Reverend Father Billot's discourse," it said, "supposes a lot, but proves nothing."[2] Within a short time, however, Billot would get more of a hearing as like-minded men came to make up the majority of the consultors of the commission.

Billot would have done little harm, had he been either an insignificant figure or an aberration. Unfortunately, he was neither. He joined the faculty of the Gregorian University in 1888, the year after Mazzella received his red hat. In 1911, he, too, was named a cardinal, but was forced to resign in 1927, because of his support of *Action Française*. He died in 1931, but he left behind his theological legacy. In 1904, he published *De sacra Traditione contra novam haeresim evolutionismi*. Confidently he traced all the errors of Loisy and the other Modernists back to Immanuel Kant's notion of relative truth. To this he opposed the immutability of dogmatic propositions in which concepts were similar to the letters of the alphabet put together to form words. Contrary to Loisy's statement that "the concepts which the Church presents as revealed dogmas are not truths fallen from heaven," Billot asserted that concepts, though human in origin, once put together to form doctrines proposed to faith on the authority of God who reveals, do in fact come from heaven. Billot's book was to go through four editions, the last of which was published in 1929. But a clue to his orientation can be seen in the change in the title of the second and subsequent editions. It then became *De immutabilitate traditionis contra modernam haeresim evolutionismi.* [3] The concept of the "immutability of tradition" was worlds apart from the lived experience of the Church, espoused by Kenrick, Hogan, Gigot, and others. Yet, this was the notion of immutable tradition taught at the Jesuits' Woodstock College up to the 1950s.[4]

Billot, of course, was not alone. He had his collaborators and imitators. But his type of theology would contribute to the intellectual slumber of the American church. The American philosopher, Josiah Royce, had remarked that "St. Thomas' spirit is more potent than his letter."[5] By the late nineteenth-century, however, enthusiasm for the spirit of Thomas soon gave way to slavery to the letter. Neo-Thomism became the Catholic bastion in the United States against a world that was either hostile or irrelevant. George Bull, S.J., dean of the Graduate School of Fordham University, summed up this mentality in 1938. The purpose of secular graduate schools, he said, was "to add to the sum of human knowledge." The purpose of a Catholic graduate school was different, for the Church was already in full possession of the truth. Bull relished the intellectual isolation of the Church from contemporary culture. "The Catholic mind," he said, had a "totality of view, as an attitude, a spontaneous direction, a thing taken for granted whenever it thinks at all. . . ." That "totality of view" was

the simple assumption that wisdom has been achieved by man, and that the humane use of the mind, the function proper to him as man, is contemplation and not research. . . . In sum, then, research cannot be the primary object of a Catholic graduate school, because it is at war with the whole Catholic life of the mind.[6]

And where better to find the true expression of that "totality of view" than in pre-Reformation Catholicism, especially as expounded by Thomas?[7]

The ideas of Billot and his fellow neo-Thomists would have had little impact on the American church, however, if there had not also been an ecclesiastical reform of the Church along Roman lines. When Leo XIII condemned Americanism in 1899, he not only spoke to the American hierarchy; he also acted. Vatican officials were intent on appointing bishops in the United States who were known for their loyalty to Rome in accordance with the new theological understanding. William H. O'Connell was the first of a new breed of American bishops who owed their advancement to Roman patronage. He embodied the trend toward Romanization of the hierarchy. In 1895, he had succeeded Denis O'Connell as rector of the American College in Rome. In 1901, he was named Bishop of Portland, Maine, though he had not been placed on the lists of three candidates submitted to Rome. In 1904, Archbishop John Williams of Boston had requested a coadjutor. As was seen above, the first name on the canonical lists of nominees was Bishop Matthew Harkins of Providence, who was accused not only of Americanism but also of allowing his diocesan newspaper to publish stories favorable to the higher criticism of Scripture—he would, of course, later be one of the two episcopal supporters of Henry Poels. How seriously the accusations were taken in Rome is unknown, but he was not named to the post. Instead, in 1905, O'Connell became Coadjutor Archbishop of Boston, though he was not on the lists of candidates. He owed his rise to his close friendship with Merry del Val and he would use his position to Romanize the metropolitan province of Boston and, if he had the chance, the rest of the American hierarchy.[8] Among those he saw impeding his program were the Sulpicians, who were then running his seminary. But his motives were complex. Not only did he hold their theological orientation suspect; he also bore them a grudge for dismissing him or asking him to leave St. Charles College, their minor seminary, in Ellicott City, Maryland.

BRUNEAU AND THE SULPICIANS AT BRIGHTON

Francis E. Gigot had been one of the most promising biblical scholars in the American church, but other Sulpicians who had written on the biblical question also fell under suspicion. Joseph Bruneau, S.S., as was seen, left Dunwoodie for St. John's Seminary, Brighton, Massachusetts, in 1906, when Driscoll, Gigot, and three Dunwoodie colleagues left the Sulpicians. Early in 1909, the Sulpicians at Brighton were well aware of O'Connell's dislike of them, but initially they seemed unaware that Bruneau was the particular object of his attack.

In February, Wendell S. Reilly, S.S., a newly appointed member of the Brighton faculty, told Edward R. Dyer, S.S., the American vicar general, of the situation. Canadian-born, Reilly had just completed his doctorate in Scripture (S.S.D.) at the Biblical Commission, the first American citizen to do so. O'Connell, he said, had chastised the faculty for failing to instill proper ecclesiastical decorum in the seminarians—one of the archbishop's complaints was that too frequently, when he extended his hand to students, they shook it rather than kiss the ring adorning it. Since O'Connell was then on his way to Rome, Reilly thought it imperative to bring "to the attention of the Holy Father, a fact that is perfectly plain to us here, that the Archbishop is so prejudicial against S. Sulpice and Sulpician methods as to render him utterly unappreciative of anything good that may proceed from them." Yet, he continued, "the position of S. Sulpice is strong in Rome. Fr. Vigouroux & Fr. [Marie F. X.] Hertzog [the procurator general] are held in the highest esteem by the pope." He, therefore, recommended that perhaps Hertzog "could get a word in on the subject before the Archbishop." Turning to more personal matters, he reported that Bruneau was then finishing up "some lectures . . . on the internal evidence for the authenticity of the Gospel . . . before letting me take hold." Reilly would himself start with a course on the Prophets and was perhaps more of a prophet than he realized in remarking that "anyway all knowing critics may find it prudent to practice a certain amount of reserve now."[9] Reilly was at Brighton to replace Bruneau, who was being considered for a post at St. Mary's Seminary in Baltimore. If anything, his letter indicated that Bruneau was extremely cautious. Shortly after O'Connell had gone to Rome, however, the Vatican called Bruneau's orthodoxy in question.

In the spring of 1909, the superior general, Henri-Pierre Garriguet, S.S., requested that Hertzog ascertain the nature of the charges against Bruneau. Hertzog spoke with Cardinal Gaetano de Lai, secretary of the Consistorial Congregation, to which the American church reported after 1908, and to Nicola Canali, substitute secretary of state. Though the charges were not serious, he wrote Dyer, Merry del Val wanted the opinion of Archbishop Falconio, the apostolic delegate. Hertzog, therefore, recommended that Dyer furnish the delegate with all the necessary information. In the meantime, he had an audience with Pius X and explained that the purpose of his visit was "to verify an accusation brought against one of our confrères and to guarantee his orthodoxy so that he could be named a professor in Baltimore." "The Holy Father, in listening to me," Hertzog continued, "had a very serious air and said to me: you have reason to take some precautions, lest some professors be named who present dangerous teaching." Hertzog assured the pope that he would soon have the apostolic delegate's testimony in Bruneau's behalf. To Dyer, however, he added his opinion that "the passage of M. Bruneau to New York has provoked this question: did he have to write in the review which came to be suppressed?"[10] In theory, of course, the *New York Review* had not been suppressed, but it was clear that Bruneau's association with the journal made him suspect. But there was more to the story. O'Connell was by that time simply looking for an excuse for removing the Sulpicians from St. John's Seminary.

In July 1909, Dyer had an interview with O'Connell concerning his reservations about the Sulpicians in general and Bruneau in particular. A few days later, Dyer wrote O'Connell to summarize their conversation. He reminded O'Connell that he had "expressed a high regard for the personal character of Father Bruneau, for his candor & sincerity, as well as for his real ability." But, as Dyer recalled the interview for O'Connell,

you said that the motive for which you demand his removal from your Seminary is that in Rome he is suspect in regard to modernist tendencies; that questions have been asked you even in this country about the character of his teaching; that you have no knowledge of his having taught anything that could fall under any censure whatsoever; that you do know however that he is tempermentally inclined towards the views generally enough looked upon as characteristic of recent Catholic scholarship.

Dyer feared that O'Connell's removal of Bruneau would be used by enemies of the Sulpicians and asked that the archbishop simply put into writing the substance of their interview.[11]

There is no record of whether O'Connell responded to Dyer's request, but, in the meanwhile, Bruneau had been transferred to Baltimore. In November, however, Hertzog reported that he had spoken with Merry del Val, who had received Falconio's letter. For the time, he thought it important "that dear M. Bruneau be extremely prudent in his teaching and in his words," in order not to draw further attention to himself.[12]

Bruneau had drawn attention because of his translation into French of Henry Oxenham's *Catholic Doctrine of the Atonement,* originally published in 1865. In his introduction, Bruneau said that he recommended the book to his students and to other priests and, hence, thought it would be useful to a French audience. Bruneau's translation was harshly reviewed in both *Civiltà cattolica* and *Osservatore Romano.* In February 1910, Hertzog feared that this might be a step toward having the Index condemn the work. Should this happen, it would be the first time a Sulpician had been so condemned and thus the entire Society would be under a cloud of suspicion.[13]

In the meantime, O'Connell had the Boston *Pilot,* his diocesan newspaper, publish a notice of the attack. "The Civilta Cattolica," said the paper,

reviews a book recently translated by the Rev. Joseph Bruneau, a Sulpician professor of theology. The Roman periodical dissects the book learnedly and points out that it is without any value whatever to the Catholic student, and moreover that it is full of pernicious ideas.

The book bears besides the name of the translator the title of 'professor of theology at Brighton Seminary.' To set at rest all inquiries, it is due the Seminary to say that there is no such professor at our diocesan seminary at present.[14]

The notice was, of course, a scarcely veiled attack on the Sulpicians at St. John's Seminary. *Civiltà* had criticized Bruneau for recommending the book to his students. This now became an added excuse for O'Connell to have the Sulpicians withdraw from his seminary. Bruneau considered writing a letter to the *Pilot* "for the sake 'of fairness to the Brighton Seminary' " to point out that no English-language Catholic paper had found any difficulty with the book up to this point. As he told Dyer, the letter might assure O'Connell "perhaps of the reciprocal joy I, who need not claim any apology from him, feel about being no longer in St. John's."[15]

O'Connell's hatred for the Sulpicians bordered on paranoia. On February 24, 1910, he vented his emotions about them to Merry del Val. The occasion was the appointment as Bishop of Hartford of John J. Nilan. O'Connell was pleased that

He is at least not a Sulpician [i.e. Sulpician trained]. Anything which breaks that blighting tyranny in this Province is a thing to be grateful to

God for. It was true—further propagation of it meant a speedy misfortune to the Church here and its relations with Rome.
That to every unbiased man is now the great question. We must have the spirit of Catholics surely—reenforced and at once—else God alone can foresee the perils of the future.
It will not be so easy now to manage and manipulate the ternae—hitherto that was a very easy and simple matter.
The Civiltà Cattolica has done a noble duty in exposing Bruneau. That is a wound which will smart in certain quarters. But, thank God, it is not the Church and true doctrine which will feel the smart. A few men must be pulled down and we shall know just where we stand, here as well as in Europe. Of all things, God deliver us from the hypocrisy of these pharisees.[16]

In the meanwhile, Merry del Val requested that Falconio notify Cardinal Gibbons of *Civiltà*'s review of Bruneau's translation and ask for an evaluation of the Sulpician's orthodoxy.[17] Gibbons's initial response to Falconio illustrated the ecclesiology that Briggs feared was developing in the aftermath of Modernism. The cardinal was subservient in replying to the delegate that he had already instructed Bruneau to draw up a statement and had "taken steps towards preventing a recurrence of such cause of complaint."[18] Bruneau's defense was straightforward. Oxenham's work in English had been highly recommended in the *Catholic Encyclopedia,* he stated, and the French translation had received positive reviews in a variety of European journals.[19] Gibbons then forwarded Bruneau's statement with a letter of his own directly to Merry del Val. In words perhaps aimed at Merry del Val's friend, O'Connell, Gibbons stated that "this incident is very painful to myself and to the Sulpitian [*sic*] Father[s], who since they came to Baltimore (where is situated their Mother House for this country) at the end of the 18th century, . . . have always been conspicuous for piety, orthodoxy and devotion to the Holy See." Nevertheless, he wished that the pope "be assured that so long as Father Bruneau remains in my Seminary, he shall write and teach nothing but what is in strict accordance with sound Catholic doctrine."[20]

With Gibbons's defense, the controversy over Bruneau ended. Bruneau's case had, however, coincided in time with the final stages of the Poels ordeal. Gibbons's strong defense of the Sulpicians contrasted with his high-handed treatment of the exegete. It may well have been that he did not fully understand the issues involved in the biblical question or was basically sympathetic with the reaction against the new exegesis. Yet, he may also have decided to draw the line in the heresy hunt, when it concerned professors whom he knew, even if Merry del Val was on the other side. In Boston, however, O'Connell used the Bruneau case as one of his excuses for demanding that the Sulpicians leave St. John's Seminary. After first giving them a year to leave, he reduced the time to a semester and requested their withdrawal by June, 1911.[21] In transferring the seminary to his own diocesan clergy, O'Connell ordered the rector and faculty to "maintain a certain distance and aloofness from the Clergy of the Diocese, contenting themselves with the companionship and friendship that they will find among themselves."[22]

Even after the departure of the Sulpicians, O'Connell remained vindictive. Elevated to the cardinalate in November 1911, he was feted at his alma mater, Boston College, the following March. In his address, he recalled his student days there. Not prone to modesty, he declared that "from the day of my entrance I was a competitor for the scholastic honors, and I won more than my due share of the highest of them. But in all the competition, there was no antagonism." This, he thought, "was the distinctive spirit of this College, and I think of every Jesuit College." Then he added: "I had been a student elsewhere and certainly that large manly spirit of honorable competition was often conspicuous by absence." He was "proud to say that both here and in the American College in Rome, the training developed the sort of manhood which can win without elation and lose without peevishness." But in case his audience had missed his earlier allusion, he immediately stated: "I was fortunate enough to escape the other sort of college spirit early in my scholastic days, and I am grateful for the illness which was its accidental cause."[23] "The other sort of college spirit" was, of course, that of St. Charles College, then located in Ellicott City, Maryland, which he had briefly attended. The Boston *Pilot* published his speech. Never one to cherish the truth, however, he later claimed that he was not responsible for what appeared in the *Pilot*, though he had published the entire address himself in his collected sermons.[24]

Now armed with his red hat, O'Connell set about to continue to make the church in New England "Roman," and this meant, in part, to keep from promoting to the episcopate any priest who was Sulpician trained.[25] The progressive breeze, which had begun to blow through at least Sulpician seminaries in the 1890s, gave way to an intellectual freeze, in which theology gave way to the mere repetition of Roman manuals.[26]

Yet, there was a link, a living one, between the liberal Sulpician spirit and the emergence of biblical scholarship in the 1940s. In 1904, as will be seen, Edward Arbez, S.S., began teaching at St. Patrick's Seminary, Menlo Park, California. Using Gigot's works, he raised all the critical questions with his seminarians, though he would also explain the decisions of the Biblical Commission. He was cautious, however, not to publish any of his research.

INTEGRISM AMERICAN-STYLE

Catholic publications on biblical subjects reflected an ultraconservative tendency. No one symbolized this more than the Jesuits at Woodstock College. Their contributions on biblical topics marred the otherwise scholarly *Catholic Encyclopedia*. Maas wrote the articles on "Deluge," "Deuteronomy," "Exegesis," "Logia Jesu," "Knowledge of Jesus Christ," "Pentateuch," and "Scripture." There was no separate article on "Genesis"—Maas treated it under "Pentateuch." He continued his assaults on biblical criticism in the *American Ecclesiastical Review* until 1912, when, after serving as rector of Woodstock, he was named provincial superior of the Maryland-New York Province. His spirit remained alive in the *Review*, however, through one of his disciples, Walter Drum, S.J.

WALTER DRUM AND THE *American Ecclesiastical Review*

Drum's father was Captain John Drum, U.S.A., killed at the battle of San Juan Hill in the Spanish-American War. His brother was also a professional military officer and rose to the rank of general.[27] Raised on army bases, Drum saw his career as a Jesuit professor and writer as a military campaign against Modernism. He had given an early indication of his close affinity for Maas's approach to historical criticism of Scripture. In January 1904, in notes he seems to have taken in one of Maas's lectures, he queried how Gigot could argue that historical criticism had begun in Catholic circles with Astruc and Geddes, when Astruc left his wife and children to live with another woman and Geddes was suspended from the priesthood and refused a Catholic funeral.[28] Maas's review of Gigot's *Special Introduction to the Old Testament* in the *American Ecclesiastical Review* had, of course, raised that question at least in regard to Astruc.[29] The point seemed to be that the new American Catholic intellectual spirit was not to investigate the value of new theories, but to assassinate the character of the theorists. Drum was also a noted retreat director who could get away in 1915 with asking a group of working women, "What is the difference between the feelings of a little lap dog and a girl?" His answer was that "your feelings are elevated by reason and the puppy's are not."[30]

After completing his studies at Woodstock, Drum spent two years studying oriental languages and biblical theology, first at St. Joseph's University, Beirut, and then at Innsbruck. In 1907, he had a personal audience with Pius X, whose parting advice became the guiding force in his life. "Remember," said the pontiff, "stand by the traditional doctrines of the Church!"[31] For Drum, the words became a pontifical hunting license for heretics wherever they were to be found. He may, in fact, have been a member of the "Sodalitium Pianum."[32] Drum, too, contributed to the *Catholic Encyclopedia*. His articles on Scripture included: "Hexateuch," "Incarnation," epistles of St. John, Josue, the books of Judges, Psalms, psalms of Solomon, epistles to the Thessalonians, Tobias, and numerous short articles on biblical commentators. In a fortunately never published commentary on "John the Historian," he leveled his attack on all the progressive exegetes. In a lengthy exposition, he concluded that von Hügel simply could not be considered a Catholic.[33]

In 1912, Drum began his regular column in the *American Ecclesiastical Review*. From this vantage point, he regarded himself as the guardian of orthodoxy, and fearlessly wielded his foil against all comers. In 1913, Cuthbert Lattey, S.J., professor of Scripture at St. Bueno's College, the house of studies for the English Province of the Jesuits, published the Epistles to the Thessalonians. It was the first fascicle of the Westminster version of the New Testament, a translation from the Greek, under the auspices of the English hierarchy. In the preface, he noted that this was the first English Catholic translation of the New Testament into the vernacular since Lingard's work in 1836. In a footnote, he added, erroneously, that Archbishop Kenrick's translation "unfortunately caused the abandonment" of the translation from the Vulgate "entrusted . . . to J. H. Newman."[34] Sending a copy to Drum, Lattey asked his assistance in the translation project. He also noted that he had differed from Drum's article in the *Catholic Encyclopedia*, which had argued that Paul did not expect the parousia in his lifetime, for such an error would have to be attributed to the Holy Spirit.[35] Drum agreed to help in the project and asked to translate the Gospel of John. Lattey further requested his opinion about getting Maas to do the Johannine epistles and Gigot to do either the Apocalypse or the Pastoral and Johannine epistles.[36]

In the meantime, Drum expressed his indignation at Lattey's criticism of his own article in the encyclopedia and then reviewed Lattey's translation in both *America* and the *American Ecclesiastical Review*. Drawing upon his own article, Drum said he regretted "to see that Fr. Lattey seems to hold that St. Paul erred in what he wrote," for "Catholics insist that St. Paul cannot have said the Parousia would be during his lifetime. Had he said so, he would have erred; the inspired word of God would have erred; the error would be that of the Holy Spirit more than of Paul."[37]

Lattey then published a rejoinder in the *Review*, in which he cited both Christian Pesch, S.J., and Ferdinand Prat, S.J., in support of his position that inspiration was not endangered by the sacred writer's display of ignorance.[38] The controversy continued, with Lattey remaining restrained, until, in October 1914, he informed Drum that "I eventually decided to submit the matter to Father [Franz X.] Wernz [the general]." "If he thinks another view had better appear in the next edition of Thessalonians," Lattey continued, "appear it shall. I did this of my own accord, as I did not wish any serious doubts to arise as to the orthodoxy of our Version."[39] Lattey either was unaware that Wernz had died the previous August or was under so much strain that his reference was a slip of the pen.

Lattey continued to exhibit heroic patience. On May 18, 1915, the Biblical Commission issued a decree stating that 1 Thes

4:15–16 need not be interpreted to mean that Paul expected the parousia in his lifetime. Drum jubilantly wrote in the *American Ecclesiastical Review* that he had been vindicated.[40] Lattey was less certain that the commission had said "that the interpretation which I was defending imputes formal error to the sacred writer." He had, in the meantime, written an article about the commission's response in the London *Tablet* and did not wish to continue the controversy any further. He had, however, arranged to substitute the *Tablet* article for his references to Drum in the first edition of his translation of the epistles to the Thessalonians. He also found it opportune to point out to Drum that he had had a very cordial conversation with Janssens, the secretary of the commission, and had received supportive letters from Cardinal Wilhelm van Rossum, the president of the commission, and Merry del Val, then the secretary of the Holy Office. Despite his differences with Drum, he still begged his American colleague to produce his translation of John.[41]

As it turned out, Drum never did complete the translation of John—at least not to the satisfaction of Lattey and the other editors. That task was taken over by Wendell Reilly, S.S., who was then teaching at St. Mary's Seminary, Baltimore. Gigot was the only other American contributor to the New Testament translation, with his rendering of the Pastorals, the Johannine epistles, and the Apocalypse.

BENEDICT XV

In the meantime, dramatic changes occurred in Rome which would influence biblical scholarship. In 1913, the integrists drew up a list of cardinals with a designation of their orientation in the event of a conclave. Their unique definition of terms revealed their mentality. For them, "reactionary" was a compliment and, hence, their favorite was Merry del Val, "The Terror." Rampolla was a "superior man, a spirit full of illusions, a dreamer, the Jules Verne of ecclesiastical politics, the Crispi of papal government, a megalomaniac." There were then only three American cardinals. Gibbons was an "old-style American liberal," and Farley was "liberal in the American fashion." If O'Connell had many enemies, then the evaluation of his integrist friends is even more telling. He was a "friend of Merry del Val from youth," they said, "was consecrated by him, became Roman, represents Romanism in America, very shady, an unscrupulous man through his money."[42] Absent from the list was Giacomo della Chiesa, former substitute secretary of state under Rampolla and not yet a cardinal. Later that year, Rampolla died, and Pius X appointed no successor to his dual posts of secretary of the Holy Office and president of the Biblical Commission.

In August 1914, Pius X died. In the conclave to elect his successor, only one American, Farley, was present. To the probable disappointment of the integrist supporters of Merry del Val, O'Connell had been prevented from getting to Rome on time through a series of fatal or providential mishaps. He and Gibbons arrived in Rome to the sound of church bells proclaiming the election of Cardinal della Chiesa, Archbishop of Bologna, who took the name Benedict XV.[43] Della Chiesa, as Rampolla's substitute in 1892, had defended John Ireland's controversial plan for Church-State cooperation in the operation of parochial schools. This provoked Archbishop Corrigan to remark of him that he was "a gentleman without any influence whatever in theological circles, and whose name consequently, if published, would carry absolutely no weight with it."[44] The election of Benedict prompted Ireland to say, "of Della Chiesa it could not be said, as it could of Sarto—non cognoverunt Joseph. . . . I felt that the pendulum would swing to Leo & Rampolla—and that meant Della Chiesa."[45] The old liberals thought their day had come again.

That year, 1914, was one of transition for the Jesuits as well. Some of them had already run afoul of the integrists; others were calling for greater moderation in ferreting out heresy. Only the intervention of Cardinal Désiré Mercier, Archbishop of Malines, prevented the condemnation of the Bollandists. Even *Civiltà cattolica* was becoming more moderate than Pius X wanted and he appears to have contemplated removing the general of the Jesuits, F. X. Wernz, S.J.[46] Wernz died on August 19, 1914, the day before the pope. His successor, elected in February 1915, was Vladimir Ledochowski, S.J. It would still be years, however, before the Jesuits emerged on the side of biblical criticism.

One of the new pope's first acts was to name a new Secretary of State, Pietro Gasparri, a canonist, who had once evoked from Merry del Val the remark: "Gasparri is . . . I must say honestly at times hardly orthodox. I don't know where he has learnt or unlearnt his theology."[47] Merry del Val then became secretary of the Holy Office, but not president of the Biblical Commission. That post fell to Cardinal Wilhelm van Rossum, whom the integrists had described as "good, with us."[48] Benedict XV's pontificate was ambivalent toward biblical studies. On the one hand, on November, 1, 1914, he issued his encyclical *Ad beatissimi Apostolorum* appealing for world peace. In it, he stated that, where there was no harm to faith or morals and where the Holy See had not authoritatively spoken, "there is room for divergent opinions." Calling for charity in discussions of such "divergent opinions," he demanded that "Catholics abstain from certain appellations which have recently been brought into use to distinguish one group of Catholics from another." Such "appellations," he continued, were to be "avoided not only as 'profane novelties of words,' out of harmony with both truth and justice, but also because they give rise to great trouble and confusion among Catholics."[49] He then ordered the Sodalitium Pianum to disband and thus stopped the witch-hunt against suspected Modernists.[50]

On the other hand, in 1920, the fifteenth centenary of the death of St. Jerome, he issued the encyclical *Spiritus Paraclitus.* Drafted by Leopold Fonck, S.J., the rector of the Biblical Institute, it marked the further repression of Scripture studies.[51] The encyclical commended those who used "critical methods . . . to seek to discover new ways of explaining the difficulties in Holy Scripture, whether for their own guidance or to help others." But it warned scholars "that they will only come to miserable grief if they neglect our predecessor's injunctions and overstep the limits set by the Fathers." In particular, the pope seemed still to be concerned with the relationship between inspiration and inerrancy. In words probably intended for Lagrange, he stated:

Yet no one can pretend that certain recent writers really adhere to these limitations. For while conceding that inspiration extends to every phrase—and, indeed, to every single word of Scripture—yet, by endeavoring to distinguish between what they style the primary or religious and the secondary or profane element in the Bible, they claim that the effect of inspiration—namely absolute truth and immunity from error—are to be restricted to that primary or religious element. Their notion is that only what concerns religion is intended and taught by God in Scripture, and that all the rest—things concerning "profane knowledge," the garments in which Divine truth is presented—God merely permits, and even leaves to the individual author's greater or less knowledge. Small wonder, then, that in their view a considerable number of things occur in the Bible touching physical science, history and the like, which cannot be reconciled with modern progress in science![52]

The pope was even harsher in regard to the claim of contemporary scholars that Leo XIII justified their assertion that "the sacred writers spoke in accordance with the external—and thus deceptive—appearance of things in nature." This position, said Benedict, was "a rash and false deduction" from Leo's thought, "for sound philosophy teaches that the senses can never be deceived as regards their proper and immediate object." To argue otherwise would be to assert that inspiration was compatible with error. Nor could scholars legitimately appeal to Jerome in asserting that the Scripture writers did not observe historical truth.[53]

Benedict, however, reserved special reproach for those who resorted to "implicit quotations," "pseudo-historical narratives," or "kinds of literature," which went against "the mind and judgment of the Church" and could not "be reconciled with the entire and perfect truth of God's word." In this category, he placed those who

refuse to allow the things which Christ said or did [to] have come down to us unchanged and entire through witnesses who carefully committed to writing what they themselves had seen or heard. They maintain—and particularly in their treatment of the *Fourth Gospel*—that much is due of course to the Evangelists—who, however, added much from their own imaginations; but much, too, is due to narratives compiled by the faithful at other periods, the result, of course, being that the twin streams now flowing in the same channel cannot be distinguished from one another.

Finally, the pope exhorted exegetes, in accord with his interpretation of Jerome's method, always to adhere to the literal sense of the Scripture.[54] Historical critics were quite clearly put on notice.

Although there was little indication that Rome would encourage historical criticism of the Scripture, there were no new restrictions. The Biblical Commission issued its last decision in 1915, when it addressed the question of Paul's ignorance of the parousia—the decision to which both Lattey and Drum appealed to uphold their respective positions. Its next decision would not be issued until 1933 in regard to a relatively insignificant matter of the erroneous interpretations of two scriptural texts (Ps 15:10–11; and Mt 16:25; Lk 9:25).

In January 1922, Benedict XV died. The conclave to elect his successor cast fourteen ballots before choosing Achille Ratti. Former prefect of the Vatican Library, he had engaged in an extensive correspondence with Henry Hyvernat of the Catholic University.[55] At the time of his election, he had been Archbishop of Milan and a cardinal for only eight months. Despite having a scholar on the chair of Peter, however, Scripture scholars were still not free from trial. On December 12, 1923, A. Brassac's version of *Manuel biblique ou Cours d'Écriture Sainte à l'usage des Séminaires* was put on the Index. Merry del Val explained the reasons to Pierre-Henri Garriguet, S.S., the superior general of the Sulpicians. Though Fulcran Vigouroux had written the original edition, Brassac's revision, said the cardinal, was so fraught with error that any "revision would be impossible." Among Brassac's errors was what he taught "about the inspiration of Sacred Scripture and its inerrancy, especially about historical events, where he distinguishes between the substance of the narration and additional material, [and] about the authenticity and historical truth of many inspired books." This teaching, the cardinal continued, went against "the dogmatic decrees of the sacred Councils of Trent and of the Vatican and other documents of the ecclesiastical magisterium, as for example the encyclicals of Leo XIII and Pius X, the decrees of the Holy Office and the Pontifical Biblical Commission."[56] Like Gigot before him, Brassac was accused of neglecting the traditional arguments for scriptural inspiration and inerrancy and of showing a decided tendency to "commend new opinions" without showing "the inefficacy and weakness of their bases."[57] Early in his pontificate, therefore, Pius XI gave no indication of any appreciation of critical studies.

The pontificate did, however, witness the appointment of the first American as rector of the Biblical Institute in Rome. In 1913, John J. O'Rourke, S.J., of the Maryland-New York Province joined the faculty of the institute as professor of biblical Greek and papyrology. From 1916 to 1918 and again from 1921 to 1926, he taught New Testament exegesis. In 1924, he succeeded Fonck as rector. Under his administration, the Biblical Institute realized one of Fonck's long-standing dreams—the opening of a house in Jerusalem (1927). When Fonck had first proposed the plan, Lagrange heard that "what had totally decided the Pope [to found a Jerusalem house of the Biblical Institute] was the need to remedy the lack of orthodoxy found in other *institutes* of the same type." There was, of course, only one other institute in Jerusalem, Lagrange's own *École biblique.*[58] After 1916, the Biblical Institute had been allowed to grant the baccalaureate and licentiate in Scripture in the name of the Biblical Commission. In 1928, under O'Rourke's rectorship, the Institute gained the authority to grant all degrees, including the doctorate, in its own name. O'Rourke ended his term as rector in 1930, but he was to return as superior of the Jerusalem house during the Arab-Jewish war from 1947 to 1949.[59] O'Rourke, however, was a teacher and administrator, not a scholar.

DRUM AND MARTINDALE

In the meantime, Walter Drum continued his vigilance against heresy. He needed no encyclical, such as *Spiritus Paraclitus,* in order to be reminded of the danger of using historical criticism, especially on John's Gospel. His was a caricature of an approach to Scripture that depended not on scientific research but on slavish adherence to the letter of Roman decisions. In 1920, he again lined up his sights on an English Jesuit. But this time he came into conflict with Herman Heuser, who failed to be convinced of the propriety of publicly accusing C. C. Martindale, S.J., of Modernism. In 1919, Martindale had published two articles in *The Catholic World,* in which he raised questions about the historical value of the Gospel of John.[60] Drum may have already been alerted to what he considered Martindale's dangerous tendencies through the latter's affinity with the thought of Lagrange, who considered the English Jesuit among his supporters.[61]

Drum chose his regular column in the *American Ecclesiastical Review* as the forum for accusing Martindale of Modernism. Heuser, however, thought that Drum should raise any charge of possible heresy indirectly, without mentioning Martindale by name, and should seek "other methods of remonstrance through different channels than public pilloring [*sic*]." He feared that both Martindale and the English Jesuits would take offense at a public challenge to their orthodoxy. Moreover, he was concerned that Father John Burke, C.S.P., editor of *The Catholic World,* would "resent the attack as a belittling of his judgment if not a questioning of his orthodoxy (which is a sore point with the congregation to which he belongs)." Acknowledging that Drum was a "soldier" ready to do combat, Heuser suggested that he bring the matter before the appropriate superiors within his order, rather than create a public scandal.[62] Heuser had thus raised the Paulists' sensitivity to the specter of Americanism as well as the propriety of airing in public one Jesuit's suspicions of heresy in another.

Unpersuaded by Heuser's argument, Drum wrote a second letter, which is no longer extant. In reply, Heuser agreed that Drum's "attitude toward Father Martindale" was "justified," but disagreed that a "public exposition" was necessary,

when it is possible for the authorities, to whom Fr. M. is solemnly bound in obedience, to be convinced, so as to call on him to withdraw and explain, and cease from utterances which his brethren plainly disapprove. Is it not correcting one scandal by an other [sic] to strike at a brother in public when it can be done by not only fraternal correction but by the command of the Father of the Family; and is not Fr. M. likely to move with open bitterness when so attacked that all the world realizes his fault, so far suspected only to those who see as you do. But perhaps I am still at sea in some way. The matter pains me. Yet I cannot view it otherwise.[63]

Drum had, in the meantime, sent Burke a copy of his proposed article on Martindale. Burke attacked Drum head-on. He would gladly publish Drum's article in *The Catholic World,* he wrote, if he thought for a moment the journal was subject to "the possible charge of Modernism." But he had decided on another tack. Since Drum had accused "a fellow member of your own religious order with approximation of heresy" in articles, which had originally been lectures to religious communities in England and which had received the approval of the English censors, Burke believed he owed "it in all justice and charity to the Society of Jesus to have the superiors thereof make what correction they wish either public or private." He had, therefore, forwarded copies of both Martindale's and Drum's articles to Father Joseph Rockwell, S.J., the Provincial of the Maryland-New York Province, to "ask him to give me his judgment and also to obtain the judgment of the Father General of the Society." If Rockwell approved, Burke would send both sets of articles to the general "and ask him to take the matter to the Biblical Commission for judgment and advice." The Paulist thought this appeal to "the supreme authority" preferable to having *The Catholic World* lend itself "to the exposition of a public and ugly disagreement between two members of the same great religious order."[64]

Though Drum remonstrated that Burke had done him an "injustice" by sending the article to the provincial, Burke stuck to his position and informed Drum that Rockwell had promised to take the matter to Ledochowski.[65] Rockwell did in fact refer the case to the general, who responded on March 19, 1920. "After careful examination" by his consultors, he informed Rockwell,

all gave with one mind their opinion that something should be published in order to take away the scandal given. Wherefore, I approve that some article of public law be written, which would correct the errors of Father Martindale. Since, however, care must always be taken, lest the mode of writing give a just cause for offense to anyone—especially to a religious; when the errors of one of ours are denounced, even greater care must be taken that there be avoided sharp words and strong style, which would rather offend a brother in the Lord than lead him to recognize his errors . . . according to which, the writings of Father Drum are to be edited before they are published.[66]

Though Drum thus received a mild rebuke for the tone of his criticism of Martindale, Ledochowski did agree that there were certain "errors."

The Martindale episode, however, drove a wedge between Drum and Heuser. Several months later, Drum asked Heuser's permission to republish a series of articles on Christology in the New Testament. In granting permission, Heuser declared his desire to give them "the widest possible propaganda." He only regretted "that our views as to what is 'ad aedificationem Ecclesiae' in the matter of Biblical Criticism, as it should appeal [*sic*] in the Review, do not fully meet. It is difficult to supply the place you have filled after dear Fathher [*sic*] Maas for so long a time; but I trust we may do so in the end."[67] Heuser was thus severing Drum's relationship with the *American Ecclesiastical Review*.

In one of Drum's final columns, he favorably mentioned a commentary on the New Testament by Charles Callan, O.P., and Maas's commentary on Matthew, but he added: "If any one desires to see John the Historian juggled into John the Mystic, we regretfully refer him to the recent articles by Father Martindale in the *Catholic World.*"[68] Drum had managed to get in the parting shot in the dispute, but, in a little over a year, he had died. His obituary stated that "his great work" had been "to uphold conservative scriptural opinion and the authority of the Biblical Commission."[69] It was a rather dubious distinction, but one of which he would have been proud. His place as professor of Scripture at Woodstock College was taken by Father William McClellan, S.J., a former Episcopal priest and gentle commentator on scriptural matters, who confined his reflections, for the most part, to the classroom.[70] For some time to come, Jesuits in general and those at Woodstock College in particular would express no sympathy for modern Scripture scholarship.

THEOLOGICAL EDUCATION IN THE UNITED STATES

While seminaries and periodicals slipped into intellectual slumber, the Catholic University attempted to maintain a semblance of the academic study of Scripture. As was seen above, the university had attempted to hire Joseph David as associate professor of New Testament in 1910.[71] A year later, they recommended that a professor of Old Testament "be secured at once," to relieve Hyvernat, who would be on leave, and A. A. Vaschalde, who were then giving two lectures a week.[72] In October, they accepted the resignation that Charles Grannan had tendered in July when he was "appointed to perform some service to the Holy See."[73] At the same meeting, they appointed Franz Cöln from the University of Bonn to replace Poels and also to teach New Testament.[74] The days of specialization and progressive scholarship in Scripture were temporarily at an end. Grannan, a proponent of the progressive spirit of the 1890s, came to be a reactionary symbol of the new era. In 1921, he published a four-volume work, *A General Introduction to the Bible.*[75] While noting the contributions in certain areas of higher criticism, he was decidedly conservative in his treatment of inspiration, in which he made no mention of Lagrange, except in his bibliography.

THE CATHOLIC UNIVERSITY OF AMERICA

The Catholic University did, however, attempt to increase its role in the study of Scripture. Early in 1913, the faculty of theology and

Shahan, the rector, developed a plan to establish a Biblical Institute. As Cöln proposed it, the institute should be allowed to award the degrees of licentiate and doctorate in Scripture, degrees that at this time were restricted only to the Biblical Commission. The faculty of theology would temporarily, therefore, award the decree of doctor of theology, with a concentration in Scripture.[76] On April 2, the trustees approved the establishment of the institute, "except as regards degrees."[77]

In the spring of 1924, the university found its institute in jeopardy. On April 27, Pius XI issued a *motu proprio* stating that no one could teach Scripture in seminaries unless he had obtained his degree from either the Pontifical Biblical Commission or the Biblical Institute.[78] On June 11, Michael J. Curley, the Archbishop of Baltimore and chancellor of the university, and Shahan wrote to Cardinal Gaetano Bisleti, prefect of the Congregation of Seminaries and Universities, to protest this policy. They pointed out that Leo XIII had urged bishops to affiliate their seminaries to the university and that many religious orders had also established houses there. The policy of requiring a Roman degree, they feared, would result in

a slacking of interest on the part of the Bishops and the Religious Orders as regards the University in general and in particular the Faculty of Theology. For if the University cannot prepare professors for the seminaries it will not only suffer curtailment of its 'rights and privileges' but it will also see the number of its students in theology reduced to zero.

They had no objection to a requirement that all the university's professors of Scripture be trained in Rome and noted that Father Heinrich Schumacher had, in fact, a decree from the Biblical Institute. They, therefore, asked that the university be allowed to train professors of Scripture and proposed, as an alternative to the new decree, that:

a. Our professors of Scripture to be trained in Rome;
b. Our course of study, method of teaching, text-books, and requirements for degrees, to be approved by the Biblical Commission;
c. Annual reports to be sent to the Commission with copies of all articles, publications and dissertations on biblical questions written either by the professors or by the students;
d. The University to see to it that those who receive degrees and teach

Scripture conform in every respect to the rulings of the Biblical Commission.[79]

Curley's and Shahan's letter was not arguing for the right to award degrees in Scripture, as such, but for the right to train seminary professors of Scripture. The new decree, in their mind, diminished the university's rights as a pontifical institution. Bisleti attacked this point.

On July 31, the cardinal informed Curley that Pius XI could not accept the argument that "there would be a slacking of interest" among bishops and religious orders in the university, since the university never had the right to confer degrees in Scripture. Moreover, the new decree did "not hinder the giving of regular courses in Sacred Scripture at centers of study, provided that they be in charge of professors who hold degrees in this subject and that the other regulations and cautions laid down by the Holy See be observed." Bisleti reminded Curley that, even before the decree, academic degrees in Scripture, "for the gravest reasons, could be conferred only by the Biblical Commission and the Biblical Institute." The university, then, could give advanced courses in Scripture, but could confer degrees only in theology, as was the case with the recently established Catholic university in Holland.[80]

In the meantime, Father Schumacher wrote out his reflections for Curley. The archbishop replied that the decree "put an end to all study of Scripture, and has had a very marked destructive effect on the whole School of Sacred Science, in the Catholic University." He could see no reason why priests who came to the university to study Scripture would any longer come,

since even they after a three years' Post-graduate course during which they are taught by yourself, a Roman Dr. in Scripture, are not permitted to teach Sacred Scripture in any Seminary. We might expect at least that men who have taken their Doctorate in Sacred Scripture in Rome might be permitted and trusted to prepare other men in this same subject, but not even that is allowed as is evident in your own case. The men you directed in their Scripture study may never teach Scripture in any Seminary of this Archdiocese, but might teach Scripture in the dangerous free Universities of Germany and Austria.

He concluded by saying that he would ask Cardinal Franz Erhle, S.J., the librarian and archivist of the Roman Church, to see if he could have some changes made in the decree "to permit you and your co-workers to carry on the splendid work you have done since you came to the University."[81]

The Americans were obviously failing to distinguish between degrees in Sacred Scripture and degrees in theology, which might entail the study of Scripture. Rome, on its part, wished to retain centralized control over the sensitive area of Scripture studies. Curley and the university trustees would make another attempt to gain Roman permission for the university to grant degrees in Scripture during the Second World War, when it was impossible for Americans to study abroad. Again, Rome would refuse permission.

There were, however, other professors either at the university or associated with it who were beginning to lay the groundwork for the later emergence of biblical scholarship. Romain Butin, S.M., taught Hebrew and ancient Near Eastern languages. A member of the executive board of the Society of Biblical Literature, he was named annual professor and acting director of the American School of Oriental Research in 1926. In 1930, he participated with Kirsopp Lake in a joint Harvard-Catholic University archeological expedition to the Sinai Peninsula.[82] Butin would later give the opening address to a meeting which led to the founding of the Catholic Biblical Association. Outside of the university, there were some harbingers of a new age dawning.

Diocesan Seminaries

In 1928, Edward Arbez, S.S., joined the faculty of the Divinity College, later named Theological College, in Washington, D.C. With the exception of a year of graduate work at Catholic University in 1917–1918, he had been teaching, as was seen above, at St. Patrick's Seminary, Menlo Park, California since 1904. His lecture notes were carefully color-coded to indicate the year in which he added references. In 1907–1908, he was still using Gigot's *Special Introduction to the Old Testament.* He would explain the reasons for the four-source theory of the composition of the Pentateuch in great detail and then briefly state what the Biblical Commission had said.[83] The same year, he also taught a course on the epistles of Paul. Updated over the years, his course notes explained at the outset that he would be treating only some of the "Pauline" epistles. Hebrews, he noted, was considered Pauline, at least in orientation, but its actual authorship presented a difficulty. The Pastoral letters, he acknowledged, also presented unique problems and would be treated in a separate course.[84] Hence, he treated in his course only those letters which critical biblical scholars of the time agreed were authentically Pauline. In notes for a course on Isaiah, which unfortunately he did not date, he said that "the book of Isaias falls into 2 main parts of pretty near equal size (1–35, 40–66), but (rather different in matter and form) separated by a long historical narrative (36–39)."[85] Arbez may well have confused some of his seminarians with his creative way of getting around the literal interpretation of the Biblical Commission's decisions, but at least he alerted them to the problems of the contemporary biblical world. He cautioned them, however, not to repeat what he said outside of class.[86] After twelve years at the Divinity College, he joined the university faculty.

The continued affinity of the Sulpicians for Gigot's work earlier in the century did not please everyone. In his memoirs, published in 1982, Cardinal Lawrence Shehan, former Archbishop of Baltimore, wrote of his days as a seminarian. He particularly recalled his professors of Scripture. In 1917, he was a student at St. Mary's Seminary in Baltimore, where Bruneau was rector. His Scripture professor used Gigot's *Special Introduction to the Old Testament.* Shehan still remembered that:

At the time we might have been said to be still living under the shadow of Modernism. Some thought that Gigot was too far advanced, but Father Daniel Duffy found no difficulty with him. In fact, my criticism of Father Duffy would have been that he adhered too closely to Gigot's text and accepted everything he said without question.

In 1920, Shehan transferred to the North American College, still affiliated with the Urban College of Propaganda. There, his professor of Scripture was "Dr. Ernesto Ruffini (later Cardinal Archbishop of Palermo), sometimes criticized by present-day Scripture scholars as an arch-conservative."[87] Shehan gave no indication that he could appreciate the negative evaluation of Ruffini by Scripture scholars. From a participant in Vatican II, it is clear that the anti-Modernist reaction had taken its toll.

Sulpician seminaries were not the only American institutions to keep alive the memory of Gigot. Yet, caution, if not conservatism, continued to be the hallmark of biblical studies. In 1911, for example, Father Edward J. Byrne joined the faculty of St. Bernard's Seminary in Rochester. He had a doctorate in theology from the seminary and then had spent two years at the École biblique in Jerusalem under Lagrange and then another year at the Biblical Institute in Rome under the Jesuits—an unusual academic background for the age. In his classes, he privately recommended Gigot, but publicly used no textbook. He would sometimes even inspect students' notes at the end of the year, explaining that he knew they had been used for dismissing professors in other institutions. When A. Brassac's version of the *Manuel biblique* was put on the Index, Byrne told his students to dispose of their copies—they had a public book burning accompanied by speeches. Perhaps they were on a lark, but their action indicated how little aware they were of the gravity of the situation.[88] In his few publications, Byrne gave little indication of his sympathy for progressive scholarship, though he maintained an extensive correspondence with Lagrange.[89] Silence was the way of survival for even potential biblical scholars.

At the Immaculate Conception Seminary in Darlington, New Jersey, John J. Dougherty, fresh from a licentiate in Scripture at the Biblical Institute, began using Gigot in 1937.[90] His lectures, while safe, at least alerted his students to the questions the historical critics were raising. But this relative openness during the 1930s was still restricted to a few institutions. American Jesuits still gave little hint that a new age was dawning.

THE JESUITS IN THE 1930S

In 1934, Michael J. Gruenthaner, S.J., was finishing his doctorate for the Biblical Commission. He agreed to write a chapter, "The World of the Old Testament and Its Historicity," for *European Civilization: Its Origin and Development,* edited by Edward Eyre and published by the Oxford University Press. Gruenthaner produced a lengthy 466-page chapter, which was virtually a paraphrase of the Old Testament, which he treated as a scientifically historical account.[91] One reviewer commented that, "ignoring both modern criticism and modern knowledge, it might have been written by a devout pre-Voltairean, and is occasionally amusing, as when it speculates whether Adam's lost rib was replaced or whether he had an extra rib to start with, and whether the angel made Balaam's ass speak by 'manipulating the animal's organs of sound' or by ventriloquy."[92]

The reaction to Gruenthaner's fundamentalism was so intense that his chapter was omitted in subsequent editions of Eyre's work, thus creating a library cataloger's nightmare. The next printing of the work kept the original table of contents, but without Gruenthaner's chapter in the text. Only the revised edition managed to omit both Gruenthaner's chapter and the reference to it in the table of contents.[93] There is no evidence, however, that Gruenthaner, then teaching at the Jesuit theologate at St. Mary's, Kansas, was chastened by the experience, for, in 1940, he requested and received his provincial's permission to have his piece published by the Catholic Truth Society of Hong Kong.[94]

Gruenthaner was by no means alone in his interpretation of the Scripture. Back at Woodstock College, Francis X. Peirce, S.J., had continued the tradition established by Maas and Drum. In the *American Ecclesiastical Review,* he revealed his orientation with an article, "Again the Synoptic Problem." Responding to the *Expository Times*'s fiftieth anniversary issue, he noted the lack of any citation of Catholic scholarship. He then took the occasion to praise Dom John Chapman's *Matthew, Mark, and Luke.* Summarizing Chapman's work, Peirce found "attractive" the theory that there were "two eye-witnesses and ear-witnesses, St. Matthew and St. Peter" to an original "Aramaic catechesis"; that Matthew wrote first in Aramaic and was later translated into Greek; that Peter used this as "a guide and memory-help" which Mark then recorded; and that Luke, desiring "to produce a complete work," used Mark as "a general background," inserted material from "Matthew and from private sources," but, "as his work is too long for a single scroll," he omitted the Marcan doublets and abbreviated Matthew's discourses. Peirce had begun his article by criticizing Vincent Taylor's assertion that few contemporary New Testament scholars "would contend that the Gospel [of John] was written by the Son of Zebedee." Peirce had countered that "obviously, Catholic exegetes, of whom there are a good few, and all of whom hold that St. John is the author of the Gospel which bears his name, are either non-existent or outside the rank of scholars."[95] Peirce had not intended any irony, but his statement did, indeed, indicate that Catholic exegetes were not in "the rank of scholars."

The state of Catholic biblical scholarship in the United States at the end of the 1930s was bleak. Whatever scholarship there had been at the beginning of the century had either been destroyed in the wake of Modernism or had gone underground with men like Arbez. The type of neo-Thomism, formulated in the nineteenth century to combat rationalism, had become so pervasive that Catholic writers confused theology with doctrine. Jesuit professors like Peirce and Gruenthaner took as their starting point, not the criticism of texts, but the declarations of the popes or the Biblical Commission. Until the late 1930s, moreover, there had been no scholarly publication since the demise of the *New York Review*. In effect, integrism had become a habit of mind, even after Benedict XV had condemned it. The American church gave little indication that it was ready to undertake any type of scholarly endeavor. Yet, that is what, perhaps unwittingly, Bishop Edwin Vincent O'Hara of Great Falls now asked the teachers of Scripture to do.

10. The Confraternity Edition of the New Testament

From the time of Kenrick, there had been little American Catholic effort to provide a new translation of the Bible. In 1899, a Bible was published in Baltimore with a preface by Cardinal Gibbons. Based eclectically upon Challoner's three revisions of the New Testament, it made no reference to Kenrick. In 1935, James A. Carey, professor of Scripture at Dunwoodie, published a version of the Challoner text, with some slight revisions of punctuation, grammar, and expression to make the text more readable to an American audience. Francis Aloysius Spencer, O.P., however, undertook a more ambitious project. In 1898, he published a new translation of the Gospels from the Latin. Three years later, he published a translation of the Gospels from the Greek, with a preface by Cardinal Gibbons. In 1913, the year of his death, he had completed his translation of the other New Testament books from the Greek. But only in 1937 was his work, revised by Charles J. Callan, O.P., and John A. McHugh, O.P., published. Between 1940 and 1946, it went through five reprintings.[1] The appearance of the Spencer translation coincided with the first major effort since Kenrick to provide an officially approved American translation from the Vulgate.

BISHOP EDWIN VINCENT O'HARA AND THE CONFRATERNITY OF CHRISTIAN DOCTRINE

A new translation of the New Testament from the Vulgate was the project of Edwin Vincent O'Hara, Bishop of Great Falls, Montana. Chairman of the bishops' committee for the Confraternity of Christian Doctrine, he had long recognized the inadequacy of the Challoner-Rheims translation. On January 18, 1936, he called a meeting of a select group of Scripture professors at the Sulpician

Seminary (later Theological College) in Washington. O'Hara quite consciously wished to involve in the project a cross section of religious and diocesan priests. The thirteen priests at the first meeting determined that the Clementine Vulgate would be the basis of their work, but they left it to the editorial board to "decide later whether it is to be known as a revision of the Rheims or a new translation." Each book of the New Testament was entrusted to a reviser, who was to indicate variants from the Greek text in notes. The entire work was to be submitted to an editorial board, with Edward Arbez of the Sulpician Seminary, as editor, Romain Butin, S.M., of the Catholic University, as associate editor, and William L. Newton of St. Mary's Seminary, Cleveland, as secretary. Callan was to do the final English editing. Butin also suggested that the gathering of biblical professors for the translation project be used as the occasion for forming a permanent association of Catholic biblical scholars.[2]

From the beginning, the work of translation was fraught with difficulty. Callan, who was present for the first meeting, shortly afterward urged O'Hara that the Spencer edition, which he had revised, be officially adopted as the American version.[3] This was but the first of a whole series of challenges that Callan, who was also editor of the *Homiletic and Pastoral Review,* would make to the Confraternity edition. There was yet a further note of criticism of the project—the use of the Vulgate as the basis for the revision. In 1935, the Westminster Version of the New Testament had been completed, with, as has been seen, contributions from Reilly and Gigot. Under the continuing editorship of Lattey, the translators then began work on the Old Testament. In 1934, however, the Dutch bishops had asked the Pontifical Biblical Commission if it was permissible to read in churches the pericopes of liturgical texts, translated, not from the Vulgate, but from the original languages. The commission responded that the translation to be "publicly read" was to be done "from the text approved by the Church for the sacred liturgy," that is, the Vulgate.[4]

This was actually the first time that the Holy See had mentioned the relationship between vernacular translations and the Vulgate—and then only of the pericopes used in the liturgy. The decision meant that, in England, the public proclamation of the liturgical texts could not be from the Westminster Version. Because the Americans wanted their new translation used in public worship and did not want to present the public with too unfamiliar a text, they decided to make their translation from the Vulgate, with reference to the Greek text in footnotes. They were to adhere as much as possible to the English style of the Challoner revision of the Rheims New Testament.[5]

Not everyone agreed with this decision. Callan, for his own personal reasons, had already urged use of the Spencer edition. Advocacy for the use of the Greek text came from an even more surprising quarter. Father A. E. Breen, who had accused Hanna of heresy at the beginning of the century, was then teaching at the archdiocesan seminary of Milwaukee. He emphatically told Newton that "the Rheims NT can not be adequately revised. The only thing that would be effective is to make a version such as the Revisers of Oxford have made. Rome will not permit this. The Gasquet revision [the revision of the Vulgate entrusted by Pius X to the Benedictines, under the direction of Aidan Gasquet, O.S.B.] will put back the real revision of the Vulgate another thousand years."[6]

In the meantime, the editorial board had met with O'Hara, on April 19, 1936, to determine the final norms for revision. It approved, in principle, Butin's earlier suggestion to form an association of Catholic biblical scholars. It, therefore, issued an invitation to all professors of Scripture to attend a meeting in New York on October 3, 1936, in conjunction with the national convention of the Confraternity of Christian Doctrine (CCD). At the New York meeting, the editors reported that about one quarter of the New Testament had already been translated. Butin suggested that, while use of the Greek text "should not be allowed to interfere with our plan of close adherence to the Vulgate," nevertheless, "more attention should be given the Greek in clarifying the Latin."[7] That meeting, as will be seen, led to the formation of the Catholic Biblical Association (CBA) and its journal, *The Catholic Biblical Quarterly.*

American Catholic biblical scholars were becoming a cohesive group, but they did not yet realize the difficulties of a translation. At its meeting in St. Louis on October 9, 1937, the editorial board decided to circulate a printed version of Newton's revision of John's Gospel, in order to get constructive criticism of the text as an aid to the remainder of the revision.[8] Though it would be almost a year before the text was distributed, the plan already created the first of several controversies. Callan, who was to do the final English editing, angrily wrote Newton that he had not seen the manuscript. As Newton informed Arbez, Callan threatened, "that if he is not accommodated with this last word he may retire from the Board."[9] A few months later, Newton learned of other objections to his text. Bishop O'Hara had informed him that one of the theological censors had questioned certain passages. In the meantime, Callan had read the manuscript and criticized Newton's use of "shall" and "will."[10]

By April, O'Hara had approved the circulation of a printed version of John's Gospel. Since Arbez was to write an introduction, the bishop recommended that he include in it a letter that Father John Baptist Frey, C.S.Sp., secretary of the Biblical Commission, had sent the editors praising the principles of the revision and, in particular, the decision to have recourse to the Greek text in order to clarify the Latin.[11] This preliminary version of John's Gospel was scheduled to be printed and circulated in August. In the meantime, the remainder of the New Testament had been completed and the editors had started to work on the Old Testament.

WILLIAM NEWTON AND ROMAN SUPPORT FOR THE TRANSLATION

During the summer of 1938, Newton traveled to Rome and England. His purpose was to publicize the newly founded Catholic Biblical Association and to sound out Roman officials on the text to be used as the basis for the translation of the Old Testament. In Rome, he first met with Frey, who advised him that, since the American hierarchy had not officially requested the Biblical Commission's opinion, he should consult members of the commission individually. Newton then interviewed Augustin Bea, S.J., rector of the Biblical Institute, Alberto Vaccari, S.J., a professor in the institute, Ernesto Ruffini, secretary of the Congregation of Seminaries, and Jacques-Marie Vosté, O.P., who subsequently became secretary of the Biblical Commission. These Roman officials, Newton reported to O'Hara, were divided in their opinion on whether to make the translation of the Old Testament from the Vulgate or from the original languages. If the work was translated from the original languages, however, it would have to "remain in 'campo scientifico.' " The American bishops could request a "formal decision" on the matter from the Biblical Commission, but Newton felt that could take years and would delay the American project.[12]

Leaving Rome, Newton went to England. As he told O'Hara, his main purpose would be to see whether English scholars would be willing to cooperate in producing "a better English version." Ronald Knox, he said, had "already expressed the desire to see all English-speaking [sic] cooperating in this work."[13] In England, his "general impression was not too encouraging" about collaboration on a translation from the Vulgate. Lattey preferred that the Americans "work out from the original languages, and that we should adopt the Westminster," but agreed to serve on the editorial board. The Jesuit even suggested some form of collaboration between the Catholic Biblical Association and the Westminster edition of the Old Testament. He also noted the "rather general English prejudice against American work," but thought that the presence of English and Irish members on the editorial board might make the translation more successful and even gain adoption by the English hierarchy. Monsignor J. M. T. Barton, an English consultor to the Biblical Commission, likewise preferred a translation from the original languages, but offered his cooperation. Canon Patrick Boylan also offered to serve on the editorial board. Newton had been unable to consult Knox personally, but recommended that he too be included among the editors and revisers.[14]

Within a few months, however, Newton learned from Lattey that the English hierarchy had requested Knox to make a translation from the Vulgate. This disturbed Newton, for Knox had to be aware of the American project and the English bishops should also have been cognizant of it, either from Knox or Lattey or from the news releases about it. "History," Newton wrote O'Hara,

seems to be repeating itself in this matter. Newman and Kenrick went about their revisions in this same way. The result was that neither came to full recognition. I have no fear for the circulation of our revision, for your plans offer an excellent guarantee. But this new move in England in [sic] no help to what you already have expressed as a desire of our own Hierarchy, the accomplishment of a universal English Revision.[15]

Newton, of course, was mistaken about Newman's having actually undertaken a revision of the Douay Bible. Later, he suggested to

O'Hara that the English bishops be encouraged to join the American project and send Knox over to join the editorial board.[16] As will be seen, however, the English biblical scholars were far more enthusiastic about the Catholic Biblical Association, which would gradually gain American Catholic biblical scholarship international acclaim.

Newton's trip to Europe had provided him with conflicting views of translating the Old Testament from the Vulgate. Several years later, his recollection of the attitudes he found in Rome was somewhat different from what he reported to O'Hara at the time. In 1943, he stated that all the consultors of the Biblical Commission he questioned

were agreed that, if the Bishops insisted, we might follow the Vulgate; but that, in such a case, we should have to make extensive corrections of the Latin text by comparing it with the Hebrew. At the same time they each of them urged that we go directly to the Hebrew text as unquestionably superior to the Vulgate. Most of the thoughts offered here are drawn from the arguments they advanced.[17]

In retrospect, it is difficult to determine precisely how Roman officials felt toward translations from the original languages in 1938. What is clear is that they did acknowledge that the text of the Vulgate was defective. Until a critical text of the Vulgate was available, the Clementine text would have to be used with great caution and only after comparison with the original languages— the procedure that Kenrick had fundamentally followed a century before. In October 1938, the editorial board of the Confraternity edition adopted the policy of using a "criticized Vulgate" as the basis not only for the translation of the Old Testament but also for further revision of the New Testament.[18]

While the editorial board was now beginning to realize the difficulties inherent in translating Scripture, in August 1938, it finally circulated Newton's recension of John's Gospel. Accompanied by a brief commentary, it was sent to every American and Canadian bishop, member of the CBA, and English-speaking biblical scholar. All were invited to comment on the text. Newton followed up the distribution of the text with a letter, which may have indicated his anticipation of problems arising from the change in the traditional language of the Douay. To justify the new version, he quoted from Cardinal Barnabò's letter to the American hierarchy in 1868, calling for a group of experts to examine the various versions of the Douay translation and any other English translations and to produce a standard edition. The purpose of the Confraternity revision, Newton continued, was "to provide a version, ultimately of the entire Bible, clearly expressed in the idiom of our time, and worthy, for its accuracy, of official recommendation to the faithful." John's Gospel was being distributed as "evidence of the work" to date, in order to elicit "a criticism which will assure the acceptability of the completed revision." Enclosed was a questionnaire on the style of the translation and suggestions for the commentary.[19]

THE FIRST ATTACKS OF THE *Homiletic and Pastoral Review*

Within a few months, the editorial board had received numerous favorable comments, but soon had to ward off the first of a series of attacks. In the summer of 1939, Thomas J. Kennedy charged in the *Homiletic and Pastoral Review* that the wording of the new translation of Jn 1:15 was "unquestionably incorrect, if not heretical." The translation read "He who is to come after me, has been made above me, because he was before me." In Kennedy's mind, this translation denied the divinity of Christ. Even casual reference to the Greek would have shown the impossibility of this rendering, he argued, and after a tedious lesson in Greek grammar, he concluded that the new version was "to say the least, strongly tinged with Arianism."[20]

Newton was furious. He immediately wrote O'Hara, who had been transferred to Kansas City. "Mr. Kennedy's rather confident charge of *proxima heresi* should be challenged," he stated. Kennedy, he believed, had been Callan's unsuccessful candidate for the editorial board and was

now manifesting his disappointment and at the same time serving the ends of the editor of the Spenser [*sic*] version. If this type of attack goes without notice, while the text is still in the process of editing, we may imagine what will be done when we come to publication.

The article itself hardly warrants an answer. The suspected heresy in the verse in question goes back to St. Jerome, if not earlier, from whom we have in the Vg. "factus est." But beyond this the tone of the entire article is plainly mean, intending to convey the notion that the revisor, and the editors, knew so little Greek that so obvious a point escaped them. He did not see my discussion of this very point in the second issue of the Biblical Quarterly. I am trying to overlook the personal affront that I suffer in the matter, that being of less concern than the interests of the Revision itself. For this reason I have not, and do not intend to write Callan.[21]

O'Hara protested to Callan for publicizing the text, intended for circulation only among the bishops and scholars, and for publishing an article, charging the new text was heretical.[22] Edward Cerny, S.S., professor of Scripture at St. Mary's Seminary in Baltimore then defended Newton's preliminary text in the *Catholic Biblical Quarterly*. He noted that Newton's translation was not dissimilar to that of either Wendell Reilly's in the Westminster Version or to Callan and McHugh's edition of the Spencer edition.[23] This was, however, not to be the last objection which Callan raised to the project.

THE CONFRATERNITY EDITION OF THE NEW TESTAMENT

In the spring of 1941, the Confraternity edition of the New Testament was finally published. It was entitled officially "A Revision of the Challoner-Rheims Version." The disputed text in John's Gospel had been revised to read: "He who is to come after me has been set above me, because he was before me." The introductions, however, were distinctly conservative. The Gospel of Matthew, for instance, was attributed to the Apostle Matthew, who had originally written in Aramaic. The version, for example, made no reference to the disputed authorship of the Pastoral Epistles. It did, however, acknowledge that Paul may not have been the author of the Epistle to the Hebrews, but that the work was at least "conceived by Paul and written under his direction," though the "excellent literary style . . . is generally superior to that found in the other Epistles of St. Paul." This, however, was well within the bounds of the Biblical Commission's response of 1914.[24]

O'Hara procured the assistance of the Holy Name Society, established in every parish, to distribute the new edition. Moreover, he had printed in the frontispiece a letter from Cardinal Eugène Tisserant, president of the Biblical Commission, and Vosté, the secretary, congratulating him on the completion of the work and praising his decision to have the Holy Name Society distribute it to insure "easily and quickly the widespread dissemination of the written word of God in the Catholic homes of your beloved country."[25] Both the publication of this letter and the publication of a lectionary of the Sunday readings caused, as will be seen, further controversies. The Confraternity edition, however, received little notice in non-Catholic scholarly circles, though Newton later informed O'Hara that Sperry of the Harvard Divinity School had written that the editors of the "American Revised Bible" were referring to the new translation.[26]

Members of the Catholic Biblical Association were well aware of the limitations of their translation. From the outset, Newton foresaw the difficulties of translating from the Vulgate. In his presidential address to the association in November 1941, Edward J. Byrne of St. Bernard's Seminary in Rochester made this point. In many instances, he pointed out, the

readings of the Vulgate as followed do not agree with the critical edition of the Greek text. These facts help to emphasize the truth that the Vulgate readings which are at the basis of our revised version are from the standpoint of textual criticism only one of the many sources of information which have to be weighed in judging what was the original text. It would consequently be regrettable if the Confraternity Edition were to be used by our seminarians as an adequate foundation for the laying of the foundations of our faith. No version from the viewpoint of textual criticism can adequately fill the place of a critical text based on the study of the best Greek manuscripts. . . .[27]

Byrne's address was but a reminder of papal teaching since *Providentissimus Deus* that serious students of the Scripture should have recourse to the original languages, though the Vulgate was to be the text used in theological disputations and in the liturgy. While American scholars were thus expressing their reservations about their new translation, strong criticism came from both inside and outside the Catholic Church.

On December 8, 1941, Callan patronizingly told O'Hara he still had difficulties with portions of John's Gospel and with numerous grammatical points. Newton, he declared, "showed from the beginning that he had no more scientific knowledge of the use of these verbs than a boy in grammar school [and] opposed me in this matter, though you had appointed me, and not him, as English editor of the Revision." In particular, he was objecting to Newton's substitution of the "Protestant 'will' for the Catholic Challoner 'shall.' " For Callan, these changes significantly altered "the meaning of innumerable texts, taking American Protestant authorities as our guide in place of Catholic, traditional and classical authorities." This was not simply a matter of grammar, for "these changes mean nothing to Protestants, who for the most part regard the Bible as mere literature; but with Catholics it is a question of expressing exactly in the idiom of our language what the Holy Ghost as principal author and the hagiographer as secondary writer intended and wanted to say." In other words, Callan seemed to believe that updating the language of translation to make it conform with contemporary usage endangered inspiration itself. He came dangerously close to doing what Loisy feared would happen by accepting Franzelin's theory of inspiration—attributing to a translation the inspiration of the Scripture in the original languages.

CHARLES CALLAN, O.P. AND THE PONTIFICAL BIBLICAL COMMISSION

But Callan had another ploy. He had been named a consultor to the Biblical Commission several years before. He now informed O'Hara that

> there has been considerable misunderstanding about the attitude up to date of the Biblical Commission towards our New Revision. I am authorized to make known and make clear that the Biblical Commission has given no official approval of our finished work on the Confraternity New Testament. Individual members of the Commission did approve of the *project,* the President and the Secretary wrote a letter expressing their best wishes and congratulations; but I am authorized to declare that no word of the Commission so far uttered is to be construed into meaning a formal approval by that authoritative Pontifical body of the Confraternity New Testament as it now stands.[28]

Callan had, of course, neglected to mention that neither the Holy See nor the commission had ever approved of any vernacular translation.

O'Hara took offense at the Dominican's insinuations. Thanking him for his suggestions about translation of some of the verses, the bishop stated he was

surprised that you should deem it necessary to seek authorization to make known that the Biblical Commission has given no official approval of the Confraternity New Testament. Whoever supposed it had! No one to my knowledge asked the Biblical Commission to give such official approval. I should regard the publication of such a statement in regard to the Biblical Commission as silly.[29]

O'Hara sent copies of his letter to Archbishops John T. McNicholas, O.P., of Cincinnati and John G. Murray of St. Paul, both of whom served on the bishops' committee of the Confraternity of Christian Doctrine. He was mustering his forces for the battle he knew was in the offing.

Not to be put off by the polite reprimand of a mere bishop, Callan now sought to enhance his influence in the American church, at least in regard to biblical studies. On April 17, 1942, Cardinal Tisserant, the president of the Biblical Commission, wrote O'Hara. Callan's influence on the letter was patent. The Pontifical Biblical Commission had compared the Confraternity New Testament and the Challoner version, said the cardinal,

and certain stylistic divergencies have been revealed which seemed less favorable to the new text. In view of the high esteem and authority in which Challoner's Version has always been held in all English-speaking countries by reason of the excellency of its classical style and theological accuracy, the new version should not depart from the primitive text except for very serious reasons and for definitely justified corrections.
Therefore, as the intervention of the Pontifical Biblical Commission in this matter has been formally requested by the Confraternity of Christian Doctrine—an intervention accepted most willingly in the interests of your praiseworthy and splendid enterprise—, I esteem it my duty, for the benefit of the new Catholic Version, as well as for the name of the Biblical Commission, to recommend a serious revision, which should be entrusted to the representative of the Pontifical Biblical Commission in America, the Very Reverend Father Charles J. Callan, O.P.
I wish to avail myself of the present opportunity to state that the letter of March 6th (N.21/41) was intended as an encouragement and a recom-

mendation of your enterprise, but not as a formal approbation of a text which had not as yet been published at the date of our letter.[30]

The letter could not have been more of an affront to the American hierarchy. O'Hara lost no time in mobilizing opposition.

First, he drafted a response to Tisserant. He thanked the cardinal for the "continued interest in the work undertaken by the episcopal committee of the Confraternity of Christian Doctrine . . . to revise the English text of the Sacred Scriptures through the collaboration of the group of thirty Scripture scholars who hold chairs of Scripture in the seminaries of this country." The episcopal committee had already begun further revision, he continued, even while the first printing was being distributed. The Holy Name Society's "cooperation" in that distribution, he noted, had "won the recognition of Your Eminence in the letter published as a foreword to the Holy Name edition." Then O'Hara came to the point. Callan, he said, had attempted "to thwart the work of the episcopal committee by publishing a reprint" of the Spencer edition "at a moment when the episcopal committee had announced the new edition of the Scriptures." The Dominican had, furthermore, engaged Kennedy, "who knew nothing of patrology or hermeneutics to criticize a version of the Gospel of Saint John from a purely etymological angle." The suggestion to have "the work of all Scripture scholars of the United States . . . submitted" to Callan, therefore, "would seem to deserve further consideration on the part of Your Eminence lest irreparable harm might be done to the work of the organization of Scripture Scholars who have consecrated themselves to a monumental task and as doctors of the Biblical Institute at Rome are aware of the manifest limitations of Father Callan in the field of biblical research."[31] On May 15, O'Hara sent copies of Tisserant's letter and of the draft of his response to Archbishops McNicholas and Murray. To Newton he forwarded only Tisserant's letter.[32]

McNicholas's response was a devastating critique of Callan's delusions of being recognized as the country's foremost biblical scholar. His proposed strategy was first to enlist the aid of Archbishop Amleto Cicognani, the apostolic delegate, and then to thank Tisserant for his continued interest in the Confraternity edition. He had heard, he continued, of Vosté's "opinion about Father Callan," but he was "entirely convinced" it was "very much exaggerated." McNicholas had been student master when Callan was a student in 1904. He thought Callan was a "good theologian," but "not an eminent Scripture scholar." As for Callan considering "himself a master of English," it was an "opinion," said McNicholas, which "I personally cannot accept." But of one thing the archbishop was "certain, in all the years I have known Father Callan he has resorted to scheming, which has seemed to me very unworthy." While McNicholas thought the episcopal committee should proceed delicately in presenting its case to the Biblical Commission, he was also "convinced that Father Callan is capable of using this Pontifical Commission for selfish reasons, for an approval which he is likely to interpret as singling him out as the most outstanding Biblical scholar in the United States, and for publicity reasons which he is apt to turn to his own advantage even if the Pontifical Biblical Commission is somewhat compromised."[33]

McNicholas also recalled that the bishops of the Province of Cincinnati had signed a protest to Cardinal Patrick Hayes of New York about the articles which had appeared in the *Homiletic and Pastoral Review*. But Hayes personally told McNicholas that, despite the reproof he had given to Callan and McHugh, his assistant editor, they "had another scheme of advertising their publication which the Cardinal considered very dangerous and morally untenable." McNicholas thought that the episcopal committee should frankly tell Tisserant

that we as Bishops charged by the whole American hierarchy to undertake the work of the new translation are not willing to assume the responsibility of entrusting a "serious revision" to Father Callan. Let us ask if we may appoint a commission to make this "serious revision," of which Father Callan will be only a member.

After this strong attack on Callan, McNicholas, nevertheless, disagreed with O'Hara's proposed response to Tisserant and recommended that he immediately consult Cicognani.[34]

Newton's response focused on Tisserant's reference to "stylistic divergencies" between the Challoner and Confraternity editions. He pointed out that the Code of Canon Law clearly gave the bishops the authority to supervise translations into the vernacular. If the commission members thought Challoner's version enjoyed such "high esteem and authority," they were simply misinformed, for it had "never been the 'official' text of the United States" and the Westminster, Spencer, Confraternity, and forthcoming Knox editions indicated the strong reservations about it. In regard to Challoner's "classical style," Newton could only call to mind that both Newman and Wiseman believed a revision was necessary and that only Callan had criticized the Confraternity's "use of 'shall' and 'will.' " Newton was further "unaware that a formal request for the intervention of the Pontifical Biblical Commission had been made on the part of the Confraternity of Christian Doctrine." The only correspondence between the Confraternity and the commission, which he could recall, had occurred at the beginning of the project, when Frey, then the secretary of the commission, concurred with the principles suggested for the revision.[35]

Newton objected more strongly to Tisserant's recommendation of a "serious revision," which would take "the work out of the hands of a carefully selected group of trained scholars, two of whom have the Doctorate in Scripture, sixteen the Licentiate in Scripture, and ten the Doctorate in Theology with special work in Scripture," and would place "it under the responsibility of one man whose training in this field is rather limited." The revision committee, already appointed, had called for criticisms at its meeting in November, when "Fr. Callan was present and said not a single word." Newton suspected that, though the letter was signed by Tisserant, it was written by Vosté, who was now contradicting what he had written in his own introduction to the Spencer version where he favored translations from the original languages. In fine, Newton thought the letter ignored the fact that the revision had taken place under the auspices of the episcopal committee. Were the letter to be implemented, he concluded,

it would deal a mortal blow to the biblical scholarship of this country, a scholarship which is just wakening from its lethargy. It will mean the indefinite postponement of the much needed revision of our Old Testament in English, and of the commentary on the New Testament which is ready for the press.[36]

O'Hara put together the responses and requested a meeting with Archbishop Cicognani early in June. Enclosing a copy of McNicholas's letter, he stated that it represented the unanimous opinion of the episcopal committee. He also asked McNicholas if he would be the spokesman with the delegate.[37] On June 10, however, O'Hara went to Washington alone. The delegate "read carefully the first draft of the letter to Cardinal Tisseront [*sic*]," the bishop told McNicholas, "and suggested that it be made even stronger in its references to the unsuitability of Father Callan as chief editor." Cicognani agreed to forward the letter to Tisserant and to write the cardinal "that he has seen the letter and approves it and will furthermore add his own representations."[38]

To McNicholas fell the task of preparing the final draft of the protest to Tisserant. Thanking the cardinal for the interest of the Biblical Commission in the revision project, the letter stated that the bishops felt sure he would want "them to speak with complete frankness" on several points. First, the Challoner version had been long felt to be inadequate and "the Episcopal Committee begs to state that the Confraternity revision has had the assurance of eminent theological censors which the Challoner version did not have." Second, the bishops "did not petition the Pontifical Biblical Commission to intervene," and did not consider Frey's letter, approving the principles of revision, "to be official." Third, the letter addressed the principal issue of Callan's involvement. "The members of the Episcopal Committee," the letter stated, "are most anxious that the Biblical scholars of the country, under the guidance of the American Hierarchy, continue their studies so that the Confraternity revision can bring out new editions from time to time." Accordingly, the bishops felt compelled to declare that

The request of Your eminence asking that "a serious revision" should be entrusted to one priest gives us Bishops very serious concern. Moved by the greatest sense of reverence due to the Holy See and with loyalty to the Pontifical Biblical Commission, it is our considered judgment that we of ourselves cannot assume the responsibility of asking Father Charles J. Callan, O.P., to bring out another edition of the Confraternity revision which will be a "serious revision." We cannot regard Father Callan as an eminent Biblical scholar. We wish to assure Your Eminence that the Scriptural scholars of the United States do not consider him in any sense an outstanding Scriptural scholar. Father Callan has certain merits as a theologian, but, even in this field, the theological censors appointed for the Confraternity revision rejected, after very careful consideration, the objections made by Father Callan.

There were yet more telling reservations about Callan's competence. Several years earlier, he had published in the *Homiletic and Pastoral Review* several articles on hell, for which he was "condemned by many of our Bishops and by Cardinal Hayes." The apostolic delegate demanded a retraction from Callan or else would bring the *Homiletic* "to the attention of the Holy Office." These articles showed Callan "lacking in judgment," wishing "for publicity at any price," and "consequently unqualified to be placed in charge of a revision of the New Testament." In view of all these objections, McNicholas declared:

To put Father Callan, now, in a position where all the Scripture scholars of the United States will have to accept the "serious revision" made by him will shock our Bishops and priests; it will belittle the work of the Commission of Scripture scholars representing the Bishops of the United States, and it will be interpreted as a withdrawal of the confidence of Rome in the work of this committee. We can assure Your Eminence that the Scripture scholars, who are wholeheartedly devoted to the Church and the inspired text, do not regard Father Callan as a serious Biblical scholar.

McNicholas concluded the letter by stating that the members of the episcopal committee never considered Tisserant's letter of March 6, 1941, as an explicit "approval" of the translation. "For some unknown reason," he continued, "Father Callan seems obsessed with the idea that the Episcopal Committee so considered it or that it was necessary for him, as a member [*sic*] of the Pontifical Biblical Commission, to announce to the country that no official approval had been given by Your Eminence." The committee had merely taken the letter as encouragement to the Holy Name Society and would omit it from future printings of the Confraternity New Testament.[39] The letter was strong, and it certainly did not hurt the cause of the American bishops that such opposition to Callan came from a fellow Dominican.

The committee dated the final letter June 27 and sent it to Cicognani, who promised to add "a personal letter of my own urging the viewpoint manifested by the Bishops."[40] With mail during wartime slowed down, Tisserant did not reply until October 14. The committee was "correct," he said, in stating that the Biblical Commission did "not wish to be associated officially with the work of revision," for

it is the unquestioned privilege of the Episcopal Hierarchy to procure for the faithful committed to their care suitable translations in the vernacular of the Sacred Scriptures. The recommendation, therefore, of Father Callan, O.P., . . . was intended simply as a suggestion submitted to the Episcopal Committee, which we cordially thank for the frankness of its statement in his regard.

While it was "not the intention of the Commission to discuss this matter," Tisserant thought it important to note that, when he visited the United States in 1927, he heard the proposal "to over-throw the traditional use of the auxiliary verbs *shall* and *will*, a change which, so long as it were not universal, might easily result in discrepancies as to the exact signification of certain sentences in texts of theological interest." Only for that reason had he spoken of the Challoner version "as a standard for the observance of grammatical rules, rather than for the value of its style." He admitted that he "should have expressed [his preoccupations] more clearly," but, he continued, "it is enough for me to know that the Members of the Episcopal Committee are personally supervis-ing the preparation of the revised English Translation of the Sa-cred Scriptures; I had never doubted their capacity and zeal."[41] Tisserant's response, couched in curial rhetoric, was, of course, a complete retraction of his earlier letter.

On the same day as Tisserant's letter, Vosté wrote Callan in a tone that suggested, as McNicholas had already intimated, that the two of them were in collusion. The bishops, he said, had written Tisserant "explaining the difficulties they had against our proposal to submit to your revision the new version of the Bible." He noted that "my first idea was that we had not to interfere in that local business of litterary [*sic*] nature," but now the bishops would have to "take their responsibility" for the edition. Tisserant, neverthe-less, hoped that, in the future revisions, "you will help the com-mon enterprise." Vosté had already informed Monsignor Barton that "the critics should also have full liberty to reveal the mistakes of the new version," but his final counsel to Callan was "not to move war against the Bishops" and seek "the advice of dear Father McHugh."[42]

The exchange between the bishops and Tisserant ended Cal-lan's conspiracy to undermine the Confraternity edition. But the issue concerned not only Callan's ambition, but also the authority of the American bishops. Either they were to have the right, ac-cording to the Code of Canon Law, to supervise vernacular translations of the Scripture or they were to be totally dependent on a Roman congregation in what pertained to the exercise of their pastoral ministry. Callan was neither the first nor the last American cleric to attempt to exercise extraordinary Roman authority in the American church. He represented the trend toward Romanization which had begun in the beginning of the century. The bishops' support of the nascent American scholarship was a step away from that process of Romanization and toward the collegiality and the recognition of the particular needs of a national church, which the Second Vatican Council would recognize. Callan, however, was not yet silenced and would raise his voice in opposition in regard to another issue several years later.

CHARGES THAT THE CCD NEW TESTAMENT WAS ANTI-SEMITIC

No sooner had the bishops temporarily leashed Callan than the Confraternity edition received attacks from a different quarter. First, the National Conference of Christians and Jews, and then the Jewish Anti-Defamation League protested that the translation was anti-Semitic. Both organizations objected to the rendering of Apocalypse 2:9. The translation read: "and thou art slandered by those who say they are Jews and are not, but are a synagogue of Satan." A note explained: "the Jews are the *synagogue of Satan*. The true synagogue is the Christian Church."[43] "How sensitive the Conference is on the Jewish side," Newton retorted, "and how lethargic when Jews offend Christian feelings."[44] He responded to the criticisms, but then proposed that the notes be changed in subsequent editions.[45] Though such complaints were relatively minor, the new edition was not reviewed in any non-Catholic journals.

THE BIBLICAL COMMISSION AND VERNACULAR TRANSLATION FROM THE ORIGINAL LANGUAGES

In the meantime, while World War II was still raging, Pius XII turned his attention to biblical scholarship. In August 1943, the Biblical Commission issued a clarification of its response to the Dutch bishops in 1934. It now explicitly stated that translations for the use of the faithful could be made from the original languages, but that the pericopes used in the liturgy were to be translated from the Vulgate.[46] In September, the pope issued his revolutionary encyclical, *Divino Afflante Spiritu,* which called for scholars to apply the historical method to the sacred books. The encyclical also stated that Trent had not forbidden "translations into the vulgar tongue, even directly from the original texts themselves, for the use and benefit of the faithful and for the better understanding of the divine word, as We know to have been already done in a laudable manner in many countries with the approval of Ecclesiastical authority."[47] It was not the encyclical, however, but the Biblical Commission's response that, as will be seen, provided American Catholic scholars with the encouragement to undertake their translation from the original languages. That response also occasioned another attack from a now familiar source.

"AMATOR EVANGELII" AND THE CONFRATERNITY NEW TESTAMENT

Early in 1944, the *Homiletic and Pastoral Review* published the commission's response of the previous August, but Callan and McHugh concentrated their analysis only on the section pertaining to the liturgical pericopes. In their mind, the response unequivocally required that the translations used at Mass strictly conform to the Vulgate, which, they said, the Confraternity did not. Next, there appeared a letter from a reader, "Amator Evangelii," who was probably Callan himself. "Amator" stated that "in view of the reiterated ruling of the Holy See contained in the response, I do not see how the Confraternity renderings of many of the Sunday pericopes can be read from the pulpit." As examples, he cited two passages that he asserted were inaccurate translations of the Vulgate. John J. Collins, S.J., of Weston College, had translated Phil 2:6 as: "Christ Jesus, . . . though he was by nature God, did not consider being equal to God a thing to be clung to." "Amator" challenged "whether the orthodoxy of this particular rendering was 'diligently examined by men excelling in . . . theological science,' as ordered by the Holy See." In his opinion, the verse was not only a bad translation of the Latin, but also endangered the doctrine of the equality of Father and Son.[48]

The second passage was Newton's rendering of Jn. 2:4 as "What wouldst thou have me do, woman?" For "Amator," this was more than a bad translation. In a display of creative exegesis, he argued that it "would . . . deprive Mary's clients of the most explicit confirmation by Our Saviour of their confidence in the efficacy of Our Lady's intercession."[49]

Joseph L. Lilly, C.M., general secretary of the Catholic Biblical Association, with O'Hara's encouragement, protested against the attack in the next issue of the *Homiletic and Pastoral Review*. The Confraternity edition had been approved by the American bishops, as required by the Biblical Commission's response, he stated, and it was not for "Amator Evangelii" or any other priest to take it upon himself to decide "to approve or reprobate vernacular versions." The Biblical Commission did not require that a "version must be slavishly literal before it can conform to the requirements of the Biblical Commission for pulpit reading," he continued, and the Challoner-Rheims version itself fell far short of this norm.[50]

The *Homiletic and Pastoral Review*, however, was hardly the forum for a scholarly discussion. Printed with Lilly's letter was a response from "Amator Evangelii." No priest had the right to determine the proper version of Scripture, he argued, but every priest had the right to choose between two approved versions. Continuing his attack on the two passages he cited, he contended that "I did not dream of suggesting that my interpretation should be *imposed on anyone*—much less that it should be imposed *on everyone* by being incorporated into an official version to be read in the public services of the Church, as the Confraternity Version has done with its purely private and personal surmise."[51] "Amator Evangelii" was, of course, contradicting himself by first acknowledging the right of the bishops to approve vernacular editions and then arguing that the Confraternity edition contained "purely private and personal surmise."

Since "Amator" had attacked the ecclesiastical authority, with which the Confraternity edition was published, this became the focal point of the next stage in the debate. Michael J. Gruenthaner, S.J., editor of the *Catholic Biblical Quarterly*, defended the edition in an article in the *American Ecclesiastical Review*, which had as large a circulation among priests as the *Homiletic*. After refuting "Amator's" grammatical and theological arguments, he concluded that

we hope that *Amator Evangelii* will gird himself like a man and make the *amende honorable* to Fr. Lilly, the theological censors, and the bishops whom he has insulted with so little cause and so grievously. We regret that the editors of the *Homiletic and Pastoral Review* were so beguiled into accepting these communications of *Amator Evangelii*.[52]

Gruenthaner, of course, was well aware that Callan and McHugh, the editors of the journal, were not only responsible for "Amator" but had also tried to undermine the Confraternity project from the beginning. O'Hara ordered copies of Gruenthaner's article distributed to every bishop and priest in the United States.[53] Even this overt ecclesiastical defense, however, did not silence "Amator," who published one more criticism of the new version. But by this time his arguments were becoming too tendentious to gain much of a hearing.[54]

"Amator's" criticisms of the Confraternity were reminiscent of the difficulties Kenrick had particularly with Reynolds. Moreover, they illustrated the extent to which certain Catholics would resist any change in the familiar language of their Bible—a resistance that would again be voiced in the 1960s when the liturgical pericopes, translated from the original languages, were first read in the Mass. But, by 1944, biblical scholarship, including translations of the Bible, was undergoing dramatic change. In retrospect, "Amator's" attack was a last-ditch effort. The Biblical Commission's response of August 1943, which had occasioned "Amator's" diatribes, provided the basis for O'Hara to instruct the translators of the Old Testament to work from the original languages. This represented the abandonment of the translation of the Old Testament from the Vulgate, one third of which had been completed late in 1941.[55]

THE CONFRATERNITY BEGINS THE TRANSLATION FROM THE ORIGINAL LANGUAGES

By February 1944, the text of *Divino Afflante Spiritu* had still not arrived in the United States. Newton, nevertheless, urged O'Hara to use the Biblical Commission's clarification on vernacular translations as the basis for having the episcopal committee approve the translation of the Old Testament from the original languages. He recalled his visit to Rome in 1938 and noted that Vosté, who had urged the use of the original languages, had now become the secretary of the Biblical Commission, which had issued the new response. He further argued that the British and American tradition of translating the Vulgate had developed in the midst of Protestant controversy, but had not been required either by the Council of Trent or by the Code of Canon Law. By attempting to correct the Clementine Vulgate against the Hebrew text, he continued, the revision procedures were unwieldy. Nor could he accept the argument that a translation from the Hebrew "might result in a disturbance of our laity," for "the fact is that the Catholic laity do not know or use the Old Testament. The current text has discouraged all but rare hardy souls from reading any of it."[56]

O'Hara was already sympathetic with Newton's proposal. He first circularized other members of the editorial committee and then wrote Archbishops McNicholas and Cicognani. The Biblical Commission's response, he wrote McNicholas, "if not directive, seems strongly to advise that the translation be from the original languages." Enclosing a copy of Newton's memorandum, he mentioned that he had also received a letter from Cuthbert Lattey, who urged that the Old Testament be translated from the original languages, except for the Psalms, which were used in the divine office. O'Hara was particularly concerned that, since the translation from the Vulgate was already underway, the episcopal committee would have to decide on the matter as quickly as possible.[57] With Cicognani, O'Hara used similar arguments.[58] But the task of using the original languages was not as simple as it at first seemed. Arbez pointed out that, while he certainly preferred a translation from the Hebrew, "it must be a critically corrected Hebrew."[59]

Early in March, O'Hara informed Newton of the episcopal committee's decision. The biblical scholars were to abandon their translation of the Old Testament from the Vulgate and begin their work from the Hebrew text, except for the Psalms, a critical Latin edition of which was then being completed in Rome.[60] Late in April, the bishop also notified Newton that he was to be chairman of a new committee to study a translation of the New Testament from the Greek.[61]

In August, the Catholic Biblical Association held its meeting at St. Mary's College, Notre Dame, Indiana. Shortly before the meeting, O'Hara received a letter from Cicognani praising the efforts of the association in undertaking to translate the Old Testament from the original languages. Citing *Divino Afflante Spiritu,* the delegate said this work was conformable "to the recommendations of

His Holiness." But he also recognized the "magnitude and importance of this undertaking," which he thought,

should elicit the interest, sympathetic understanding, and aid, as far as possible of both clergy and laity. The difficulty of this noble work arises from the very nature of things. Each language has its own proper genius and idioms. The difficulty is enhanced when the translator is dealing with ancient languages such as biblical Hebrew and Greek. The books of the Old Testament were composed in centuries long since past, and all of us are well aware how distances of time and divergences of custom can be obstacles to the acquisition of adequate knowledge of the events and of the language and manner in which they are narrated. Not infrequently the simple fact of translation must be an interpretation. Hence, perfection cannot be demanded, and no translation can ever hope to win the unreserved approval of every scholar. In the light of modern findings in the fields of archaeology and philology, the divine message of the Scriptures is constantly being set forth with ever greater clarity.

Cicognani, then, was sensitive to the problems that would arise from such a new endeavor. He was aware that any translation would have its detractors, but he reminded his readers of the words of Pius XII in his encyclical, that all "should bear in mind that the efforts of these resolute laborers in the vineyard of the Lord should be judged not only with equity and justice, but also with the greatest charity; all moreover should abhor that intemperate zeal which imagines that whatever is new should for that very reason be opposed or suspected."[62] Written within a few months of the "Amator Evangelii" diatribes against the Confraternity New Testament, Cicognani's letter may well have been intended to silence future detractors. It was published in the front of the October 1944 issue of the *Catholic Biblical Quarterly*.

It would, however, take more than two decades for American Catholic scholars to produce a translation of the entire Bible from the original languages. The translation project became only one of the aspects of biblical scholarship. When O'Hara summoned biblical professors to Washington to begin work on a new translation or revision of the Douay Bible, he set in motion a broader and more significant movement—the founding of the Catholic Biblical Association and the development of a mature American Catholic biblical scholarship.

11. The Catholic Biblical Association: The Formative Years

The primary intention of the Scripture professors' meeting in Washington on January 18, 1936, was to discuss the translation of the New Testament. They also voted to meet again at the annual convention of the Confraternity of Christian Doctrine in order to consider founding a permanent biblical society. All priests teaching Scripture, both diocesan and religious, were invited to attend the convention that began in New York on October 3, 1936.

THE FOUNDING OF THE CATHOLIC BIBLICAL ASSOCIATION.

Bishop Edwin V. O'Hara opened the meeting of Scripture professors and designated Edward Arbez to lead the proceedings. Thomas à Kempis Reilly, O.P., who had earlier in the century unsuccessfully attempted to explain Lagrange's theory of inspiration to Anthony Maas, then delivered an address on "The Bible and the Laity." Thomas Plassman, O.F.M., read a paper entitled "Nova et Vetera." Afterwards, Romain Butin, S.M., took the floor to pose a series of questions to be discussed in preparation for the founding of the association. All present unanimously voted to establish the association. Initially, they considered calling their organization the "St. Jerome's Society," but then decided on "The Catholic Biblical Association of America," under the patronage of St. Jerome.

Butin's statement of the association's purpose was twofold: to provide the episcopal committee of the Confraternity of Christian Doctrine with "a body of men qualified to study and work out biblical problems" and to afford an opportunity for Scripture professors to become better acquainted, to encourage the development of scriptural scholarship, and to enable the laity "to cooperate in the advancement and diffusion of biblical knowledge." In regard to membership, the assembly voted to make no distinction between clerical and lay members, since "a layman might be able to contribute to the advancement of Biblical science" and "there is here no question of teaching authority."

The association was to meet annually in conjunction with the Confraternity of Christian Doctrine, but the members strongly recommended that regional associations be formed and meet semiannually. The assembly postponed decision, however, on Butin's further suggestion to start a periodical and other projects. The association was to have a two-tiered organization: an "episcopal board of moderators" appointed by the bishops and a "regular board" consisting of a president, two vice presidents, two consultors, a corresponding secretary, an executive secretary, and a treasurer. The funds of the association were temporarily to be deposited with the Confraternity of Christian Doctrine. This first meeting of the association concluded by electing officers: Edward P. Arbez, president; William L. Newton and William J. McGarry, S.J., of Weston College, vice presidents; Wendell S. Reilly, S.S., of St. Mary's Seminary, Thomas Plassman, O.F.M., of St. Bonaventure's, consultors; Edward H. Donze, S.M., of the Marist Seminary in Washington, corresponding secretary; John F. Rowan of St. Charles Seminary, Overbrook, in Philadelphia, executive secretary; and John E. Steinmueller of the Seminary of the Immaculate Conception, Huntington, New York, treasurer. These officers, together with the representatives of the episcopal board, were to draw up the constitution and bylaws of the new association.[1]

THE CONSTITUTION OF THE CBA

On April 11, 1937, the officers met with O'Hara at the Sulpician Seminary in Washington. All were present except McGarry and Rowan. By that date, the association already had eighty-three members. In the morning, the officers drafted a constitution, and, in the afternoon appointed committees to carry on the work of the association between general meetings, the first of which was to take place at the Confraternity's next convention in St. Louis on October 10–11, 1937.[2] The proposed constitution made some changes from the general outline of the association agreed upon at New York the previous fall. There was to be only one vice president, but there were to be new offices: an editor, two associate editors, and a librarian. All were to be elected to a term of one year at the annual meeting, except the consultors, who were to be appointed by the episcopal committee of the Confraternity. The president and vice president were ineligible for immediate reelection. One additional change was a minor one—the office of "executive secretary" was renamed "general secretary."[3]

The officers then drew up bylaws. The association was to have its headquarters at the Catholic University of America and the general secretary was to reside in the vicinity. The establishment of standing committees, particularly the program committee, showed the close relationship they envisioned between the hierarchy and the biblical association. The program committee was to consist of the president, the consultors, appointed by the episcopal committee, the general secretary, and the editor; it was to approve all papers to be read at the annual meetings. The nominating committee was to draw up lists of candidates for elective office, but nominations from the floor of the meeting were to have equal standing. The committee on membership, appointed by the president with the approval of the executive board, was to examine the credentials of prospective members, which, according to this first constitution, included "all Catholics, duly elected members and paying regular dues," stipulated to be $5.00 a year. There was no other qualification for membership. Finally, the committee on enlargement of resources had the charge of raising funds for the association.[4]

The constitution and bylaws were relatively straightforward. On the one hand, the Catholic Biblical Association was now beginning to take shape. On the other, the officers did not yet seem to have a clear idea of the nature of a scholarly organization. The association's close connection with the Confraternity of Christian Doctrine was understandable in light of the translation project, but it would create a tension between scholarly and catechetical objectives in the future. Moreover, the lack of any scholarly credentials for membership would cause future difficulties. More indicative of emerging American scholarship was the list of eight papers approved for the program in St. Louis, all concerning revision of the

Scripture. One, merely from its title, however, was provocative. Butin's was entitled "Some Evidence of Revision of the Hebrew Text in Ancient Times."[5]

The Catholic Biblical Association held its first general meeting in St. Louis on October 9 and 10, 1937. After O'Hara opened the proceedings, the members present voted to adopt the constitution. While most of the discussion centered on the revision project, Butin's paper presented a cautious, yet scholarly approach to the issue of the Mosaic authorship, which had so preoccupied biblical scholarship at the beginning of the century. "We shall not attempt here to prove that the Pentateuch substantially goes back to Moses," he said,

It does; on this point there is not a dissenting voice in all the Biblical and Jewish tradition. Moses was inaugurating a new nation with a definite program of conquest and eventual settlement in Palestine, and he wanted to provide for it. To say that Moses promulgates only such laws as were to meet the conditions in which the Israelites were placed in the desert while Moses was present, supposes that Moses knew nothing of Palestine or of Mesopotamia or of Egypt where there were settled populations, with a well established set of laws. He was legislating both for the present and also for the future. Nor did the legislation of Moses consist only of oral decisions. All of our authorities speak of a written code, the Book (Sepher), or the law of Moses. On this point, also, there is no dissenting voice in tradition. However, it does not mean that there has been no addition, or no change of any kind. A code of laws is an organic element of the life of the people, and hence it is to be expected that some of the enactments should be expanded, paraphrased, interpreted so as to meet conditions that may arise in the course of time.[6]

Butin was well within the norms of the Biblical Commission's decision on the Mosaic authorship, but he did add certain nuances.

Butin was careful not to speak of the sources of the Pentateuch. Unlike the Biblical Commission, which had spoken of uninspired glosses and additions, however, he noted a series of "insertions and expansions [which] were written under inspiration and their inerrancy, therefore, is beyond question."[7] He left open the question of what theory of inspiration he espoused, but would seem to imply that it extended to subsequent redactors. He, furthermore, pointed to the evidence for the modernization of language. Such revision, he concluded was "likely to occur at times when there

[was] . . . a renewal of literary, religious, or national activity," such as during the period of David and Solomon, of Ezechiel, and of the exile and restoration.[8] Cautious though Butin may have been, he did at least indicate the difficulty of interpreting the statement literally that Moses was the author of the Pentateuch. The possibility of his taking a bolder stance in the future was abruptly cut off when he was killed in an automobile accident on December 8, 1937, less than two months after delivering his address.

The first general meeting of the Biblical Association also voted to establish a periodical, *The Catholic Biblical Quarterly (CBQ)*, and then proceeded to elect officers, according to the newly approved constitution. Newton was elected president with William A. Dowd, S.J., of the Chicago archdiocesan seminary in Mundelein, Illinois, as vice president. The members then voted to designate as "charter members" the one hundred Scripture professors, who had already joined the association, and the bishops who had offered their support, either financially by becoming a "patron" or "life member" or in some other fashion by becoming an "associate member."[9] One of the purposes of the Biblical Association was to encourage communication between biblical scholars. Initially, the CBA consisted solely of priests. A side effect was, therefore, to establish an organization that brought religious and diocesan priests together on both a professional and fraternal basis. From this viewpoint alone, the CBA was notable, for *Pascendi Dominici Gregis* had specifically forbidden meetings of priests, for these had been "among the means used by the modernists to propagate their opinions."[10] The passage of the encyclical occurred immediately before the command that bishops establish vigilance committees.

The association next turned to what would develop into its principal scholarly contribution to the American church—the founding of the *Catholic Biblical Quarterly*. At their meeting on April 24, 1938, the association's officers voted that the first issue of the new quarterly would appear on January 1, 1939, but they were ambivalent about its purpose. They stated that the journal was to be "both technical and practical so as to appeal to the biblical scholar and to the Priest and educated layman—helpful to the Leaders of the Confraternity of Christian Doctrine." It was to be "coextensive with the field of Bible study" and would include: "Research material and scholarly articles; Practical articles, (homiletics, select exegetical studies); News of the biblical world; Book reviews (the C.B.A. will set a high standard for its book reviews); Digest of current biblical literature; Work of biblical schools and institutes." It was to be "an organ of expression for the Active Members of the Association" and "all writers who could provide material worthy of the aims and interest of the Association."[11] The initial proposal for the *CBQ* was certainly ambitious and displayed the naïvete of the association at the time. As the CBA became more of an organization of scholars, it became impossible for the journal to publish both "technical" and "practical" articles.

EUROPEAN REACTIONS TO THE CBA

In the meanwhile, the proceedings of the first general meeting of the CBA were sent to John Baptist Frey, secretary of the Biblical Commission. Pleased with the founding of the CBA, he encouraged Newton that "by reason of your intelligent activity and fidelity to the doctrine of the Church," he would "contribute to the development of biblical studies, with a profoundly Catholic orientation which will receive the blessings of heaven upon your labors." Frey had not yet read all the articles of the proceedings, but he had carefully studied the constitution. He especially noted the importance of always acting "in a spirit of filial obedience to the directives of the Church," and was, therefore, pleased to see that the organization was "placed under the patronage of the bishops and that each of your meetings is presided over by one of them giving a complete guarantee of an excellent orientation." Frey may well have had in mind the proscriptions against priests' meetings in *Pascendi.* He concluded by saying he was looking forward to seeing Newton in Rome that summer.[12] Frey envisioned the association at this juncture as reflecting the mind of the bishops and taking its guidance from them. There was not yet an open espousal of scholarship.

Newton's primary purpose in going to Rome and England was, as was seen, to sound out Roman officials and English scholars about the new translation. But he also wanted their opinion on the CBA. Though he had no "special commission to speak of the Association in Rome," he told O'Hara, the topic frequently came up. He took with him bound copies of the proceedings of the first meeting and presented them to Pius XI and Cardinal Marchetti-

Salvaggiani, secretary of the Holy Office. He also gave copies of the constitution to Monsignor Alfredo Ottaviani, assessor of the Holy Office, and to English-speaking students at the Biblical Institute. Frey, as he had already written Newton, thought the association would "lead to a revival of biblical interest." Ottaviani was "enthusiastic" about the constitution, "deeming it particularly assuring of the orthodoxy of our undertakings, [but] . . . he warned of the need of vigilance when more biblical work is under way." This led Newton to comment that "our relations with the Hierarchy of the United States is a source of protection both for us and for the Church." Augustin Bea, S.J., rector of the Biblical Institute, thought the CBA "will be an occasion not only of more biblical work, but also of work of a higher scientific standard." The English-speaking students were uniformly positive about both the association and the proposed journal. Robert Dyson, S.J., had already written a review of the proceedings and gave notice to the CBA in both *Biblica* and *Verbum Domini*.[13]

Newton's report of his reception in England indicated that, at this point at least, he hoped the CBA would embrace the English-speaking world. He had received "particular instructions," he told O'Hara, "to interest the biblical men of England and Ireland in the Association." He found an opportunity at the Summer School at Cambridge to address the audience about the association. Cuthbert Lattey was enthusiastic and saw "no difficulty in forming a branch of the Assoc. in England and Ireland," but, continued Newton, he "suggested that we must work some means of making the Engl. branch of the Assoc. autonomous, since they will hardly agree to being merely an appendage on the American group." Barton thought the English members should have their own meetings and have their own officers "who might have a voice on the executive council," but publish their proceedings in the *CBQ*. He also offered his opinion that, if the organization was to be founded in England, it would need the support of the English hierarchy. Barton, therefore, recommended that the CBA's constitution be sent to the English and Irish bishops with an invitation to establish the association. Alexander Jones, professor at St. Joseph's, Upholland, suggested that the full title of "Catholic Biblical Association of America" be dropped, and that separate groups be formed in England and Ireland. He acknowledged, however, that the Americans would have to bear the brunt of the financial burden. Richard Foster of St. Mary's, Oscott, thought that, after a sufficient number of English members were enrolled, they could approach the English hierarchy to make the association part of the English Confraternity of Christian Doctrine. Canon Patrick Boylan, formerly of Maynooth, echoed the concern of "making either the Engl. or Irish branch appear as a tail on the American kite," though he himself planned to join and would work to establish an "Irish branch."[14] Newton's plan was grandiose, but it did illustrate his desire to have American scholars take the lead in biblical scholarship. As it turned out, however, while some English and Irish scholars joined the CBA, it was to become the association of biblical scholars of North America alone.

Newton was prepared to give a very optimistic report at the second annual meeting of the CBA in conjunction with the CCD convention at Hartford on October 1–2, 1938. As he prepared to issue a program for the meeting, however, O'Hara had one reservation. "In regard to the Biblical Quarterly," he wrote, "I think nothing should be said until we have time to consider the matter more carefully."[15] O'Hara seems to have dropped any opposition to the project, however, and the meeting voted to initiate the *Catholic Biblical Quarterly*, with Wendell S. Reilly, S.S., the first American to obtain the S.S.D. degree, as editor. Newton's presidential address, possibly reflecting the criticism his translation of John's Gospel had received, warned against destructive criticism. Alluding to Pius XI's encouragement to undertake scholarly criticism, he noted the amount of work done in biblical languages since the Council of Trent.[16]

The Catholic Biblical Quarterly AND *A Commentary on the New Testament*

The *Catholic Biblical Quarterly* provides a good barometer of the development of American Catholic biblical scholarship. The first issue appeared, as was hoped, in January, 1939. Reilly's editorial gave a preview of the articles, with particular attention to an article by Callan on "The Synoptic Problem." Callan disagreed with Dom Chapman's hypothesis that Mark depended on Matthew and argued that Peter could have had a copy of Matthew in Aramaic and that the Greek version of Matthew was essentially the same as the

Aramaic original. He preferred the theory of Vosté, which had a fivefold development of the Synoptics. First, Matthew and Peter had a primitive Aramaic catechesis. Second, there emerged an Aramaic version of Matthew. Third, Mark was derived from both Peter and Aramaic Matthew. Fourth, the Greek version of Matthew was compiled from both Aramaic Matthew and from Mark. Finally, Luke was dependent on Mark, St. Paul, the Virgin Mary, witnesses to the earthly life of Jesus, and perhaps *logia* taken from Greek Matthew.[17] Callan—and Vosté—was a bit ingenious in placing Peter at the basis of the synoptic tradition, as Maas had done at the end of the last century. But, at least he acknowledged that, in its present form, Mark was the oldest of the Gospels. Reilly advanced this argument still further the next year, when he asserted that Greek Matthew need not be the same as the lost Aramaic and may have depended on Mark.[18] American Catholic scholars were still hedging about the question that had been so controversial during the Modernist crisis. How traditional they were can be illustrated by their *Commentary on the New Testament.*

At their third annual meeting in Toronto, on August 27–28, 1940, the members of the CBA voted in favor of a commentary on the New Testament to accompany the new CCD translation.[19] Meeting in Philadelphia the following year, the CBA formally voted that one of its functions should be to provide up-to-date commentaries on Scripture. It decided to entrust the commentary on the New Testament to those who had translated the various books. O'Hara added the encouragement that the bishops were anxious to see a popular commentary published as soon as possible.[20] The commentary, which appeared in 1942, illustrated the state of American Catholic biblical scholarship at the time. Wendell Reilly did the introduction on "The Literary Relations of the First Three Gospels." "A solid tradition almost as old as the books themselves," he wrote, "tells us the order of their composition, an order which is still preserved in our modern New Testament." This tradition, he continued, taught that Matthew wrote first, but

the tradition says his Gospel was originally composed in Aramaic, the current language of the Jews. It was not until some years later that it would have been translated in Greek, whether by Matthew himself or by some other inspired writer. By that time, it may be supposed, St. Mark's Greek

Gospel had already appeared. Therefore, the order of composition of the Greek Gospels may have been (1) Mark, (2) Matthew, (3) Luke. This sequence is generally accepted today by scholars and must be kept constantly in mind in any treatment of this question of the literary relationship of the Gospels.[21]

Reilly dismissed the theory that, rather than there being a literary dependence of the Gospels, there was a common oral tradition behind each of them. As a strong argument against such a postulation, he cited the "fact that the most important words of Christ—on the Eucharist, for instance—differ considerably in the different Synoptics; yet, the oral theory demands an identity of language on much less important points." In treating the literary dependence of Matthew and Luke upon Mark, Reilly was still cautious. Not only had there been an Aramaic form of Matthew before Mark's Gospel, "tradition makes it certain, according to the Biblical Commission, that the Aramaic and Greek of St. Matthew are substantially identical." Just how the Biblical Commission had such certitude Reilly did not specify. In regard to the relationship between Matthew and Luke, he favored the theory presented by Dom Butler that "the resemblance or identity may best be explained by the dependence of St. Luke on St. Matthew." To postulate "Q" behind the similarities of Matthew and Luke, Reilly did not find "objectionable," but "there does not appear to be sufficient reason to admit its existence," when the "simpler view" would be to see Luke's dependence on Matthew.[22]

Less open in his treatment of the synoptic problem was Mark Kennedy, O.F.M., who contributed a commentary on Matthew. For him, the theory that Matthew, the apostle, had indeed composed a collection of the sayings of Jesus, which had later been put together by "some unknown writer" with the life of Jesus was not only contrary to the testimony of the Fathers but had also been explicitly condemned by the Biblical Commission. He further argued that "even in the Greek the sentence structure and rhythm are typically Semitic." Then Kennedy lapsed into a contradiction. The similarity between the three Synoptics, he said "may be explained by supposing that in his work the translator [of Matthew] followed a Greek catechesis parallel to the Aramaic oral catechesis used by Matthew and similar to those followed by Mark and Luke, or that he used the Gospels of Mark and Luke as his guide, or that this translation is older than these two Gospels and was used by these Evangelists."[23] By thus allowing for a possible literary dependence of Matthew upon Mark and Luke, Kennedy seemed to go beyond the decision of the Biblical Commission, which he was trying to defend.

Edward Cerny, S.S., was more progressive in his introduction to the Epistle to the Hebrews. He cited the difficulties of its canonicity and of its Pauline authorship and noted that "Catholics, since the decree of the Biblical Commission (June 24, 1914), maintain the Pauline authorship of the Epistle at least in the sense that it was conceived by him and written under his direction." He also acknowledged, however, that "the excellent literary style . . . is generally superior to that found in the other Epistles of St. Paul."[24] Cerny's comment was well within the limits of the Biblical Commission's decree and mirrored what Arbez had been teaching first at Menlo Park and later at the Sulpician College in Washington. In treating the "Johannine Comma" (1 Jn 5:7–8), Albert Meyer, then professor of Scripture at St. Francis Seminary in Milwaukee, had added a note in his translation. "According to the evidence of many manuscripts," he wrote, "and the majority of commentators, these verses should read: 'And there are three who give testimony, the Spirit, and the water, and the blood; and these three are one.' The Holy See reserves to itself the right to pass finally on the origin of the present reading."[25] In his commentary, Meyer, later the Archbishop of Milwaukee and then Archbishop of Chicago and a cardinal, alluded to his note on the text. Without emphasizing the point, he stated that "according to the reading of the Vulgate, there are three heavenly witnesses corresponding to the three witnesses on earth, the three divine Persons."[26] Meyer's commentary had at least alerted the conscientious reader that there was a problem with the text, though it was well within the limits of the decree of the Holy Office in 1927, allowing Catholic scholars freedom critically to study the text, as long as they submitted their findings to the final judgment of the Church.[27]

John J. Collins, S.J., perhaps still smarting from the attacks of "Amator Evangelii," commented on Phil 2:6 that "the Son of God did not think He must selfishly cling to all His glory and enjoy to the full His dignity, but He laid them aside to become man." He acknowledged, however, that others interpreted the text to mean

"although He fully realized His equality with God was no usurpation, yet He put it aside."[28] On other controverted issues, however, the commentary made less of an effort to inform its readers
of scholarly debates. Leo P. Foley, C.M., for example, did the
commentary on the Pastoral Epistles, but made no allusion to the
controversy over their Pauline authorship.[29]

BROADENING HORIZONS

The CBA's commentary on the New Testament was a good indication of the state of American Catholic biblical scholarship in 1942.
It contained flashes of insight, but was basically safe and conservative. It had been composed in extreme haste with the principal
intention of providing a companion piece for the new translation
of the New Testament. But, even as it made its appearance, the
CBA and its members were beginning to move beyond narrow
Catholic circles onto a more ecumenical plane.

On the Eve of *Divino Afflante Spiritu*

The first indication of a change in a approach was in the mode of
education of Scripture scholars. The norms of the Holy See required that all priests preparing to teach Scripture in seminaries
receive a degree from either the Biblical Commission or the Biblical Institute in Rome. The Second World War made such Roman
study impossible. In 1940, Bishop Joseph M. Corrigan, rector of
the Catholic University, obtained through Ernesto Ruffini, then a
consultor to the Congregation of Seminaries and Universities, oral
permission to prepare students for the licentiate, for which they
would later be examined in Rome. Michael Gruenthaner, with his
doctorate from the Biblical Commission, was to teach one of the
special courses in preparation for the examination.[30] In 1942, after
the United States entered the war, Corrigan again made overtures
to Cardinal Giuseppe Pizzardo, prefect of the Congregation of
Seminaries and Universities, to allow the university to grant at
least the licentiate in Scripture. He argued that the university had
inaugurated a special course in Scripture, taught by Gruenthaner
one semester each year. There were in the United States, he continued, three men, besides Gruenthaner, who had doctorates in
Scripture: Wendell S. Reilly, S.S., of St. Mary's Seminary, Balti-

more, Edward J. Hodous, S.J., of the Jesuit scholasticate in West Baden Springs, Indiana, and William Newton of St. Mary's Seminary, Cleveland. These four could constitute an examining board. He noted that there was also Charles Callan, a consultor of the Biblical Commission. He added that Newton had resigned from the faculty the previous year for "personal reasons and left the university with great resentment."[31]

Corrigan's efforts to have the university empowered to grant degrees in Scripture, like previous ones, were unsuccessful. But the wartime situation made necessary a new Catholic approach to the preparation of Scripture scholars—priests began attending secular universities for their language training before going to Rome to obtain their degrees in Scripture.

In September 1942, Roger T. O'Callaghan, S.J., fresh from theology studies in Rome and a year of teaching at Fordham University, enrolled in the Oriental Seminary of the Johns Hopkins University in Baltimore. His professor, William F. Albright, later recalled their first meeting.

I can never forget a day in early September, 1942, when a tall and handsome young Jesuit came to my office and said that he wished to study "the historical background of Scripture." As usual, I gave him an immediate informal quiz, and was delighted to find that he possessed a fluent command of French, German, Italian, and Spanish, as well as the classical languages. Before the end of the year he was speaking Hebrew and Arabic, and had acquired a fair reading knowledge of several other Semitic tongues.[32]

O'Callaghan was but the first of a new generation of Catholic scholars who would receive their language training first at the Johns Hopkins University and later at other secular institutions. The attraction of Hopkins in the 1940s and later was the presence of Albright, whose work in archeology and ancient Near Eastern languages provided an irenic milieu in which Catholics could study what had previously been so controversial—the "historical background of Scripture."

Albright's *From The Stone Age to Christianity* had already gained a generally favorable review in 1942 from William H. McClellan, S.J., in the new Jesuit journal, *Theological Studies,* though the Jesuit still had some reservations about the sources of the Pentateuch and the assertion that the decalogue relied upon other law codes.[33] Moreover, as will be seen shortly, Albright rapidly became a friend of the nascent CBA. Archeology was an important point of contact between Catholic and non-Catholic scholars. Butin had already participated in a joint Harvard-Catholic University excavation of a nonbiblical site as early as 1930. In 1942, Edward Cerny began the "Archeological Corner" as a regular feature in the CBQ.[34] World War II, however, slowed down archeological research and made continuous reporting of it difficult.[35]

In the meantime, Gruenthaner had succeeded Reilly as editor of the CBQ in 1942. He split the academic year by teaching one semester at the Catholic University in Washington, D.C., as was noted above, and the other at the Jesuit scholasticate at St. Mary's, Kansas. His editorship coincided with important developments in Catholic biblical studies. With Catholics studying in secular universities and cooperating in archeological excavations with non-Catholic scholars, the way was being prepared for the emergence of full-blown biblical scholarship, which reflected the shifting winds of attitudes toward historical criticism in Rome itself.

Rome and, in particular, the Pontifical Biblical Institute were undergoing changes in the late 1930s and early 1940s. In 1933, Augustin Bea, S.J., rector of the Biblical Institute, defended the Mosaic authorship of the Pentateuch, but acknowledged that Moses may have used preexisting sources.[36] In this regard, he had not advanced much beyond Eichhorn, whom Kenrick had admired so much in the previous century. On the other hand, he was also beginning to reject Franzelin's theory of inspiration in favor of certain aspects of Lagrange's thought.[37] Americans who studied at the Biblical Institute during this period of transition recalled Bea's conservatism in regard to the documentary theory, but they also noted that Alberto Vaccari, S.J., the vice rector, raised questions about the Mosaic authorship of the Pentateuch.[38] Bea, the rector, however, gave little indication of the role he would play in being one of the drafters of Pius XII's encyclical Divino Afflante Spiritu. Nor did the CBA seem to sense any shift in Roman thought on the eve of the encyclical's publication.

In its second number for 1943, the CBQ published three articles commemorating the fiftieth anniversary of Providentissimus Deus. Anthony J. Cotter, S.J., of Weston College summarized the circumstances that led up to the encyclical. The First Vatican Council, he said, had "defined that the books of the Bible are inspired and canonical because, written under the inspiration of the Holy Ghost, they have God for their author and as such were given to the Church." Franzelin, Cotter explained, was among those theologians who analyzed the significance of the council's decrees and "placed the ultimate metaphysical essence of inspiration in this that God is the *author of the Bible,* and that therefore in inspiring Scripture He did whatever one must do to become an author."[39] Cotter failed to note that Franzelin was also instrumental in drafting the council's decrees and ignored the problem of applying to God the anthropomorphism of authorship.

But neither the council nor Franzelin's formulation settled the issue, Cotter continued, for there still remained the question, not of inspiration, but of inerrancy. For Cotter, this was the Catholic "Biblical Question" and he proceeded to present the positions of various scholars, who attempted to reconcile errors in the Bible with inspiration: August Rohling, François Lenormant, John Henry Newman, Salvatore di Bartolo, Giovanni Semeria, Jules Didiot, Maurice D'Hulst, and Alfred Loisy. Each had, in one way or another, "forgotten . . . the true Catholic doctrine" that "the sacred writers, being inspired throughout by the Holy Ghost, could not err." Cotter showed little awareness of the problems of biblical criticism or, for that matter, the precise nature of the "tradition" and "doctrine" he was defending. For him, the encyclical settled the question, for it stated

emphatically that inspiration may not be restricted to certain parts of Scripture, and that inspiration makes error metaphysically impossible; it also answered the arguments, one by one, by which the writers mentioned had tried to make their solution of the problem plausible; finally it pointed out the correct method by which Catholic scholars may meet the objections of higher critics.[40]

Though more irenic, Cotter would have been at home with Maas and gave little indication of the new intellectual winds beginning to blow in Rome.

Richard T. Murphy, O.P., of the Dominican House of Studies in Washington followed with "The Teachings of the Encyclical *Providentissimus Deus."* Covering some of the same material as Cotter and attacking those Protestants who either impugned the Genesis account of creation or held that the historical-critical method destroyed the notion of "infallible inspiration," Murphy's article took a strange twist. He too accepted as his starting point that God was the principal author of Scripture, but then he gave to his understanding of the human author as an instrument a new connotation. For him, instrumental causality meant that the human author had to remain free in such a way that "in this book there will be nothing the human author has not produced, and absolutely nothing that does not proceed also and primarily from the divine author." This interpretation of instrumental causality, which Murphy argued was in the encyclical, led him to espouse Lagrange's theory of verbal inspiration. Without mentioning Franzelin by name, he wrote, "that God should supply the ideas and man the words is a plausible theory, but it would destroy the authorship of God and the instrumentality of man."[41]

Murphy then moved to draw the distinction, already familiar to those who knew Lagrange, between inspiration and revelation. In choosing the human instrument, he argued, God

did not destroy, hamper, or hinder His chosen instruments but He did guarantee the truthfulness of their inspired judgments. Not every inspired judgment is a dogma or revealed truth. Inspiration is compatible with opinion, rumor, and the like; all of these things are inspired, for they are certainly part of the canonical Scriptures, but not all of them are revealed. The light which God gives to the sacred writer enables him to form a judgment, wherein alone logical truth, or error, is to be found. The author's judgment, freely formed with God's special help, must be therefore true to the extent that he intends to affirm or teach.

Though Murphy was endeavoring to present Lagrange's views, he remained basically conservative. On the one hand, all doubts about appealing to "history according to appearances" were for him removed by Benedict XV's *Spiritus Paraclitus*. On the other, while acknowledging that all exegesis must conform to the tradition of the Church, he reminded his readers that "the Church has only rarely declared in an official manner the precise meanings of texts."[42] Murphy, then, a Dominican product of the École biblique with a licentiate in Scripture from the Biblical Commission, was more progressive than the Jesuit Cotter in regard to the nature of the biblical question, but still seemed unable to reconcile his own instincts about scriptural difficulties with statements of the magisterium.

Stephen J. Hartdegen, O.F.M., of Holy Name College in Washington, concluded the commemorative issue of the *CBQ* with a broad survey of "The Influence of the Encyclical *Providentissimus Deus* on Subsequent Scripture Study." Among the introductions to Scripture, he lumped together Ruffini, Breen, Gigot, Grannan, and Steinmueller. In listing the institutions that owed their origin directly or indirectly to the encyclical, he gave pride of place to the Biblical Institute and its branch in Jerusalem, but made no mention of the École biblique. He likewise made short shrift of von Hummelauer, Batiffol, Prat, and Lagrange, who proposed either theories of historical appearances, literary forms, or implicit citations, each of which was definitively repudiated by Benedict XV. He concluded his treatment by mentioning "the ecclesiastical sanctions pronounced against the writings and the persons of those who persisted in opposing its teachings." Here he mentioned not only Loisy and Ernesto Buonaiuti, who refused to submit to Church teaching, but also A. Brassac, who did submit.[43]

Divino Afflante Spiritu

The orientation of the three articles indicated how little prepared American Scripture scholars were for a change in the Church's teaching. All accepted "tradition" as something static and unchanging and statements of the Biblical Commission as unconditioned by historical circumstances. Pius XII's own commemoration of *Providentissimus Deus* came as a shock to most Americans. The pope noted that, at the time of Leo, archeological excavations of biblical sites and textual criticism were only beginning. In light of this, he urged the study of the Bible in the original languages. This, he continued, did not derogate from the decree of Trent declaring the Vulgate to be authentic, for "this special authority or, as they say, authenticity of the Vulgate was not affirmed by the Council particularly for critical reasons, but rather because of its legitimate use in the Churches throughout so many centuries."[44]

The encyclical proceeded to exhort Catholic exegetes: "Being thoroughly prepared by the knowledge of the ancient languages and by the aids afforded by the art of criticism, let the Catholic exegete undertake the task, of all those imposed on him the greatest, that, namely, of discovering and expounding the genuine meaning of the Sacred Books."[45] The pope then virtually reversed the thrust of *Spiritus Paraclitus.* The present age with its discoveries, he said, could contribute to a deeper understanding of Scripture, "for not a few things, especially in matters pertaining to history, were scarcely at all or not fully explained by the commentators of past ages, since they lacked almost all the information which was needed for their clearer exposition." As an example, he cited the various ways in which the Fathers had explained the first chapters of Genesis.[46] The Catholic interpreter was now urged, "with all care and without neglecting any light derived from recent research," to "endeavor to determine the peculiar character and circumstances of the sacred writer, the age in which he lived, the sources written or oral to which he had recourse and the forms of expression he employed."[47]

Fully to understand the meaning intended by the author, the interpreter was to "go back wholly in spirit to those remote centuries of the East." As his tools, he was to use "history, archaeology, ethnology, and other sciences" to determine the particular "modes of writing" an author of a given age was likely to use.[48] "The Sacred Writers," like "other ancient authors," used "certain fixed ways of expounding and narrating, certain definite idioms, especially of a kind peculiar to the Semitic tongues, so-called approximations, and certain hyperbolic modes of expression, nay, at times, even paradoxical, which even help to impress the ideas more deeply on the mind." It was only to be expected, the pope continued, that the human author would use his own language and form of expression to express his thought and here he drew an analogy with the Incarnation, so frequently used by the progressives of the last century. "For as the substantial Word of God became like to men in all things, 'except sin,' " he stated, "so the words of God, expressed in human language, are made like to human speech in every respect, except error."[49] To prove the Scripture immune from error, the Catholic exegete had to determine the "manner of expression or literary mode adopted by the sacred writer" in order to provide "a correct and genuine interpretation." Furthermore, the Catholic scholar had to "be convinced that this part of his office cannot be neglected without serious detriment to Catholic exegesis." As an example of the need to determine the "literary mode," the pope used history. Too frequently, he said, "some persons reproachfully charge the Sacred Writers with some historical error or inaccuracy in the recording of facts," when, in reality, "it turns out to be nothing else than those customary modes of expression and narration peculiar to the ancients, which used to be employed in the mutual dealings of social life and which in fact were sanctioned by common usage."[50] Von Hummelauer, Lagrange and Poels would have been gratified to have found themselves vindicated on this point. Cotter, Murphy, and Hartdegen may well have been mystified to have learned that, even as they were publishing their articles on what they believed to be the authentic and timeless teaching of the Church, an encyclical was being drafted that changed that teaching.

Pius concluded his exhortation to exegetes by reminding them that progress would be slow and that they should seek to refute adversaries but also "satisfy the indubitable conclusion of profane sciences." In the passage, which Cicognani quoted in urging the CBA to undertake the translation of the Old Testament from the original languages, the pope reminded "other sons of the Church" to have charity and not be suspicious of whatever was new.[51] Pius XII had thus reversed a trend in Catholic biblical scholarship, which had begun toward the end of Leo XIII's pontificate, developed under Pius X, and was reinforced under Benedict XV, at least in regard to historical criticism. The new encyclical had, in fact, cited *Spiritus Paraclitus* only three times and one of those seemed to take Benedict's condemnation of "historical appearances" and reverse it.[52] The pope dated his encyclical September 30, 1943, the feast of St. Jerome. Though Vosté, the secretary of the Biblical Commission, and Bea, the rector of the Biblical Institute, were reputed to have been the major drafters of the encyclical, an American, Vincent McCormick, S.J., former rector of the Gregorian University, recorded in his diary for September 2, 1943, that he was assisting in drafting the letter, probably in terms of its style.[53] The encyclical would alter the direction of American Catholic biblical scholarship.

NEW DIRECTIONS IN THE CBA

Because of the war, the encyclical did not arrive in the United States until after February 1944. At that time, as was seen above, the principal interest of American biblical scholars was the encouragement to undertake translations of the Bible into the vernacular from the original languages. The war slowed down the influence on American scholars of other aspects of the new encyclical. There were, nevertheless, some signs of changing American attitudes toward critical scholarship.

ECUMENICAL CONTACTS

Because of the difficulty of wartime travel, the CBA did not hold an annual meeting in 1943. The 1944 meeting of the CBA at St. Mary's College, South Bend, Indiana, however, represented a turning point in the association. In February, while the debate with "Amator Evangelii" was in full tilt, O'Hara approved the suggestion of having Albright address the meeting.[54] Next, Edward Cerny, in the name of the association, extended a formal invitation to Albright, who submitted a list of possible topics. Joseph Lilly, the association's secretary, selected the topic "Canaanite and Hebrew Literature."[55] Albright refused an honorarium, and Cerny offered a suggestion to Lilly. Albright's wife was a convert to Catholicism and could be invited to accompany her husband at the association's expense. Moreover, he continued, "she is as talkative as he is reserved (he is a good lecturer, however) and would be the best person to make him feel at ease."[56]

As promised, Albright delivered his lecture on August 22 on "The Old Testament and Canaanite Language and Literature." Subsequently published in the *CBQ,* it was the first article by a non-Catholic to appear in the journal.[57] The association also voted at the meeting to make Albright an honorary life member, the first Protestant accorded that title.[58] Albright, for his part, was delighted at the meeting and his reception. "I enjoyed the meetings," he wrote Lilly,

and my associations with the members of the Association immensely. I had not realized quite how many old friends and acquaintances there would be at the meeting. What I liked particularly was the fresh enthusiasm and interest, which were most stimulating by comparison with the rather bored attitude characteristic of most members of the Society of Biblical Literature. Nor do I blame them, in view of the waste of time involved in listening to the numerous papers which expose half-baked theories and wild hypotheses of various kinds. Such papers are not likely to be presented at meetings of the Catholic Biblical Association.[59]

Here was high praise from the man widely regarded as the foremost American authority on the ancient Near East. It would, however, be almost a decade before the CBA lived up to Albright's expectations and began to absorb and express the new directions of *Divino Afflante Spiritu*. Albright had, nevertheless, begun his formal contact with the CBA and its members.

From August 16 to 26, 1946, the CBA sponsored its first Summer Biblical Institute at Niagara University, Buffalo, New York, as part of the association's original purpose of disseminating knowledge of biblical scholarship. Albright was part of a faculty consisting of Patrick W. Skehan of the Catholic University, Gruenthaner, Collins, and Vosté, secretary of the Biblical Commission. Sixty-seven priests attended the lectures.[60]

In the summer of 1947, the CBA sponsored its second biblical institute at St. Thomas Seminary in Denver. Again, there was a Protestant member of the faculty, John A. Wilson of the University of Chicago. Lilly thought "the Biblical Summer Schools . . . are the best thing the Association ever started and should be continued." He saw them also as a means of promoting ecumenism. As he wrote Hartman:

I particularly like the idea of calling in non-Catholic scholars, such as Albright and Wilson. Dr. Wilson was very deeply impressed at Denver. It was the first time he had ever been in a Catholic Seminary or associated to any extent with priests, and I am sure that he was most favorably impressed. There has been a recent pronouncement from Rome against cooperation with Protestants, but I am sure that nothing of the sort we are doing in our Biblical summer schools was in the mind of those who drew up this decree. However, I defer to your Dr. [Francis] Connell and the Canonists on that point. I think it does the Church a lot of good to have these leading lights come in contact with us priests; they are favorably impressed, and one more obstacle to the operation of grace is removed. And it helps the Protestants too.[61]

Like Albright, Wilson was elected to honorary life membership in the CBA. Lilly, however, was a bit too optimistic about how the Holy See regarded "cooperation with Protestants." Whether or not it was because of the ecumenical overtones of the summer biblical institutes, the CBA sponsored only one more—for sisters in New York in 1947.[62] But ecumenical contacts would continue. Several members of the CBA joined the Society of Biblical Literature and regularly attended its meetings.[63]

Albright, however, was the key figure in gaining recognition of American Catholic biblical scholarship in Protestant circles. In September 1947, moreover, he asked Patrick Skehan, professor of Semitic languages at the Catholic University, if he could take his place at the Hopkins University for twelve weeks and teach Aramaic and Syriac to enable him to go on an archeological expedition.[64] Skehan readily agreed and Albright enthusiastically reported on his most outstanding students. Two Jesuits, Francis J. McCool and a seminarian, Mr. William Moran were "even better than I thought—in other words, they are very good men." He was also sure Skehan would "like our two star men, [David Noel] Freedman and [Frank] Cross, very much."[65] Thus, Skehan began a tradition of several years of replacing Albright, whenever the archeologist was absent on an expedition. By the late 1940s, therefore, young scholars, both Catholic and Protestant, were studying under the same professors.

DEVELOPING BIBLICAL CRITICISM

Only gradually, however, did the CBA emerge as a scholarly organization. In 1943, the *CBQ* had begun a "Survey of Periodicals." The Old Testament section was edited by Skehan and John P. Weisengoff of the Catholic University and the New Testament by Anthony Cotter, S.J., and John J. Collins, S.J., of Weston College. The latter survey would finally lead to *New Testament Abstracts,* founded at Weston in 1956 and separated from the *CBQ.*[66] The war slowed down the assimilation of the new thrust in biblical studies. As the CBA prepared to hold its annual meeting in 1945, two issues absorbed the attention of the association's officers. First, the Pontifical Biblical Institute had published a revised edition of the Psalms from the Latin. Through Archbishop Cicognani, the apostolic delegate, the CBA requested permission to publicize the new "Liber Psalmorum" and to translate it into English. Augustin Bea, S.J., rector of the institute, replied on May 23, 1945, readily sending four copies of the translation but strongly recommending against "a translation of a translation." Bea urged that instead the Americans make a translation directly from the Hebrew.[67] The second issue was more political. Many members of the

CBA questioned whether the association should hold an annual meeting in 1945, scheduled for St. Joseph's Seminary, New York, due to the government's restriction of all nonessential travel. Lilly, the secretary, expressed his reservations to O'Hara, who thought the meeting could be held without publicity, except for letters to the members.[68] William McClellan, S.J., the president, thought the CBA should set an example of compliance with the government regulations.[69] But Lilly had other reasons for proceeding with the schedule. "A meeting in New York," he wrote McClellan, "should also serve to win over Archbishop Spellman who has already been contacted and has offered to attend our meeting."[70] Hayes, it will be recalled, had been one of the original sponsors of the CBA, but Spellman had held himself aloof.

The meeting itself was not noteworthy. Spellman delegated his auxiliary bishop, James F. McIntyre, to celebrate the Mass on August 22. McClellan was unable to attend. Lilly read a paper on F. R. Hoare's thesis that the order of John's Gospel had been changed, but concluded that there was no proof. John Steinmueller, however, treated "Genesis and the Antiquity of Man" and concluded that there was not evidence in the Bible to fix the date of man and woman with certainty. Skehan then presented the new Latin edition of the Psalms and Stephen Hartdegen reported that the first draft of twenty-six books of the Old Testament had been submitted. Arbez was hopeful of having Genesis in print within the year.[71] The CBA, at this point, was still more preoccupied with its translation project than with issues of criticism. Gradually, it lost this preoccupation.

The annual meeting of the CBA, held in Boston in the summer of 1946, shortly after the first Summer Biblical Institute, indicated the developing scholarly awareness of the association. Prior to the meeting, Cardinal Tisserant, the president of the Biblical Commission, wrote to commend the association's work and its invitation to Vosté, the secretary of the commission, both to lecture at the biblical institute and to attend the meeting of the CBA. The cardinal reminded the members that Pius XII had insisted "on the absolute necessity of a critical and historical exegesis" of Scripture. Vosté gave two lectures at the meeting. In the first, he spoke of the context of Trent's decree on the authenticity of the Vulgate, but stated that preference was always to be given to the Scripture in the original languages. In the second, he narrated the history of Scripture studies from *Providentissimus Deus* to *Divino Afflante Spiritu,* a period in which, he fully acknowledged, Catholics had not been in the forefront of biblical scholarship.[72]

In his presidential address, Matthew Stapleton of St. John's Seminary, Brighton, Massachusetts, picked up an ecumenical theme. The Bible was common to Catholics as well as Orthodox and Protestants, he noted, and called for greater collaboration with non-Catholic scholars in all areas of biblical research. Such a cooperative approach to exegesis, he thought, could not help but lead to a greater understanding of Scripture.[73] Richard Murphy, O.P., of the Dominican House of Studies in River Forest, Illinois, introduced what would have been a daring topic earlier in the century. The arguments for a twofold authorship of Isaiah, he noted, were not compelling, but he considered that opinion probable. Not all the participants, however, appreciated the significance of the new Catholic scholarship. Charles Callan prepared a paper, read in his absence by McHugh, on "The Bible in the Summa Theologica of St. Thomas Aquinas." Since the *Summa* was based on the data of revelation contained in Scripture, he concluded, it contained "an exact and literal interpretation of all the essential passages of the Bible."[74] Other papers were of a more pastoral nature. It would still be some years before the CBA's meetings became gatherings of scholars.

At its Denver meeting in August 1947, the CBA made the first change in what until then had been an exclusively clerical organization. Albright had, of course, been voted honorary membership, but at the meeting Mother Kathryn Sullivan, R.S.C.J., of Manhattanville College was elected to the association. Other people began to take on prominence. John L. McKenzie, S.J., of the Jesuit scholasticate at West Baden, Indiana, spoke on El and Elohim, but much of the meeting was still devoted to discussion of the translation of the Bible. Gruenthaner delivered a paper critical of Ronald Knox's translation for being too arbitrary. Stephen Hartdegen reported that thirty-seven books of the Old Testament had been translated and that Genesis would be published in 1948.[75]

The Kleist-Lilly Translation of the New Testament

Genesis was actually published on August 25, 1948, during the CBA's annual meeting at St. Joseph's Seminary, Dunwoodie, New

York. By that time, thirty-nine books were complete. In addition, the association heard a report on the status of the translation of the New Testament from Greek. James A. Kleist, S.J., of St. Louis University had completed the Gospels, but his translation ran into difficulties with the episcopal committee. A month before the meeting, O'Hara explained the problem to Lilly. The bishops, he said, had a "rather definite conviction . . . that the translation of the New Testament they will wish to authorize should not avoid the use of the traditional English where the language expresses the meaning of the original in idiomatic English." The bishops were concerned that "the language of the New Testament is in the minds of the thousands of priests and teachers and people and there is no gain but much loss in departing from the accustomed language where Scripture scholarship and good English use permit it to be retained."[76]

Kleist was deeply upset when Lilly communicated O'Hara's information to him. O'Hara's letter, said Kleist,

seems to rule out any expressions not found in the Douay Challoner or the Confraternity versions. This would destroy my work utterly and funditus. Our conviction was at the very start that we should modernize the Douay and not merely touch it up. Of course many priests would welcome a version that would recall to them the old translation. Whether the faithful, the people, I say, would welcome it also, I doubt very much, after they had been shwon [sic] a specimen of the new version. When the Bishop read my chapter 17 of St. John he wrote: I like it very much. Well, but that is radically different from anything he had ever read before. My opinion is this: if I am expected to go oerv [sic] the whole of my manuscript before it is planographed, and revise it with a constant eye on the old version, then I respectfully beg to be excused from any further work on it. You cannot teach new tricks to an old dog. The work would be extremely nerve racking; and I think it is not worth that much. If the Bishop wants the wishes of the High Committee to be carried out, he must look for another collaborator.[77]

At the CBA meeting, there was a simple report that Kleist had completed the Gospels and that Lilly and Dominic J. Unger, O.F.M.Cap. were completing the rest of the New Testament, but the episcopal committee was hesitating to approve the new text.[78]

Still piqued at the rejection of his translation, Kleist resigned from the committee of revisers a short time later.[79] Within a few months, he was dead. O'Hara requested the return of his manuscript to the episcopal committee.[80] Paul Reinert, S.J., president of St. Louis University, then informed O'Hara that he had arranged to have the Bruce Publishing Company publish not only Kleist's translation of the Gospels but also Lilly's translation of the rest of the New Testament. O'Hara finally notified Reinert that the CCD was surrendering the copyright to the New Testament.[81] It was, however, only in 1954 that the Kleist-Lilly translation would appear in print.

Scripture and the Theologians

In the meantime, even as the CBA was discussing its translation projects, some of its members were indicating their growing independence of dogmatic theology. At the annual meeting in 1948, Edward Siegman, C.PP.S., of the Precious Blood Seminary in Carthagena, Ohio, noted the tendency in textbooks on dogmatic theology to ignore Scripture. He called for a "readjustment of the attitude which uses Scripture for controversy and loses the idea of the living spirit of Scripture. The scholastic method might be balanced with a presentation that would begin with the scriptural data and arrive at the thesis."[82] It was a similar attitude toward Scripture that had characterized the liberal exegetes at the beginning of the century. This new attitude had received encouragement from a letter of the Biblical Commission to Cardinal Suhard, Archbishop of Paris, on January 16, 1948. In regard to the composition of the Pentateuch, the commission stated that its earlier decisions were "in no way opposed to further and truly scientific examination of these questions according to the results obtained during the past forty years." The commission had earlier allowed for the possibility that Moses had used preexisting sources in compiling the Pentateuch, but now it stated that "there is no one today who doubts the existence of such sources and does not admit that there has been a progressive increase in the Mosaic laws, which is due to the social and religious conditions of later times, and which comes to light even in the historical narrations." Now the commission exhorted "Catholic scholars, without party spirit, to examine these questions in the light of sane criticism and according to those findings, which other sciences have obtained in regard to the matter." The commission left open the question of what type of history the opening chapters of Genesis was narrating and only gave the caveat that, in the eyes of some people, to deny that Genesis narrated history in the contemporary sense was paramount to denying that it narrated history at all.[83]

Although the *CBQ* published the Biblical Commission's letter, no one mentioned it at the CBA meeting in 1948. The following year, however, the association met at Emmitsburg, Maryland. John L. McKenzie gave a paper on "Polygenism and Exegesis," in which he argued that, according to both *Divino Afflante Spiritu* and the commission's letter, polygenism was not clearly ruled out of legitimate Catholic exegesis. A heated debate ensued. Gruenthaner attacked McKenzie for speaking of Adam and Eve as representative figures and said that next he would speak of a "collective Christ." Siegman said that St. Paul had already spoken that way. Gruenthaner had the last word—he rejected McKenzie's paper for publication in the *CBQ*.[84] The tension expressed at the Emmitsburg meeting was a sign that American Catholic biblical scholarship was beginning to mature. Yet, the relationship between biblical questions and the findings of paleontology bore a striking resemblance to the intertwining of those issues at the beginning of the century. At that time, the Holy See's reaction was to condemn Modernism. In 1950, as will be seen, Pius XII would issue his encylical *Humani Generis*.

As the CBA developed into a scholarly organization, some of its founders gradually faded into the background. William Newton, against O'Hara's advice, accepted a parish in Cleveland in 1945.[85] One of his last contributions to the biblical field was an article in *The Priest* in 1947 surveying Catholic translations of the Bible in English. He reminded his readers that the Confraternity edition was at best a revision of the Challoner version and suffered from that fact.[86] For reasons not altogether clear, he ceased taking an active role in the association. While acknowledging that he was the real driving force in founding the CBA, some early members believed that he could not surrender control of it once it had grown beyond its infancy.[87]

Other changes in the association's leadership reflected its growing scholarship. Michael Gruenthaner, S.J., had been the editor of the *CBQ* since 1942. In its earliest years, the *CBQ* was ambivalent as to whether it was to be a journal intended for a scholarly or more general audience. In one of his first editorials, Gruenthaner had called for articles that avoided technical language not familiar to the average priest.[88] By the late 1940s, the association and its journal had grown well beyond this attitude. One year after the Gruenthaner-McKenzie altercation, the CBA met in St. Louis in 1950. Without forewarning Gruenthaner, the officers demanded his resignation.[89] They already had a replacement in mind, Edward F. Siegman, C.PP.S., professor of biblical theology at St. Charles Seminary, Carthagena, Ohio. Siegman arrived at the Catholic University to assume his editorial duties at the end of January, 1951.[90] He would be responsible for transforming the *CBQ* into the scholarly journal that the association's members were now demanding. In the process, he and the CBA would draw increasingly hostile attacks.

Before the controversy unfolded, however, the CBA had won important allies within the hierarchy who would play influential roles during the next decade. O'Hara, of course, continued his support. In 1950, the association met in St. Louis, at the specific request of Archbishop Joseph Ritter, who addressed the meeting and warmly praised the work of biblical scholars.[91] Albert G. Meyer, a charter member of the CBA, remained an active member for most of his years as Bishop of Superior, Wisconsin, Archbishop of Milwaukee, and later Archbishop of Chicago and cardinal.[92] Patrons—those who contributed $250 or more—by the late 1940s included Cardinal James McGuigan, Archbishop of Toronto, Archbishop Richard J. Cushing, O'Connell's successor in Boston, Archbishop McNicholas of Cincinnati, and Bishop Thomas E. Molloy of Brooklyn. Among the life members, who had contributed $100, were Cardinal Tisserant and Archbishop James Francis A. McIntyre of Los Angeles. Four cardinals were among the associate members: Edward Mooney of Detroit, Francis Spellman of New York, Samuel Stritch of Chicago, and Ernesto Ruffini of Palermo. There were altogether eighty-one bishops, who were listed under various categories of membership.[93] In retrospect, it was a rather strange association of disparate personalities, for the next decade would see them sharply divided over the biblical question and other issues.

12. The Catholic Biblical Association Comes of Age

During the 1950s, American Catholic theology in general, and biblical studies in particular underwent rapid change. Many of the issues of the turn of the century again came to the fore, such as historical criticism and religious liberty. Biblical scholars, moreover, received mixed signals from Rome, as the older form of Thomism gradually gained a hold on Pius XII. On the one hand, the pope issued *Humani Generis* in 1950 against "la nouvelle théologie." On the other, the officials of the Biblical Commission seemed to give greater encouragement to biblical scholars in 1956. Throughout the decade, moreover, progressive American scholars came under increasing attack from Joseph C. Fenton, professor of dogmatic theology at the Catholic University of America. By the end of the decade, Pius XII had died and John XXIII had been elected. Through all this change, the CBA would develop into a mature scholarly organization, but it was left to Edward Siegman to steer the course of the *CBQ* in the new direction.

SIEGMAN'S EDITORSHIP OF THE *CATHOLIC BIBLICAL QUARTERLY*

Siegman's appointment as editor of the *CBQ* represented the first sign of the maturing of American Catholic biblical scholarship. He had a doctorate in theology from the Catholic University, but not a degree in Scripture. Initially, he was to be employed solely in editing the journal, but was not to teach.[1] During the spring semester of 1951, he studied Hebrew, while he was also translating the Second Book of Chronicles and Jeremiah for the new edition of the Old Testament. In the meanwhile, he had substituted for one professor who was ill.[2] By the beginning of the fall semester, however, he was under pressure from Bishop Patrick

J. McCormick, rector of the Catholic University, to teach at least part-time.

THE CATHOLIC UNIVERSITY AND SCRIPTURE

The study of Scripture at the university was deplorable, as he described to his provincial, Father S. W. Oberhauser, C.PP.S.:

A week or so after I got here, I met the Bishop at a cocktail party. He asked me whether I am teaching now. Of course, I wasn't. The picture gradually became clearer. The Scripture department here is not in good order. I've heard that from any number of profs, e.g. Dr. [Johannes] Quasten, Father Arbez, Father Skehan, to mention just a few. Dr. Quasten spoke to me a whole evening about it. He is most anxious that I teach in the Department. They have two men: Dr. Gruenthaner, S.J., who teaches here one semester each year and tries to cover in one semester what should be done in two. He teaches at the Jesuit Seminary the first semester, and is the Dean of the Theology School, St. Mary's, Notre Dame, during the summer. You can figure out how much attention he can give his students here. And he is the only one teaching graduate Scripture.

The other man is Dr. Weisengoff, an able fellow, but a veritable enfant terrible. I don't think it exaggerated to say that he was giving public scandal. His students were utterly disgusted with him. A dozen of them walked out of his class in protest one day. When a number of seminarians heard (through a former seminarian of ours) that I was on the place, they made no bones about expressing their hope that I would take his place. Of course, this all got to Archbishop [Patrick A.] O'Boyle, who was on the point of giving Dr. Weisengoff his walking papers, when someone or something mysteriously intervened. Now, the two men who should have asked for me to help them were the last two who would push the matter. A third man is badly needed. Dr. Weisengoff has over a hundred seminarians in one class. But he was in no position to ask for help, and Dr. Gruenthaner is not interested.[3]

This was a rather sorry comment on the university, which had been on the cutting edge of Scripture studies in the United States at the beginning of the century. And the situation was to get worse.

In November, Gruenthaner submitted his resignation, and Siegman found himself under consideration for the position. Among his supporters was Francis Connell, C.Ss.R, the dean of the school of theology. Then there was a delay, and Siegman learned that one reason for it was that the budget committee of the university was disposed to drop graduate studies in Scripture altogether and retain one professor for seminary courses alone.[4] Only on March 31, 1952, did he receive an appointment as assistant professor, effective for the fall semester.[5] Siegman came to the Catholic University and to the editorship of the *CBQ* during a period of theological transition. Within a few years, some of his initial supporters, such as Connell, would be among the strongest opponents to biblical scholarship, as the Church again went through a period of retrenchment.

Humani Generis

On August 12, 1950, Pius XII issued *Humani Generis*. Aimed primarily at the "New Theology," then developing in France, the encyclical rebuked those theologians who sought to abandon scholasticism, so long approved by the Church, in favor of theological pluralism, who blurred the distinction between nature and grace, and who practiced a false irenicism that glossed over dogmatic differences between Catholics and Protestants and that was too enamored of modern philosophical tendencies. In what pertained more directly to Scripture scholarship, it dealt with three issues, which were becoming controversial. First, it spoke of "the sources of divine revelation," which were found "in the Sacred Writings and in divine 'tradition.' "[6] Second, it warned about polygenism, "since it is in no way apparent how an opinion of this kind can be reconciled with what the sources of revealed truth and the acts of the Magisterium of the Church propose about original sin, which proceeds from the sin truly committed by one Adam. . . ."[7] It is important to note, however, that the encyclical did not condemn polygenism, but only pointed to the difficulty of reconciling it with the doctrine of original sin.[8] Finally, it cautioned those in historical disciplines who used the letter of the Biblical Commission to Cardinal Suhard to justify their assertion that the first eleven chapters of Genesis presented merely a figurative and not, in any true sense, an historical account.[9]

Humani Generis was a balanced document. Yet, it represented the beginning of a decade of increased warnings to biblical scholars and others. The encyclical had stated, for instance, that "some go so far as to pervert the sense of the Vatican Council's definition that God is the author of Holy Scripture, and they put forward again the opinion . . . , which asserts that immunity from error extends only to those parts of the Bible that treat of God or of moral parts of the Bible."[10] The phrase "God is the author of Holy Scripture" had of course provoked controversy at the turn of the century. Did one, as Franzelin had, therefore, attribute to God all that a human author did in writing a book? This, in fact, was Augustin Bea's interpretation, but he nuanced his answer to show how Scripture bore "the traces of the human instrument adopted by God in writing it."[11] Conservative interpreters, however, would use the same phrase to argue that the encyclical was condemning the analysis of the human author that was so essential for the application to Scripture of the historical method. Moreover, the encyclical stated that certain contemporary trends in biblical exegesis were "foreign . . . to the principles and norms of interpretation rightly fixed by our predecessors of happy memory, Leo XIII in his Encyclical 'Providentissimus Deus,' and Benedict XV in his Encyclical 'Spiritus Paraclitus,' as well as by Ourselves in the Encyclical 'Divino Afflante Spiritu.' "[12] *Divino Afflante Spiritu,* as was noted above, had cited *Spiritus Paraclitus* only three times, and, in one of those citations, pertaining to "historical appearances," had virtually reversed the meaning of the earlier encyclical.[13] Conservative theologians would again find encouragement to charge that Pius XII's *Divino Afflante Spiritu* had not changed the norms imposed on Catholic exegetes.

Balanced though *Humani Generis* may have been upon close theological scrutiny, it ushered in a period of new warnings and reprisals, similar to the integrism that characterized the anti-Modernist crusade. In France, Yves Congar, O.P., Marie-Dominique Chenu, O.P., and Henri de Lubac, S.J., leading proponents of the New Theology, were deprived of their teaching posts.[14] Unlike the earlier crusade against Modernism, however, the Jesuits at the Pontifical Biblical Institute would be on the defensive against the reactionary onslaught and in the forefront of the progressive movement of biblical exegesis. Their battle in Rome would have ramifications for biblical scholarship in North America.

At first, the CBA took little official notice of the encyclical. Its meeting on August 22, 1950, recorded no mention of the papal pronouncement, which the association's members had hardly had time to absorb. Individual scholars, however, were soon aware of its application to biblical studies. Siegman later reported that as he was preparing to leave Carthagena in the fall of 1950, one of his colleagues charged that his class notes on the first eleven chapters of Genesis were contrary to *Humani Generis*. Siegman's provincial asked him "about publishing a corrective" in the congregation's journal, "in case I had anything in the Notes contrary to the 'Humani Generis.' " Siegman promised to make a careful study of the periodical literature since the encyclical. In January 1952, he wrote to assure his provincial that "everything in those Notes is perfectly orthodox, that nothing need be retracted or corrected." His notes, he continued, reflected the moderate exegetical approach taken by Edward Arbez, S.S. in the *American Ecclesiastical Review*.[15] Siegman, at least, was cognizant that some conservatives would apply the encyclical to the emerging biblical scholarship.

From November 8 to 10, 1951, the CBA met together with the Confraternity of Christian Doctrine in Chicago and may have studiously avoided the issue by having no Old Testament topic among its papers. Some scholars, especially John L. McKenzie, were determined to remedy that situation in the next meeting, scheduled to be held on August 26–27, 1952, at St. Procopius Abbey, Lisle, Illinois.[16]

Granted the limitations, under which biblical exegetes were working, and the divisions, which were beginning to appear at the CBA meetings, the presidential address of John E. Steinmueller was remarkable for its openness toward the ecumenical movement, all the more so because he had been a consultor to the Biblical Commission since 1947. Steinmueller began by reporting on a papal audience granted in April to the Society for Old Testament Study, most of whose members were Anglicans. Recognizing the complexity of contemporary biblical research, he stated, the Holy See saw the need for collaboration between Catholic and non-Catholic scholars, for there was truth outside the Catholic Church. He noted the paradox that, whereas the Bible had first divided Christians and Jews and later Catholics and Lutherans, it had now become the common meeting ground for scholars of all nations. "Perhaps in the Providence of God," he declared, "it will be the Bible, God's written message to all mankind, that will reunite divided Christianity and even help to revivify, spiritualize and personalize benumbed Christianity. Perhaps it will be even the Bible that will bring Judaism into the true fold to recognize Jesus

Christ as its Messiah."[17] While Steinmueller said nothing specific about biblical exegesis, he was clearly countering any misinterpretation of *Humani Generis* that there could be no truth outside the Catholic Church and that, therefore, there should be no collaboration with non-Catholic scholars.

In the meantime, McKenzie was successful in having the CBA deal with Old Testament exegesis. He addressed the meeting on "The Hebrew Attitude toward Mythological Polytheism." Ermenegild Florit, a guest from the Lateran Seminary in Rome, delivered a Latin response about the unique fact of monotheism among the Israelites. Roderick MacKenzie, S.J., of Regis College in Toronto, then treated the "Genus Litterarium of Gn 1–11." Recalling that the Biblical Commission's letter to Cardinal Suhard had declared that the historical nature of these chapters was still not settled, his paper called for the need to answer three questions: the provenance of the literary material, whether direct revelation, primitive tradition, or pre-Abrahamic, non-Israelite traditions; the intention of the sacred writer; and the very definition of "genus litterarium," which he preferred to call "religious prehistory." MacKenzie's paper provoked a lively discussion that had to be curtailed.[18] In the eyes of many conservatives, MacKenzie was calling in question the teaching of *Humani Generis*. His paper and John L. McKenzie's were, nevertheless, published in the *CBQ*.[19]

In the background of the discussion was the desire of some CBA members to state explicitly the association's loyalty to the magisterium. Immediately after the debate over MacKenzie's paper was cut off, the members voted to suspend the constitution until a new clause could be inserted into its statement of purpose.[20] The primary purpose of the CBA now became:

To devote itself to the scientific study of the Bible and to such branches of learning as are connected with it, in conformity with the spirit and the instructions of the Catholic Church, which the Association acknowledges to be the only divinely appointed custodian and authoritative interpreter of the Holy Scriptures.[21]

Virtually a paraphrase of the encyclical, the new clause was officially adopted at the association's meeting in Ottawa in 1953.[22] In the context of *Humani Generis* and of the debate in 1952, the new clause was a warning to scholars that statements of the magisterium were still to be their starting point.

THE NEW DIRECTION OF THE *Catholic Biblical Quarterly*

Despite its caution and divisions among its members, the CBA began to display new boldness in its approach to scholarship. Under Siegman's editorship of the *CBQ,* David M. Stanley, S.J., of Toronto, began publishing a series of articles applying form criticism to the New Testament and exposing his readers to the new discoveries of Catholic and Protestant scholars in France and Germany.[23] This new orientation became apparent at the same meeting in 1953, at which the CBA modified its constitution. Stanley delivered a paper on "St. Paul's Original Treatment of the 'Suffering Servant' Theme, and the Authorship of the Hymn in Phil 2, 5–11." His conclusion that the hymn was non-Pauline provoked a discussion, in which the participants were reluctant to admit such a Pauline Christology could, in fact, be non-Pauline. Roland E. Murphy, O.Carm., then surveyed the literature on the Canticle of Canticles. Following A. Robert and A. Feuillet, he preferred to consider the canticle as a unity and an allegory of the relation of God with his people, rather than as an anthology of poems.[24]

In the meantime, new archeological and manuscript discoveries were having their impact on Old Testament studies. In 1947, a Beduin shepherd boy discovered the first in a series of scrolls in a cave in Qumran. War between the Arabs and Jews, however, prevented the first excavations of the site until 1949.[25] Joseph S. Considine, O.P., used his presidential address in 1953, to report on the significance of the Dead Sea scrolls. Skehan then pointed out the affinities between some of the scrolls already studied and Isaiah. William Moran, S.J., who had completed his doctoral work at the Johns Hopkins and had just been ordained, read a paper on "The Canaanite Background to the Hebrew Cohortative." Mitchell J. Dahood, S.J., a seminarian who had also received a doctorate from the Hopkins, treated "The Language and Date of Psalm 47 (48)." Finally, André Legault, C.S.C., of the Scolasticat Sainte-Croix, Quebec, applied form criticism to the anointings in Galilee and Bethany to show the significance of each of the narratives in their own contexts and maintain the distinction between the sinful woman of Galilee and Mary of Bethany.[26] The CBA meetings were becoming increasingly technical and drawing more younger scholars. Gone were the days of less than a decade before when the CBA would also hear papers on more pastoral and catechetical issues. For the time, however, Old Testament scholars would have no difficulty as long as they remained within the confines of ancient Near Eastern languages. It was a different story, if they dealt directly with the composition and dating of the various books.

The Translation Project

On September 30, 1952, the five hundredth anniversary of the Gutenberg Bible, the CBA published the first volume of its translation of the first eight books of the Old Testament from the Hebrew. The introduction to Genesis still reflected a conservative orientation. "The Pentateuch," it said, was "substantially the work of Moses," which constituted "a closely knit literary unit and was originally conceived as one work written for a single purpose." Only later, was the Pentateuch "divided . . . into five parts or books." Printed in front of the volume was a letter of Pius XII to O'Hara commending the work. Dogmatic, rather than critical, considerations still determined the interpretation of certain texts. A note on Gn 3:15, for example, stated that the enmity placed between the serpent's and the woman's seed "refers principally to Jesus Christ, the Conqueror of Satan."[27]

YEARS OF TRANSITION

The CBA was becoming more of a scholarly organization. Yet, its definitive reorientation would take place only with the loss of influence of older, more conservative members and the admission of new ones trained in the historico-critical method.

THE CHANGING OF THE GUARD

Prior to the 1953 meeting, a young Sulpician aspirant, Raymond E. Brown applied, with Siegman's encouragement, for membership. He had already published an article in the *CBQ* on the *sensus plenior*, the subject of his doctoral dissertation in theology at St. Mary's Seminary.[28] He was then to pursue his Ph.D. in Semitic languages at Johns Hopkins, before taking the S.S.L. before the

Biblical Commission. Older members, however, resigned. From Woodstock College, Francis X. Peirce, S.J., who had been professor of Old Testament since 1932, wrote of his forthcoming retirement from teaching and resignation from the association. "My Scripture days will finish at the end of this term," he wrote Louis Hartman, the CBA secretary, "and I shall not weep any tears if I never see a Scripture book again." He noted, however, that George S. Glanzman, S.J., was replacing him at Woodstock. Glanzman, he continued,

has an L.SS from the Biblical, and will have his doctorate in Oriental languages from Hopkins by the end of this month. I could have murdered him cheerfully for taking so long to get here to relieve me (he has been in studies since 1947), but now that he is here I love him like nobody's business.[29]

Peirce had never been active in the CBA, but the tone of his resignation was that of a defeated man. In the pages of the *American Ecclesiastical Review,* he had carried on in the obscurantist Jesuit tradition of Maas and Drum. For the *CBQ,* he had contributed articles attempting to prove that Mary was the woman of Gn 3:15.[30] His optimistic expectation for Glanzman to finish his doctorate, however, was never fulfilled. Yet, even in retirement, he fired one last salvo at the new exegetes.

In 1953, McKenzie had completed a book on the Old Testament incorporating the new orientations in Catholic biblical scholarship, but intended for a more general audience. At that time, Jesuit Scripture scholars had to have their work submitted not only to ordinary censors but also to a "suprarevisor." Against McKenzie's advice, his provincial superior, Joseph M. Egan, S.J., sent the manuscript to Peirce. McKenzie's presentation of the meaning of Gn 3:15 could not have been farther removed from Peirce's. For the younger scholar, the "Hebrew Storyteller" did not "see in vision the figure of the Man who was to overcome sin and death on behalf of the race." "Still less," he continued, "can we detect in his mind any awareness of the mother of Jesus; she who was to be truly the Ideal Woman, and who was to raise her sex to a dignity undreamed, was too great a figure for the comprehension of those times."[31] Peirce, as might have been expected, rejected the manuscript.

Only in the fall of 1955 did McKenzie learn of the reason for the delay in receiving permission to publish the book. William J. Schmidt, S.J., the new provincial, decided to resubmit it to different censors. This time the censors were David M. Stanley, S.J., in Toronto and Frederick J. Moriarty, S.J., of Weston College; the suprarevisor was Roderick MacKenzie. With the approval of these new censors, *The Two-Edged Sword* was finally published in the fall of 1956.[32] McKenzie's book played a large role in introducing Catholics and non-Catholics alike to the new world of Catholic biblical scholarship. His conflict with Peirce was symbolic, for he and other Jesuits were now on the cutting edge of the exegesis, which their predecessors had done so much to thwart. Peirce's own institution of Woodstock moved to the forefront of that movement.

RELIGIOUS LIBERTY AND THE BIBLICAL QUESTION: ISSUES IN CONTROVERSY

Between 1955 and the first session of the Second Vatican Council, the Church watched the drama over Americanism and the biblical question reenacted. Religious liberty had again surfaced in American theological discussions. This time, its proponent was John Courtney Murray, S.J., professor of dogmatic theology at Woodstock College and editor of *Theological Studies*. At the time, it is doubtful whether either Murray or the biblical scholars realized they had anything in common, other than a common enemy. Just as at the turn of the century, Delattre attacked first Americanism and then Lagrange and other biblical exegetes, in the 1950s, Joseph C. Fenton, editor of the *American Ecclesiastical Review*, first condemned Murray and then turned his attention to Scripture scholars. As in the previous period, so in the 1950s, the American battle was but a reflection of the war raging in Rome. Fenton and his disciples mirrored the theology of Cardinal Alfredo Ottaviani, named prosecretary of the Holy Office in 1953. If the proponents of religious liberty and of biblical scholarship had looked more closely, they would have realized that they had more in common than Fenton's and Ottaviani's opposition. Both were arguing for a particular view of human nature in relationship to grace. Murray repudiated the notion that "error had no rights," in favor of the assertion that the human person, even when in error, has certain rights. The biblical scholars were arguing for the human element in Scripture, to which could be applied the same human, scientific methods of criticism, which were applied to other ancient Near Eastern literature.

Murray first broached the question of religious liberty and the American separation of Church and State in *Theological Studies* in 1943, the same year as *Divino Afflante Spiritu*. He initially met opposition from Archbishop Samuel Stritch of Chicago and Archbishop John T. McNicholas, O.P., of Cincinnati, for whom the difficulty was the notion of the development of doctrine on Church-State relations from Leo XIII to Pius XII. By 1948, however, both were won over, but Murray then drew the attention of Fenton in the *American Ecclesiastical Review*. For Fenton, Murray was simply reviving Americanism, which the Holy See had formally condemned. In March 1953, Ottaviani, recently named a cardinal, spoke at the Lateran Seminary. Catholics were obliged, he stated, when in the majority, to have their Church established as the sole religion, but, when in the minority, their Church was to have freedom. He argued on the premise that "error has no rights." Ottaviani's elevation to the sacred college and his statement on Church-State relations have to be seen in the context of the general Roman retrenchment in the years after *Humani Generis*. In the United States, Fenton continued his attacks on Murray. By the summer of 1955, Murray, on the advice of his Roman superiors, ceased writing on religious liberty and the separation of Church and State. While Murray was subjected first to attack and then to silence, biblical studies seemed untouched.[33] But this would not be the case for long.

Although some of the papers at the CBA meetings continued to be oriented toward a more general public, some were becoming increasingly technical. Still, the neuralgic questions of inspiration or of the relationship of Scripture to tradition were not yet of concern to the biblical scholars. The translation project continued to occupy much of their attention. In 1954, the "Kleist-Lilly" translation of the New Testament appeared, but it received mixed reviews for its English style.[34] The CBA meeting at St. Mary's Seminary in Perryville, Missouri, in August, sounded the note of an organization in transition. Sebastiano Pagano, O.M.I., of University Seminary in Ottawa, gave his presidential address on the suitability of the Bible for dramatic reading. Bruce Vawter, C.M., of Kenrick Seminary in St. Louis, however, spoke on the Canaanite background to Gn 49. But always the scholars had their eyes peeled on Rome. An entire afternoon of the meeting was devoted to a panel discussion on the teaching of Scripture and the interpretation of the decrees of the Biblical Commission. Barnabas Mary Ahern, C.P., of the Passionist Monastery in Chicago, Richard T. A. Murphy, O.P., of St. Rose Priory in Dubuque, and Stanley presented their views respectively on Hosea, Genesis, and Matthew, in light of the commission's decrees. Fear of Modernism continued to lurk in the background. At the business meeting, Stephen Hartdegen proposed that the preamble to the CBA constitution be modified to place the association "under the patronage of St. Jerome and Saint Pius X," because the recently canonized pontiff "had done so much for Scripture studies."[35] The motion was unanimously carried, and the secretary was to submit the proposed amendment to all the active members before the next general meeting. The officers of the association, however, seemed to have decided that St. Jerome provided sufficient patronage without adding that of the pope who had been so opposed to biblical scholarship. The minutes for the annual meeting in 1955 record no response to the proposed change.

Some members were now becoming critical of the failure of biblical studies to make their way into college teaching. At Providence College in 1955, the presidential address of Daniel W. Martin, C.M., of Perryville, read in his absence by Thomas Aquinas Collins, O.P., of the Dominican House of Studies in Washington, chastised American Catholic colleges for using books, whose authors presented views of the Old Testament, out-dated for at least fifty years. He called for a popularization of the scholarly work to reach a more general public.[36] What, of course, was needed was some sign from Rome that those outdated interpretations were no longer synonymous with orthodoxy, that the early decrees of the Biblical Commission were historically conditioned.

THE MILLER-KLEINHANS INTERPRETATION OF THE BIBLICAL COMMISSION'S RESPONSES

The sign from Rome came from no less authorities than Athanasius Miller, O.S.B., secretary of the Biblical Commission, and Arduin Kleinhans, O.F.M., the undersecretary, but they chose an unusual way of giving their sign to the scholarly world. Reviewing a new edition of the *Enchiridion Biblicum*, Miller in the *Benediktinische Monatschrift* and Kleinhans in the *Antonianum*, virtually repealed the early responses of the commission. Miller wrote in German and Kleinhans in Latin, but their texts were substantially identical—and no one missed the importance of this semiofficial declaration.

The *Enchiridion*, they wrote, displayed "how Sacred Scripture has always been the primary source and foundation of the truths of Catholic faith" and recorded the history of "the fierce battle that the Church at all times has had to fight, though with varying degrees of intensity, to maintain the purity and truth of the Word of God." But, whenever the commission's responses "propose views which are neither immediately nor mediately connected with truths of faith and morals," they continued, "it goes without saying that the scholar may pursue his research with complete freedom [plena libertate/in aller Freiheit] and may utilize the results of his research, provided always that he defers to the supreme teaching authority of the Church." Here seemed to be an assertion that the commission's decrees were concerned only with the religious and moral truths of Scripture. The two officials of the Biblical Commission admitted that "today we can hardly picture to ourselves the position of Catholic scholars at the turn of the century, or the dangers that threatened Catholic teaching on Scripture or its inspiration on the part of liberal and rationalistic criticism, which like a torrent tried to sweep away the sacred barriers of tradition." But now, they asserted, "the battle is considerably less fierce," many "controversies have been peacefully settled and many problems emerge in an entirely new light, so that it is easy enough for us to smile at the narrowness and constraint which prevailed fifty years ago."[37]

They concluded by mentioning the "apologetic value" of the *Enchiridion*, for it showed "the Church's untiring vigilance and her perennial solicitude for the Scriptures." In particular, they mentioned the encyclicals *Providentissimus Deus* and *Divino Afflante Spiritu*—they passed over *Pascendi* and *Spiritus Paraclitus*—for presenting "with admirable clarity the basic principles of Catholic interpretation which hold for all times and effectively close the door to subjective and arbitrary expositions."[38] Contemporary scholars could perhaps "smile at the narrowness and constraint" a half century earlier, but Henry Poels, it will be recalled, had been compelled to submit "in conscience" to the commission's responses.

Siegman reported the news in the *CBQ* for January, 1956. He reminded his readers that Pius X had stated that the Catholic scholar was "bound in conscience to submit to the decisions" of the commission and could not "escape the stigma both of disobedience and temerity nor be free from grave guilt" if he "impugns these decisions either in word or writing." On the other hand, said Siegman, "since the decisions are not infallible and hence are revocable, as all Catholic theologians teach, may he trust the indications that the decisions have been tacitly revoked?" Siegman was a bit too optimistic about what "all Catholic theologians" taught on this matter, as he would soon discover.[39]

Siegman welcomed the distinction Miller and Kleinhans had made between the decrees pertaining to "truths of faith and morals" and those concerning "questions of literary and textual criticism," such as "authorship, date of composition, and integrity." These questions, he said, "no longer have the crucial importance attached to them fifty years ago" and were "independent of the inspiration and inerrancy of the text."[40] As Siegman would soon discover, however, he had underestimated the importance conservative theologians still attached to the relationship between inspiration and authorship.

Siegman acknowledged that some of the commission's responses about the "historical character of certain parts of the Bible have a relation to truths of faith," but these responses also had to be properly interpreted. In a note, he told his readers that most Catholics then regarded Job "as a parable" and Tobit, Judith, and Esther "as at least partly fictitious." Yet, there were other responses "that safeguard the historicity of the Gospels, the Acts of the Apostles, and Gn 1–3." The Catholic exegete now interpreted these responses in terms of the instructions of *Divino Afflante Spiritu* and the later letter to Cardinal Suhard and sought to determine "the literary forms of the Bible in order to evaluate the sacred author's intention." In *Humani Generis*, furthermore, the pope had reaffirmed "the Catholic's obligation to interpret Gn 1–3 as implying the unity of the human race, but admits the probability that the narratives of the creation of Adam and Eve are to be understood metaphorically." In Siegman's interpretation of the encyclical, "Pope Pius says equivalently that the immediate creation of Adam's body and Eve's body by God is a probable opinion (no longer *certain,* or *proxima fidei,* as some have held), that the metaphorical interpretation of the Yahwistic account is also *probable,* so that the bodies of our first parents may have evolved from other living beings."[41] Siegman could justify his interpretation of the historicity of Gn 1–3 by appeal to *Divino Afflante Spiritu,* but conservatives would also challenge that interpretation.

Miller's and Kleinhans's actions and Siegman's interpretation of their significance did not, however, meet with universal acceptance. John E. Steinmueller, who had joined Callan as an American consultor to the Biblical Commission in 1947, accused Siegman of falsely concluding that the commission's responses were only of historical interest. He further stated that Miller and Kleinhans were saved from being brought before the Holy Office only through Cardinal Tisserant's direct intervention. Cardinal Pizzardo, the Secretary of the Holy Office, had written the Biblical Commission demanding that it disown the Miller-Kleinhans statement and that it censure them. Cardinal Tisserant, the President of the commission, replied with a strong rebuttal that the two officials were speaking the mind of the commission. That ended the Holy Office protest. Neither secretary was every brought up on charges and no Roman official ever countered their statements.[42]

MATURING CATHOLIC BIBLICAL SCHOLARSHIP

Siegman's was one of the first statements in the *CBQ* about inspiration and its independence of authorship and about metaphorical interpretations of Gn 1–3 that did not deny the historical and theological fact of the unity of the human race. In September, 1956, the CBA cautiously approached these questions at its annual meeting in Buffalo, the last time the association met in conjunction with the CCD, its parent organization. The program consisted of fifteen papers on Messianism in the Bible. The topic seemed innocuous enough, but the treatment given it provoked disagreement. Eugene Maly, of Mt. St. Mary's Seminary, Norwood, Ohio, discussed the need to define messianism and showed that Hosea prepared the ground from which grew the notion of a personal messiah. Frederick L. Moriarty, S.J., of Weston College, addressed the question of whether Is 7:14 was to be taken literally or typically as a messianic prophecy. R. A. F. MacKenzie was more daring. While the postexilic version of Deuteronomy was inspired, he argued, there was no criterion for judging the original version. Richard T. A. Murphy, O.P., spoke of messianism in Deutero and Trito-Isaiah, but noted the difficulty of determining whether there was one or multiple authors of either.[43] All these were subjects that previous American Catholic biblicists would have avoided. Yet, the Americans had still not directly addressed the issue of inspiration. This was to be the principal topic of the CBA's next meeting, held at the College of the Holy Cross, Worcester, Massachusetts.

JOSEPH C. FENTON AT THE CATHOLIC UNIVERSITY

In the meantime, some biblical scholars were beginning to feel the first gusts of reaction, blowing from a familiar direction. Siegman was planning a summer institute of theology and Scripture at the Catholic University. As he told his provincial, he ran into strong opposition from Joseph Fenton, who was "feared by many people here, including the Rector, because of his supposed influence with certain Roman Cardinals." Fenton had been named a counsellor to the Congregation of Seminaries and Universities, "apparently because he is a friend of Cardinal Pizzardo." He had been dean of the School of Theology, but "was so obnoxious that he was voted out unceremoniously, and ever since the faculty is fearful of the prospect of his getting back in; he has never forgiven the people who voted him out (this was before I got on the scene) and still speaks of Fr. Connell as 'the guy that has my job.' "[44]

Siegman then proceeded to describe his own relations with Fenton. Before he arrived at the Catholic University, Lilly had told him Fenton was "an abominable teacher," a description that Siegman could confirm for himself. Fenton's "classes are completely disorganized, punctuated with wild statement like, 'Newman did more harm to the Church than all the Protestants of the 19th century,' or, 'Sulpician spirituality has sent more souls to hell than Luther has.' " After Fenton had held up the approval of the summer institute, Siegman had a meeting with the vice rector, a meeting which brought upon him the personal venom of Fenton. As Siegman continued his report to his provincial,

In the course of the discussion [with the vice-rector] I mentioned that since this is something new we have to be careful about the teachers appointed, since a bad one can prejudice a community against a project of this kind. I had heard, after a talk I gave recently, that a superior of a certain community was sending no more of his men to the summer theology here because of the complaints he had heard about one of the profs. I took care to mention no names, but within a few hours the story was carried to Joe, who assumed (correctly, as it turned out) that he was the one meant. Since then his violence against me has been unrestrained. At our last faculty meeting he shouted at me, "You're no gentleman and never were!" After the meeting, he referred to me in the hearing of quite a group as "that pig Siegman." The other day he ordered Fr. [Robert] Mohan, book review editor of the *Ecclesiastical Review* to send Fr. Benard and myself no more books for review, and he kicked Fr. Benard off the staff.

I may sound like an injured innocent. Actually, I've done my best not to offend the man, though I must confess I loathe him and have loathed him from the very beginning. He has an inquisition mentality, he is vulgar and uncouth, and has absolutely no regard for anyone but himself; when aroused his language is revolting and he hasn't the least regard for truth. Actually, I think he works himself into such a mental state that he believes himself the wild statements he makes.[45]

These were extremely harsh words from the gentle Siegman. And there was more.

Fenton felt slighted for being left off Catholic University's summer faculty and argued that the university owed him the salary, "because he has to go to Rome every summer for business with the Congregation." This was "absurd," remarked Siegman, for "Frankie Connell has a higher post (consultor) on the Congregation, and is not going to Rome this summer." Siegman's motivation for informing his provincial of the situation was "in case Joe makes trouble. I am warned that he will stop at nothing when aroused, and he is aroused. Perhaps his next step will be to protest to Rome." Siegman was careful to point out, however, that he himself faced no opposition from the university administration and, in fact, had been promoted to associate professor the previous year.[46] Curiously, at this point in the developing saga, Siegman seems not have suspected any antagonism from Francis Connell, but he was aware of a gathering storm.

INSPIRATION AND THE HISTORICITY OF THE GOSPELS

Just as Siegman was giving the first indications of trouble from Fenton, the CBA began to treat some of the theological issues that arose from current biblical scholarship. The annual meeting, held at the College of the Holy Cross in Worcester in September 1957, was devoted to inspiration. This was at the suggestion of R. A. F. MacKenzie. As he told Hartman, a discussion of inspiration seemed necessary, for

Our knowledge of the process, on the human and historical levels, of composition of the sacred books, has increased tremendously in the last 50 years, but there hasn't been any corresponding application of the inspiration-doctrine to these new data. There are all kinds of problems here, which the commentator or translator or biblical theologian needs to have solved, or at least clarified. And this theme has the advantage of applying both to the OT and NT (last year Messianism was mainly OT).

MacKenzie then addressed the issue, which had been so crucial for biblical scholars at the beginning of the century—the relationship between inspiration and authorship. With an appended note that there should be "plenty of specific examples," he outlined his proposal:

1. Inspiration applying to authorship as we find it historically. Where does authorship lie in anthologies? in compilations? in "second (third, fourth) editions"? in citations, annotations, glosses? If St Paul told somebody else to write a letter to Ephesians, who was inspired? etc. Who is the author of 2 Peter?

2. Inspiration and translation, esp. of LXX. Tradition in the Church, pro and con? Benoit's position. Evidence of NT citations.

3. Inspiration and the *sensus plenior.*

4. Inspiration and the *sensus typicus.*

5. Inspiration and "myth," in Bultmann's sense.

6. Inspiration and inerrancy (connected with 5). Is there place for a distinction in the concept of inerrancy? Should we (departing from tradition) use the word "error" of sentences in Scripture? especially in historical contexts. [*sic* in original]

7. Inspiration and modern editing. What liberties may the textual critic or translator take with the text of an inspired book? Is it any different from editing a non-inspired text? How would you handle the book of Tobias? What about the LXX Daniel? or Liber III . . . ?[47]

In bald outline, MacKenzie was raising all the questions, which had been left unanswered since Modernism, and which would have to be answered if biblical scholarship was to progress any further.

When the meeting convened at Worcester, MacKenzie gave his presidential address on "Some Problems in the Field of Inspiration." "Instead of 'the inspired author' of a given book or pericope or phrase," he said, "we should accustom ourselves to speak of 'the inspired authors.'" The charism of inspiration should, therefore, be considered not individually, but collectively, for "theologically, the viewpoint from which the work of the various part-authors must be examined is that of the completed canonical book."[48] Other papers addressed similar themes, which would have been foreign to Catholic biblicists of a generation earlier. The minutes of the meeting, however, record no debate on the issue.[49]

While the American biblical scholars were now taking the initiative in discussing theological topics, they still approached certain issues cautiously. On the one hand, at the meeting in 1958, Stephen Hartdegen, gave his presidential address on the parallel between the Bible as *verbum inspiratum* and Christ as *verbum incarnatum.* On the other hand, Richard G. Philbin, S.J., of Holy Cross, strongly criticized certain Protestant trends in interpretation. He argued for the necessity of seeing the respective roles of both biblical criticism and dogmatic theology in establishing faith in the historical Jesus. Carroll Stuhlmueller, C.P., of the Passionist theologate in Chicago, then explained the development of the theology of creation in the Old Testament and showed the influence of Second Isaiah on both Paul's concept of the new creation and on John through Wisdom literature. The Americans had also not lost their interest in the Dead Sea scrolls. Joseph A. Fitzmyer, S.J., a fellow of the American School of Oriental Research for 1957–1958, reported on the progress of the work at Qumran.[50]

By the late 1950s, the CBA and its journal were becoming bolder as Catholic biblical scholarship entered into the mainstream. But the maturing of biblical scholarship was not without its opponents.

In the January issue of the *CBQ* in 1958, David Stanley published "Balaam's Ass, or a Problem in New Testament Hermeneutics." Originally read as a paper at the annual meeting of the CBA the previous September, it drew the distinction between the *Sitz im Leben* of the events and sayings of Jesus and the *Sitz im Evangelium,* which "has endowed it [the "setting in life"] with a theological dimension which, to say the least, was not immediately evident in its original form and setting." Stanley's purpose was "to throw some light upon the sacred writer's attitude towards 'the historical,' as well as upon what we mean by saying that our Gospels contain no error." As one illustration, Stanley used the centurion's remark on Calvary in Mk 15:39. In the *Sitz im Leben Jesu,* the pagan declaration that Jesus was "God's son" would have meant only "some sort of superstitious admiration for a man whose awe-inspiring death indicated that he was one of those divine heroes or supermen extolled in ancient mythology." In the hands of the evangelist, however, the original statement provided the Christian reader "with a formula of faith in Christ's divinity, as the story of Jesus' life reaches its significant climax."[51]

Stanley further illustrated his argument by contrasting the Matthean and Markan versions of Jesus walking on the lake and the Petrine profession at Caesarea Philippi. In both instances, Matthew transformed the Markan versions into "a profession of faith in Christ's divinity." Stanley explained in a note that "these Marcan accounts square with the fact that only at Pentecost would the disciples receive the full Christian faith."[52]

Stanley then explained the parallel he was trying to draw in the provocative title of his article. The reason for the inclusion of the story of Balaam's ass in Numbers was to instruct its readers "upon a point of OT doctrine of first-rate importance"—the "theological principle that God can, and does, make use of His creation, animate and inanimate, rational and irrational, as bearers of His Word of salvation to men." The evangelists, Stanley argued, employed this same theological "principle which they found in the OT writers in order to express the revelation of the Word Incarnate." Only at Pentecost would the apostolic community receive the full revelation of "Christ's divinity and the personality of the Spirit," but "still Jesus' public ministry had served as introduction to the meaning of the Pentecostal revelation." Stanley then summarized his views on the distinction between strict "historical" truth and theological inerrancy. "The aim of our Gospels was *didache*," he stated,

a deeper theological instruction intended to nourish the initial response of faith to the apostolic kerygma. Granted the didactic purpose of the evangelists and their insight into the Christophanic nature of the traditions about Jesus' earthly ministry, these inspired authors made use of their materials to present an account of Jesus' life which is not primarily "historical" (in our sense), but a *theological interpretation.* That the Gospel narratives contain much that is also "historical" is easily demonstrable from the fact that the modern critic can still recover the original *Sitz im Leben* of so many of its narratives. That they necessarily remain *didache,* however, revealing the Person of Christ to the reader with faith, is equally clear from the new theological dimension which the evangelists so frequently add to them.[53]

Though Stanley's position was relatively conservative, his efforts to distinguish between the inerrancy of the Gospels and historical truth in the modern sense drew strong criticism.

In February 1958, Siegman received a letter of protest against Stanley's article. The writer argued that the article's publication in the *CBQ* implied the editors' approval of the content. He also feared that Stanley's argument that the apostles fully recognized the divinity of Christ only at Pentecost would impugn any historical value of the Gospels. Siegman forwarded a copy of the letter to Stanley, and noted that he had "ever increasing evidence that we must bring this out in the open and discuss it freely." He had, in the meantime, already drafted an editor's response, but he asked Stanley to pen his own reply.[54]

Siegman's response first addressed the editorial policy of the *CBQ.* The assumption that publication in the *CBQ* meant that the editors found an article "acceptable" was "justified in the case of Fr. Stanley's article," he said, but "the assumption is not universally valid." Not only had three recent articles been published "which did not convince the editor," but "the staff of *CBQ* has from the beginning regarded as betrayal of trust any policy which would make of this journal an organ of propaganda for the staff's viewpoints." Siegman then proceeded to give a detailed defense of Stanley's position.[55]

Though Stanley had already obtained the assistance of Roderick MacKenzie in writing his response, Siegman ran into objections from the editorial staff about publishing the exchange. One staff member thought that it cast doubt on Stanley's orthodoxy, that it would draw attention to the *CBQ* itself, and that the matter could be better discussed at the annual meeting. Though Skehan and Hartman had agreed with Siegman that the letters should be published, Siegman ultimately accepted the advice of other staff members and suppressed the original protest and his own comments, which were already in galley proof.[56] Siegman had originally welcomed the opportunity of using the pages of the *CBQ* for a scholarly exchange on the significance of form criticism for understanding the New Testament. Unfortunately, the controversy occurred at the very moment that the CBA and its journal were under attack from Bishop Matthew Brady of Manchester, New Hampshire, who had succeeded O'Hara as chairman of the episcopal committee of the Confraternity of Christian Doctrine. As Siegman informed Stanley, Brady had remarked that the *CBQ* was "not much of a success anyway," and Matthew Stapleton, a consultor of the CBA, was "afraid that the Bishop may use this controversy as further ammunition to cause us trouble and perhaps even bring about the suppression of the CBA and *CBQ.*"[57]

CONTROVERSY WITH BISHOP BRADY

The controversy with Brady arose over the disposition of the royalties of the Confraternity edition. On November 12, 1957, the revision committee of the Old Testament met with Brady and requested that the CBA receive forty percent of the royalties. In a covering letter to the entire episcopal committee the next day, Hartdegen, the president of the CBA and secretary of the Old Testament editorial board, and Hartman, the executive secretary of the CBA and chairman of the editorial board, quoted the CBA's original constitution and subsequent amendments to show the close relationship between it and the Confraternity. As early as 1941, the CBA entered into a formal agreement with Bishop O'Hara to receive part of the royalties. The arrangement was a logical one, they continued

since the purposes of the Confraternity and the Biblical Association are closely allied, and since all the work of revising and translating of the Scriptures was accomplished by the special editorial boards of the Catholic Biblical Association and their associate members, a request was made of the Episcopal Committee for some share in the royalties, not as payment for any service of individual scholars, but for use in the realization of popularizing the Bible and the other express purposes contained in the Constitution of the Catholic Biblical Association.[58]

The CBA was, moreover, now planning on undertaking "a popular Biblical monthly periodical"—a move which would enable the *CBQ* to be strictly a scholarly journal. An increased share in the royalties would not only help support this new endeavor but would also cover all the expenses connected with the translation project. They, therefore, asked the episcopal committee "to reconsider the policy of wishing to pay individual scholars for service rendered, since we never worked with this spirit and purpose in the past, and if all the service of the years of scientific work were estimated on a material basis for personal renumeration [*sic*] it would be great."[59]

In a separate letter to Brady the same day, Hartman quoted a contract agreement from 1947, in which the Confraternity formally assigned royalties to the CBA. He also included an account of the royalties received for each year from 1949 to 1957.[60] In other words, the CBA was arguing that it had a direct relationship with the Confraternity and that the revision committees were among its functions. This was, however, not the way Brady interpreted the situation.

Only on March 7, 1958, did Brady respond to Hartdegen and Hartman. At the outset, he accused them of not presenting a complete financial report. He then went on to distinguish between Hartdegen and Hartman as the president and secretary of the CBA and as chairman and secretary of "the Old Testament Editorial Board." He demanded "that there be a clear declaration of the separation of the two groups." The episcopal committee, through O'Hara, he argued, had arranged "with the *Superiors* of these scholars," engaged in the translation project. Subsequently, when funds became available, "actual arrangements were made with the Superiors of these scholars as to salary and expenses." The existence of the CBA was merely accidental in relation to the translation project. In Brady's interpretation,

We now come to the situation wherein these scholars decided to establish an organization to be known as the Catholic Biblical Association of America, presumably with the approval of their Superiors. It was so established but with no approved authorization of the Body of the Bishops, who, through the Episcopal Committee of the C.C.D, had authorized the translation of the Bible.

Brady asserted that the CBA had no claim to any royalties for the work done "by fortuitous instance of a few of its scholars." The episcopal committee, which commissioned the translation, would recognize only the "Old Testament Editorial Board."[61]

Brady then addressed the proposed popular biblical periodical. The episcopal committee, he said, "approves the idea but not the subsidizing of it." In the passage that had alarmed Siegman in regard to Stanley's article, Brady stated: "this proposition (monthly magazine) in view of the questionable success of *The Catholic Biblical Quarterly* is a subject for further consideration for the C.B.A." He further challenged the CBA's dedication to promoting the Confraternity edition. On this point, he quoted a letter from O'Hara to Hartman in January, 1952, which complained that

the Association (C.B. of A.) has done little to encourage the production of the Confraternity text. When the New Testament appeared the only full length criticism was one which compared the confraternity revision unfavorably with the Knox translation. This would have ended the entire project if the Episcopal Committee had not determined to see it through. Subsequent efforts of prominently placed members of the Association to wreck the work are well known; fortunately their intrigues were defeated.[62]

Brady had moved well beyond the issue of granting the CBA a share of the royalties to challenging the right of the association to exist at all.

On March 27, Hartman informed the CBA's executive committee of Brady's letter, to which he had sent a simple acknowledgment. He suggested that the members attend the regional meeting to be held at Manhattanville College in Purchase, New York, on April 8, in order to prepare a more adequate response. He suspected that Brady's letter had actually been written by Miss Miriam Marks, executive secretary of the National Center of the Confraternity, and that "Bishop Brady evidently believes the malicious calumnies which Miss Marks told him about our Association and its relationship with the CCD."[63] When the executive board met, it had before it a draft of a response to Brady, probably composed by Hartman. It provided the essential outline of the letter, which Hartman and Hartdegen, in the name of the executive board, sent to Brady on May 25—one major difference was that the final version omitted any reference to founding a popular periodical.[64]

The letter repeated the history of the relationship between the Confraternity and the CBA, which Hartdegen and Hartman had already communicated to Brady. They then took up each of the Brady charges. Without mentioning the name of Miriam Marks, they stated that "the compilation of statements contained in the letter of Their Excellencies obviously depended on subordinates of the National Office of the C.C.D.," which "show a lack of correct information about the Catholic Biblical Association." The only scholars with whose superiors the Confraternity had made any financial arrangements were Hartman, Siegman, and Hartdegen and this was because it was O'Hara's "idea . . . to offer some compensation due to the fact that these scholars, during the period of their full time work would not be of teaching service to their own Communities." The officers challenged Brady's assertion that O'Hara had announced that "the C.B.A. had separated from the Confraternity." They noted that "we who have been attending the annual general meetings know of no time in the history of the C.B.A. when the Association separated or wished to be separated from its affiliation with the Episcopal Committee of the Confraternity." As further evidence, they cited O'Hara's speech at the annual meeting in 1955 praising the close relationship between the CBA and the Confraternity.[65]

The officers of the CBA then turned to Brady's reference to the "questionable success of the Catholic Biblical Quarterly." They acknowledged that it had "not been a financial success," for "scholarly journals are not expected to make money." The *CBQ* had kept its costs down, "because the editors work without compensation and the contributors agree to work for the small sum of a dollar a page." But "the success of the magazine as regards credit to the Church needs to be determined by other standards." Here, they cited Albright's public praise of the *CBQ* as the "best biblical journal published in North America." Answering the charge that the CBA had not promoted the Confraternity edition, they pointed out the use of the text in classrooms as well as its promotion in annual Bible weeks. They then narrated the context of the reference to the Knox translation. At the annual meeting in 1945, Siegman read a paper on Knox's English style, in order "to point out ways in which the English of the proposed Confraternity Old Testament, then in the process of translation, might derive some benefit." This was "a little self-criticism within our own circle," however, and did not imply a rejection of the Confraternity edition.[66]

The letter concluded by rejecting Brady's interpretation of O'Hara's letter to Hartman. "We cannot subscribe to the statement . . . ," they said,

that "subsequent efforts of prominently placed members of the Association to wreck the work are well known," as though this were in any way representative of the Association in reference to its own work. A categorical assertion such as this has seemed unfair. If this is a reference to the "Amator Evangelii" episode relating to the New Testament revision then it is only fair to say that the entire Association along with the Episcopal Committee and the Apostolic Delegate cooperated to preserve the translation from the danger that arose out of the misgivings which a member of the Association had concerning the dogmatic import of Philippians 2,7 and the action he took concerning it.

They reminded Brady that Lilly and Gruenthaner both responded to this charge and that the *CBQ* reprinted Gruenthaner's article from the *American Ecclesiastical Review*.[67]

On the same day as their letter in the name of the executive committee of the CBA, Hartman, Hartdegen, and Skehan, wrote Brady in their capacity as respectively the chairman, secretary, and vice chairman of the editorial board of the Old Testament. They fully acknowledged that all royalties from the Confraternity edition were "the exclusive property . . . of the Episcopal Committee of the Confraternity of Christian Doctrine." "The Board of Editors," they continued, "respectfully request continued recognition as a regular committee of the Catholic Biblical Association, constituted within the framework of the Constitution of the Association." They pointed out that seventy-six members of the association, living and dead, had contributed to the work, and that O'Hara had agreed to have "the title pages of the volumes of the Old Testament translation indicate that the work was accomplished by members of the Catholic Biblical Association." In light of the cooperation of so many who were not officially members of the editorial board, they noted that "we cannot but regret reference to ourselves in your letter as 'a few of its (the C.B.A.'s) scholars.' " The policy had been for the board to enlist an individual scholar on the basis of his competence and availability, but "no question of compensation was raised either by the Board or by those whose help was enlisted." They wished this policy to continue, for "only on these grounds can we enlist any further help that may be needed in the future, never on terms of personal compensation, or in any way that would disassociate the project from the Catholic Biblical Association." Concluding their letter, they returned to Brady a check for $4000, since the present work entailed only the reading of galley and page proofs. Since there was no need for a typist's service, they were also sending back the money Brady had designated for that purpose.[68]

This did not end the disagreement, however. In November 1958, the Old Testament committee refused to accept anything from the Confraternity until the dispute was settled. But then Brady sent "tokens of appreciation" to members of the New Testament committee who had not been informed of the Old Testament committee's stance. David Stanley and Richard Kugelman, C.P., both accepted the money and their superiors did not want them to become involved in the controversy. In the summer of 1959, Myles M. Bourke, professor of Scripture at St. Joseph's Seminary, Dunwoodie, New York, recommended to Roland Murphy that the executive board of the association rule that no one should accept any remuneration until the dispute was settled.[69] The controversy with Brady and the Confraternity was just one sign of growing tension between the CBA and certain members of the hierarchy.

TRANSITIONS IN THE CHURCH AND THE CATHOLIC BIBLICAL ASSOCIATION

In the meantime, there were important changes in the CBA. In 1958, Siegman stepped down as editor of the *CBQ*. He had a sabbatical from the Catholic University and had arranged to go to the Biblical Institute in Rome to earn the S.S.L.[70] He was replaced as editor by Roland E. Murphy, O.Carm., professor of Old Testament at the Catholic University. Murphy would continue the orientation of the *CBQ*, begun under Siegman. Moreover, he would be the helmsman for the CBA through the storms, which were about to break.

That year, 1958, was also one of transition for the American church and the Church universal. In March, Cardinal Samuel Stritch, Archbishop of Chicago, had been named proprefect of the Congregation of Propaganda in Rome, where he died only a few months later. In Chicago, he was replaced by Archbishop Albert Meyer, a charter member of the CBA, who was transferred from the Archdiocese of Milwaukee. In October, Pope Pius XII died. Prior to the conclave, which elected his successor, John XXIII, Cardinal Mooney, Archbishop of Detroit, died. His successor was John F. Dearden, former Bishop of Pittsburgh. Soon after his election, John XXIII named new cardinals. Among them were Richard Cushing, Archbishop of Boston and Archbishop Amleto Cicognani, the apostolic delegate for twenty-five years, who had so forcefully defended the rights of the American bishops when Callan had been named the sole censor of biblical material in 1941. He was replaced as delegate by Archbishop Egidio Vagnozzi, who soon formed an alliance with Fenton in attacking biblical scholarship.

For the time being, however, the CBA showed little awareness of the growing opposition to biblical scholarship. In August 1959, it met at Manhattanville College in Purchase, New York. Brendan McGrath, O.S.B., of St. Procopius Abbey, used his presidential address to remind Catholic scholars that they should see the advantage in finding the truth in what others were saying. Scripture scholarship would advance only by discovering the truth, whether it was uttered by Gregory of Nyssa or Martin Luther or Rudolph Bultmann. Neil McEleney, C.S.P., reported that the Paulist Press would soon begin a pamphlet Bible series, intended to disseminate more widely both the new translations of the Old Testament and scholarly commentaries on the books. Eugene Maly spoke on the antimonarchical tradition in Isaiah and Frederick Moriarty on the retrospective type of historical writing in the Old Testament, especially in Joshua and Deuteronomy. Bruce Vawter, C.M., of St. Thomas Seminary in Denver, addressed the issues of apocalyptic and prophetic literature. John Collins, S.J., of Weston College, discussed Oscar Cullman's argument for the rejection of immortality on the basis of the New Testament. One paper, however, would contribute to the growing controversy. In the words of the printed minutes, "Fr. Myles M. Bourke analyzed the literary genre of Matthew 1–2, which precipitated more discussion on midrashic elements; the speaker distinguished between historical nucleus and midrashic development in certain events of the infancy narrative."[71] Subsequently published in the *CBQ*,[72] the paper became, as will be seen, one of the articles cited as the basis for a conservative attack on the Biblical Institute.

Aside from the papers, the meeting in 1959 was important because of two other developments. First, the Society of Biblical Literature (SBL) took the initiative in voting to exchange official delegates with the CBA. Robert C. Dentan was introduced as the SBL's first representative to the CBA, which then passed a similar resolution to send a delegate to the SBL. Second, present for one afternoon session was Cardinal Francis Spellman, Archbishop of New York.[73] Not himself an intellectual, he would become a strong supporter of biblical scholars, especially against the attacks of Vagnozzi, with whom he had had strained relations, since both of them had arrived in the United States on the same ship in 1932—Spellman to become the auxiliary bishop of Boston and Vagnozzi to take up duties as an assistant to Cicognani.[74]

Despite the ecumenical recognition that Catholic biblical scholarship was gaining in the United States, that recognition was not universal. Vawter complained in 1959 that the *Journal of Biblical Literature* still misrepresented Catholic exegesis. During that summer, moreover, Oxford was to host the Third International Congress for the Study of the Old Testament. Of the twenty-three papers on the program, not one was allotted to a Catholic. Siegman, then in Rome, had told Vawter that the Biblical Institute was tempted to boycott the congress. As a member of the organization sponsoring the congress, Vawter protested that "nobody has any right to turn it into a non-Catholic organization." He suggested to Roland Murphy, "after we see how the final disposition is by the people at Oxford, that the *CBQ* publish an open letter on the subject, signed by the President of the Association, deploring this major set-back in interconfessional co-operation in the Scripture field."[75] Siegman added his own advice to Murphy that, "since we contributed so generously to the Congress, you might ask [William

F.] Albright, when you run into him, why no Catholics were invited, which had hurt the people at the PIB [Pontificio istituto biblico] considerably."[76]

In the meanwhile, there were other clouds appearing on the European horizon that would burst forth in a storm against biblical scholarship. In February 1958, the Congregation of Seminaries and Universities had declared that Robert-Feuillet's *Introduction à la Bible* was unsuitable for use in seminaries, though both the Biblical Commission and the Holy Office refused to proscribe it. In November, Siegman learned in Rome that Antonino Romeo, a professor at the Lateran Seminary and consultor to the congregation was "so anxious to kill the French work" because "his own Introduction (a collective work also; he has written the section on Inspiration) has just appeared!" He strongly recommended that the *CBQ* have "someone review it who will do a job on it."[77] Romeo would become an increasing critic of biblical scholarship and would soon level his attacks on the Biblical Institute. These attacks came at a critical time, for on January 25, 1959, John XXIII announced that he was calling a council. For the moment, Scripture scholars were uncertain how the new pope regarded them and what a council would mean. The next four years were a period of crisis, as they now found themselves on the defensive against an entrenched form of theology.

By 1959, the CBA was dramatically different from the group of biblical professors who had first assembled in Washington in 1936 to discuss the translation of the New Testament. It had passed through its infancy of naïvete and fundamentalism, its adolescence of ambiguity as to whether it was a popular or scholarly organization, to an adulthood of assimilation of critical scholarship. Its members were now at home with issues, such as form criticism, literary criticism, and whether Isaiah was written by one man. An increasing number of its members had received not only the S.S.L. or S.S.D., but had also the Ph.D. from leading secular institutions, such as Johns Hopkins. Those who received their pontifical degrees from the Biblical Institute in Rome no longer reflected the obscurantism of that institution's early days, but the progressive scholarship, which emerged with *Divino Afflante Spiritu*. Among its members were some leading members of the hierarchy, principally Archbishop Meyer, who was elevated to the cardinalate in December, 1959. It had gained, if not the support, at least no opposition from the most politically powerful of the American cardinals, Spellman. American Catholic biblical scholarship, almost alone among Catholic scholarly disciplines, was prepared to take a leading role in the Second Vatican Council, which John XXIII had called. But it would still have to face overt opposition on the eve of the council and through its first session.

13. American Catholic Biblical Scholarship on the Eve of the Second Vatican Council

The CBA now included among its members some of the nation's outstanding biblical scholars. Yet, from time to time in the annual meetings during the 1950s, tensions had surfaced between the old theology, shaped in defense against rationalism and Modernism, and the new scholarship, encouraged by Pius XII. On the eve of the Second Vatican Council, the CBA had to defend biblical scholarship against a rising crescendo of attacks emanating particularly from the *American Ecclesiastical Review* and its editor, Monsignor Joseph C. Fenton. Orchestrating these attacks was Archbishop Egidio Vagnozzi, the apostolic delegate. As had happened at the turn of the century with Americanism, the conflict in the United States was but a reflection of the campaign in Rome, where the Biblical Institute was engaged in an identical ideological controversy over the new scholarship with Cardinal Alfredo Ottaviani, Secretary of the Holy Office, and his associates. In the United States, biblical scholars found support from a powerful, though unlikely ally, Cardinal Francis Spellman, Archbishop of New York. But the battle was to have its casualties. Edward Siegman at the Catholic University became the principal target of both Fenton and Vagnozzi.

JOSEPH C. FENTON, THE *AMERICAN ECCLESIASTICAL REVIEW,* AND ARCHBISHOP EGIDIO VAGNOZZI

One of the earliest of the *American Ecclesiastical Review*'s attacks on the new biblical scholarship appeared in the column "Answers to Questions" by Francis Connell, whom Siegman had previously seen in a friendly light. In January 1959, Connell answered the question whether there was a "trend among some Catholic scripture scholars nowadays to interpret the Bible in such wise as to seem to weaken its historical value." Connell's answer quoted from *Divino Afflante Spiritu*, and more particularly from *Humani Generis*, but his conclusion was the more offensive part of his answer. "I believe, also," he wrote,

that it is opportune to remind Catholic scholars of their duty to join to their research prayer for divine guidance. It is true, we do not hold that by prayer alone a scholar will be assured of special divine guidance in the pursuit of his studies. But prayer will obtain gifts of grace, which will surely aid those who are engaged in the delicate task of investigating religious truth. It is pathetic to meet a Catholic scholar so busy with his studies that he limits his prayers to the minimum. An occasional hour before the Blessed Sacrament will help him more in his studies than many hours of painstaking research.[1]

It was difficult for biblical scholars, some of whom were Connell's colleagues at the Catholic University, not to feel their spiritual lives had been called in question.

Six months later another attack came in the same journal, this time from Fenton. He claimed that a question had been sent in concerning whether "recent trends" had now repudiated "the traditional method found in most manuals and set forth in most seminary courses," which held that the Gospels were "historical documents." The topic was too important to be relegated to the "Answers to Questions" column, Fenton declared, and must be answered in the light of the magisterium. In *Providentissimus Deus*, he argued, Leo XIII "means that the Church's teaching power is what it is precisely because Our Lord actually did and said what the inspired books, and particularly the four Gospels, state that He did and said." At the turn of the century, some of the liberal scholars had attempted to show that the Church had nothing to fear from historical criticism of the Scripture, because, even if there were no Scriptures, there would still be a Church. Fenton reversed this. In his interpretation of Leo's thought, "Catholic teachers are called upon to assert and to vindicate at least the human or natural historical trustworthiness of these writings, not because it is the policy of the moment, but because the authority of the Church itself depends upon the fact that what is set down in these books is really true." The Church, therefore, depended solely on Scripture, and the veracity of her dogmatic pronouncements depended on the historical credibility of the Gospels. Anyone who denied "that the four Gospels are reliable historical documents is certainly being recreant to the task set before him in the *Providentissimus Deus.* "[2]

But Fenton was not done with the matter. He reminded his readers of the Holy Office's decree *Lamentabili,* which had condemned the proposition that John was "only an outstanding witness of the Christian life, or of the life of Christ in the Church, towards the end of the first century." The Gospel of John, he continued, had been the object of "particular attack" of the "original Modernists." But "recently" it had "apparently become fashionable to make this statement with reference to all four of the canonical Gospels"—a statement that Fenton asserted was "impossible for any loyal and instructed Catholic." Fenton went on to list other propositions in *Lamentabili* concerning the Gospels and instructed his readers in the "binding force" of the syllabus and of the decisions of the Biblical Commission as explained by Pius X in *Praestantia Scripturae Sacrae.* The pope had declared that anyone who contradicted either *Lamentabili* or *Pascendi* incurred "*ipso facto* the censure" of excommunication. Though the pope had stated that those who disagreed with the decisions of the Biblical Commission incurred "the note of disobedience and of *temeritas* and consequently are guilty of serious sin,"[3] Fenton lumped all Roman decisions and statements together as binding under pain of excommunication.

For a true approach to "apologetics" that displayed "the historical reliability of the four Gospels," Fenton recommended both Bishop Hilarinus Felder's *Christ and the Critics* and Léonce de Grandmaison's "classical work *Jésus Christ.* " De Grandmaison was so persuasive, Fenton argued, because he simply presented "the essentials of that traditional apologetic [which] were enunciated by the Vatican Council as a part of the dogmatic constitution *Dei Filius.* "[4] Fenton's theological objection to the new approach to Scripture was consistent. Magisterial pronouncements, and not history, were the starting points for any discussion. But his objection was also dishonest. Absent from consideration as part of the magisterium was any reference to *Divino Afflante Spiritu* or the letter to Cardinal Suhard. Yet, he claimed that he was finding the authentic teaching of the Church in the *Enchiridion Biblicum,* which contained both of those documents.

Fenton, however, did not limit his attacks to the printed page. At the Catholic University in the fall of 1959, Geoffrey Wood, S.A., submitted to Siegman a dissertation proposal on the literary genre of Lk 1–2. When the dissertation outline was submitted to the faculty, Siegman reported that "Msgr. Fenton objected vehemently, and cited it as an example of the neo-modernism which he had been combatting in *AER.*" Siegman then rewrote part of the proposal to remove any ambiguity. The faculty then approved the dissertation outline, but Fenton still voted against it. Some months later, Siegman received a letter from his provincial, John E. Byrne, C.PP.S., asking whether he held that "the historical accuracy of Lk 1–2 is governed by our judgment on the literary form." Byrne could not reveal the source of his query, but Siegman recognized the phrasing as the first version of the proposition in Wood's dissertation outline, which he had rewritten. He subsequently learned that it was Vagnozzi who had written to his provincial and that, therefore, Fenton had given the delegate the information.[5]

Siegman had already filled in his provincial on Fenton's attitude toward Scripture scholars. Early in 1960, Siegman had been asked to serve as subeditor for the New Testament under Skehan in preparation of the *New Catholic Encyclopedia.* As he told Byrne,

I don't know how well you are familiar with the Msgr. Joseph Clifford Fenton phenomenon that stalks our C.U. campus and strikes dread into fearful hearts who have ecclesiastical ambitions and quail at Joe's veiled threats to fix clocks in Rome. Joe has been giving the Scripture men a bad time with his accusations of "neo-modernism." He just spoils anything he puts his hand on, witness the *American Ecclesiastical Review.* Well, since I have reached the peak of my ambitions and since Scripture profs are somewhat scarce, I don't exactly fear Joe, and so I told Msgr. Skehan quite bluntly (and he agreed whole-heartedly with my stand) that if the big Monsignor is going to be an editor, or have any job in which he can throw his weight around, I would not accept any job on the staff, although I would write the articles I am asked to write. I hardly expected my condition to be accepted, but I am told that it was; at least, the steering committee all agreed that Joe makes too many enemies and so could not work on a job like this. He is being made a "consultant" instead, and generally consultants do not die from being over consulted.[6]

During the summer, after Siegman had explained his position in regard to literary forms and Lk 1–2, he provided Byrne with additional information about his situation. He also drew the parallel with what was then happening in Rome. "I should warn you," he wrote his provincial,

that I cannot guarantee that you will hear no more complaints about me. The reactionaries are fighting hard. I wish their competence were as great as their doggedness and fanaticism. The Lateran University, you doubtless know, is trying hard to gain prestige, and since most of their men are mediocre, they have resorted to attacking the men who are making real contributions, especially the French. Msgr. Romeo is the spearhead of the attack, he enjoys the patronage of Cardinal Ottaviani, formerly on the faculty, and in this country the Apostolic Delegate and Msgr. Fenton are the most prominent agitators. The Delegate is a big disappointment to all of us. He apparently is quite rash in using hearsay information, and takes action before he knows what it is all about. He had mentioned Fr. David Stanley's name at gatherings, though I doubt seriously whether he ever read anything that Fr. Stanley wrote. He tried, I understand, to persuade Cardinal Spellman to deny the Imprimatur to the Paulist Bible Pamphlets. After consulting with his seminary faculty, the Cardinal backed the pamphlets. Most priests and bishops, however, will assume that the Delegate speaks for "Rome" no matter what irresponsible nonsense he spouts forth, as when he remarked at a banquet, "President Eisenhower does not like Catholics, I understand." No wonder the Philippines were glad to have him promoted to the U.S.A.[7]

Even though Siegman did not yet know that Vagnozzi had written his provincial accusing him of heresy, he and others were fully cognizant of the existence of a Fenton-Vagnozzi-Ottaviani axis. His mention of Spellman's support of the Bible Pamphlet Series, moreover, indicated that he knew that biblical scholars were gaining support from an unexpected source.

In January 1960, the Paulist Press began publication of the Pamphlet Bible Series, to which members of the CBA contributed. The series was edited by Neil J. McEleney, C.S.P, of St. Paul's College in Washington, D.C. The first to appear was an introduction to the Pentateuch by McEleney; the second was on Genesis by Ignatius Hunt. The series had received Spellman's *imprimatur,* which Vagnozzi then asked him to withdraw. On April 2, McEleney received a phone call from John Carr, the editor of the Paulist Press, stating that Spellman wished to see the two of them, together with John Mitchell, C.S.P, the general of the Paulists, on April 8. No reason was given for the meeting. When McEleney arrived, he found Father Myles Bourke, then professor of New Testament at Dunwoodie, Joseph Nelson and Charles O'Conor Sloane, former Scripture professors at the seminary, and John A. Goodwine, the diocesan censor, none of whom knew the purpose of the meeting to which they had been summoned. Spellman pointed out to McEleney several marked passages in the pamphlets. McEleney and Mitchell both explained that the two pamphlets merely reflected the commonly accepted approach of most Catholic Old Testament scholars. When Spellman then queried why Vagnozzi was therefore objecting to them, Bourke explained that the delegate was on good terms with a group of theologians who had been making increasing attacks on biblical scholarship, especially since the death of Pius XII in 1958.[8] Learning Vagnozzi's motivations, Spellman was now swinging toward support of the biblical scholars.

At the end of the meeting, McEleney promised to send Spellman a written explanation. In the meantime, he called Hunt to alert him to the situation. Once back in Washington, McEleney called Roland Murphy to warn him of what had happened, and then on April 13, wrote Spellman the letter he had promised. He cited the encouragement given to biblical scholarship by Pius XII in *Divino Afflante Spiritu,* but then pointed out that both he and Hunt had closely followed the line of thought of Albert Clamer and Roland de Vaux, O.P., each of whom was a consultor to the Biblical Commission.[9] McEleney learned a short time later from Patrick Skehan that Spellman had commented about the affair: "They knew what they were doing so I supported them."[10] Spellman then wrote Vagnozzi stating that he would not withdraw his *imprimatur* and that the series would continue.[11] Spellman had long been at odds with Vagnozzi and was not about to tolerate the intrusion of a delegate into the authority of an ordinary. At the council, as will be seen, his enmity for Vagnozzi, as well as for Ottaviani, led him to espouse a number of progressive causes.

In the meantime, Fenton continued his assaults in the *American Ecclesiastical Review*. In March 1960, he wrote that "it is unfortunately possible for a man, while retaining the supernatural virtue of divine faith, to build up within himself dispositions which are hostile to this virtue." "Since the early days of Modernism, these dispositions" advanced "under cover of learning." The priest concerned for "a properly ascetical care for the virtue of faith" would make his own the words of Vatican I's *Dei Filius* that, "although actually faith is above reason, there can still never be any true opposition between faith and reason." Such a priest was "not going to be stampeded into accepting as true any proposition contradictory to or incompatible with that teaching [Catholic dogma], even when that proposition is represented as the fruit of modern science." He would take to heart the words of Pius IX in *Tuas libenter*, addressed to the Archbishop of Munich in 1863, that "Catholic savants" should "submit themselves to the doctrinal decisions which are set forth by the Pontifical Congregations as well as to those points of doctrine which are held by the common and constant consent of Catholics as theological truths and conclusions which are so certain that, even though the opinions opposed to these points of doctrine cannot be designated as heretical, they still deserve some other theological censure."[12]

Fenton's ideal priest had to resist the temptation to "gullibility" in "accepting something . . . incompatible with Catholic doctrine," without being "shown conclusive *evidence.*" "The ascetical cultivation of . . . faith" demanded of "the believer a realistic attitude with reference to sources which are supposed to be scientific or scholarly." Then Fenton began focusing his attack on accepting truth from outside the Catholic Church. "The Catholic who is prone to offer servile adulation to everything that is represented as the fruit of scholarship in non-Catholic or anti-Catholic circles," he declared,

is, by his very attitude, endangering the force and the perfection of his own faith, and thus of his own spiritual life. The man who is certain, on the authority of God Himself, that what God has revealed is true, is not in a position to be deluded into imagining that statements incompatible with the divine teaching are backed by any genuine evidence. The tragedy of Modernism in the twentieth century has centered around the fact that men who should have known better were led to imagine that teachings incompatible with Catholic faith and Catholic doctrine were legitimate scientific conclusions.

Having worked himself up to a peroration, Fenton now attacked those who argued that there was a distinction between scientific knowledge and "the faith of the ordinary Catholic." Here, he used as an example Friedrich von Hügel. It was not, as some said, that he exposed his daughter to "religious and historical truths" when she was too young to comprehend, but that she and "the unfortunate priests," who were "under the influence of the old Modernist," abandoned the faith because of "a mass of errors which Von Hügel deluded all of them into accepting as religious and historical truth." In case there was any doubt of what he intended, Fenton concluded that "the ascetical development of the divine faith" meant "the repudiation of the fancy that religious or historical truth can be harmful to the faith." For this, nothing was more dangerous than those who failed to embrace the entire truth, for

> It is also a matter of record that, during the earlier stages of the Modernist crisis, far more harm was done to the faith of Catholics by men who piously professed acceptance of the Church's teaching, but who, at the same time, bitterly opposed all of those who actually contradicted the Modernist writers, than was done by the Modernists themselves. The man who works for the advancement and the strengthening of the faith within him definitely cannot be an anti-anti-Modernist.[13]

Without ever having mentioned them, Fenton clearly considered the new biblical scholars as, at least, "anti-anti-Modernists," if not Modernists.

In the summer of 1961, the *American Ecclesiastical Review* grew even bolder. Two articles in the July issue alone warned of the danger of the new exegetes. Gerald T. Kennedy, O.M.I., warned of the dangers of applying form criticism to the New Testament. It was one thing, he said, to speak of the prodigal son as imaginary; it was quite another thing to reject the existence of Mary Magdalen, a "case [in which] the evangelist records as flesh and blood example of a prodigal daughter and teaches the same divine truth [of forgiveness]." There had been numerous attempts to apply to the sacred text the "types" of narrative used in analyzing profane history, he continued, but "since the advent of Modernism, . . . the philosophical motives which stirred the protagonists of the movement were basically those of the positivists who accepted only what they could measure in a concrete way." This led to a rejection of "an historical Christ and a divinely established Church." Though "the *Lamentabili* and the *Pascendi* cleared the air of [the] virus of Modernism," he asserted, "its after-effects . . . lingered" with those who were "imprudent" or "half-trained" or "untrained" failing to make "the proper distinctions" when treating "certain historical topics in the New Testament."[14]

Why "deny the existence of the star which attracted the Magi," queried Kennedy, and argue that it was a piece of Midrash, when "one would be more in line with honesty to admit a similarity and affirm that God is the God of nature and controls the creatures of his Hand." Lest there be any doubt of his outlook, Kennedy advised his readers: "let those who fear that modern scriptural studies are tearing the Bible to tatters be assured that there was an annunciation, a nativity, a visit by the Magi, a flight into Egypt and a return to Nazareth just as surely as there was a wedding feast in Cana, a multiplication of the loaves and fishes and a sacrifice on Calvary."[15] Kennedy, of course, made no distinction between the various events narrated in the Bible; they were all of equal importance for preserving the historical truth of the existence of Christ.

The second article in the July issue of the review was by the associate editor, John L. Murphy, who traced to Friedrich Schleiermacher the influence on "biblical criticism in the developing liberal theology of the last century [which] meant treating the Scriptures as purely human creations, as expressions of the religious experience of the primitive Christian Church alone." It was essential that Catholic exegetes "spell out more distinctly the philosophical or theological basis upon which we are working." Only this would "separate the scriptural position of Catholic scholars today from the context of liberal theology." Nor was it correct to argue that Catholics were allowed more freedom under Pius XII than under Pius X, for Pius XII and, before him, Leo XIII condemned "the philosophical basis coloring all of the interpretations offered both by the Protestant Liberals and the Modernists within the Catholic Church." This "complicated web of Schleiermachian thought," underlying biblical criticism "was condemned by Rome then" and "is condemned today."[16]

Murphy granted that it was "considerably easier for the scriptural scholar to advance his findings today quite independent of the philosophical matrix into which similar findings were inserted by Liberals and Modernists at the turn of the century." While "the Roman Pontiffs have given frequent encouragement to such scriptural studies," however, they attached the condition "that the data would be related to the philosophical and theological basis proper to Catholicism." If this was "neglected in any way," Murphy warned,

difficulties recur. The student of Scripture may ask that all give to him that charitable understanding urged by Pius XII, but at the same time, it would possibly be more prudent and would help matters no end if he himself would state in as clear a manner as possible the relationship of his data to Catholic theology. The exegete has a responsibility, certainly, to the whole of Catholic doctrine, and cannot, on the pretext of specialization, absolve himself from this further duty. To do so will only cause misunderstanding on the part of the dogmatic theologian, and may possibly be the occasion of others inadvertently interpreting the data for themselves in the context of something like that of Schleiermacher's philosophy.

Biblical scholars, he concluded, should be aware of "precisely what did happen in the Modernist crisis" and be cautious of "the use . . . of the exegetical conclusions of non-Catholic scriptural scholars," for "apart from the more simple determination of texts, the meaning of words, and the like, it is obvious that any exegete must labor within the framework of his own philosophical or theological background."[17] An ecumenist, Murphy certainly was not. His was still the *aprioristic* method of starting with dogma as interpreted in light of a particular type of theology. But he never paused for a moment to question whether that theology was itself historically conditioned.

The *American Ecclesiastical Review* and its contributors were not the only public critics of biblical scholarship. Early in the summer of 1961, Archbishop Vagnozzi gave an address at Marquette University in Milwaukee. He listed everything that he saw undermining the life of "the Catholic intellectual," from new theological developments to the movement for the vernacular liturgy. But he reserved some of his sharpest comments for biblical scholarship. There was a dangerous movement among some Catholic intellectuals, he declared, "to build a bridge between modern secular thought and Catholic thought, even to the point of digressing from positions traditionally accepted in the past, in the expectation of being acknowledged and accepted in the intellectual circles of today." Sometimes, these people introduced "interpretations of Catholic teaching which would often appear to be contradictory to what has been believed not only in the last century but in the preceding centuries as well." In this context, Vagnozzi addressed the issue of the "dispute amongst Catholic scholars concerning the idea of history as applied to both the Old and New Testaments." On the one hand, he acknowledged that "this dispute takes its foundation from the request made by Pope Pius XII . . . that exegetes lay stress upon and diligently investigate the 'literary meaning' of the Sacred Text," in order to know "the mind of the authors" and deepen "our knowledge of the Word of God." On the other hand, though he admitted that it was not his prerogative to say whether "recent efforts to give us this literary meaning are in consonance with the teaching of the Church," he did think exegetes should not "insist on presenting as definitive truth—to be accepted by all right-thinking people—theories and opinions which can receive the definitive stamp of truthfulness only from the 'magisterium' of the Church."[18]

Vagnozzi concluded his remarks by stating that "the Sacred Books of the Bible are too basically fundamental, too basically essential to be left to the individual and private interpretation of even a large number of scholars."[19] No American Catholic biblical scholars had, of course, argued in favor of "individual and private interpretation," but Vagnozzi put them on notice that he saw them already in the camp of the Protestants. Vagnozzi's address was published in the *American Ecclesiastical Review.*

THE ROMAN DIMENSION TO THE AMERICAN BATTLE: ATTACKS ON THE BIBLICAL INSTITUTE

What Vagnozzi and the writers in the *American Ecclesiastical Review* were saying, however, was but an American version of the scene then being played in Rome. There, biblical scholars and particularly the Biblical Institute had been coming under increasing attack during the late 1950s, but especially after the death of Pius XII. In January 1955, Cardinal Giuseppe Pizzardo, secretary of the Holy Office, had written Ernest Vogt, S.J., the rector of the institute. Both Robert Dyson, S.J., English-born, but a member of the

New England Province, and Robert North, S.J., of the United States, said the cardinal, had been accused of espousing the critical methods of "liberal Protestants" to the detriment of the doctrine of revelation in the Old Testament. Vogt soon learned that the accusations were made by Monsignor Antonino Romeo, professor of theology at the Lateran Seminary and a consultor to the Congregation of Seminaries and Universities. Vogt refuted the charges, but then learned from Pizzardo in May, 1955, that there were still efforts being made to remove Dyson and North from the institute. At this time, however, Pizzardo encouraged Vogt and told him that the institute still enjoyed Pius XII's favor. During 1958, Romeo continued his attacks, usually in unsigned articles. In December, after the election of John XXIII, Pizzardo assured Vogt that he had ordered members of the Congregation of Seminaries not to meddle in biblical affairs. When Vogt responded that they continued to make accusations, the cardinal replied decisively, "yes, yes, they have ceased."[20]

For a time, the attacks did cease, but the silence was only the lull before the storm. In the December 1960 issue of *Divinitas,* published in January 1961, Romeo wrote a signed article attacking Luis Alonso-Schökel, S.J., and Max Zerwick, S.J., both professors at the institute. He accused them of going against the teaching of *Divino Afflante Spiritu* and of *Humani Generis*. Romeo also specifically cited Myles Bourke's article on "The Literary Genus of Mt 1–2," which had originally been given as a paper at the CBA meeting in 1959. One of Romeo's correspondents in the United States, probably Fenton, had referred to the article as an example of "a flood of new biblical 'modernism,' " proponents of which won applause "only because they say new things, that is they repeat the old things of the rationalists."[21] Archbishop Vagnozzi had already made objections to the article to Spellman. In an initial reply to Romeo, which was subsequently withdrawn from circulation, the Biblical Institute charged that Romeo spoke of the dangerous influence of the institute on its students, but that he had ignored the hundreds of graduates who were beyond reproach and had cited "a particular case" of a graduate who had not learned his ideas from the institute. Bourke was the "particular case," and the Biblical Institute, in its defense of the orthodoxy of its teaching, argued on the technical grounds that he had never formally taken a course in the Gospel of Matthew as a student in Rome.[22]

Romeo's article, said Vogt, created such a "scandal" that in March he received a letter from Athanasius Miller, in the name of all the consultors of the Biblical Commission, expressing their "keen regret" for Romeo's attacks. The consultors wished "publicly to reaffirm their unchangeable adhesion and solidarity with the Biblical Institute."[23] Cardinal Pizzardo, furthermore, wrote Cardinal Bea on February 3 to say that neither he nor the secretary of the Congregation of Seminaries and Universities knew anything of Romeo's article before it was in print. "The responsibility for the article," continued Pizzardo, rested "exclusively upon the person who wrote it." "The tone of the publication," he declared, "is so personal as obviously to exclude any official or quasi-official character." Pizzardo gave Bea permission to communicate his letter to anyone he wished.[24] The Biblical Institute then countered these charges in its journal, *Verbum Domini.*[25] A copy of this was then sent to Roland Murphy, the editor of the *CBQ.*

Murphy had already been watching the Roman controversy, so similar to the American one. On March 13, he wrote Vogt to offer the services of the *CBQ.* He had heard—erroneously as it turned out—that copies of the reply to Romeo in *Verbum Domini* had been ordered "recalled." While some members of the CBA had suggested "that the *CBQ* print the reply over the names of the editorial staff," he hesitated to "print anything that will make things difficult for the Biblical Institute." Murphy himself thought that what was needed was "a good stiff reply or observation on our own part (if Frank McCool or Bill Moran are minded to phrase such a comment, we would welcome it.)" For the time being, he would do nothing until he received Vogt's advice.[26]

Vogt replied on March 25. He had sent copies of the *Verbum Domini* article to all the Italian bishops, to whom Romeo had sent copies of his article. In the meantime, Silverio Zedda, S.J., president of the Associazione Biblica Italiana, which "had also been an object of the Monsignor's wrath," had prepared a protest and response. The Biblical Institute had "received numerous letters protesting against the libellous statements of Romeo and expressing sympathy to us," Vogt continued, and was now receiving important signs of papal support. Not only had Miller written the institute in the name of the consultors of the Biblical Commission, but John XXIII had recently named Vogt "consultor of the Theological Commission for the coming Council, thus showing that His confidence in the Biblical was unshaken." In view of these actions of "the Roman authorities," Vogt had ordered the institute's bookstore to stop selling the *Verbum Domini* article, in order not "to prolong this controversy one moment longer than is absolutely necessary."[27]

Since the situation in Rome was then quiet, Vogt suggested that the *CBQ* print only "a note of clarification on the Roman controversy." The note, he said,

you can phrase as you wish but in our judgement it should be brief, impersonally stated and should contain the following points:

1) This attack was aimed not only at the Biblical Institute but against the developments in biblical studies as promoted by Pius XII.

2) It was in no way official or semi-official in character, despite the position of Monsignor Romeo; but represents at the most the views of a small group in Rome which has not had training in modern biblical studies and which is hostile to the pontifical directives given on these matters during the past 20 years. . . .

3) It has been strongly disapproved of by very many persons in high authority in the Church, some of whom have termed the attack "unjustifiable from the scientific, moral and Christian point of view" and have stated that "it [the attack] has rendered all modern Catholic exegesis suspect in a way which is totally alien to the love of truth or to Christian charity."

Vogt thought that, if the editors of the *CBQ* "joined their voice" with those who had already spoken in behalf of the institute, "this would be an affirmation of solidarity which we should appreciate and which would be useful in the present situation." He also suggested that the letters of Miller to the institute and of Pizzardo to Bea be distributed to the members of the CBA, in order to "close the mouths of those who attribute official value to Romeo's charges."[28]

Murphy then hastily wrote a brief notice, "The Close of a Controversy," in time for the April issue of the *CBQ*. Following Vogt's suggestions, he briefly narrated the controversy, without mentioning Romeo's name. "In retrospect," he said, "the affair illustrates the difficulty that many people have had in accepting the principles laid down in the *Divino Afflante Spiritu* by the late Pope Pius XII." "Perhaps the most salutary effect of all this," he continued, "will be to highlight the need of many to inform themselves concerning scholarly methods and principles involved in the understanding of Sacred Scripture." The Biblical Institute, he pointed out, had received "warm support . . . , which the *CBQ* heartily seconds." He concluded by stating that "former students of Father Ernest Vogt, S.J.," among whom was Murphy himself, would "rejoice" at Vogt's recent appointment to the Theological Commission.[29] Murphy, of course, was not being naive, but diplomatic in referring to the "close of a controversy." It would only get worse, but, in the meantime, he had also distributed copies of the letters of Miller and Pizzardo to all members of the CBA.

THE HOLY OFFICE ADMONITION

On June 20, 1961, the Holy Office, in agreement with the cardinal members of the Biblical Commission, issued a *monitum*. Mixing praise with admonition, it stated:

Now that there is evidence of laudable efforts to study the Biblical sciences, judgements and opinions are being spread in many countries which gravely imperil the exact historical and objective truth of Holy Scripture, not only in the case of the Old Testament, as Pope Pius XII had cause to lament in '*Humani Generis*', but also in the case of the New Testament, involving even the words and events of the life of Christ.

Since these judgements and opinions are disturbing Pastors and Faithful, the eminent Fathers who are the guardians of faith and morals, have decided to notify all those whose work concerns the Sacred Books that they should treat them with the prudence and respect demanded by a subject of such great importance and that they should keep before them at all times the doctrine of the Fathers and their way of thinking together with the *magisterium* of the Church, so that the consciences of the Faithful be not troubled nor the truths of Faith damaged.[30]

In the midst of the preparation for the Second Vatican Council and in the wake of assaults on biblical scholarship, the *monitum* gave rise to a series of contradictory interpretations.

On August 19, less than ten days before the CBA's annual meeting, Vagnozzi addressed the second national conference of religious at the University of Notre Dame. "This Monitum," he declared,

did not originate in the personal worries or limited views of a small group of Vatican officials. Nor was it issued without serious and weighty reasons. It came from that Sacred Congregation which is supreme among the authoritative organs of the Apostolic See and of which the Holy Father himself is the head and Prefect. A Monitum is only a warning, but it is designed to prevent the adoption of stronger and more direct measures. . . . See to it, therefore that all those under your authority respond to this Monitum with a filial acceptance which is sincere and that they observe its prescriptions with exactness.[31]

As will be seen, the meaning of the *monitum* would provide cause for further controversy.

The summer of 1961 was filled with mixed signals for biblical scholars. On July 6, 1961, John F. Whealon, a member of the CBA, was consecrated auxiliary bishop of Cleveland. Acknowledging Louis Hartman's congratulations, he remarked, "Maybe now I can do something to keep all of us from being burned at the stake."[32] Whealon had his first chance to "do something" at his episcopal consecration. Due to the illness of Bishop Edward Hoban of Cleveland, the principal consecrator was Archbishop Vagnozzi, who used every opportunity after the ceremony to question Whealon about what the Scripture scholars were teaching.[33] Whealon, who subsequently was named Bishop of Erie and Archbishop of Hartford, later reflected that Vagnozzi's difficulty was that he honestly believed that the inspiration of each Pauline letter, for example, was directly linked to its having been written by Paul himself.[34] In this, of course, Vagnozzi was merely reflecting the thought of Cardinal Ottaviani. But his discourses gave added weight to Fenton's charges, and he now joined with the Catholic University professor to cleanse the university of the dangerous exegesis.

ATTACKS ON EDWARD SIEGMAN

In the meantime, Siegman had learned that not only was he the particular object of Vagnozzi's offensive but also that it was the delegate who had written to his provincial the previous year. Siegman had been asked by Father James Healy, Catholic chaplain at Yale University, to give a series of lectures on Scripture. At the same time, Healy was negotiating with Archbishop Henry O'Brien of Hartford to approve the establishment of a chair of Catholic studies at the university. In July, O'Brien had not yet approved either the establishment of a chair or the extension of Healy's invitation to Siegman. Siegman feared that O'Brien's delay was due to several factors. First of all, Roland Murphy had been invited to be a visiting professor at Princeton University in the fall semester of 1962, but Bishop George Ahr of Trenton vehemently refused his permission and even requested that the Congregation of Seminaries and Universities gain the Carmelite General's prohibition of Murphy's accepting the post. But Siegman had obtained far more ominous information.[35]

Siegman, who had recently recovered from a heart attack, was then teaching in the summer institute at the Catholic University, in which one of his students was a religious sister. Vagnozzi visited her convent and learned that she was taking Siegman's course. As Siegman narrated the story to his provincial, Vagnozzi "told her to quit . . . , because she would become perverted with us. He bandied around the terms [sic] heretic quite freely, and mentioned me by name as apparently the main villain." The sister also told Siegman that the delegate stated that he had already written his provincial the year before. "Evidently," Siegman continued, Vagnozzi "is following the line of thought that Msgr. Fenton used in 1957 when we first began this program, i.e., that we shouldn't be teaching these things to Sisters and Brothers because we will disturb their faith." He further suspected that the delegate "will succeed in killing the program here, and will also persuade the Rector to knock out all Scripture in the Religious Education Department." He knew that "somebody is feeding him fuel about me," but could think of nothing he had done, except to write a rejoinder to an article in *The Priest* by Francis Filas, S.J., of Loyola University in Chicago. Vagnozzi had praised that article in a letter, a copy of which Filas jubilantly sent to Siegman.[36]

Siegman thought that perhaps Vagnozzi's hostility toward him might have entered into "Archbishop O'Brien's hesitation." He did not know, he went on,

whether Bishops consult the Delegate about something like this, but if my name is mentioned to the Delegate, he will surely speak his mind about how undesirable I am in this matter. He must have suggested to the Rector to get rid of me. I would be glad to resign, of course, but this would be admitting guilt. Moreover, I don't care to do anything that would compromise my chances to be invited to Yale.

Siegman noted that his doctor had "been eloquent about my avoiding tensions," but that a recent cardiogram had indicated that the damage was healed.[37] Siegman's weak heart, as will be seen, soon provided the excuse for him to be summarily dismissed from the university.

THE CBA RESOLUTION AGAINST THE *AMERICAN ECCLESIASTICAL REVIEW*

During the summer of 1961, it was impossible for either Siegman or other biblical scholars to avoid tension. The progressive members of the CBA, therefore, decided to launch a counterattack against their critics.

THE CBA MEETING, 1961

From August 28 to September 1, 1961, the CBA met at Mt. St. Mary's Seminary of the West, Norwood, Ohio. Geoffrey Wood, whose dissertation topic had prompted Fenton's and Vagnozzi's attack on Siegman the previous year, gave the first paper on the "Literary Form of the Angelic Message in the Lucan Annunciations." Robert Krumholtz of the seminary faculty then delivered the presidential address. His topic was the recent *monitum*. There were, he said, certain dangers, that the laity were either unprepared for the new biblical scholarship or were "victims of popularization," or that some scholars might assert as fact what was only a probable opinion. He summarized the debate that had gone on in Rome and mentioned the letters of Pizzardo to Bea and of the consultors of the Biblical Commission to Vogt. He cited Vagnozzi's speech earlier that summer in an effort to show the context of the *monitum*. Krumholtz reminded his audience that the *monitum* had begun with praise for biblical scholarship, but had warned against too hasty conclusions about the historical truth of Scripture.[38] Krumholtz's address was relatively mild, but his archbishop, Karl J. Alter, asked him to send a copy to Vagnozzi, who had requested it.[39]

Other papers read at the meeting gave little indication that the CBA was in retreat. Barnabas Mary Ahern, C.P., showed the value of form criticism in interpreting the Gospels as records of the Christian message of the first century. He traced the formation of the Gospels from the historical level of the words and deeds of Christ, through the level of the importance of those words and deeds in the life of the community, to the level of the written Gospels, where the synoptic writers, who "were not eyewitnesses of our Lord's life," incorporated material into their works for their own specific purposes.[40] John L. McKenzie, S.J., spoke on the social character of inspiration, for which he thought Pierre Benoit, O.P., and Karl Rahner, S.J., had made significant contributions. Following the two European theologians, McKenzie had thus moved inspiration away from authorship to the community's recognition and acceptance of the sacred writings. His presentation provoked lively discussion.[41] But all of this was but a buildup to the main event of the meeting, not a scholarly exchange, but what is usually the most tedious part of a scholarly meeting—the business session on August 30. Geoffrey Wood took the minutes.

Louis Hartman, the secretary, read a resolution from the executive board calling for restriction of the meetings of the association to active members only. The resolution was proposed in light of the *monitum,* but it presented various difficulties. According to the constitution, both "active" and "associate" members enjoyed the same privileges. Moreover, as Hartman pointed out, it might also be necessary to redefine qualifications for active membership, which at that time included those who had degrees in Scripture or had published or taught in the field, or were recommended by another active member. There were, therefore, actually two issues before the meeting: on restriction of meetings to active members and on qualifications for active membership. On the first, the members voted unanimously to adopt the resolution that "to implement fully the directive of the Holy See in such wise that the general meeting of the CBA will be closed meetings for the active members exclusively," with the provision that the president could "invite individual non-active members who in his judgement have the required competence." The redefinition of qualification for active membership came up when the names of new active members were proposed. Joseph Fitzmyer, S.J., introduced a resolution that only those "with biblical degrees be admitted to membership," but all the applicants were unanimously approved.[42] Since the resolution required a change in the CBA's bylaws, it had to be submitted to the entire membership, before it could be formally voted on at the next general meeting.

With the question of qualifications for membership temporarily set aside, the meeting was open for new business. A week before the meeting, Monsignor Patrick Skehan of the Catholic University had written Hartman with a proposal that the executive board adopt

a resolution to the effect that the implications of Modernism as existing in Catholic Biblical studies, specifically in North America in our day, as they are contained in the American Ecclesiastical Review for Dec. 1959, vol. 141, pp. 406–416, and in the issue of July, 1961, are false, derogatory, and disgraceful in a responsibly run Catholic periodical. I would like to see such a resolution addressed both to the Rector of this University and to their Eminences of the Pontifical Biblical Commission.

I am writing to this effect to all the members of the Executive Board.

If this be a headache, I'm sorry: but I think we ought to stand on our minimum rights.[43]

Skehan was never one to make his position unclear. At the meeting of the executive board, he submitted a formal resolution concerning both Fenton's article on apologetics in 1959 and the more recent articles in the *Review* in July. Failing to win the board's support, he withdrew the proposal. But that did not settle the fate of the resolution or of Skehan's role in promoting it.[44]

The discussion began quietly enough when Richard Kugelman, C.P., suggested the formation of a permanent " 'watch-dog' committee . . . to prevent distortion in the Catholic Press of biblical activities." John L. McKenzie, S.J., had a bolder plan. Skehan had approached him about drafting a resolution condemning the *American Ecclesiastical Review*. McKenzie and Bruce Vawter, C.M., then wrote a resolution, which McKenzie proposed from the floor of the meeting. Because it was already late in the morning, he promised to be brief, but stated that the purpose of the resolution was "to repudiate the insinuations of certain individuals and a certain organ concerning the theological soundness of the biblical movement in this country." He then passed out copies of what he called "a Declaration against Defamation." The meeting then adjourned until a special afternoon session. At that time, there were still two motions on the floor from the morning—the one called for a suitable celebration of the CBA's Silver Jubilee and the other for an expression of filial homage toward John XXIII and a request for his blessing upon the association's work. Skehan quickly seconded each, and both were unanimously adopted. The real business of the meeting could now begin.[45]

Kugelman again rose to propose his "watch-dog" committee. After considerable discussion, including the suggestion of hiring a professional public relations expert, the resolution carried by a voice vote. McKenzie then took the floor with his resolution from the end of the morning session. It read:

Whereas
During the last few years the *American Ecclesiastical Review* has carried a large number of articles on contemporary biblical studies, which articles do consistently charge Catholic scholars with gross ignorance of basic theological truths, if not of deliberately malicious perversion of these same truths, no evidence being adduced of any particular error published by any scholar:
And whereas:
Such blanket unsupported defamation cannot possibly advance either the investigation of truth or fraternal sacerdotal charity,
Be it resolved:
That this association does declare that it repudiates any and all such attacks, and affirms its desire and intention of promoting discussions which join honesty and candor with genuine friendship and mutual esteem.
to be signed for the Association by the President, Vice-President, and Executive Secretary.

McKenzie urged the necessity of "direct action," just like that which the Biblical Commission had taken in defending the Biblical Institute in Rome.[46]

As the discussion warmed up, Krumholtz informed the audience that the executive committee had voted down a similar resolution and mentioned that someone "had promised to do something quietly about the problem." McKenzie and Roland Murphy both reminded Krumholtz that the members of the CBA had the right to act independently of the executive committee. John L. Murphy, author of one of the offending articles, then took the podium. The *American Ecclesiastical Review,* he stated, was "a pastoral magazine," which had published numerous articles on scriptural topics by members of the CBA. In his opinion, the issue was "a clash of personalities," and he suggested "Msgr. Fenton and Fr. Connell be specifically mentioned," in order not to cast aspersions on the review as such. The tone of the meeting then shifted to a semblance of a made-for-television movie. From the back of the room, Skehan moved to the podium. Not only had he been on the executive committee which voted down the resolution, he declared—he did not mention that he had actually proposed it—he also wanted to be delegated by the association "to deliver the resolution personally to the Rector of the Catholic University of America." Singling out the articles by Connell and Fenton, he asserted that Fenton's "response to a question concerning modern biblical studies and apologetics" was "a caricature of present day Gospel study, deliberately vague and associates biblical scholars with a known heresy, Modernism." John Murphy again took the rostrum to argue that the resolution would be "futile" in changing Fenton's "attitude." Skehan returned to the rostrum. According to the minutes, he stated that

during 20 years on the campus of Catholic University he had been engaged but once in conversation with Msgr. Fenton on Sacred Scripture. He noted Msgr. Fenton's influence with Church authorities and emphasized that the men at Catholic University want this resolution on the campus! He concluded that dogmatic theologians have as much an obligation to read biblical arguments as scripturists have to be clear in their presentation. He reminded the members that the editor, Msgr. Fenton, is on his way to Rome and before he goes this resolution should be made public in order to offset any false coloration he may give there.

In a style worthy of the best nineteenth-century newspaper reporting, Wood, the secretary of the meeting, recorded that "there was spontaneous applause for these statements by Msgr. Skehan."[47]

The debate then began in earnest. When John Murphy, "during one of these intervals," rose to remind the members that not all the articles in the review were reprehensible, McKenzie responded that he "was willing to amend his resolution by adding a footnote which would specify volume, page and author of the articles in question." Monsignor Francis Rossiter argued that the resolution was really aimed only at Fenton and the Catholic University, but Roderick MacKenzie countered that the problem extended beyond the Catholic University, for "the *AER* comes from that campus and carries with it the authority of the University." James

Solari, O.S.B., asked to whom the resolution would be given. McKenzie replied that that should be left to the determination of the CBA officers, though the resolution would of course be printed in the *CBQ*. Skehan reminded the members "that he would like to give a copy to the Rector of the Catholic University." When some members objected that they could not vote on the resolution if they had not read the articles, Skehan offered to pass around one of Fenton's articles. After over a hour and a half of discussion, Wood recorded, "the resolution was VOTED ON AND CARRIED BY AN OVERWHELMING MAJORITY and with APPLAUSE." The final resolution was substantially the same as that originally proposed, with specific references added to the offensive articles. The minutes included among these Vagnozzi's address at Marquette, to which Krumholtz had alluded in his presidential address. But this reference was omitted in the official version signed for the association by V. Bruce Vawter, C.M., newly elected president, Eugene H. Maly, vice president, and Louis F. Hartman, C.Ss.R., secretary. This was, however, not the end of the debate. John Murphy had ominously "cautioned that the Apostolic Delegate might enter into the matter."[48]

The drama now shifted from the meeting in Cincinnati to the editorial offices of the *CBQ* at the Catholic University. The CBA issued a press release containing the resolution to the National Catholic News Service, which did not run it. The Religious News Service did, however, pick it up.[49] On September 18, as Roland Murphy, the editor of the *CBQ*, was preparing the galleys of the resolution for publication in the October issue, he received a summons to Vagnozzi's office. The delegate did not want the resolution published. As Murphy pointed out, however, it had always been the policy of the *CBQ* to publish the resolutions and this one was already in galleys. Vagnozzi then appealed to Archbishop Patrick A. O'Boyle of Washington, who called Murphy to meet with him the next day. O'Boyle, as the ordinary who gave the *imprimatur* to the journal, refused permission for the publication. Murphy then suggested a compromise in which the *CBQ* would only allude to the resolution. O'Boyle initially accepted this, only to change his mind because Vagnozzi preferred to delay publication "into November till the opposing parties had come together for a discussion." Murphy succeeded in persuading O'Boyle that, since there would be no publication of the full resolution, the *CBQ* should come out as scheduled. On September 24, Murphy again met with O'Boyle, who had further modified the wording of Murphy's compromise statement to the form in which it appeared in the *CBQ.*[50]

The published version simply stated that John L. McKenzie had offered a resolution passed by a majority "rejecting what are considered unwarranted attacks by a Catholic Publication upon Catholic biblical scholars in America."[51] Vagnozzi and the *American Ecclesiastical Review* had triumphed—at least for a time. The only Catholic newspaper to report on the resolution with specific reference to the *Review* was the Cleveland *Catholic Universe Bulletin* for September 8, 1961, probably because Bishop Whealon passed on the information to the editor.[52]

THE RESPONSE OF THE *AMERICAN ECCLESIASTICAL REVIEW*

On October 3, 1961, John L. Murphy wrote Vawter—he made mimeograph copies for wider distribution. He had learned only through a third party that one of his articles was to be on the now suppressed list. He protested that no one could find in his article any unwarranted attack on biblical scholars. Moreover, he considered himself to be "one of the best informed men" in the country on "the delicate question of the relationship between Scripture and tradition." As he sought to defend himself, however, it became clear that he was not nearly as objective or scholarly as he asserted. In his article, he had stated that a biblical scholar could not shirk his responsibility of relating his findings to other branches of theology. In his protest, he noted that Barnabas Ahern had made an admittedly "facetious" remark about "how happy he was to be able to limit his attention to scriptural topics, and not have to consider the philosophical and historical questions which the theologian must discuss." What Murphy was urging in his article was "prudent foresight in answering expected questions," in much the same manner as had been written by Karl Rahner, "who I would suppose now becomes a candidate for next year's condemnation by the Association." He had every reason to be concerned about such lack of "foresight," he continued, when he read Avery Dulles's statement that "Son of God" used in the Gospels did not necessarily mean "strict divinity," for this was clearly condemned by *Lamentabili*. David Stanley had also been imprudent in not spelling out what he meant by the "gradual psychological awareness of the meaning of the Church on the part of the primitive community."[53]

Murphy then turned his protest to the conduct of the meeting, which "hardly seemed to express the spirit of a sedate, scholarly gathering of men interested in scriptural studies." In particular, he found Skehan's attitude offensive, especially when he admitted that he had discussed biblical matters only once with Fenton, but had never written on the topics in question. Since the resolution had not been published in its complete form, however, "the Catholic Biblical Association has conveniently cast a cloak of doubt on the qualifications of those authors cited."[54] There was, of course, a certain irony in Murphy's complaint. He had predicted at the meeting that the delegate would get involved and now he was protesting the secrecy that had resulted from that involvement. Yet, he also had a point. During the Modernist crisis, biblical scholarship had been curtailed as a result of a theological system that could not deal with historical criticism. Biblical scholarship was again in jeopardy because of the same theology. No one had made a new synthesis, and there was a danger that each branch of sacred studies would in fact become isolated. The solution, however, was not to curtail biblical scholarship, but to find a cohesive theology. But Murphy, Connell, and Fenton were not finished with the matter.

On November 7, 1961, Connell wrote to each of the bishops defending his plea that scholars should join prayer with research. He had heard of the CBA resolution censuring him. "The matter is serious," he continued, and, "if I am guilty of this charge, I have committed a mortal sin." But, he insisted, "if those who made the accusation have not adduced adequate proofs to support the charge, they have committed, at least objectively, a mortal sin." In justification of his original statement, he cited the address of John XXIII to the Biblical Institute, calling for "prayer" to "be the nourishment and inspiration of his life of study." Connell concluded his letter with the "hope that His Holiness will not be condemned by the Biblical Society for implying that biblical scholars as a group do not pray enough."[55]

On the same day, Murphy and Fenton also sent a joint letter of protest to every member of the hierarchy. Enclosed in their letter was a copy of the original resolution. They cited the "unorthodox manner" in which the resolution had been drafted with the actual citation of the particular articles "turned over to an *ad hoc* committee of two," Skehan and McKenzie, after the meeting. "The entire discussion," they charged, "was conducted in a highly emotional manner from start to finish," and "the vote represents quite clearly a mentality geared to an attempt to silence any discussion of questions in which others might disagree with or question the current positions of certain Catholic biblical scholars." The articles in question, they asserted, had called for "prudence and caution," and the charge of "defamation" and "calumny" could more properly be leveled against those "who passed and signed this resolution." At no point, they argued, had biblical scholars tried to engage in a "serious discussion . . . of the articles cited from our periodical," but "the entire matter" had in fact "been taken out of the realm of scholarship and thrust into the area of mass pressure attacks."[56]

In all the articles in question, they continued, the authors "have expressed their own personal opinions, have given their reasons for their views, and have signed their names to the articles published." Fenton and Murphy challenged biblical scholars to express their "disagreement . . . in writing as well, in a systematic and scholarly manner, without the emotionalism associated with the passing of this resolution." For themselves, they concluded,

In our efforts in *The American Ecclesiastical Review*, we have been and are concerned solely with the proper presentation and discussion of Catholic truth. May we assure Your Excellency that not even what these men have done will prevent us from teaching and writing in such a way as to explain and defend the principles of the Catholic faith, in exactly the way we have done in the articles indicated in the resolution.[57]

It was clear that Fenton and Murphy had a different concept of "Catholic truth" than biblical scholars. Moreover, they had now themselves distributed the resolution which the CBA had obediently not publicized except to its own membership.

Rumors of Fenton's tactic abounded before he and Murphy actually sent their letter. Vawter found it "ironical that JCF should be answering a resolution that was never officially published, publishing it in the process. I think the authorities owe us one on this silly exercise of suppressing power."[58] The Committee for Public Relations, also established at the Cincinnati meeting, and the officers of the CBA now answered Fenton with a letter addressed to all the American bishops. Fenton's and Murphy's letter, they noted, represented "the first general distribution of the text of this resolution that has been made by anyone." The CBA now felt "called upon to explain the purpose and spirit of the resolution as it was adopted." The committee pointed out that "this is not the first time that Catholic scholarship in America has found it necessary to dissociate itself from the performance of the *American Ecclesiastical Review* under the present editorship," for only the year before by a vote of seventeen to zero the School of Sacred Theology of the Catholic University of America expressed its will that this journal not be advertised in the future as the official organ of the School of Theology."[59]

Quoting from Fenton's article on "Traditional Apologetics," the CBA submitted "that . . . Monsignor Fenton has charged numerous unidentified, but allegedly indentifiable [*sic*], American Catholic biblical scholars with magnifying the original error of modernism by applying modernist principles of interpretation to all four of the canonical Gospels." Fenton had specifically stated in his article that, if anyone might "be impressed by people who 'know or suspect' that the Gospels are *merely* expressive of the Church *sentiments* about our Lord some sixty or seventy years after His death on the Cross, he owes it to himself to examine and to appreciate the evidence adduced by De Grandmaison and by other Catholic writers in the field. . . ." The CBA had emphasized those words to show that Fenton had in fact defamed biblical scholars and "the Church in the United States, which contains no person or group to whom this language, or the position it reflects, is in any way attributable."[60]

The CBA then turned to answer Connell, who stated that the resolution could only be "justified at the expense of accusing him of mortal sin." The CBA merely pointed out that when Connell issued his injunction that the biblical scholar should pray, "the implication is that he has found him derelict in these duties." In regard to Fenton's claim that he was calling for "serious discussion," the CBA responded that the articles cited "have presented the scholar with nothing to discuss," for they showed "no acquaintance with modern exegetical literature" nor did they cite "a single book or article by any modern biblical scholar to illustrate their imputations." The CBA would not "shrink from any legitimate theological debate" and, in fact, this was one of the purposes of the resolution. Murphy was scheduled to give a paper at the next year's meeting and Fenton, too, if he so desired, "would be most certain of receiving a cordial invitation to address our meeting." "Innuendoes and imputations of heresy, however, are not discussible," the CBA declared, for "a priest's reputation for orthodoxy is his most precious possession." The letter reminded the bishops that most biblical scholars had been "licensed by the Holy See for the delicate work of seminary instruction, and all of them must enjoy the confidence of the Most Reverend Ordinaries in whose jurisdictions they labor."[61]

The CBA acknowledged that it had "made a serious charge," for, it argued, casting "doubt on the orthodoxy of a large body of American Catholic scholars is no trifling matter." The association was pleased that Fenton and Murphy had not made any attempt "to prove any charges of dangerous doctrines or neo-modernism in respect to biblical scholars," and, in fact, had stated in their letter that "such charges were never intended." Yet the CBA could not accept the closing words of their letter that they would continue to "explain and defend the principles of the Catholic faith." To this the CBA objected: "if these articles are defenses of the Catholic faith, they can be such only on the assumption that the biblical issues they discuss have obscured the faith or attacked it," which, of course Fenton and Murphy had stated they had no intention of stating. The CBA concluded its letter with a defense of the way in which the final wording of the resolution was left to the work of a committee, a standard practice with learned societies.[62] In retrospect, the CBA statement was relatively restrained. It had not, for example, challenged Fenton's intellectual integrity in defending "Catholic truth" while omitting any reference to *Divino Afflante Spiritu* and later official pronouncements. But the matter was still not settled.

On December 7, Vagnozzi wrote Bishop Whealon asking his opinion of the CBA's circular letter to the hierarchy and of its meeting the previous August. He also requested the bishop's "ideas in regard to the Biblical movement in general in the United States," especially about "any attitudes, techniques, trends, etc., that could have dangerous doctrinal consequences for the orthodoxy of the Faith."[63]

On December 18, Whealon responded. "The contemporary American Catholic Scripture movement," he wrote, "is a development of *Divino Afflante Spiritu,*" and, in particular, of the section in which "the Scripture professor was forcefully directed to study ancient literary forms and the literary forms of the Sacred Scriptures." He praised the American scholars for faithfully following these directives. "When the first criticisms of their work were heard," he continued, "they continued to follow the available guides: the Scriptural Encyclicals of the Holy Fathers, the teachings of the faculty of the Pontifical Biblical Institute, the writings of Catholic scholars in other nations, and their own mutual example." The result was "a group of scholars with a general reputation for scholarship—something perhaps novel in American Catholic intellectual life."[64]

The difficulty and confusion, Whealon wrote, arose not so much from the professional scholars as from popularizers of various theories. In his own experience, the biblical scholars were positive in their response to the Holy Office's *monitum* and had told him "of their concern and their desire to exercise prudence." At the Cincinnati meeting, he found "a moderate tone in regard to scholarly subjects." He turned then to the business section of the meeting. "The theologians and the Scripture scholars," he continued, "misunderstand one another in several areas," and "the need now is for mutual understanding and discussion, and not for accusation." The articles in the *American Ecclesiastical Review,* he thought,

were most unfortunate as general condemnatory statements with imputation of heresy. Such general name-calling does, I believe, a disservice to charity and to Catholic scholarship in America. I opposed the resolution—not because it was undeserved, but because it would lead to further misunderstanding and might do a disservice to the cause of Sacred Scripture. The general membership, after a thorough discussion (I was present for most of it) voted for the resolution. It is regrettable that the theologians subsequently carried the matter further, since this publicized the controversy further and provoked the recent reply of the "Committee for Public Relations." In this last exchange my sympathies lie with the Scripture group. Their letter impressed me as necessary and satisfactory.[65]

In conclusion, Whealon expressed his belief that "a dialogue" between Theology and Scripture "will be needed for many years to come." He suggested that "both sides in this current controversy" be "told authoritatively to stop this bickering and this negative approach to the current problem," that "the theologians" be "reminded to study the current Scripture work in the light of *Divino Afflante Spiritu* and with an open and yet positively critical mind," and that "the Scripture scholars" be "reminded that their primary task is to present the Holy Bible to modern man as a meaningful *spiritual* book." Only in this way did he think there would be "the beginning of a project of cooperative study on the effects on theology of the developments in Biblical Science."[66]

As the Church prepared for the opening of the Second Vatican Council, Catholic biblical scholars in North America and elsewhere were on the defensive. In Rome, the Biblical Institute continued to be on the defensive against attacks that sometimes seemed to have John XXIII's tacit approval. At the Pauline Congress held in Rome in September 1961, for example, the biblical scholars were not accorded a special audience, but were included in a general one, at which the pope made only a passing reference to their presence.[67] In North America, the CBA was now in the forefront of scholarship. But it faced the united opposition of Vagnozzi and Fenton in the United States and of Ottaviani and his supporters in Rome. From the American hierarchy, biblical scholars had received the limited support of Cardinal Spellman, but other bishops had remained aloof from the controversy. Many of the bishops either did not understand the issues or did not wish to counter Vagnozzi's influence. Before the council opened, the scholarly community would receive a yet more severe setback. In the United States, Siegman was dismissed from the Catholic University.

14. The Second Vatican Council: The First Phase

In many ways, the American church was ill prepared for the Second Vatican Council. The nineteenth-century tradition of episcopal collegiality had long since given way in the twentieth to a tradition of Romanization.[1] On an intellectual level, the form of Thomism shaped in the nineteenth century to combat rationalism had become confused with the doctrine it was meant to preserve. A distorted interpretation of papal infallibility had made it seem unlikely, if not totally unnecessary, for there ever to be another ecumenical council. But a council was being called and preparation for it and the progress of the council itself brought out into the open many of the theological tensions, which had plagued biblical and other scholars for the previous decades. John Courtney Murray, as was seen, had been silent on the question of religious liberty since 1955. On the question of biblical scholarship, Edward Siegman fell victim to Vagnozzi's vendetta, even as the bishops were making their plans to attend their historic meeting.

SIEGMAN'S DISMISSAL FROM THE CATHOLIC UNIVERSITY

In the spring of 1961, Siegman had a mild heart attack. In September, he suffered a second attack and was granted a semester's sick leave from the Catholic University. In January 1962, he visited the university and requested another semester's leave. At the same time, however, he agreed to offer a summer course. A short time later, Gerald Sloyan phoned to tell him that the rector, Monsignor McDonald, "had vetoed my summer appointment as well as Fr. [Godfrey] Diekmann's." The alleged reason was Siegman's health.[2] Siegman informed John E. Byrne, C.PP.S., his provincial, that Sloyan thought McDonald was "trying to squash the summer

Scripture program on the assumption that it is too avant-garde for Sisters and Brothers." He recalled that he had himself initiated the program in 1957, which "earned for me the wrath of Msgr. Fenton and, I suspect, the disaffection of at least one of his friends."[3] Sometime around this date, McDonald subsequently claimed he phoned Siegman's provincial, "and suggested . . . that in view of Father Siegman's state of health and serious illness, he should not resume his teaching duties at the Catholic University of America. The Very Reverend Provincial at this time agreed."[4] As events unfolded, there would be considerable discrepancy between McDonald's and Byrne's recollection of the nature of this telephone conversation.

In the meantime, Siegman was well aware that McDonald was trying to use his health to pressure him into resigning. Late in March, he told Roland Murphy: "I agree with you whole-heartedly that I should not resign, and have no intention of doing so, unless the doctor forbids me to go back." His doctor, he continued, was "confident" that he could return to teaching, but questioned "going back to C.U. because of the possible tensions I may have to be exposed to." For Siegman's own part, "to resign would be practically a surrender and/or confession of unorthodoxy." Murphy had asked about the length of Siegman's contract. In Siegman's mind, "since I am an associate professor, it goes on indefinitely; the University would have to prove good cause for not keeping me, as far as I know."[5] Unfortunately, the university administration would not give the same interpretation to the meaning of an associate professorship.

On April 7, Siegman informed Walter Schmitz, S.S., dean of the School of Sacred Theology, that he was then being tested for possible tuberculosis. He assured Schmitz, however, that his physician

consistently assumes that I shall be able to resume teaching in the fall. From this I gather that even if active tuberculosis is found, he thinks it can be cured within a short time. You can be sure that I shall inform you just as soon as I know the probabilities regarding my future.[6]

Siegman's reference to possible tuberculosis now became another issue. On April 18, McDonald wrote Byrne that Schmitz had informed him that Siegman had "suffered further complications in his state of health." He reminded the provincial that "at the time of his [Siegman's] heart attacks, . . . I discussed the situation by telephone with you, and we agreed that in fairness to Father Siegman he should go on sick leave for this academic year." Here the documentary evidence becomes vague. If this was the only telephone call McDonald made to Byrne, then he later seriously misrepresented it, when he stated that Byrne had agreed that Siegman's relationship with the university should be permanently severed. In view of Siegman's heart condition and the threat of tuberculosis, the rector continued, "and of our being pressed to make permanent plans for our faculty, I believe we must be reconciled to Father Siegman's uncertain state of health and to his not returning to the University."[7]

When Byrne received McDonald's letter, he was himself ill and communicated its contents to Siegman only several weeks later. Having ascertained that Siegman's health was improving, he wrote a night letter to McDonald on May 1 to say: "Father Siegman is mending steadily. Can plan to resume teaching at Catholic University Sept. 1962."[8] By the time of Byrne's letter, however, McDonald had already presented the case to the university Board of Trustees. On May 2, he telegraphed Byrne:

In accordance with my letter had presented matter to Board of Trustees. Permanent replacement already secured. Regret unable to change decision. Grateful for your interest in the University. Assurance of prayers for Father Siegman.[9]

Byrne responded immediately. Since Siegman was an associate professor and had tenure, he argued, "it is my understanding that Father Siegman . . . cannot be dismissed from the faculty of the Catholic University without grave cause." He found "it difficult to understand how Father Siegman can be dismissed so abruptly," and was "anxious to hear a more complete explanation."[10]

On May 8, Siegman himself wrote McDonald. "Since I have given the University no cause for this unilateral action," he said, "my understanding is that my contract will be automatically renewed January 30, 1963." He thought there had to be a "misunderstanding," for he had written Schmitz, the dean, that he would inform him if his health would prevent his return to the university in the fall of 1962.[11] This letter to Schmitz was, of course, the basis on which McDonald had argued that there were "further complications" in Siegman's health. On May 9, before receiving Siegman's letter, McDonald had already met with the vice rector, Monsignor Joseph B. McAllister, and the procurator of the university, James A. Magner. They discussed Siegman's health and "the fact that his appointment as Associate Professor, which was of three year's duration, would routinely cease as of January 31, 1963." The university administration "decided to abide by the decision not to renew Siegman's appointment but to continue his salary of $4,700.00 for the academic year 1962–63."[12]

Word of McDonald's action had by this time reached the university faculty. The rector offered to appear at the next faculty meeting of the School of Sacred Theology, but Schmitz thought his presence was unnecessary. At the meeting on May 16, Roland Murphy introduced the following resolution:

In view of the following situation:
1) the present adequate health of Father Edward Siegman, and his desire to return to the University,
2) in view of the tenure in keeping with his status as Associate Professor,
3) the wish of the Right Reverend Rector to terminate his services at the University because of reasons of health, of which he was notified through his Provincial during the week of April 30
the faculty of Sacred Theology of the Catholic University of America wish to state that they are profoundly disturbed by the move to release this revered colleague, and they respectfully request that Father Siegman's own wish to return to the University should be honored.

Adopted by a vote of 18 to 2, the resolution was transmitted to the rector.[13] The Graduate School of Arts and Sciences unanimously adopted a similar resolution.[14] In his own memorandum on the case, McDonald argued that Siegman, his provincial, and the faculty were in error in stating that associate professors had tenure, for, according to the university statutes approved by the Holy See, only ordinary professors enjoyed that status.[15]

Making no allusions to what had transpired, Siegman wrote Schmitz on May 30 to say that his tests for active tuberculosis were negative and that, "there is, consequently, nothing to prevent my returning to The Catholic University in September and resuming my duties as associate professor of Sacred Scripture."[16] There is, unfortunately, no record of a reply.

On June 16, Byrne appealed to O'Boyle with a letter that implies that McDonald had, in fact, seriously misrepresented their telephone conversation. He could "hardly believe," he asserted, "that a year's leave of absence for sickness, granted with the promise that he could return at any time, justifies this breach of contract. To date I have received no answer from Msgr. McDonald, and so I am making this appeal to you as Chancellor of The University." He regarded "this cavalier treatment of one of my priests . . . as an affront not only to him personally, but also to the entire American Province of the Society of the Precious Blood." He reminded O'Boyle of the number of Precious Blood students who had studied at the university and the several members of the society who had taught on the faculty. This had "often . . . meant a sacrifice," but was one "made cheerfully," while "the action which the Rector wishes to take against one of our members hardly indicates that this good will is reciprocated." Byrne concluded by stating that he was "confident" that O'Boyle, "as the highest authority in The Catholic University of America, will intervene to make certain that justice will be done."[17]

O'Boyle consulted McDonald and gave him Byrne's letter. On June 25, McDonald replied with a memorandum on the Siegman case. Again, he argued that Byrne had made no reference to "our telephone conversation of last February, in which he agreed that, in view of Father Siegman's severe heart attacks, it would not be in his best interest to return to the University." It is unclear, of course, whether this was the same conversation in which Byrne agreed only that Siegman should have a full year's leave of absence because of his health.[18] What is clear is that McDonald had vetoed Siegman's appointment to the summer institute in February and had chosen to place on Siegman's own letter to Schmitz the interpretation that he now had tuberculosis. O'Boyle then forwarded this correspondence to Byrne, with the comment that he believed that McDonald had "acted in good faith and also in the best interests of Father Siegman."[19] Siegman's immediate reaction was to remark: "There's a strange inconsistency in the Rector's decision to pay me for all of next year. I don't think I've ever been venal or grabby in my life, but I'll get an unholy glee out of collecting those checks next year!"[20]

Although some of Siegman's friends urged him to appeal to the Congregation of Seminaries and Universities, he accepted the decision as final. Only a year later did his dismissal become public. The context was McDonald's ban of Diekmann, Murray, Gustave Weigel, S.J., and Hans Küng from speaking at the university. In the uproar that ensued, the story of Siegman's dismissal came to light. McDonald alleged that he had not renewed Siegman's contract only because of his health, but then he admitted that he had obtained approval for his action from both the apostolic delegate and the Congregation of Seminaries and Universities. If his health were the real reason, Siegman later wrote, "why did he cover his tracks with help from the Apostolic Delegate and from the Congregation?" No one had sought a medical opinion on Siegman's health. As he himself noted, "I do not believe that anyone who knows the facts is deceived about the real reason for my dismissal from C.U."[21] At the CBA meeting at Maryknoll, New York, in August, Skehan introduced a resolution, which was unanimously adopted, "that the membership of the CBA assembled in its annual meeting wish to convey to Rev. Edward F. Siegman, C.PP.S., their fraternal sympathy in his present anxieties and to assure him of their earnest good wishes and their prayers."[22]

In 1963–1964, Siegman was the assistant chaplain at St. Thomas More House at Yale University. At one point, Father James Healy, the chaplain, had hoped he might be appointed to a part-time position at the university, but that proved impossible.[23] In 1964, he returned to the Precious Blood Seminary in Carthagena, Ohio, which he had left in 1951 to edit the *CBQ*. In 1966, he went to Notre Dame, where he died in 1967.

THE CBA ON THE DEFENSIVE

The dismissal of Siegman from the Catholic University was reminiscent of what had happened to Poels in 1910, although in Poels's case no excuses of ill health were used to mask the real issue of his scholarly orientation on the biblical question. Unlike Poels, moreover, Siegman did have like-minded colleagues in the United States. But they, like him, were decidedly on the defensive in the period between their meetings of 1961 and 1962, as a rising crescendo of attacks on biblical scholarship came from conservative journals.

INCREASING ATTACKS ON BIBLICAL SCHOLARSHIP

In October 1961, the *Homiletic and Pastoral Review* published what can only be construed as a mistranslation of the Holy Office's *monitum* of the previous June. The opening paragraph, for instance, was rendered as: "Through praiseworthy enthusiasm for Biblical studies, assertions and opinions are being spread in many quarters, bringing into doubt the genuine historical and objective truth of the Sacred Scriptures, not only of the Old Testament (as Pope Pius XII had already deplored in his encyclical letter *Humani Generis*, cf. *Acta Apostolicae Sedis* XLII, 456), but even of the New, even to the sayings and deeds of Christ Jesus."[24] The *Homiletic and Pastoral Review* followed this with a long quotation from Vagnozzi's warning to the superiors of religious orders the previous summer. The CBA's public relations committee, consisting of Roland Murphy, Joseph Fitzmyer, and Thomas Barrosse, C.S.C., immediately responded with a letter challenging the translation and the failure to note the *monitum*'s acknowledgement of "the praiseworthy progress of current biblical studies." The journal responded by publishing a more accurate translation in its December issue.[25]

Also in December, the *American Ecclesiastical Review* published a translation of an article by Cardinal Ernesto Ruffini, whom Cardinal Shehan later remembered with such fondness. The Italian original had been published on the first page of the *Osservatore Romano* on August 24, 1961. Fenton appended a note that the Congregation of Seminaries and Universities had distributed the article to all diocesan seminaries in Italy, with a letter from Cardinal Pizzardo, the prefect, requesting that it be brought to the attention of all Scripture professors. Ruffini argued that the use of form criticism led to the denial of the historicity of the first chapters of Genesis and of the Gospels. Furthermore, he questioned the usefulness of a type of criticism, which was unknown to the Church for nineteen centuries.[26] Ruffini's article virtually repudiated *Divino Afflante Spiritu*. John L. McKenzie, in fact, lined up passages in parallel columns from both the cardinal's article and the pope's encyclical to show the disagreement.[27] He sought, unsuccessfully, to have the *American Ecclesiastical Review* publish it.

Next, the *American Ecclesiastical Review* again entered the fray. Gerald Kennedy, who had authored one of the offending articles the previous summer, gave his own interpretation of the *monitum* of the Holy Office, which he termed "an unusually strong directive," and predicted that stronger action would be forthcoming.[28] In March 1962, Fenton devoted virtually the entire issue of the *Review* to the biblical question. First of all, William Moran, then teaching at the Pontifical Biblical Institute in Rome, wrote what he later admitted was a too hasty rejoinder to Kennedy.[29] He took Kennedy to task for his interpretation of the *monitum*, which he himself found to be "in perfect accord with the teaching of Pope Pius XII." He thought that the only explanation for the views of Kennedy and others like him lay "in their love for the Church." But, he continued, "curiously blinded by this love to the full scope of the Church's teaching, Father Kennedy has been led to a one-sided and false exegesis of the *Monitum* and to censures of men whose loyalty and devotion to the Church are beyond question."[30]

Immediately after Moran's article was a response from Kennedy, who argued that "there were very serious reasons for the issuance of the *Monitum*."[31] As evidence for this, he quoted Vagnozzi's address to the Second National Conference of Religious at Notre Dame the previous summer.[32] Reminiscent of Connell three years earlier, Kennedy cited John XXIII's address to the faculty and students of the Biblical Institute calling them to combine their study with prayer. Prayer was not a substitute for research, said Kennedy, but it would "obtain special gifts of grace to assist him in the very difficult task of investigating and explaining religious truths. The same might be said of the virtue of humility whose necessity in research is all too evident to bear repetition." Kennedy concluded his rebuttal of Moran by quoting from his fellow Jesuit, Gustave Weigel of Woodstock College, who complained that some Scripture scholars "show a tendency which would impoverish theology" and "show an impatience with any theology which is (not but) exclusively biblical."[33] Fenton then followed with his own rebuttal of Moran. For the most part, it was an ardent defense of Kennedy's interpretation of the *monitum* and a syllogistic *ad hominem* argument against Moran.[34]

In the April, 1962 issue of the *CBQ*, Patrick Skehan decided to take the offensive against these criticisms. He chose as his target Kennedy's original article in the *American Ecclesiastical Review*, included in the CBA's resolution. In "Why leave out *Judith?*", Skehan referred to Kennedy's article with the remark that "some discussions of the Holy Scriptures would, it seems, make it mandatory to presume that all narratives written in prose, with the verbs in the past tense, 'have the form of history.' " Sprinkling his text with lengthy footnote quotations from papal documents, he argued that Pius XII had encouraged the scholar to discover precisely what type of history the sacred author was writing. The Book of Judith was a prime example, for the author exercised considerable literary license with the historical facts, in order to tell a story on a far higher level. Appealing to the "admirable *monitum* of the Holy Office of June 20, 1961," Skehan concluded:

There can be no question of the need for prudence in Biblical studies; and the present writer trusts that he will not be found wanting. But to discuss explicitly the form of Biblical narratives in terms which suggest that nothing happened in 1943 is to do less than justice to the memory of a great Pope, and to show, it seems to me, a lack of gratitude and appreciation for that *vera filiorum Dei libertas* of which he was the exponent.[35]

Scripture scholars had to defend themselves not only from conservative theologians in the United States, but also from what many Catholics regarded as official spokesmen in Rome. For over a month in the spring of 1962, the CBA's public relations committee, Fitzmyer, Barrosse, and Roland Murphy labored over a statement explaining the "new direction" of biblical studies. Some of the new scholars were accused of being "the Modernists of the present generation," they said, giving footnote references to several of the articles included in the resolution of the CBA the previous summer. *Divino Afflante Spiritu* had ushered in a new age of Catholic exegesis, they asserted, for "the emphasis which is found in that encyclical on the study of history, archeology, ethnology, and of literary forms in particular, is something that one will not find in ecclesiastical documents pertaining to Scripture prior to about one hundred years ago." In regard to Pius XII's demand to use "literary forms," they drew attention to Ruffini's article in a footnote.[36]

While they acknowledged that there was "a rift which has unfortunately opened in recent times between the results of modern biblical study and certain approaches to fundamental and dogmatic theology—to say nothing of popular piety," they also noted the efforts to "build the bridges" through Bible weeks and biblical institutes. They admitted that "one of the aspects of the situation which creates the greatest amount of concern is the study of the *literary forms* of the Old Testament and the New Testament." But they mentioned that this was one of the areas of study, "which Pius imposed on all Catholic commentators of the Bible." The recent *monitum* had, indeed, called for "prudence" and "reverence" in treating the Sacred Books, and, in regard to exegetes, "it should be presumed that men loyally devoted to the Church have taken it to heart." But they also recalled that Pius XII had called for charity in judging the legitimate work of trained Catholic commentators.[37]

There was, then, a "new direction" in biblical studies, they continued, and this necessitated "a certain abandonment of some modes of exegesis which were fashionable for centuries." This new development, they concluded, was part of divine Providence and

the study of literary forms of the Bible is part of that providential development. It has not yet fully come to term, and perhaps some of the confusion and concern today about such study is due to the transitional character of the phase in which it finds itself. The situation will certainly not be helped by baseless accusations, recriminations, and unworthy controversy. "Bridge-building" of a solid and serene nature will do more good.[38]

The committee members had taken several weeks to hammer out the statement, and it was already in galley form, when they decided not to publish it. As Fitzmyer remarked to Murphy, in view of the heated battle then raging, "I am afraid that if we were to publish something now, we might give the impression that we are worried."[39]

The biblical debate in the Catholic church had by now drawn outside attention. In the spring of 1962, William S. Schneirla published an account of the battle between biblical scholars and both the *American Ecclesiastical Review* and *Homiletic and Pastoral Review* in the *St. Vladimir's Seminary Quarterly*. He pointed out that the future of Catholic scholarship would have a direct impact upon the Orthodox Church.[40] By the summer of 1962, the Catholic debates over Scripture studies were no longer only in-house.

The CBA Meeting of 1962 and Change in Membership Qualifications

From August 28 to 30, 1962, the CBA met at Maryknoll Seminary, Maryknoll, New York. The papers presented gave little evidence of the tension seething beneath the surface. In a surprisingly progressive paper, John L. Murphy treated Scripture and tradition and rejected the "two-source" interpretation of Trent's decree—a point which would be highly controverted during the first session of Vatican II, which opened only a month later.[41] Luis Alonso-Schökel, S.J., who had drawn the wrath of Monsignor Romeo, talked about the necessity of interpreting the Bible in the context of general hermeneutics.[42]

The business section of the meeting then picked up the change in qualifications for membership proposed the previous year. The constitution was amended to provide for three classes of membership: active, associate, and sustaining. The bylaws were then amended to state the qualifications for each class. An active member had to "have the Licentiate in Sacred Scripture, or the equivalent in graduate training or in scholarly publication, and this equivalent is to be determined and explained in each case by the Committee on Credentials." Associate members had to "have taught Sacred Scripture for at least one year at major-seminary level or at least two years at college level, or must be engaged in higher studies in the biblical or allied field." Candidates for either active or associate membership had to be sponsored in writing by an active member. The general meetings were open only to active and associate members, and only active members or others designated by the president of the CBA could present papers.[43] The purpose of the new qualifications for active membership was to limit the meetings in the future to professional biblical scholars.

At the meeting, Louis Hartman also announced the inception of a long-felt need of the association—the publication of a popular biblical journal, *The Bible Today*. One of the issues controverted with Bishop Brady, the new venture would enable the *CBQ* to concentrate strictly on scholarly articles. Raymond Brown then reported on the progress of the two-volume commentary on Scripture, *The Jerome Biblical Commentary*, which had been planned the previous year. Brown was to edit the general introductory articles, Fitzmyer those on the New Testament, and Roland Murphy those on the Old Testament. The project was to be solely the effort of Catholic scholars, in order to show the maturity of Catholic biblical studies. But most of the members had not forgotten the attacks on biblical scholarship. The meeting passed a resolution expressing sympathy for Siegman, as was seen, and George Glanzman, S.J., called for the wide circulation of Schneirla's "Roma locuta . . . ?"[44]

THE SECOND VATICAN COUNCIL

A little over a month before the council convened, there was little sign that biblical scholars, American or otherwise, would play any large role in the proceedings. Of the American biblical scholars, only Barnabas Ahern was chosen to be a *peritus*. Joseph Fenton, however, was chosen to be a *peritus* for Cardinal Ottaviani. The official American theological delegation to the council was weak both in the biblical and in other areas. As Fenton headed for the council, John Courtney Murray remained at home at Woodstock College, "disinvited," to use his term, by Ottaviani and Vagnozzi.[45] The first session of the council would be a learning experience for the American bishops, but learn they did.

THE FIRST SCHEMA ON THE SOURCES OF REVELATION

When the bishops assembled for the first session of the council on October 11, 1962, they were confronted with a series of schemata for discussion, which illustrated their conservative origin in the Theological Commission, presided over by Ottaviani. The schema pertaining to the biblical question was entitled "On the Sources of Revelation," and sought to present Scripture and tradition as separate deposits of revelation.[46] Nothing could have more represented the confusion between doctrine and theology, which had been created in the nineteenth century. It was far removed from Francis Kenrick's position that Scripture was the written part of tradition. Moreover, the schema totally ignored the magisterial work of Hubert Jedin on the Council of Trent, which showed that the council had not in fact spoken of two separate sources—a point, which even John L. Murphy acknowledged.[47] As Joseph Ratzinger put it, this schema "amounted to a canonization of Roman school theology." While recognizing that various "schools" had existed in the past, the advocates of the "Roman school" failed to see "that Catholic theology has remained alive, that new 'schools' and conflicts have formed within it and that these new groups and their questions are also legitimate forms of Catholic theological work."[48]

The schema was merely part of the ongoing battle in Rome against biblical scholars, of which the American dispute was only a reflection. At the end of the academic year 1961–1962, two professors at the Biblical Institute, Stanislaus Lyonnet, S.J., the dean, and Max Zerwick, S.J., had been removed from their teaching posts. On the eve of the council, Monsignor F. Spadafora, a former student of Romeo and then a professor at the Lateran University, published a pamphlet attacking Lyonnet and Zerwick for denying the historicity of the Gospels. It was widely distributed to many of the council fathers. It prompted a reply from the Biblical Institute, "A New Attack against Catholic Exegesis and against the Pontifical Biblical Institute." Printed in French, German, Spanish, and English, it was distributed to all the bishops.[49] The institute also distributed reprints of Joseph A. Fitzmyer's "A Recent Roman Scriptural Controversy," which had been published in *Theological Studies* in 1961, and which summarized the earlier attacks of Romeo on Scripture scholarship and on the institute.[50] Both sides on the biblical question were trying to influence the bishops on the schema.

On November 14, the bishops began formal debate on the schema with an introductory defense of it by Cardinal Ottaviani. As subsequent speakers took the podium, their arguments reflected the division between biblical scholars and conservative theologians. Ruffini, as might have been expected, defended the schema. But then, one after another bishop spoke against it. Bea took the microphone to charge that the schema was the work of a particular school of theology, "not what the better theologians today think." In all the references to biblical scholars, he continued, only one was positive. He called for the schema to be redone to make it shorter, clearer, and more ecumenical.[51]

Only four Americans spoke on the schema during the session. The first was Cardinal Joseph Ritter of St. Louis. Bluntly he stated that "the schema . . . must be rejected so that another may be proposed." The purpose of the council, he continued, was

to help and direct, not reprimand and dissuade. If the Council has solutions to actual problems, let it show them as clearly, as distinctly as possible. If there are no solutions, indeed, let the Council say so or remain quiet. If errors exist, let the Council remonstrate and even condemn them.

But let the Council abstain from statements that lack any use, imperil unity and engender suspicions.

Cardinal James Francis McIntyre of Los Angeles, however, strongly defended the schema, for it contained "positive action aimed at correcting new theories which are not acceptable—and action against scientific theories, and against scientific theories *which should be considered only as theories.*" Cardinal Albert Meyer, a charter member of the CBA, seconded Cardinal Bea's call for a new draft. He wanted the council to declare itself in three areas:

First: Express confidence in Catholic exegetical endeavors. Second: recommend to exegetes their duty to follow the teaching set forth by supreme pontiffs up to the present on the interpretation of Sacred Scripture. Third: Make special mention, in referring to the supreme pontiffs, of Pius XII of happy memory who is recognized as the architect and promoter of biblical renewal in our century.[52]

One of the more surprising interventions against the schema came from James Griffiths, auxiliary bishop of New York. Arguing for the retention of the positive elements in the present schema, he noted that the biblical controversy was "something real and actual in the Church." He called for the council "faithfully [to] take up discussion of this matter, with the advice of experts from both sides and from widely diverse schools, considering the schema not necessarily as it was proposed in the beginning, but emending, abbreviating and polishing it where we can, going into and correcting it in its very essence."[53] The schema was clearly attracting opposition from bishops representing a broad spectrum of opinion.

On November 19, Ahern addressed the weekly meeting of the American bishops at the North American College. He explained to them the significance of literary forms and of their application to the study of the Bible. Afterwards, Vagnozzi took the floor, and spoke critically and disparagingly of Ahern and the new exegesis. One of his points was that scholars were arguing that the Gospels, as they exist, represent expressions of a later faith community, rather than of eyewitnesses. This, he thought, denied that the Church had the actual words of Jesus. At the end of the delegate's speech, the bishops requested Ahern to offer a rebuttal. Ahern fully agreed with Vagnozzi that the words of Jesus should be retained, but pointed out the problem that there were divergent traditions about what Jesus said on three crucial occasions—the words of the institution of the Eucharist, the Lord's Prayer, and the Beatitudes.[54]

On November 20, the bishops voted on whether to reject the schema or retain it for discussion. For rejection, 1,473 votes were required, but the bishops against the schema mustered only 1,368—822 voted to retain it. Archbishop Pericle Felici, Secretary General of the Council, therefore announced that the bishops would immediately take up the first chapter of the schema. The conservatives had won, but only temporarily. The next morning, Pope John XXIII ordered the schema withdrawn and submitted to a special commission, jointly presided over by Ottaviani and Bea. The progressives had finally received a papal hearing. That afternoon, the Biblical Institute held a dissertation defense by Norbert Lohfink on Deuteronomy. Twelve cardinals, 150 bishops, and numerous other visitors were present—so many, in fact, that the defense had to be moved from the institute to the main hall of the Gregorian University across the street.[55] William Moran, who had drawn the fire of Fenton for his efforts to challenge Kennedy, was the director of the dissertation. The defense had been made public, in order to show the council fathers that the institute was not trying to undermine the faith. Though all the cardinals had been invited, Ottaviani did not attend. After the defense, Moran recalled, there was a formal reception for all the distinguished visitors, after which the biblical scholars moved back across the street to the Biblicum, where they held a real celebration.[56]

Some American bishops, nevertheless, were slow to absorb what had happened during the session. On November 23, the Theology Committee of the American hierarchy approved a series of "recommendations concerning current problems in Scripture about historicity of Gospels." Their intention was to avoid the abuses mentioned in the *monitum* of the Holy Office. The committee stated that "any absolute denial of the real existence of traditionally historical personages in the Gospels is rash." Bishops were to curb "any Catholic preaching such a doctrine, or teaching it unqualifiedly, or writing it unqualifiedly in popular journals." The committee then addressed the issue of form criticism. "As applied to the Gospels," it said,

the literary form known as *midrash* remains in the realm of theory. It is often misunderstood and easily misinterpreted. Prudence demands that it be predicated of a Gospel pericope with extreme caution, and (a) never in sermons, (b) only to an audience of intellectually mature Catholics and (c) by an exegete who is prepared to demonstrate the reasons for supposing *midrash* in a particular Gospel pericope, never overlooking the Church's teaching in a given instance.[57]

On December 15, 1962, Bishop Whealon, who was also an official consultor of the CBA, forwarded the recommendations to Hartman. The committee, he noted, was also seeking the Biblical Institute's opinion of the recommendations, but wanted Hartman's confidential opinion "as to whether they would promote or would hinder the progress of true Scripture studies."[58] Hartman had no problem with the recommendations as such, but he feared the way some conservative bishops would interpret them. He also wondered

why the American Hierarchy are so anxious to jump the gun and express themselves on this matter before the whole Hierarchy of the Universal Church decides the matter in the Ecumenical Council. To speak the truth (which you asked me to do), I cannot help thinking that the hand of our Apostolic Delegate is behind this—which will not be to the good.

Hartman urged Whealon to prevail on the bishops' committee to "give most serious consideration to the reaction of the Biblical Institute."[59] Whealon agreed with Hartman's observations, and, in January, informed him that the committee had decided to postpone issuing any recommendations until the council had completed its discussion on Scripture.[60] As it turned out, the council's final constitution on Revelation was so revolutionary to the American hierarchy that the episcopal committee never issued any set of guidelines.

THE CATHOLIC BIBLICAL ASSOCIATION BETWEEN THE FIRST AND SECOND SESSIONS

The decision to refer the schema on revelation to a joint commission was a victory for the biblical scholars and progressives, but the war was not yet over. During the interim between the first and second sessions, scholars received mixed signals from the Vatican. On April 4, 1963, John Courtney Murray became a council *peritus*. His sponsor was Cardinal Spellman.[61] Yet, Lyonnet and Zerwick were still banned from teaching. Moreover, the only American consultor to the Biblical Commission was John Steinmueller. In May, Roderick MacKenzie had just completed a negative review of a new edition of Steinmueller's *Companion to Scripture Studies*. Steinmueller's being the only American consultor led MacKenzie to comment that "it's really a disgrace." He asked Roland Murphy, "Is there any way we could work on Cardinal Meyer, perhaps on Cushing and Spellman, to get others named, and more representative ones?"[62] A short time earlier, five outstanding European biblical scholars had been named consultors to the commission, R. Schnackenburg of Germany, C. Spicq, O.P., of Switzerland, X. Léon-Dufour, S.J., of France, B. Rigaux, O.F.M., of Belgium, and G. Castellino, S.D.B., of Italy. They were "all good men, and not notably conservative," MacKenzie commented, but he still wanted "to propose at our business meeting that CBA send some sort of petition, to *all* the Cardinal members and *all* Consultors, asking that a few Americans be added." He would himself propose Siegman, Roland Murphy, Myles Bourke, Barnabas Ahern or his fellow Canadian, David Stanley. John L. McKenzie, he "would love to see . . . in there, but I doubt if he'd stand a chance."[63]

MacKenzie did not have a chance to make his proposal at the CBA business meeting, for, late in the spring, he was named rector of the Biblical Institute. He attributed his appointment to Francis McCool, S.J., an American at the institute, whose faculty feared that, in the midst of the attacks made on their orthodoxy, an outsider might be imposed on them.[64] McCool was, in the meantime, concerned at the negative review MacKenzie had given of Steinmueller's book, for he feared the only American consultor "would be stung and bring the matter to the attention of his friends in Rome with repercussions which, without exaggeration, could be very harmful to Rod and the Institute."[65] MacKenzie had, in fact, toned down his review, but that still did not suit Father E. Robert Arthur, the *censor deputatus* for the Archdiocese of Washington. Steinmueller had accused John L. McKenzie of lack of orthodoxy. Roderick MacKenzie, in turn, praised McKenzie and suggested that "the reader who turns from these pages of the

Companion to re-read chapter IV of *The Two-Edged Sword* may judge for himself which of the two Catholic writers treats the subject of 'historicity' with greater seriousness and competence."[66] MacKenzie's "sharpness," said Arthur, went contrary to O'Boyle's policy that "nothing resembling personal attack should be published."[67]

Meanwhile, though MacKenzie could not be present for the CBA meeting in 1963, the question of an American consultor to the Biblical Commission did come up. At the meeting, Hartman, the executive secretary of the association, was commissioned to approach Barnabas Ahern about the situation. The American scholars "are not only being slighted," wrote Hartman, "they are being completely ignored." Steinmueller, furthermore, "can hardly be said to be representative of Catholic biblical scholarship in this country." The members of the association were not optimistic about receiving any help from the American bishops, even those who were active members, but did think Ahern could broach the question with Cardinal Meyer.[68] Meyer was a charter member of the CBA and his aid had already been enlisted in support of biblical scholarship.

In 1963, the CBA celebrated its twenty-fifth anniversary. In honor of the occasion, the *CBQ* published a jubilee edition of two enlarged issues for January and July. In view of the attacks made on biblical scholars both in the United States and Rome, the editors of the *CBQ* had Cardinal Richard Cushing of Boston and Cardinal Meyer each write an introductory letter to the respective issues. In the introduction to the January issue, Cushing commented that, though "the Church in the United States is comparatively young . . . , it is surely one of the signs of her maturity and progress that your biblical association is observing such a Jubilee with an impressive record of scholarly achievement." This opinion, he noted, was shared by Cardinal Bea in a recent interview with *America* magazine. "The teaching and pastoral role of the Hierarchy," he continued, "has benefited immeasurably from the painstaking scholarship that made possible the Confraternity of Christian Doctrine version of the New Testament," though he acknowledged that "American Catholics needed a few years to grow accustomed to the contemporary idiom that replaced the more familiar phrasing of the Challoner-Rheims version of yesteryear." "The Church will always have need of dedicated bible scholars," he went on, "to meet the challenge to her teaching mission that progress in education and research invariably bring." Cushing made no specific references to papal teaching on the Bible, but he concluded that "the patience and loyalty of the dedicated bible scholar must be matched . . . by the encouragement and sympathy of the Clergy and Faithful if the Mystical Body of Christ is to be properly nourished by the inspired Word of God, the Bible."[69] The letter, written on the eve of the first session of Vatican II, was positive enough, but it hardly served to ward off the attacks to which biblical scholars were subjected during that session.

In April, Roland Murphy wrote Meyer asking for a letter introducing the July issue of the journal. Meyer, who had by that time distinguished himself in opposition to the original schema on revelation, suggested that Murphy draft a letter.[70] Murphy complied and sent Meyer a draft on April 28.[71]

Meyer took Murphy's draft and added several important passages. From Murphy, he took the theme that the silver jubilee of the *CBQ* was also the twentieth anniversary of *Divino Afflante Spiritu*. But he added to this John XXIII's praise of the Biblical Institute on its golden jubilee. He slightly adapted Murphy's formulation of the influence of Pius's encyclical on the biblical movement, and stated that "the success of the *CBQ* has been due in no small way to its fidelity to the principles of this important and forward-looking document." Then, he inserted a long section on the necessity of joining scientific research with a "pastoral intent," which had to be "guided by the norms of truth, prudence and charity." In describing these norms, Meyer tried to provide a balance between autonomy of research and faithfulness to the magisterium. "The norm of truth," he said

will always allow for that patience which gives science the time and freedom to make its advances. It will strive always to determine clearly the limits placed by faith and by sane science. In doing this it will never lose contact with the living magisterium of truth, which is the Church, for again to quote our Holy Father: "Only serious scholarship and perfect docility toward the 'mind of the Church' can help find the right answers to the various questions, and preserve scholars from lamentable errors."

The norms of prudence and charity are intimately connected with the principle that work done on Scripture must be done with a pastoral intent, having before one's eyes souls and their good, since this is the reason why God has given the Sacred Scriptures to men. More than once, Pius XII, in *Divino Afflante Spiritu,* advises the scholar to approach his task with prudence. The biblical student is called upon to distinguish between what is determined and what is still hypothetical. In making this position clear through thorough investigations, his work should always be guided by that equity, justice and charity with which Pope Pius XII stated that it should also be judged by others.[72]

On the whole, Meyer was giving warm praise to American Catholic biblical scholars at a time when they seriously needed it. At the same time, he was gradually emerging as a leader at the council, which was about to come under new direction.

On June 3, 1963, John XXIII died. On June 21, Cardinal Giovanni Battista Montini of Milan was elected Pope Paul VI. When the CBA assembled for its annual meeting in San Francisco in August, Eugene Maly gave his presidential address on the twenty-five years of the association's history. Granted the tension that existed between biblical scholars and many other theologians, the actions of the business meeting were even bolder than those of the one two years earlier. The association elected John L. McKenzie as president. On a motion of Bruce Vawter, the members also unanimously elected Lyonnet and Zerwick to honorary membership.[73] The official letters sent to Lyonnet and Zerwick by Louis Hartman stated that this honorary membership was "in recognition of your scholarly work in the field of Biblical studies, and in sympathy with you over the difficulties which you have encountered because of your scientific publications."[74]

Roderick MacKenzie had by then taken up his post as rector of the Biblical Institute. For him the restoration of the two scholars was of paramount importance. Of the CBA's action, he commented:

The honorary memberships for Lyonnet and Zerwick are a gallant gesture, and they will both appreciate them. L. of course has taken the suspension quite in stride—as a Frenchman, it doesn't bother him to be disapproved by a Roman congregation—rather an accolade, in fact. He is lecturing and writing, busier than ever. With Z. it is very different; he feels it keenly. As for getting them rehabilitated, my best authorities seem to think there's no question of it before the Council reconvenes; but then, if enough Cardinals and Bishops speak up for them, it may be possible. Naturally, it is item no. 1 on my agenda.[75]

Zerwick acknowledged his honorary membership "as an honor for a representative of a type of exegesis that is somewhat slow in getting general approval. But it is a personal encouragement too."[76] The CBA had now publicly sided with Lyonnet and Zerwick against the Holy Office, but MacKenzie still had the task of working for their rehabilitation.

The Second Session

MacKenzie had to wait until March, 1964, to get a personal audience with Paul VI. He made his formal report as rector, and the pope was about to end the session, when MacKenzie introduced the problem of Lyonnet and Zerwick. The pope claimed he had no knowledge of their suspension. As MacKenzie recalled the audience, the pope "listened carefully, took notes, was quite noncommittal, but said he would look into it." Sometime afterwards, Paul appointed Bea to investigate. The cardinal interviewed Lyonnet and Zerwick and exonerated them of any charges. In his mind, part of the problem was that Vogt, MacKenzie's predecessor, had not consulted him. The whole affair was shrouded in mystery. The instructions to Vogt suspending the two scholars were transmitted orally, as was their reinstatement. At no point was any apology given them; yet, neither were they required to retract anything they had written or said. Bea's exonerating them was a victory over Ottaviani.[77]

During the second session of Vatican II, which opened on September 29, 1963, the schema on revelation was still being revised, and was not submitted to the bishops for a vote. There were, nevertheless, important developments during the session that would influence the outcome of the vote on revelation. Among other things, Cardinal Meyer joined Spellman in the council's presidency. For the Americans, however, the principal schema was religious liberty. They now had as a *peritus* John Courtney Murray, who, as was seen, had been forced to cease writing on the question in 1955. Like the biblical scholars, he had as his principal opponents Joseph C. Fenton, Vagnozzi, and Ottaviani. The schema on religious liberty was originally Chapter V in the proposed schema on ecumenism being drafted by the Secretariat for Promoting Christian Unity. When the second session opened, the bishops learned that Cardinal Cicognani, former apostolic delegate to the American hierarchy and at that time Secretary of State and President of the Coordinating Commission of the Council, had removed religious liberty from the agenda. Spellman assembled the American bishops, and had Murray draft a memorandum calling for the issue to be treated and outlining the content of a proposed document. The bishops unanimously approved the memorandum and drafted a letter, which Spellman signed in the name of the hierarchy of the United States and presented to Cardinal Cicognani, the presidency, and moderators of the council. Opposition to the schema came from Ottaviani, who was president of the Theological Commission. Murray himself had the task of explaining the chapter to the commission in the presence of Ottaviani and Fenton. While the commission voted eighteen to five in favor of the chapter, the bishops in council voted to accept the first four chapters of the constitution on ecumenism, but to postpone voting on Chapter V. The Secretariat for Promoting Christian Unity itself approved this postponement, for it would now have more time to develop the document.[78] While the second session ended without approval of religious liberty and discussion of the revised schema on revelation, the American scholars on both questions lost a principal opponent. At the end of the session, Fenton resigned as editor of the *American Ecclesiastical Review* and retired to a parish in Chicopee Falls, Massachusetts.[79]

At first blush, the questions of religious liberty and of biblical studies seemed to have little in common. At the turn of the century, however, they were both intertwined and, during the first phase of the council, they continued to face the same source of opposition. Moreover, the issue in the first schema on the "sources of revelation" presented a serious ecumenical difficulty. The constitution on ecumenism, of which religious liberty was a chapter, had emanated from the Secretariat for Promoting Christian Unity, for there could be no ecumenical dialogue, unless the Catholic Church recognized that truth existed outside its institutional confines and that, therefore, there had to be religious liberty. In short, the council would have to reject Ottaviani's abstract theological formulation that "two weights and two measures are to be applied:

one for truth, the other for error."[80] The difficulty was that the problem of religious liberty had historically emerged within the context of the normative Catholic teaching on Church-State relations. Murray and Pietro Pavan, professor of theology at the Lateran University and later a cardinal, framed their treatment of religious liberty in political and juridical terms. They thus faced the opposition not only of Ottaviani but also of sympathetic theologians who wanted to ground religious liberty in an adequate theology of the person. Such a theology would ultimately come from the schema on revelation, which was now the joint work of both the Secretariat and the Theological Commission.

15. The Second Vatican Council: Approval of *Dei Verbum*

THE INSTRUCTION OF THE BIBLICAL COMMISSION ON THE HISTORICAL TRUTH OF THE GOSPELS

Before the council could vote on the new schema on revelation, however, the Biblical Commission issued an instruction on the historical truth of the Gospels on April 21, 1964. Its publication occurred during the period of the restoration of Lyonnet and Zerwick. In the context of the debate still going on in Rome, the instruction represented a victory of those exegetes who were faithful to *Divino Afflante Spiritu* in using literary form criticism to interpret the Gospels; it was also a repudiation of positions, like that of Ruffini, who denied the validity of such an approach.[1]

Reminiscent of David Stanley's controversial article on Balaam's Ass in 1958, the instruction delineated three stages in the development of the Gospel traditions: 1) the events of the life of Jesus in His dealing with his disciples; 2) the apostolic preaching about these events; and 3) the shaping of this tradition into the written Gospels. In encouraging the exegete to ferret out the meaning of each of these stages, the instruction clearly affirmed the use of form criticism. On the first level, it stated, "when the Lord was orally explaining his doctrine, he followed the modes of reasoning and of exposition which were in vogue at the time. He accommodated himself to the mentality of his listeners and saw to it that what he taught was firmly impressed on the mind and easily remembered by the disciples." On the level of the preaching of the apostles, "they preached and made use of the various modes of speaking which were suited to their own purposes and the mentality of their listeners." Finally, from what had been orally handed down, the evangelists selected certain events, synthesized some, and expanded others; "indeed, from what they had received the sacred writers above all selected the things which were suited to the various situations of the faithful and to the purpose which they had in mind, and adapted their narration of them to the same situations and purpose." As a result, the exegete was to "seek out the meaning intended by the evangelist in narrating a saying or a deed in a certain way or in placing it in a certain context."[2]

Though the instruction cautioned exegetes to be obedient to the magisterium, it carefully avoided asserting the historicity of the Gospels. The "doctrine and the life of Jesus were not simply reported for the sole purpose of being remembered," it stated, "but were 'preached' so as to offer the Church a basis of faith and of morals."[3] With this terminology, many of the censured turn-of-the-century Catholic scholars would have been quite content. It represented, moreover, a turning point in the council's discussion of revelation, for, as will be seen, it was incorporated into the council's constitution on revelation.

The *CBQ* published the instruction in its July issue and Bishop Whealon wanted reprints of it, perhaps in pamphlet form, to distribute to all the priests of the Diocese of Cleveland. "It is," he wrote, "a document so positive and beneficial to the cause that I think it would help to make it available to as many as possible."[4] By the time the instruction was published, the CBA was preparing for its annual meeting, held in New York during the World's Fair.

At one point in the preparations, the CBA was considering holding all its sessions in the Vatican Pavilion at the World's Fair. If the association did meet there, John L. McKenzie remarked with some sarcasm, "It occurs to me that we might be suspected of discourtesy, or something, unless we invite Archbishop Vagnozzi to address us." If Hartman thought Vagnozzi should be invited, he continued, "it would be my duty, as President, to extend the invitation. Believe me, I should enjoy writing this letter. I doubt that he will accept."[5] Hartman agreed that the delegate should be invited, if the CBA met exclusively at the Vatican Pavilion, but he warned McKenzie: "You better not fire till you see the white of his eyes." Mother Kathryn Sullivan, R.S.C.J., on the program committee, had already reserved the pavilion for September 1–3, but recommended that the CBA meet there only on the first day and hold the rest of its sessions at the Passionists' retreat house in Jamaica,

Long Island.[6] This arrangement avoided the necessity of inviting Vagnozzi.

At the meeting McKenzie gave his presidential address on power and authority in the New Testament. According to the published minutes, "he challenged exegesis to focus more attention on the unique nature of the Spirit's *power* within a community of love and on a charismatic authority conceived as *service* to both."[7] The CBA was now well aware of its relation with scholars elsewhere, especially as the bishops prepared for the third session of the council. Roland de Vaux, O.P., of the École biblique in Jerusalem, delivered a paper on "Recent Discussions on Biblical Theology."[8] Despite the presence of Monsignor John Steinmueller, whose re-edition of *A Companion to the Study of Scripture* had merited such a harsh review from Roderick MacKenzie, the business meeting was uneventful. In light of the Biblical Commission's recent instruction, however, there was a "Free Panel-Discussion on the Historicity of the Gospels." The panel was made up of Raymond Brown, David Stanley, Bruce Vawter, and Joseph Fitzmyer, each of whom had already distinguished himself by the use of form criticism. The members also heard a report from the board of editors of the Old and New Testaments, which were then cooperating with the bishops' committee on the liturgy. In accordance with the Constitution on the Liturgy, approved during the second session of the council, vernacular translations of the liturgical pericopes from the original languages would be ready for use for the first Sunday of Advent.[9] As will be seen, however, the final translation was still several years from completion.

THE THIRD SESSION OF THE COUNCIL

Before the third session opened, the bishops had the opportunity to submit written observations on what was now the third revision of the schema on revelation. Spellman's observations showed the influence on him of more progressive scholars. The schema, he said, was "very acceptable," but he proposed two amendments. First, he suggested:

For at one time the truth is expressed and proposed in historical texts in various ways, while at another time in didactic or prophetic texts. And so it is necessary that the exegete inquire after the sense which the holy writer expressly intended and expressed in his determined circumstances, given the conditions of his time, by means of the types of literature used at that time.

The cardinal's second proposal reflected the Biblical Commission's instruction. "The four holy writers," he continued,

wrote the Gospels, selecting certain things from the things which had been handed down both by mouth and in writing, synthesizing some things and explaining things with attention to the conditions of the churches. This, however, does not prevent the evangelists from having somewhat modified and elaborated the words and deeds of Christ the Lord. For these men wrote out the Gospels under the inspiration of that Spirit of truth who was promised to the Apostles by Christ, that He might lead them to the path of all truth. Otherwise they did not discharge the magisterium of the earliest Church, whose responsibility is to enlighten and clarify what is implicitly contained within the deposit.[10]

Probably around this time, McIntyre, who had been Coadjutor Archbishop of New York before becoming Archbishop of Los Angeles, rebuked Spellman for being too easily influenced by younger Scripture scholars. McIntyre argued that he was better informed on biblical matters, because he had had more years of Scripture at Dunwoodie, than Spellman had in Rome.[11] He boasted that he had studied under Gigot![12]

On September 30, as the bishops were formally discussing the revised schema at the council, Cardinal Meyer made the first of his two interventions. He found the schema acceptable, "particularly the manner in which it presents sacred tradition as being something alive, dynamic and whole, i.e., consisting not only of doctrinal declarations, but also the cult and practice of the entire Church." He also liked the reference to the Virgin Mary, "in which it states that the Church imitates her by considering in its heart the things and words handed down to it." He wanted clarification, however, of the section, which

presents the life and cult of the Church entirely under a positive aspect. Tradition in this paragraph is extended, in my opinion, beyond the limits of the infallible magisterium. If this interpretation is true, then such tradition is subject to the limitations and defects of the Church Militant, which is the Church of sinners and which knows divine realities through a mirror darkly.

The history of the Church amply attests to these defects, e.g., the long, obscure theological casuistry, non-liturgical piety and the neglect of Sacred Scripture. There are many other similar instances.

This paragraph, therefore, must be augmented with the addition of words which point out both these defects, which are always possible in this state of life, and their remedy.[13]

Meyer would return to the theme of tradition in his second intervention six days later.

On October 1, Cardinal Lawrence Shehan of Baltimore suggested that greater stress be placed on "that which is accomplished by the subject of revelation that is, by the human mind which receives revelation from God, interprets and transmits it to the people of God." In his proposed amendment, however, he came close to raising the old issue of the equation of inspiration with authorship and of limiting inspiration to a known author. "Supernatural revelation," he said,

truly is the communication of God with man by which God reveals Himself. This communication, *in an active and, indeed, dynamic sense*, is rightly called the speaking of God, not however necessarily as a formal speech of God, but rather as a salvific action of God toward men *along with a divine selection and movement of the witnesses*, who, by the goodness of God and the action of the Holy Spirit, understanding what had been revealed to them, gave their interpretation in the historical context of the People of God, and put it into human words.

These witnesses in the Old Testament were the Patriarchs and Prophets, while

in the New Testament, Christ Himself gives the most outstanding witness and, after Him, the Apostles called by Him. Revelation, however, *in a passive and static sense*, is regarded as that interpretation of the witnesses, accomplished by the Spirit of God, from which arise doctrines and revealed truth.[14]

Shehan's definition of "Revelation . . . in a passive and static sense" would make it appear that he still had difficulties with redaction criticism, for which the instruction of 1964 had specifically allowed.

Meyer's second intervention on October 5 repeated some of the arguments he made about tradition. Pointing to the "evidence of failings" in the history of the Church, he recommended an insertion into the section on tradition:

Nevertheless, this living tradition does not always and in all things advance and grow. For when the Pilgrim Church contemplates divine matters, it can fail in some respects and actually has failed. For this reason, it carried within itself Sacred Scripture as an abiding norm, one against which it can measure its own life and thus unceasingly correct and improve itself.[15]

Meyer was sensitive to the ecumenical dimensions of the constitution, and, therefore, wanted to stress the primacy of Scripture as a regulating norm. In his formulation that tradition "carried within itself Sacred Scripture as an abiding norm," however, he picked up the thread of thought so familiar to Kenrick in the nineteenth century.

The final American intervention came from Charles Maloney, the auxiliary bishop of Louisville. Maloney focused on the inspiration and interpretation of the Scripture. That section, he thought, "should indicate certain things held by all and should mention what will be clarified by free, yet prudent, investigation and discussion." If such a clarification were made, he continued, "the harshness of the arguments and disagreements would decrease, and the way would be cleared for that internal unity of the Church which would cleanse the blemishes of the Bride of Christ and would make her wrinkles disappear." In his mind, "popular authors have written much and imperfectly about the newness of the [historical] method, and thus they disturb the minds of the faithful and sometimes the leaders." Citing the Biblical Commission's instruction, he then recommended a series of relatively minor changes.[16]

THE FOURTH SESSION OF THE COUNCIL

Over a year would pass before the bishops gave their final vote on the schema, but the major thrust of the document represented a significant departure from the first schema on the "sources of revelation." In the meantime, other developments would deeply influence the outcome of the schema and would enhance the respect with which American scholarship was regarded, for the Biblical Commission was undergoing further changes.

NEW CONSULTORS TO THE BIBLICAL COMMISSION AND THE CBA

In 1964, three new cardinals were named as members of the commission, Bernard Alfrink of Holland, Franziskus König of Austria, and Ildebrando Antoniutti of Italy. Alfrink and König were biblical scholars. The three new members counterbalanced the conservative orientation of Ottaviani, Ruffini, and Michael Browne, O.P., who retained their membership on the commission. In 1965, Roderick MacKenzie got his wish to see more of an American representation among the consultors, though it is uncertain if this was due to the influence of Meyer, who died during the summer. The new consultors were MacKenzie himself of Canada, Barnabas Ahern of the United States, Patrick W. Skehan of the United States, H. Schürmann of East Germany, R. Lach of France, and G. Rinaldi of Italy.[17] The Americans appointed illustrated the shift on the biblical question at the council, for Ahern and Skehan had both been at odds with Vagnozzi.

When the CBA convened for its annual meeting at Notre Dame at the end of the summer of 1965, Barnabas Ahern, the president, delivered his address on the challenge of the revised schema to exegetes. In particular, he noted its stress on the social character of inspiration, that is, that inspiration involved not only the author(s) of Scripture but also the acceptance of the writings by a community under the guidance of the Holy Spirit. Moreover, the new schema called for ecumenical cooperation in translating the Bible—a momentous change from the Catholic attitude in the past. Although, as will be seen, this soon presented some political rather than theological problems, the CBA assigned the incomplete portions of its translation project to leading Protestant scholars. Frank Cross of Harvard was to do 1 and 2 Samuel; James Sanders of Union Theological Seminary in New York, 2 Kings; and David Noel Freedman was to revise Genesis, the translation of which was the first published by the CBA and CCD. John Knox and W. D. Davies, both of Union Theological Seminary, were to translate the Pastoral Epistles and Epistle to the Hebrews respectively.[18]

APPROVAL OF *Dei Verbum*

When Vatican II reconvened on September 14, 1965, for its fourth and final session, the issue paramount for Americans was the schema on religious liberty. On September 21, the bishops voted by an overwhelming majority to close debate on the schema and submit it for final revision to a mixed committee of the Secretariat for Promoting Christian Unity and the Theological Commission. Joining the committee for this final revision was the outstanding biblical scholar, Pierre Benoit, O.P.[19]

On September 20, the bishops had also begun voting on the sections of the schema on revelation. On September 24, Francis McCool, S.J., professor at the Biblical Institute and member of the American Bishops' Press Panel, addressed the assembled journalists. Acknowledging that he realized their attention was focused on the Declaration on Religious Liberty, he pointed out the significance of the schema on revelation. During the previous "three historic days" of voting, he stated, "the Second Vatican Council has placed its seal of approval on several points which theologians have seen with new clarity in the course of the last hundred years." He then traced the history of the discussion of Scripture and tradition. "The ecumenical nature of the schema," he noted,

is shown most clearly in what it deliberately did not say. Ever since the Protestant Revolt, the assertion of the Reformers that Scripture was the only vehicle which transmitted God's revelation to man offended Catholic sensibilities. The Council of Trent insisted in reply that divine revelation came to us in both Scripture and Apostolic Tradition. After Trent, some Catholic theologians developed the theory that Scripture and Tradition were complementary sources and that, therefore, Scripture alone was an incomplete source. Though this view won a certain predominance in the manuals of the nineteenth century, other Catholic theologians more recently have proposed another explanation of the relation between Scripture and Tradition. All of divine revelation is contained in both, though, naturally, in different ways. When Vatican II began, this draft, then entitled "On the Sources of Revelation," presupposed as established the first of these two positions—which caused the turmoil in which that draft was rejected. Now, two sessions later, the Council is content to reaffirm the position of Trent—revelation comes to us in both Scripture and tradition. It asserts that both are intimately related, indeed intertwined with each other. But it has reserved for a future Council the exact determination of what these relations are.[20]

By speaking of "Apostolic Tradition" and of revelation found in "both Scripture and tradition," McCool may have been playing loose with the Council of Trent, which spoke of "traditions" and avoided a formulation that would imply two separate sources of revelation. McCool was, however, expressing a theological concept, in popular terms, with which Kenrick and American Catholics would have been perfectly at home in the nineteenth century.

On November 18, by an almost unanimous vote—2,115 to 27—the bishops approved the Constitution on Divine Revelation, *Dei Verbum*. It received Pope Paul's approval and was promulgated the same day.[21] The constitution consisted of a prologue and six chapters. On revelation, it stated that "it pleased God, in his goodness and wisdom, to reveal himself and to make known the mystery of his will (cf. Eph. 1:9). His will was that men should have access to the Father, through Christ, the Word made flesh, in the Holy Spirit, and thus become sharers in the divine nature (cf. Eph. 2:18; 2 Pet. 1:4)." "This economy of revelation," moreover,

is realized by deeds and words, which are intrinsically bound up with each other. As a result, the works performed by God in the history of salvation show forth and bear out the doctrine and realities signified by the words; the words, for their part, proclaim the works, and bring to light the mystery they contain. The most intimate truth which this revelation gives us about God and the salvation of man shines forth in Christ, who is himself both the mediator and the sum total of Revelation.[22]

Revelation, then, was not a series of propositions, but primarily the Word made flesh, for Christ

himself—to see whom is to see the Father (cf. Jn. 14:9)—completed and perfected Revelation and confirmed it with divine guarantees. He did this by the total fact of his presence and self-manifestation—by words and works, signs and miracles, but above all by his death and glorious resurrection from the dead, and finally by sending the Spirit of truth. He revealed that God was with us, to deliver us from the darkness of sin and death, and to raise us up to eternal life.[23]

The constitution then turned to the transmission of revelation. This section represented the most radical departure from the original schema. "Sacred tradition and sacred Scripture," it declared, "make up a single sacred deposit of the Word of God, which is entrusted to the Church." It belonged to "the living teaching office of the Church alone," however, to give "an authentic interpretation of the Word of God, whether in its written form or in the form of Tradition." But the constitution made it clear that "this Magisterium is not superior to the Word of God, but is its servant. It teaches only what has been handed on to it."[24] Tradition was thus given a much more dynamic meaning than it had had in Roman theology since Vatican I. As Joseph Ratzinger noted, "it is not difficult . . . to recognize the pen of Y. Congar in the text and to see behind it the influence of the Catholic Tübingen school of the nineteenth century with, in particular, its dynamic and organic idea of tradition."[25] That "idea of tradition" was, of course, the one that Francis Kenrick had expressed.

In regard to the study of Scripture, the constitution instructed exegetes to determine "the intention of the sacred writers" and to use, among other methods, "literary forms."[26] They were to recognize "the marvelous 'condescension' of eternal wisdom." The constitution then drew the analogy between the human and divine elements in Scripture and the two natures in Christ: "indeed the words of God, expressed in the words of men, are in every way like human language, just as the Word of the eternal Father, when he took on himself the flesh of human weakness, became like men."[27] Lagrange and the other suspect Catholic exegetes of the turn of the century had finally been vindicated. The council, furthermore, summarized in its constitution, and thus gave conciliar sanction to, the Biblical Commission's instruction of 1964 on form criticism of the Gospels.[28] Finally, the council requested that vernacular translations be made "in a joint effort with the separated brethren," so that "they may be used by all Christians."[29] The CBA had, of course, already anticipated such "a joint effort" at its meeting the previous summer. In *Dei Verbum,* the Church officially espoused historical criticism and placed itself firmly in the mainstream of biblical scholarship.

Dei Verbum and the Declaration on Religious Liberty

Yet, if the problems of biblical criticism and of religious liberty had been intertwined at the turn of the century and on the eve of Vatican II, their solutions were also interrelated. On October 25, the bishops overwhelmingly voted to accept the revised text on religious liberty, and, on December 7, formally approved and promulgated it. It is perhaps no accident that *Dignitatis Humanae Per-*

sonae shows an affinity with *Dei Verbum,* for Benoit was on the committee that made the final revisions of both. *Dei Verbum* had stressed revelation as God's self-communication, culminating in the Word made flesh. One of the objections to Murray's and Pavan's earlier schema on religious liberty was that it stressed Church-State relations and did not adequately ground the right to freedom on a theology of the person. *Dignitatis Humanae Personae* stated that "the act of faith is of its very nature a free act," because "man, redeemed by Christ the Saviour and called through Jesus Christ to be an adopted son of God, cannot give his adherence to God when he reveals himself unless, drawn by the Father, he submits to God with a faith that is reasonable and free."[30]

The two conciliar documents, when taken together, present a theology of revelation and faith, which emphasizes God's personal freedom in communicating Himself and man's personal freedom in responding in faith. It is a theology, not of subjectivism, as the Holy See feared with Americanism and Modernism, but of personalism. When the Church reacted against Americanism and Modernism, as was seen, it saw the positive assessment of human potentiality in both of those movements as a resurrection of the old nature-grace dispute, now reshaped in the battle against rationalism. The Church expressed its reaction against those movements in terms of a form of Thomism, introduced into the Church to combat rationalism. The promulgation of the two documents on religious liberty and revelation represented the vindication of John Courtney Murray and of the biblical scholars who had all suffered for trying to remind the Church that its theological heritage, even its Thomistic one, was older than the nineteenth century. As will be seen, however, the battle between the entrenched form of Thomism and biblical scholarship would continue even after the council.

BIBLICAL SCHOLARSHIP AFTER THE COUNCIL

With the conclusion of the council, American Catholic biblical scholars still had two unfinished items on their agenda: *The Jerome Biblical Commentary (JBC)* and a complete American Catholic translation of the Bible. Begun in 1962, while the council was discussing the first schema on revelation, the *JBC* was consciously the work of Catholic scholars alone. The editors, Raymond E. Brown, S.S., Joseph A. Fitzmyer, S.J., and Roland E. Murphy, O.Carm., explained their motivation:

Everyone now knows that generally Catholic and non-Catholic biblical scholars work very well together and have the same approach to and interpretation of most biblical passages. But there remains a feeling or suspicion both within and without the Roman Catholic Church that such cooperation represents a private endeavor of only a few and that it is without any official backing in the Church. The question of *the* Catholic interpretation of the Bible constantly reappears. It seemed to the editors that the best way to expose the misunderstanding implicit in this question was to produce a commentary written entirely by Catholics.

Because the *JBC* was the product of many contributors, the editors had "no illusion that the articles are all of equal value."[31]

A glance at the arrangement of the table of contents is sufficient to indicate how far Catholic biblical scholarship had advanced since that group of Scripture professors assembled in Washington in 1936 to begin translation of the CCD New Testament. "Isaiah" and "Deutero-Isaiah" were treated in separate articles. The arrangement of the commentaries on the New Testament books followed the chronological order in which most scholars agree the books were written. Thus Mark precedes Matthew and Luke, and John came after the Epistles, except 2 Peter. In addition to commentaries on the biblical books, there were also topical articles. Gone was the unscholarly Catholic defensiveness of the past. Thus Eugene Maly wrote openly of the four sources of the Pentateuch. Frederick Moriarty, S.J., noted that Is 7:14 was not in itself a prophecy of the virgin birth of Christ[32]—a scholarly point that is not reflected in the New American Bible, as will be seen. The *JBC* achieved its purpose of showing the maturity of American Catholic biblical scholarship, but is currently being completely revised by the same editors.

In the meantime, the translation project continued. By 1961, three of a projected four-volume translation of the Old Testament had appeared—Volume I: *Genesis to Ruth*, in 1952; Volume II: *The Sapiential Books: Job to Sirach*, in 1955; and Volume IV: *The Prophetic Books: Isaiah to Malachi*, in 1961. Still, Catholic dogmatic considerations shaped the translation. Patrick Skehan informed the CBA meeting in 1960 that the episcopal committee of the CCD insisted that Is 7:14 be translated as "the virgin shall be with child."[33] As was seen above, the CBA at its meeting in 1965 enlisted the contributions of Protestant scholars for completing the translation. At the same time, the editors of the Old Testament reported that the translation of the historical books was about half done.[34]

The American Catholic laity had its first experience of the new translation in an interim form on the first Sunday of Advent of 1964, when the first changes in the liturgy were introduced. There were mixed reactions. Some problems arose from the people's unfamiliarity with a translation of the New Testament from the Greek. The CCD, for example, had translated Mat 28:6 as "He is not here, for he has risen even as he said." The new translation was: "but he is not here. He has been raised, just as he promised." Some Catholics thought this diminished Christ's divinity and was, therefore, heretical. One such critic was Father Gommar de Pauw of the Archdiocese of Baltimore, who condemned the new vernacular liturgy and led an early "traditionalist" schism. Raymond E. Brown, S.S., patiently explained the reasons for the change and pointed out that "when the New Testament says that Jesus was raised from the dead, it means that the Father raised him up."[35] Other difficulties arose from an effort to render a text into too colloquial a form of modern English. Thus, in Lk 15:8, the woman was said to have lost a "dime." This may have been a better rendition of "drachma," but hardly seemed sufficient reason for the woman to wake up her friends and neighbors when she found it. In light of a number of criticisms, the editors continued their revision of the liturgical texts.

In the meantime, the ecumenical spirit threatened to undermine the translation project. As early as 1957, R. C. Fuller of the English Catholic Biblical Association had approached the CBA about the possibility of adopting a Catholic edition of the Revised Standard Version (RSV). The new edition already had Bea's verbal approval and was to be submitted to the English hierarchy. The faculty of the Biblical Institute, he noted, was also in favor of the move.[36] Louis Hartman bluntly rejected the proposal, which would "stultify" the CCD project. He and his colleagues found it "understandable but, we think, regrettable that our English colleague [sic] are of the opinion that nothing good can come from the Nazareth of

Catholic America."[37] This ended any possible American cooperation with the English effort at this time.

After the council, there was a new threat to the CCD translation.
In 1966, Cardinal Cushing gave his *imprimatur* to an unaltered
edition of the RSV.[38] The cardinal's ecumenical enthusiasm thus
led him to be the first prelate to give approval to the denial of the
Pauline authorship of the pastoral Epistles.[39]

Despite these various setbacks, the CCD translation of the Old
Testament was completed in 1969 with the publication of Volume
III: *Samuel to Maccabees.* The following year, the *New American Bible*
appeared. It was the first Catholic translation into English of the
entire Bible from the original languages. Its publication coincided
with the introduction of the final changes in the liturgy, which gave
renewed emphasis to Scripture by providing for a three-year cycle
of readings on Sundays. The old liturgy used Old Testament readings only on four major feasts. The new one provided for an Old
Testament reading every Sunday, except during the Easter season.
The introductory material to the NAB reflected the new orientation in Scripture studies. As an example, it stated that

inspiration is related to a certain sensitivity which exists in a society at a
given time. This sensitivity inspires gifted individuals in that society.
These individuals in turn heighten that sensitivity in their fellow citizens.

It was through "this same process of mutual influence," it continued, that

Hebrew literature came into being. We see in the Hebrew people a highly
developed sensitivity for God's presence in their lives. From these pious
Hebrew communities we see arise prophets, preachers, writers, who offered their (first spoken) reflections on that shared experience of God's
presence with His people. In turn these prophets, preachers and writers
heightened that religious sensitivity in their people.[40]

Such an approach to inspiration for popular dissemination would
have been impossible only a decade before.

The NAB also sought to instruct a wider audience on some of
the scholarly issues, which had been so controversial in the past.
In introducing the Pentateuch, the edition drew attention to the
four primary sources of the five books. Reminiscent of Butin's

address to the first session of the CBA, the NAB noted that the recognition of these sources did not deny

the role of Moses in the development of the Pentateuch. It is true we do not conceive of him as the author of the books in the modern sense. But there is no reason to doubt that, in the events described in these traditions, he had a uniquely important role, especially as lawgiver. Even the later laws which have been added in P and D are presented as a Mosaic heritage. Moses is the lawgiver *par excellence,* and all later legislation is conceived in his spirit, and therefore attributed to him.

Similarly, in introducing the New Testament, the editors indicated the priority of the Gospel of Mark to that of Matthew, but were more cautious in rejecting the Pauline authorship of the Pastoral Epistles.[41] The translation was a vast improvement over the older Douay-Rheims edition as revised by Challoner and over the CCD translation of the New Testament. The editors, however, are still continuing their work. In 1987, they issued a totally new translation of the New Testament, which, while closer to the Greek original than the earlier NAB translation, avoids colloquial expressions unsuitable for public proclamation of the word of God.

In the meantime, Paul VI further changed the composition of the biblical commission. In 1971, he reconstituted it and closely affiliated it with the Congregation for the Doctrine of the Faith, as the Holy Office had been renamed. No longer were cardinals members and all others only consultors; the revised commission was composed of twenty members from around the world, many of whom were renowned biblical scholars.[42] Several members of the CBA have been appointed members of the new commission, David Stanley, S.J., Raymond E. Brown, S.S., Jerome D. Quinn, and Joseph A. Fitzmyer, S.J.

While American Catholic biblical scholarship had thus gained recognition in Rome, it was also gaining increasing prominence in the United States. Biblical scholars had been in the forefront of moving Catholic intellectual life out of the isolation, which had prevailed since Modernism. As was seen above, Catholic and non-Catholic scholars began studying in the same institutions, especially the Johns Hopkins University, in the 1940s. By the late 1960s, Catholic biblical scholars who had achieved prominence during the turmoil of the 1950s and during the council began to be elected presidents of the Society of Biblical Literature. John L.

McKenzie was the first in 1967, followed by Raymond E. Brown in 1977, Joseph A. Fitzmyer in 1979, and Roland E. Murphy in 1984. In the meantime, the number and role of women in the CBA had increased dramatically since 1947, when Kathryn Sullivan, R.S.C.J., became the first woman admitted to membership. Pheme Perkins, professor of theology at Boston College, became the first woman elected president of the CBA in 1986. The following year, another member of the CBA, Elisabeth Schüssler Fiorenza, Talbot Professor at the Episcopal Divinity School in Cambridge, Massachusetts, was elected president of the Society of Biblical Literature. On an international level, Raymond Brown became the first American Catholic elected president of the Novi Testamenti Studiorum Societas in 1986–1987.

CONCLUSIONS

Despite the advances made by biblical scholarship in the Catholic church throughout the world, but especially in the United States and Canada, some of the older problems still remain. There is a renewed conservative reaction against biblical scholars for their use of historical criticism, which, in the conservative mind, destroys dogma. On the other side of the debate, there is an ultraliberal misinterpretation of what the biblicists are doing. Biblical scholar Raymond Brown, who himself has been the target of ultraconservative criticism, objects to the statements of Thomas Sheehan as being an ultraliberal distortion of his position. Sheehan has stated, for example, that Jesus "saw himself not as God or Messiah, but as a Jewish prophet." For Brown, this "is a negative exaggeration of what most Catholic exegetes hold about the implicit christology of Jesus' ministry." Sheehan also stated that Jesus "did not know that he was supposed to establish the Holy Roman Catholic and Apostolic Church with St. Peter as the first in a long line of infallible popes." Brown objects to this as presupposing "an oversimplified understanding of church foundation, involving *explicit* intention on Jesus' part during his ministry—an explicitness not necessarily a part of Catholic doctrine on the subject." In short, Sheehan's assertions are generalizations, and at least many Catholic biblical scholars would like more nuance.[43]

Much of this contemporary debate bears an unfortunate resemblance to the battles at the beginning of the century. Then, as now, biblical scholars find themselves on the defensive against extremes. In the 1890s, Lagrange wrote against Loisy, only to find himself the object of attack from Delattre and other conservatives. In the 1980s, biblical scholars find their positions misrepresented by the far left and therefore become objects of attack from the far right. Behind this lie some of the same theological tensions of earlier periods of the Church's history.

The history of the period surveyed points out the necessity of distinguishing between doctrine and theology. What frequently led to charges of heterodoxy, for instance against Lagrange and Poels, was not their denial of any doctrine, but their disagreement with the reflection on that doctrine by a particular school of theology. What made them objects of concern to Roman authorities was their apparent affinity, according to the same theological school of thought, to objectively unorthodox thinkers, such as Loisy. The encouragement of biblical scholarship by Pius XII and the teaching of Vatican II on revelation were something new to American Catholics, who have such a short memory of history. The problem was the ensconced mode of theology that led to a confusion between doctrine and theological interpretation. From Francis Kenrick to Anthony Maas to Edward Siegman, I would argue, and from Pius IX to Leo XIII to Pius XII and Vatican II, there has been a development not so much of doctrine as of theology. Franzelin, Mazzella, and Billot formulated a theology for the interpretation of the Bible that may have been necessary to combat nineteenth and twentieth-century rationalism, but it was a theology and not doctrine. To embrace historical criticism of Scripture—and religious liberty—Vatican II had to adopt a different type of theology, one that was radically different from the form of Thomism that had dominated seminary education; yet, one that would have been intelligible to Kenrick and Newman.

The present debates are, indeed, reminiscent of the past. Until the entire theology of Vatican II is assimilated, there are bound to be misunderstandings, confusion, and even disagreement. The tragedy would be if there again arose the confusion between a time-conditioned theology and Church teaching—a confusion that led to the dismissal from teaching of Poels and Siegman and the obedient abstention from writing of John Courtney Murray. But debate can also be a sign of vitality. It not only contributes to the development of theology but is proof that the Church is a living body.

Abbreviations

ARCHIVES:

AAB	Archives of the Archdiocese of Baltimore
AABo	Archives of the Archdiocese of Boston
AANY	Archives of the Archdiocese of New York
AASP	Archives of the Archdiocese of St. Paul
ACBA	Archives of the Catholic Biblical Association
ACUA	Archives of the Catholic University of America
ACPPS	Archives of the Congregation of the Precious Blood
ADKC	Archives of the Diocese of Kansas City
ADR	Archives of the Diocese of Richmond
ASV	Archivio Segreto Vaticano
ASV, SS	Segreteria di Stato
ASV, DAUS	Delegazione apostolica degli Stati Uniti
APF	Archives of the Congregation of Propaganda Fide
AUTS	Archives of Union Theological Seminary
AWC	Archives of Woodstock College
SAB	Sulpician Archives, Baltimore

PERIODICALS AND COLLECTIONS

AAS	*Acta Apostolicae Sedis*
CBQ	*Catholic Biblical Quarterly*
DS	Denzinger and Schönmetzer (eds.), *Enchiridion Symbolorum Definitionum et Declarationum de rebus fidei et morum*

Notes

FOREWORD

1. Karl Rahner, *Karl Rahner in Dialogue* (New York: Crossroad, 1986), 258.

CHAPTER 1

1. Thomas O. Hanley, S.J., ed., *The John Carroll Papers* (Notre Dame, IN: Univ. of Notre Dame Press, 1976), 1:111.
2. Ibid., 137–38.
3. *Die Verbum*, no. 8 in Austin Flannery, O.P., ed., *Vatican Council II: The Conciliar and Post Conciliar Documents* (Collegeville, MN: The Liturgical Press, 1975), 754.
4. Carroll to Carey, Baltimore, Jan. 30, 1789, in Hanley, *Carroll Papers*, 1:348.
5. Carroll to Carey, Baltimore, Apr. 8, 1789, in *ibid.*, 355.
6. Wilfrid Parsons, S.J., "First American Editions of Catholic Bibles," *Historical Records and Studies* 27 (1937): 89, 90.
7. Hanley, *Carroll Papers*, 3:133.
8. DS, 1504. For the Florentine decree on the canon, see DS, 1334–36.
9. Hubert Jedin, *A History of the Council of Trent*, trans. Dom Ernest Graf, O.S.B. (St. Louis, MO: B. Herder Book Co., 1961), 2:55–58. The original German edition was published in 1957. See also James C. Turro and Raymond E. Brown, S.S., "Canonicity," in Raymond E. Brown, S.S., Joseph A. Fitzmyer, S.J., and Roland E. Murphy, O.Carm., eds., *The Jerome Biblical Commentary* (Englewood Cliffs, NJ: Prentice-Hall, 1968), 523–24.
10. DS, 1506–08.
11. Jedin, *Council of Trent*, 2:95–97.
12. Robert E. McNally, S.J., "The Council of Trent and Vernacular Bibles," *Theological Studies* 27 (June 1966): 226.
13. Hugh Pope, O.P., *English Versions of the Bible* (St. Louis, MO: B. Herder Book Co., 1952), 249–97.
14. Patrick W. Skehan, George W. MacRae, S.J., and Raymond E. Brown, S.S., "Texts and Versions," in Brown et al., *Jerome Biblical Commentary*, 588.
15. Ibid.
16. Pope, *English Versions*, 355–71.
17. *Collectanea S. Congregationis de Propaganda Fide seu Decreta Instructiones Rescripta pro Apostolicis Missionibus* (Rome: Typographia Polyglotta S.C. de Propaganda Fide, 1907), 1:593.
18. Parsons, "First American Editions," 90, 92–94.
19. See my "Quest for a Catholic Vernacular Bible in America," in Nathan O. Hatch and Mark A. Noll, *The Bible in America: Essays in Cultural History* (New York: Oxford Univ. Press, 1982), 164–66. See also Ray Allen Billington, *The Protestant Crusade: A Study of the Origins of American Nativism, 1800–1860* (Chicago: Quadrangle Books, 1964), 221–30.
20. Hugh J. Nolan, ed., *Pastoral Letters of the American Hierarchy, 1792–1970* (Huntington, IN: Our Sunday Visitor, 1970), 28.

21. *Acta et Decreta Sacrorum Conciliorum Recentiorum: Collectio Lacensis* (Freiburg im Breisgau: Herder, 1875), 3:28.
22. Nolan, ed., *Pastoral Letters,* 51, 52.
23. Francis Patrick Kenrick, *Theologia Dogmatica,* 2d ed. (Baltimore, MD: John Murphy & Co., 1858), 1:282–83.
24. Ibid., 288.
25. Ibid., 289, 300–301.
26. Ibid. 301, 302.
27. Ibid., 302.
28. Ibid., 306.
29. *Dei Verbum,* no. 12, in Flannery, *Vatican Council II,* 757.
30. Kenrick, *Theologia Dogmatica,* 1:365–70, 227–28.
31. Ibid., 20–21, 64–65, 357–63.
32. John P. Marschall, "Francis Patrick Kenrick, 1851–1863: The Baltimore Years" (Ph.D. diss., The Catholic University of America, 1965), 4. On Lingard's translation of the Gospels, see Joseph P. Chinnici, O.F.M., *The English Catholic Enlightenment: John Lingard and the Cisalpine Movement, 1780–1850* (Shepardstown, WV: The Patmos Press, 1980), 149–53, 155, 157, 164.
33. Anon., "New Versions and the Vulgate," *Brownson's Quarterly Review* 3 (October 1846): 473–75, 476–78.
34. Ibid., 486, 487.
35. William Foxwell Albright, *From the Stone Age to Christianity: Monotheism and the Historical Process,* 2d ed. (Baltimore, MD: The Johns Hopkins Press, 1957), 27.
36. Jack Finegan, *Light from the Ancient Past* (Princeton, NJ: Princeton Univ. Press, 1959), 235–36.
37. AAB, 3 W 8, Garnier to Carroll, Paris, Oct. 3, 1806.

CHAPTER 2

1. F. Kenrick to P. Kenrick, Philadelphia, Sept. 25, 1843, in Frederick E. Tourscher, trans., *The Kenrick-Frenaye Correspondence: Letters Chiefly of Francis Patrick Kenrick and Marc Anthony Frenaye: 1830–1862* (Philadelphia: Philadelphia Archives, 1920), 173–74. On Kenrick's translation, see John P. Marschall, "Francis Patrick Kenrick," 294–328.
2. Billington, *The Protestant Crusade,* 220–31.
3. Francis Patrick Kenrick, *The Four Gospels, Translated from the Latin Vulgate, and Diligently Compared with the Greek Text, Being a Revision of the Rhemish Translation* (New York: Edward Dunigan & Brother, 1849), 27, 29.
4. Ibid., 38.
5. Pope, *English Versions,* 462.
6. F. Kenrick to P. Kenrick, Philadelphia, Apr. 10, 1850, in Tourscher, *Kenrick-Frenaye Correspondence,* 307–8.
7. Chinicci, *English Catholic Enlightenment,* 151–54.
8. Nicholas Wiseman, "The Parables of the New Testament," *The Dublin Review* 27 (September 1849): 182–84.
9. Nicholas Wiseman, "Miracles of the New Testament," *The Dublin Review* 27 (December 1849): 291–345.
10. F. Kenrick to P. Kenrick, Philadelphia, Dec. 24, 1849, in Tourscher, *Kenrick-Frenaye Correspondence,* 302.
11. Orestes Brownson, "Literary Notices and Criticisms," *Brownson's Quarterly Review,* n.s. 3 (July 1849): 409. See also Hugh J. Nolan, *The Most Reverend Francis*

Patrick Kenrick: Third Bishop of Philadelphia: 1830–1851 (Philadelphia: American Catholic Historical Society, 1948), 394.

12. F. Kenrick to P. Kenrick, Philadelphia, Oct. 2, 1849, in Tourscher, *Kenrick-Frenaye Correspondence*, 299.

13. Francis Patrick Kenrick, *The Acts of the Apostles, the Epistles of St. Paul, the Catholic Epistles, and the Apocalypse* (New York: Edward Dunigan and Brother, 1851), v, xi–xiii.

14. Ibid., xiii, 501–2.

15. Francis Patrick Kenrick, *The Psalms, Books of Wisdom, and the Canticle of Canticles* (Baltimore, MD: Lucas Brothers, 1857), 61.

16. *Collectio Lacensis*, 3:174.

17. Newman to Lynch, Dec. 7, 1858, in John Henry Newman, *Letters and Diaries* (London: T. Nelson, 1961–), 18:531–34.

18. F. Kenrick to P. Kenrick, Baltimore, May 9, 1858, in Tourscher, *Kenrick-Frenaye Correspondence*, 413.

19. Francis Patrick Kenrick, *The Book of Job, and the Prophets* (Baltimore, MD: Kelly, Hedian & Piet, 1859), v, vi.

20. Ibid., 115–16, 134.

21. [Orestes Brownson], "Literary Notices and Criticisms," *Brownson's Quarterly Review*, 2d New York series (October 1859): 541, 542.

22. F. Kenrick to P. Kenrick, Baltimore, Oct. 25, 1859, in Tourscher, *Kenrick-Frenaye Correspondence*, 430.

23. Francis Patrick Kenrick, *The Pentateuch* (Baltimore, MD: Kelly, Hedian & Piet, 1860), vii–viii.

24. Ibid., ix–x.

25. Ibid., 17–18.

26. Ibid., 18–19.

27. Ibid., 19, 20.

28. AAB, P. Kenrick to F. Kenrick, St. Louis, Mar. 7, 1860.

29. Orestes Brownson, "Literary Notices and Criticisms," *Brownson's Quarterly Review*, 3d New York series 1 (July 1860):404, 405.

30. Ibid., 406–7.

31. Francis Patrick Kenrick, *The Historical Books of the Old Testament* (Baltimore, MD: Kelly, Hedian & Piet, 1860), ix–x.

32. AAB, P. Kenrick to F. Kenrick, St. Louis, Sept. 8, 1860.

33. F. Kenrick to P. Kenrick, Baltimore, Jan. 1, 1861, in Tourscher, *Kenrick-Frenaye Correspondence*, 454–55.

34. F. Kenrick to P. Kenrick, Baltimore, [Dec. 8?], 1861, in *ibid.*, 464.

35. AAB 37 D 3, Spalding to Kenrick, Louisville, Sept. 6, 1858, in Marschall, "Francis Patrick Kenrick," 320.

36. AAB 37 D 20, Spalding to Kenrick, Louisville, Feb. 4, 1861, in *ibid.*

37. AAB 34 K 55, F. Kenrick to Spalding, Baltimore, Feb. 20, 1861, in *ibid.*, 320–21.

38. Francis Patrick Kenrick, *The New Testament* (Baltimore: Kelly, Hedian & Piet, 1862).

39. AAB 37 D 30, Spalding to Kenrick, Louisville, Jan. 15, 1863, in Marschall, "Francis Patrick Kenrick," 322.

40. AAB, SpC Q 6, Newman to Kenrick, Birmington, July 6, 1860.

41. Newman to Acton, Birmingham, Aug. 31, 1862 in Newman, *Letters and Diaries*, 20:265.

42. *Collectio Lacensis*, 3:357, 396.

43. Marschall, "Francis Patrick Kenrick," 325–26.
44. Collectio Lacensis, 3:380.
45. Concio Petri Ricardi Kenrick Archiepiscopi S. Ludovici . . . in Concilio Vaticano Habenda at Non Habita (Naples: Typis Fratrum de Angelis, 1870), 16–17.
46. Acta et Decreta Concilii Plenarii Baltimorensis Tertii in Ecclesia Metropolitana Baltimorensi habiti a die IX. Novembris usque ad diem VII. Decembris A.D. MDCCCLXXXIV (Baltimore: John Murphy & Co., 1884), lxvi–lxvii.
47. Nolan, Pastoral Letters, 177–78.
48. Michael Heiss, The Four Gospels: Examined and Vindicated on Catholic Principles (Milwaukee, WI: Hoffmann Brothers, 1863), 6, 8, 12.
49. Ibid., 52, 73–188, 223, 228–29. Italics mine. See also p. 230.
50. There is, for instance, no mention of it in The Jerome Biblical Commentary.

CHAPTER 3

1. Vincent F. Blehl, S.J., "Newman's Delation: Some Hitherto Unpublished Letters," The Dublin Review 486 (Winter 1960–61): 298–302.
2. DS, 3006. On Franzelin, see Gerald A. McCool, S.J., Catholic Theology in the Nineteenth Century: The Quest for a Unitary Method (New York: The Seabury Press, 1977), 220–21.
3. Pierre Benoit, O.P., Aspects of Biblical Inspiration, trans. J. Murphy-O'Connor, O.P., and S. K. Ashe, O.P. (Chicago: The Priory Press, 1965), 55–56, 100–103.
4. James Tunstead Burtchaell, C.S.C., Catholic Theories of Biblical Inspiration since 1810: A Review and Critique (Cambridge: Cambridge Univ. Press, 1969), 98–99.
5. DS, 3011, 3020.
6. On Franzelin's theology of tradition and his influence on the council, see Yves Marie-Joseph Congar, O.P., Tradition and Traditions: An Historical and a Theological Essay (New York: The Macmillan Co., 1967), 196–98. See also Walter J. Burghardt, S.J., "The Catholic Concept of Tradition in the Light of Modern Theological Thought," in Proceedings of the Sixth Annual Convention of the Catholic Theological Society of America (n.p.: Catholic Theological Society of America, 1951), 48–49.
7. Roger Aubert, Le pontificat de Pie IX (1846–1878), vol. 21 of Histoire de l'église depuis les origines jusqu'à nos jours (Paris: Bloud & Gay, 1952), 354.
8. Trent had referred to the "Gospel" of Christ as "the source of all salutary truth and moral discipline," which were "contained in Scripture and unwritten traditions" (DS, 1501). In quoting Trent, Vatican I truncated the text. Instead of "salutary truth and moral discipline," "revelation" was now said to be contained in Scripture and unwritten traditions (DS, 3006). See Congar, Tradition, 198.
9. APF, Acta 252 (1883), 1088–1197. See also my Vatican and the American Hierarchy from 1870 to 1965 (Stuttgart: Anton Hiersemann, 1982), 27–30.
10. AAB, 79 O 5, Moore to Gibbons, Rome, July 6, 1885.
11. Anon., "Two of Woodstock's Founders," Woodstock Letters 29 (1900): 296–308.
12. ACUA, Minutes of Trustee Meetings, Jan. 27, 1885, 4. There is no further reference to Hogan being named rector of the university and it is possible that the trustees were actually considering him for the post of superior of the priest-students at the university, rather than rector of the university itself.
13. ACUA, Ireland to Keane, Rome, Apr. 26, 1892.
14. AASP, O'Connell to Ireland, Rome, Sept. 21, 1890.
15. Salvatore di Bartolo, I Criteri Teologici: La Storia dei Dommi e La Libertà delle Affermazioni (Torino: Tipografia S. Giuseppe, 1888), 230–31.

16. Patrick H. Ahern, *The Catholic University of America, 1887–1896: The Rectorship of John J. Keane* (Washington, DC: The Catholic Univ. of America Press, 1948), 5.

17. Joseph Schroeder, "Theological Minimizing and Its Latest Defender," *American Ecclesiastical Review* 4 (January–June 1891): 122–23, 164–65. Schroeder's articles appear on pp. 115–32, 161–78, and 286–305. See also Robert Cross, *The Emergence of Liberal Catholicism in America* (Cambridge, MA: Harvard Univ. Press, 1958), 154.

18. For Briggs's address, see H. Shelton Smith, Robert T. Handy, and Lefferts A. Loetscher, *American Christianity: An Historical Interpretation with Representative Documents* (New York: Charles Scribner's Sons, 1963), 2:275–79.

19. Anthony J. Maas, S.J., "Professor Briggs on the Theological Crisis," *American Ecclesiastical Review* 5 (September 1891): 201, 204, 209.

20. A. J. Maas, S.J., *The Life of Jesus Christ according to the Gospel History* (St. Louis, MO: B. Herder Book Co., 1947), v–vi.

21. Ibid., xxv.

22. A. J. Maas, S.J., *Christ in Type and Prophecy* (New York: Benzinger Brothers, 1893), 1:207, 184.

23. Anthony J. Maas, S.J., "Adam's Rib—Allegory or History," *American Ecclesiastical Review* 9 (August 1893): 88. For an excellent survey of the treatment of Scripture in American periodicals, see Bernard Noone, F.S.C., "American Catholic Periodicals and the Biblical Question, 1893–1908," *Records of the American Catholic Historical Society* 89 (March–December 1978): 85–108. On Maas's articles on the biblical question, see Bernard Noone, "A Critical Analysis of the American Catholic Response to Higher Criticism as Reflected in Selected Catholic Periodicals: 1870–1908," (Ph.D. diss., Drew University, 1976), 259–321.

24. Maas, "Adam's Rib," 91–93.

25. Anthony J. Maas, S.J., "The Synoptic Problem," *American Ecclesiastical Review* 13 (September 1895): 171–73.

26. A. J. Maas, S.J., *The Gospel according to Saint Matthew with an Explanatory and Critical Commentary* (St. Louis, MO: B. Herder Book Co., 1898), 181, 183.

27. Leo XIII, *Providentissimus Deus*, in Cyril Gaul, O.S.B. and Conrad Louis, O.S.B., eds., *Rome and the Study of Scripture* (St. Meinrad, IN: Abbey Press, 1962), 13, 20.

28. Ibid., 22, 23.

29. Ibid., 23–24.

30. Francesco Turvasi, *Giovanni Genocchi e la controversia modernista*, vol. 20 of Uomini e Dottrine (Rome: Edizioni di Storia e Letteratura, 1974), 93.

31. James Conroy, S.J., "The Pope and the Scriptures," *American Catholic Quarterly Review* 19 (April 1894): 425–26.

32. Ibid., 427–28.

33. Anthony J. Maas, S.J., "A Negative View of the Encyclical 'Providentissimus Deus,' " *American Catholic Quarterly Review* 20 (January 1895): 163, 165, 169, 171, 173, 174.

34. ADR, Loisy to O'Connell, Paris, July 10, 1894.

35. ADR, Loisy to O'Connell, Neuilly, Dec. 30, 1894.

36. For the background to this, see Fogarty, *Vatican and the American Hierarchy*, 139–44.

37. Charles Grannan, "Higher Criticism and the Bible," *American Catholic Quarterly Review* 19 (July 1894): 563, 564, 568.

38. Ibid., 573.
39. Ibid., 577–79.
40. Ibid., 581.
41. Charles A. Grannan, "A Program of Scripture Studies," *Catholic University Bulletin* 1 (1895): 39, 51–52.
42. ASV, SS, Rub. 43 (1903), fasc. 2, 78–80, Schroeder to Satolli, Washington, June 18, 1895. On Keane's dismissal, see Patrick H. Ahern, *The Life of John J. Keane, Educator and Archbishop, 1839–1918* (Milwaukee, WI: The Bruce Publishing Co., 1955), 178–79.
43. *American Ecclesiastical Review* 14 (May 1896): 446–57; 16 (1897): 495–503; 17 (1898): 169–78; 18 (1898): 225–33.
44. Joseph Bruneau, "A Page of Contemporary History," *American Ecclesiastical Review* 14 (March 1896): 240–44, 244–45.
45. Ibid., 245.
46. Ibid., 245–46.
47. Ibid., 246–47.
48. Ibid., 247–48.
49. Ibid., 250–51.
50. Ibid., 252.
51. Ibid., 252–53, 254.
52. Charles Grannan, "Two-fold Authorship of Scripture," *The Catholic University Bulletin* 3 (April 1897): 132, 136, 138–39.
53. Ibid., 139, 151–52.
54. Ibid., 153–155.
55. Ibid., 156–159.

CHAPTER 4

1. See Fogarty, *Vatican and the American Hierarchy*, 152.
2. *Compte rendu du quatrième congrès scientifique international des Catholiques, tenu à Fribourg (Suisse) du 16 au 20 août 1897* (Fribourg: Imprimerie et librairie de l'oeuvre de Saint Paul, 1898). For Lagrange and von Hügel, see section 2, "sciences exégétiques," 5, 10–11, 179–200, 231–65. For O'Connell, see section 4, "sciences juridiques économiques et sociales," 34–36, 74–81. For Zahm, see section 9, "sciences anthropologiques," 8–10, 166–76. For von Hügel's remark about Blondel, see Lawrence F. Barmann, *Baron Friedrich von Hügel and the Modernist Crisis in England* (Cambridge: Cambridge Univ. Press, 1972), 68–69; Fogarty, *Vatican and the American Hierarchy*, 153–56.
3. See Gerald P. Fogarty, S.J., *The Vatican and the Americanist Crisis: Denis J. O'Connell, American Agent in Rome, 1885–1903* (Rome: Università Editrice, 1974), 260, 271–72.
4. Fogarty, *Vatican and the American Hierarchy*, 157–59.
5. Fogarty, *Vatican and the Americanist Crisis*, 257; Turvasi, *Giovanni Genocchi*, 96–98.
6. Barmann, *Friedrich von Hügel*, 68n.
7. Friedrich von Hügel, "The Historical Method and the Documents of the Hexateuch," *The Catholic University Bulletin* 4 (April 1898): 198–226.
8. Marie-Joseph Lagrange, "Miscellaneous: On the Pentateuch," *The Catholic University Bulletin* 4 (January 1898): 115.
9. Ibid., 116.
10. Ibid., 116–17.
11. Ibid., 118.
12. Ibid., 119–20.

13. Ibid., 120.
14. Ibid., 120–21.
15. Ibid., 121–22.
16. Joseph Bruneau, "Biblical Research," *American Ecclesiastical Review* 18 (March 1898): 278.
17. Joseph Bruneau, "Biblical Criticism," *American Ecclesiastical Review* 19 (October 1898): 383–84, 385.
18. Charles Grannan, "The Human Element in Scripture," *The Catholic University Bulletin* 4 (April 1898): 174, 176–77, 181.
19. McAvoy, *Great Crisis in American Catholic History: 1895–1900* (Chicago: Henry Regnery, Co., 1957), 189–98.
20. Alphonse J. Delattre, S.J., *Un Catholicisme Américain* (Namur: A. Godenne, 1898). See McAvoy, *Great Crisis,* 224–26.
21. Fogarty, *Vatican and the American Hierarchy,* 161–70.
22. ADR, Grannan to O'Connell, Vincentius-Haus, July 17, 1898.
23. AASP, O'Connell to Ireland, Rome, July 12, 1898.
24. Genocchi to Fracassini, July 4, 1898, in Turvasi, *Giovanni Genocchi,* 98.
25. Rev. Henry Wansbrough, trans., *Père Lagrange: Personal Reflections and Memoirs* (New York: Paulist Press, 1985), 62–63, 67–68.
26. Fogarty, *Vatican and the Americanist Crisis,* 286–87. On this issue see also Ralph E. Weber, *Notre Dame's John Zahm: American Catholic Apologist and Educator* (Notre Dame, IN: Univ. of Notre Dame Press, 1961), 108–114.
27. ADR, "Grapeshot" [Grannan] to O'Connell, Washington, Oct. 26, 1898.
28. Leo XIII, *Testem Benevolentiae,* in John Tracy Ellis, ed., *Documents of American Catholic History* (Chicago: Henry Regnery Co., 1967), 2:539.
29. Ibid., 541.
30. Ibid., 541–42.
31. Ibid., 543.
32. Wansbrough, *Père Lagrange,* pp. 68–70, 74–75.
33. Joseph Bruneau, S.S., *Harmony of the Gospels* (New York: The Cathedral Library Association, 1898), preface. See Christopher J. Kauffman, *Tradition and Transformation in Catholic Culture: The Priests of Saint Sulpice in the United States from 1881 to the Present* (New York: Macmillan Publishing Company, 1988), 103–105.
34. Kaufmann, *Tradition and Transformation,* 5, 8.
35. John B. Hogan, *Clerical Studies* (Boston: Marlier, Callahan & Co., 1898), 427–28. See Kauffmann, *Tradition and Transformation,* 168–77.
36. Hogan *Clerical Studies,* 429–31, 457–59.
37. Ibid., 461–64.
38. Ibid., 471–72, 473, 474.
39. Ibid., 476–77.
40. Ibid., 480–81.
41. St. George Mivart, "The Continuity of Catholicism," *The Nineteenth Century* 47 (January 1900): 56, 62, 72.
42. Ibid., 58, 60, 62. Other citations of Hogan are on pp. 54, 59, 71n.
43. Ibid., 67–69.
44. On Mivart and his excommunication, see John D. Root, "The Final Apostasy of St. George Jackson Mivart," *Catholic Historical Review* 71 (January 1985): 1–25.
45. ADR, Hogan to O'Connell, Brighton, April 29, 1900.
46. Alfred Loisy, *Mémoires pour servir à l'histoire religieuse de notre temps* (Paris: E. Nourry, 1931), 2:73.

47. Roger Aubert, *The Church in the Industrial Age*, vol. 9 of *History of the Church* (New York: Crossroad, 1981), 414.
48. Emile Poulat, *Intégrisme et catholicisme intégral un réseau secret international antimoderniste: La "Sapiniere" (1909–1921)* (Tournai, Belgium: Casterman, 1969), 270–72, 582.
49. ADR, Briggs to O'Connell, Rome, Nov. 18, 1897.

CHAPTER 5

1. See Fogarty, *Vatican and the American Hierarchy*, 195–207.
2. For O'Connell's appointment as rector and the initial support he had from Grannan and others on the faculty, see Fogarty, *Vatican and the Americanist Crisis*, 296–302.
3. "The Books of the Abbé Loisy on the Index," *American Ecclesiastical Review* 30 (February 1904): 175, 176.
4. H. J. Heuser, "Father A. J. Mass, S.J.—An Appreciation," *Woodstock Letters* 58 (1929): 417.
5. See, for example, Anthony J. Maas, S.J., "Recent Phases in Bible Study," *American Catholic Quarterly Review* 22 (October 1897): 832–50; "Higher Biblical Criticism," *Messenger of the Sacred Heart* 35 (January 1900): 51–59; "Divisive Criticism," ibid., 116–26; "Biblical Criticism," ibid., 239–46, 512–22, 627–33.
6. Alphonse J. Delattre, S.J., *Autour de la question biblique* (Liege, Belgium: H. Dessain, 1904), 176, 176–82. See also p. 55.
7. Lagrange's pamphlet was entitled *Eclaircissement sur la méthode historique à propos d'un livre du P. Delattre, S.J.*. See Wansbrough, *Père Lagrange*, 111–12.
8. Anthony J. Maas, S.J., "Ecclesiastical Library Table: Recent Bible Study," *American Ecclesiastical Review* 31 (October 1904): 395.
9. Ibid., 396–97.
10. Ibid., 400, 401, 403. For the affinity between Lagrange and von Hummelauer, see Wansbrough, *Père Lagrange*, 110.
11. Louis Martin to Provincials, Nov. 4, 1904, in *Epistolae Praepositorum Generalium ad Superiores Societatis* (Rome: Typis Polyglottis Vaticanis, 1911), 258–61.
12. Wansbrough, *Père Lagrange*, 112.
13. Henry A. Poels, "A Vindication of My Honor," edited with an introduction by Frans Neirynck in *Annua Nuntia Lovaniensia* 225 (1982): 60. A copy of this lengthy pamphlet, written on March 1, 1910, is also in AAB.
14. Francesco Turvasi, *Giovanni Genocchi*, 142–43.
15. Ibid., 217. The other members of the preparatory commission were David Fleming, O.F.M., F. Vigouroux, T. Esser, F. von Hummelauer, E. Gismondi, A. van Hoonacker, A. Amelli, R. Clarke, U. Fracassini, and R. Torio.
16. Ibid., 307n, 217; Wansbrough, *Père Lagrange*, 94–95.
17. Poels, "Vindication," 76–80.
18. Ibid., 81–82, 83–84.
19. Ibid., 86–88.
20. Henry Poels, "History and Inspiration," *The Catholic University Bulletin* 11 (January 1905), 22–23.
21. Ibid., 27, 28.
22. Ibid., 33–40, 50–51, 52–53, 56.
23. Ibid., 64.
24. Henry Poels, "History and Inspiration. II. The Fathers of the Church," *The Catholic University Bulletin* 11 (April 1905): 153, 156–58.
25. Ibid., 161, 165–67, 173.

26. Ibid., 175.
27. Ibid., 179–82.
28. Ibid., 189, 190.
29. Ibid., 191, 192.
30. Ibid., 192, 193–94.
31. DS, 3020.
32. Congar, *Tradition*, 198.
33. DS, 3074.
34. Anthony J. Maas, "Ecclesiastical Library Table: Recent Bible Study," *American Ecclesiastical Review* 32 (June 1905): 647–49, 650.
35. Ibid., 654.
36. See Thomas à Kempis Reilly, O.P., "What Father Lagrange Says and Thinks," *American Ecclesiastical Review* 33 (October 1905): 422–30.
37. Henry Poels, "History and Inspiration. Saint Jerome," *The Catholic University Bulletin* 12 (April 1906): 192.
38. Ibid., 195, 198, 200.
39. Ibid., 203n.–204n. On Pesch, see Burtchaell, pp. 117–119.
40. Poels, "Saint Jerome," 204, 208.
41. Ibid., 212.
42. Ibid., 215–17.
43. Ibid., 218n.
44. Ibid., 217–18.

CHAPTER 6

1. DS, 3394–97.
2. ACUA, Lagrange to Hyvernat, Roybon, Aug. 16 [1906 or 1907].
3. Von Hügel to Briggs, Hindhead, Surrey, Aug. 28, 1906, AUTS, Briggs Papers. Unfortunately, most of these letters were transcribed by Briggs's daughter who destroyed the originals.
4. Charles A. Briggs and Baron Friedrich von Hügel, *The Papal Commission and the Pentateuch* (London: Longmans, Green, and Co., 1906).
5. Anthony J. Maas, "Ecclesiastical Library Table: Recent Bible Study," *American Ecclesiastical Review* 36 (March 1907): 55–71.
6. *The Catholic University Bulletin* 13 (July 1907): 495.
7. Colman J. Barry, O.S.B., *The Catholic University of America: The Rectorship of Denis J. O'Connell* (Washington, DC: The Catholic Univ. of America Press, 1950), 186.
8. Poels, "Vindication," 96–98.
9. DS, 3410.
10. Pius X, *Pascendi Dominici Gregis*, in *American Catholic Quarterly Review* 32 (October 1907): 719.
11. DS, 1502.
12. F. Vigouroux, *Les livres saints et la critique rationaliste: histoire et réfutation des objections des incrédules contre les saintes écritures* (Paris: A. Roger & F. Chernoviz, 1890), 1:9–10.
13. ACUA, Gibbons to Pius X, Baltimore, June 6, 1908 (copy).
14. Alphonse J. Delattre, S.J., *Le Criterium à l'usage de la nouvelle exégèse biblique: réponse au R.P.M-J. Lagrange, O.P.* (Liege, Belgium: H. Dessain, 1907), 70.
15. ACUA, Trustees Meeting, April 10, 1907, 155; Barry, *Denis J. O'Connell*, 178.
16. Poels, "Vindication," 14–15, 16–17.
17. Ibid., 17–18.

18. ACUA, Trustees Meeting, Nov. 13, 1907, 156; Barry, *Denis J. O'Connell*, 179–80.
19. Poels, "Vindication," 18–19, 5.
20. Ibid., 9–12, 33*.
21. ASV, DAUS, Università Cattolica, Gibbons to Falconio, Baltimore, Oct. 16, 1908; unsigned to Gibbons, Washington, Oct. 17, 1908.
22. ACUA, Trustees Meeting, Nov. 18, 1908, 168.
23. ACUA, Gibbons to Pius X, Baltimore, Nov. 22, 1908 (copy).
24. ACUA, Trustees Meeting, April 21, 1909, 174, 176. Poels, "Vindication," 12–13. There is a signed copy of Poels's defense before the trustees in ASV, DAUS, Università Cattolica, but it is not clear whether he sent it to Falconio personally or not.
25. ACUA, Pius X to Shahan, July 12, 1909.
26. ACUA, Gibbons to Shahan, Baltimore, Aug. 1, 1909.
27. Poels, "Vindication," 24. Merry del Val's letter is given on pp. 34*–35*.
28. Ibid. 25–27. Translation of the oath: "I, Henry Poels, do promise, vow, and swear upon God's holy Gospels that I will sincerely accept and faithfully teach all the doctrines and conclusions which the Pontifical Biblical Commission has promulgated up to now or will promulgate in the future. In testimony of this I have signed with my own hand."
29. Ibid., 29–30.
30. Ibid., 30–31.
31. Emile Poulat, *Intégrisme et Catholicisme intégral*, 587.
32. Louis Hugues Vincent, "Le Père Lagrange," *Revue biblique* 47 (1938): 347. See also Wansbrough, *Père Lagrange*, 152–55.
33. Poels, "Vindication," 32–34.
34. Ibid., 35–36.
35. AAB, 107 O 5, Merry del Val to Gibbons, Rome, Sept. 18, 1909 (cable).
36. AAB, 107 P 2, Merry del Val to Gibbons, Vatican, Sept. 19, 1909.
37. AAB, 107 P 2/1, Merry del Val to Gibbons, Rome, Oct. 19, 1909, given in Poels, "Vindication," 36*.
38. Poels, "Vindication," 38–40.
39. Ibid., 43–46.
40. ACUA, Trustees Meetings, Nov. 17, 1909, 180–81.
41. Poels, "Vindication," 54–55.
42. AAB, 107 S 9, Gibbons to Merry del Val, Baltimore, Nov. 19, 1909 (copy).
43. AAB, 107 S 14, Ryan to Gibbons, Philadelphia, Nov. 28, 1909.
44. ASV, DAUS, Università Cattolica, Falconio to Merry del Val, Washington, Nov. 23, 1909.
45. AAB, 107 T 2, Merry del Val to Gibbons, Vatican, Dec. 8, 1909.
46. Poels, "Vindication," 57–59, 63.
47. Ibid., 67–68.
48. ASV, DAUS, Università Cattolica, Aiken to Falconio, Washington, Apr. 12, 1910.
49. Poels, *Vindication*, 70.
50. Ibid., Neirynck, "Woord Vooraf."
51. Ibid., 92. See also p. 53.
52. Ibid., 42n, 95n.
53. Ibid., 100, 101–2.
54. Ibid., 107.
55. Ibid., 103–6, 107.

56. Aaron I. Abell, *American Catholicism and Social Action: A Search for Social Justice* (Notre Dame, IN: Univ. of Notre Dame Press, 1963), 144–45.

57. ASV, DAUS, Liste Episcopali, 73, Patrick Supple to Gotti, Cambridge, MA, Apr. 17, 1904.

58. ACUA, Trustees Meetings, Apr. 6, 1910, 181.

59. ASV, DAUS, Università Cattolica, Falconio to Merry del Val, Washington, Apr. 10, 1910.

60. Ibid., Merry del Val to Falconio, Vatican, Apr. 28, 1910.

61. ACUA, Trustees Meetings, Apr. 6, 1910, 184.

62. ASV, SS, Protocolli, 44702, cipher to Falconio, Vatican, June 10, 1910. This information had to be taken from the protocol books, because, at the present writing, the documents themselves are not accessible in the Secretariat of State.

63. ASV, DAUS, Università Cattolica, Falconio to Merry del Val, Washington, June 17, 1910 (draft).

64. Ibid., Merry del Val to Bonzano, Vatican, June 25, 1912.

65. Ibid., Bonzano to Merry del Val, Washington, July 18, 1912 (draft); Merry del Val to Bonzano, Vatican, Aug. 5, 1912. It is unclear whether Hyvernat was thinking of actually resigning from the university or was merely seeking a temporary replacement, so that he could go on sabbatical. See below, p. 191.

66. Ibid., Merry del Val to Shahan, Vatican, Dec. 10, 1912.

67. Ibid., Shahan to Bonzano, Washington, Dec. 29, 1912.

68. For the life of Poels, see Johannes Colsen, *Poels* (Roermond-Maaseik, 1955).

69. Roger Aubert, *The Church in a Secularised Society*, vol. 5 of *The Christian Centuries* (New York: Paulist Press, 1978), 201–2, 536.

CHAPTER 7

1. Michael V. Gannon, "Before and after Modernism: The Intellectual Isolation of the American Priest," in John Tracy Ellis, ed., *The Catholic Priest in the United States: Historical Investigations* (Collegeville, MN: St. John's Univ. Press, 1971), 334. See Kauffman, *Tradition and Transformation*, 199–223.

2. Albert Houtin, *La question biblique chez les catholiques de France au XXe siècle* (Paris: Alphonse Picard et Fils, 1906), quoted in Bernard Noone, "A Critical Analysis," 330.

3. On the *Annales de philosophie chrétienne*, see Roger Aubert, *The Church in the Industrial Age*, vol. 9 of Hubert Jedin and John Dolan, eds., *History of the Church* (New York: Crossroad, 1981), 431, 439, 515.

4. SAB, Lebas to Dyer, Paris, Nov. 9, 1901.

5. SAB, Driscoll to Dyer, Washington, Feb. 26, 1902.

6. Francis E. Gigot, S.S., *General Introduction to the Study of the Holy Scriptures* (New York: Benzinger Brothers, 1900), 517.

7. Ibid., 511–14.

8. Francis E. Gigot, S.S., *Special Introduction to the Study of the Old Testament: Part I. The Historical Books* (New York: Benzinger Brothers, 1901), 85–141. For a detailed analysis of this work, see Noone, "A Critical Analysis," 331–76.

9. Gigot, *Special Introduction*, 1:32.

10. See p. 62.

11. Anthony J. Maas, S.J., "Ecclesiastical Library Table: Sacred Scripture," *American Ecclesiastical Review* 26 (February 1902): 218–19.

12. SAB, Driscoll to Dyer, Washington, Feb. 26, 1902.

13. SAB, Dyer to Driscoll, Dunwoodie, Mar. 1, 1902 (draft).

14. SAB, Driscoll to Dyer, Washington, "Thursday 9th [Oct.]," 1902.

15. SAB, Lebas to Gigot, Paris, Dec. 24, 1902 (copy). There is, unfortunately, no copy of Gigot's letter to Lebas, the contents of which can only be surmised from Lebas's response.
16. SAB, Gigot to Dyer, Washington, Jan. 4, 1903.
17. SAB, Maher to Dyer, Brighton, Jan. 11, 1903.
18. SAB, Gigot to Dyer, Baltimore, Jan. 14, 1903.
19. SAB, Gigot to Lebas, Washington, Jan. 15, 1903 (copy).
20. SAB, Dyer to Lebas, Baltimore, Jan. 18, 1903 (copy). Dyer noted on the top of the letter that he had sent the original on Jan. 21, 1903.
21. SAB, Lebas to Dyer, Paris, Feb. 9, 1903.
22. SAB, Dyer to Driscoll, Baltimore, Feb. 22, 1903 (copy).
23. SAB, Gigot to Driscoll, Washington, Mar. 7, 1903.
24. E. R. Dyer, S.S., *Letters on the New York Seminary Secession* (Baltimore, MD: Private Printing, 1906), 10. Originally published in English and French, this was circulated among Sulpicians in the United States and France, the former Sulpicians at Dunwoodie, and the apostolic delegate. On France and its laicization, see Aubert, *Church in the Industrial Age*, 507–11.
25. SAB, Gigot to Dyer, Dunwoodie, Jan. 19, 1905.
26. SAB, Dyer to Gigot, Baltimore, Jan. 25, 1905.
27. Driscoll to Dyer, Dunwoodie, Jan. 11, 1905, in Dyer, *Letters*, 11–14; Dyer to Driscoll, Baltimore, Jan. 18, 1905, in Dyer, *Letters*, 14–17.
28. SAB, Gigot to Dyer, Dunwoodie, Feb. 4, 1905.
29. SAB, Gigot to Dyer, Dunwoodie, Feb. 13, 1905.
30. *The Tablet* (London), May 2, 1903, 690.
31. SAB, Dyer to Gigot, Baltimore, Feb. 23, 1905.
32. Dyer, *Letters*, 54–55.
33. SAB, Gigot to Dyer, Sept. 6, 1905.
34. Dyer, *Letters*, 57–67.
35. Francis E. Gigot, *Special Introduction to the Study of the Old Testament: Part II. Didactic Books and Prophetical Writings* (New York: Benzinger Brothers, 1906), 265. See also 249–65.
36. Unsigned, "Criticisms and Notes," *American Ecclesiastical Review* 35 (October 1906): 435–36.
37. The reviewer may have been reflecting the position of Christian Pesch, who had stated that, since the responses of the Biblical Commission were not infallible, no assent of divine faith was required. But there was required an "interior assent . . . an assent of which the formal motive is the supreme religious, though not infallible authority." This assent to the responses was required as long as there was no positive evidence that they were in error. The exegete was to investigate the reasons for the official teaching, which would either be accepted by the whole Church as infallible or be shown to be in error. This "religious assent," Pesch continued, "rests . . . more or less on broad moral certitude, it does not exclude error, and so, when first sufficient reasons for doubt appear, the assent may be prudently suspended." Christian Pesch, S.J., *Institutiones propaedeuticae ad sacram theologiam*, quoted in B. N. Wambacq, "Pontifical Biblical Commission," *New Catholic Encyclopedia* (New York: McGraw Hill, 1967), 11:551–54. Wambacq was the secretary of the Biblical Commission. Pesch, however, did not explain whether it was legitimate for scholars to publicize their research, so that others would know the "first sufficient reasons for doubt." In light of later developments, it was permissible for scholars to suspend their assent only in private.

38. Fogarty, *Vatican and the Americanist Crisis*, 82–83.
39. Michael J. DeVito, *Principles of Ecclesial Reform according to the "New York Review"* (New York: United States Catholic Historical Society, 1977), 262–67.
40. Lagrange's comments are in *Revue biblique* 9 (1900): 161–62 and *Revue biblique* 15 (1906): 164–65, cited in James P. Gaffey, *Citizen of No Mean City: Archbishop Patrick Riordan of San Francisco (1841–1914)* (Washington, DC: A Consortium Book, 1976), 284–85.
41. DeVito, *New York Review*, 267–72.
42. Hanna to Gotti, Dec. 16, 1907, quoted in *ibid.*, 274.
43. Ibid., 272–76.
44. See *New York Times*, Jan. 5, 1908, cited in *ibid.*, 284.
45. Ibid., 284–88.
46. Ibid., 289–91. On Gibbons's role in having O'Connell named auxiliary bishop of San Francisco, see Fogarty, *Vatican and the Americanist Crisis*, 308–9.
47. AANY, McQuaid to Farley, Rochester, Feb. 2, 1908, in Gannon, "Before and After Modernism," 379. The best discussion of the Hanna case and Breen's involvement is Gaffey, *Riordan*, 284–85, 290–93.
48. ASV, DAUS, Diocesi, 28, Merry del Val to Falconio, Vatican, Dec. 12, 1907.
49. Ibid., Falconio to Merry del Val, n.p., Dec. 24, 1907 (draft).
50. On Tyrrell, see David G. Schultenover, S.J., *George Tyrrell: In Search of Catholicism* (Shepherdstown, WV: The Patmos Press, 1981), 335–38.
51. ASV, DAUS, Diocesi, 28, Falconio to Farley, Washington, Jan. 14, 1909 (draft). See also De Vito, *New York Review*, 276–78. De Vito states that Falconio specifically objected to Tyrrell's *Lex Credendi*, which is not mentioned in the draft of Falconio's letter. The advertisement, a copy of which Falconio retained, highlighted *Through Scylla and Carybdis*, but then listed in fine print all of Tyrrell's other books.
52. ASV, DAUS, Diocesi, 28, Farley to Falconio, New York, Jan. 23, 1908 (copy).
53. Ibid.
54. Ibid. See also De Vito, *New York Review*, 276–282.
55. *Washington Post*, Sept. 17, 1908, clipping in ASV, DAUS.
56. *Washington Times*, Oct. 5, 1908, clipping in ASV, DAUS. For other newspaper accounts, see De Vito, *New York Review*, 291–96.
57. De Vito, *New York Review*, 290.
58. Ibid., 296–301.
59. Gannon, "Before and after Modernism," 343, 362.
60. Gaffey, *Riordan*, 297, 299–300.

CHAPTER 8

1. See p. 40.
2. See p. 97.
3. AUTS, Briggs Papers, X, 384–88, von Hügel to Briggs, Surrey, Aug. 28, 1906. On the difficulty of using these transcribed letters, see p. 361, n. 3 above. For Briggs's contact with Catholic exegetes, see William J., Hynes, "A Hidden Nexus between Catholic and Protestant Modernism: C. A. Briggs in Correspondence with Loisy, von Hügel and Genocchi," *Downside Review* 360 (July 1987), 193–223.
4. AUTS, Briggs Papers, X, 384–88, von Hügel to Briggs, Surrey, Aug. 28, 1906.
5. Ibid., 393–95, von Hügel to Briggs, Surrey, Sept. 14, 1906.
6. Ibid., 407–9, von Hügel to Briggs, London, Nov. 6, 1906.
7. Briggs and von Hügel, *Papal Commission*, iii–iv.

8. Ibid., 5-6.
9. Ibid., 7-9.
10. Ibid., 11-13.
11. Ibid., 15, 16.
12. Ibid., 17-18.
13. Ibid., 19.
14. Ibid., 19-20.
15. Ibid., 23-24.
16. Ibid., 32-33.
17. Ibid., 33-35.
18. Ibid., 35.
19. Ibid., 36.
20. Ibid., 37-39.
21. Ibid., 41.
22. Ibid., 42.
23. Ibid., 42-44.
24. Ibid., 45-47.
25. Ibid., 47-48.
26. Ibid., 48, 49.
27. Ibid., 49, 50.
28. Ibid., 50-51.
29. Ibid., 51-52, 53-54.
30. Ibid., 55-56.
31. Ibid., 56, 57-62. The work on the Johannine Comma that von Hügel cited was K. Küstle, *Das Comma Johanneum auf seine Herkunft untersucht* (Freiburg: Herder, 1905).
32. Alec R. Vidler, *A Variety of Catholic Modernists* (Cambridge: Cambridge Univ. Press, 1970), 116. On *Rinnovamento*, see also Michele Ranchetti, *The Catholic Modernists: A Study of the Religious Reform Movement, 1864-1907* (London: Oxford Univ. Press, 1969), 173-205.
33. AUTS, Janssens to Briggs, Rome, Jan. 29, 1907.
34. Briggs to Janssens, New York, Feb. 2, 1907, in Turvasi, *Giovanni Genocchi*, 251-54.
35. Charles Augustus Briggs, "The Real and the Ideal in the Papacy," *North American Review* 184 (Feb. 15, 1907): 356.
36. John Ireland, "The Pontificate of Pius X," *North American Review* 184: (Feb. 1, 1907): 238, 239, 240, 241.
37. Ibid., 241, 242.
38. See Neil T. Storch, "The Church and Modern Society: John Ireland and the Modernist Controversy," *Church History* 54 (September 1985): 353-65.
39. John Ireland, "Is the Papacy an Obstacle to the Reunion of Christendom?" *North American Review* 184 (Apr. 5, 1907): 705.
40. Charles A. Briggs, "The Great Obstacle in the Way of a Reunion of Christendom," *North American Review* 186 (Sept. 1907): 72, 78, 79.
41. Ibid., 80.
42. See Fogarty, *Vatican and the Americanist Crisis*, 282-83.
43. AUTS, Briggs Papers, X, 457-60, von Hügel to Briggs, London, Mar. 26, 1907. Von Hügel was a man of great complexity. He announced in this same letter his happiness that his daughter was entering the Carmelites.
44. Gaul and Louis, eds., *Rome and the Study of Scripture*, 119-20.

45. AUTS, Briggs Papers, X, 473–475, von Hügel to Briggs, Kensington, June 11, 1907.
46. Ibid., 475, Briggs to von Hügel, London, June 12, 1907.
47. Genocchi to Briggs, May 20, 1907, in Turvasi, *Giovanni Genocchi*, 293–94.
48. Genocchi to Briggs, July 14, 1907, in *ibid.*, 305–6.
49. AUTS, Briggs Papers, XI, 8–9, von Hügel to Briggs, Kensington, Sept. 28, 1907.
50. Ibid., 11–13, Briggs to von Hügel, Paris, Oct. 2, 1907.
51. Ibid.
52. AUTS, Briggs Papers, XII, 13, Genocchi to Briggs, Rome, Oct. 5, 1907.
53. Emile Poulat, *Intégrisme et Catholicisme intégral*, 65–67, 77. See also Aubert, *Church in a Secularised Society*, 201–2.
54. AUTS, Briggs Papers, XII, 20, Briggs to von Hügel, New York, Nov. 15, 1907. On *La Programma dei modernisti*, see Turvasi, *Giovanni Genocchi*, 326–28.
55. AUTS, Briggs Papers, XII, 25–27, Driscoll to Briggs, Yonkers, Dec. 8, 1907.
56. Ibid.
57. Charles Augustus Briggs, "The Encyclical against Modernism," *North American Review* 187 (Feb. 1908): 200–201. As a caricature of Loisy's position in *The Gospel and the Church*, he cited the twenty-second condemned proposition that "the dogmas which the Church gives out as revealed are not truths which have fallen down from heaven, but are an interpretation of religious facts, which the human mind has acquired by laborious effort."
58. Ibid., 202, 204–5.
59. Ibid., 205–206, 207, 208.
60. Ibid., 209–210.
61. Ibid., 211.
62. Joseph Ratzinger, "The First Session," *Worship* 37 (August–September 1963): 534. Later on, however, as a cardinal, Ratzinger said that "we must not forget that the episcopal conferences have no theological basis, they do not belong to the structure of the Church, as willed by God, that cannot be eliminated; they have only a practical, concrete function. . . . No episcopal conference, as such," he continued, "has a teaching mission; its documents have no weight of their own save that of the consent given to them by the individual bishops." See Joseph Cardinal Ratzinger with Vittorio Messori, *The Ratzinger Report*, trans. Salvator Attanasio and Graham Harrison (San Francisco: Ignatius Press, 1985), 59, 60.
63. AUTS, 3.15, von Hügel to Briggs, Kensington, Apr. 13, 1908.
64. Ranchetti, *The Catholic Modernists*, 131, 176, 178. See Schultenover, *George Tyrrell*, 345.
65. AUTS, Briggs Correspondence, XII, 42, Genocchi to Briggs, Rome, Jan. 24, 1908.
66. AUTS, 2.5, Genocchi to Briggs, May 18, 1908.
67. Ibid., Genocchi to Briggs, Rome, June 28, 1908.
68. Ibid., Genocchi to Briggs, Rome, July 16, 1908.
69. Ibid., Genocchi to Briggs, Rome, Feb. 25, 1909.
70. Ibid., Genocchi to Briggs, Caserta, June 3, 1909.
71. Ibid., Genocchi to Briggs, Rome, June 11 and June 22, 1909.
72. Ibid., 3.15, Briggs to von Hügel, Oberhofen, June 12, 1909 (copy?).
73. Ibid., von Hügel to Briggs, Kensington, Oct. 4, 1909.
74. Charles A. Briggs, "Modernism Mediating the Coming Catholicism," *North American Review* 189 (June 1909): 877–78.

75. AUTS, 3.15, Briggs to von Hügel, New York, Jan. 27, 1910 (copy?).
76. Ibid., Briggs to von Hügel, Engardine, Switzerland, July 31, 1910 (copy?).
77. Ibid., 2.51, Genocchi to Briggs, Rome Mar. 31, 1911.
78. Poulat, *Intégrisme*, 64–78.
79. *The Church Teaches: Documents of the Church in English Translation* (St. Louis, MO: B. Herder Book Co., 1955), 38. See DS, 3537–3550.

CHAPTER 9

1. Quoted in Gabriel Daly, O.S.A., *Transcendence and Immanence: A Study in Catholic Modernism and Integralism* (Oxford: Clarendon Press, 1980), 175n.
2. Quoted in Turvasi, *Giovanni Genocchi*, 222, 226.
3. Daly, *Transcendence*, 176. See also p. 174n. for a summary of Billot's life.
4. Burghardt, "Catholic Concept of Tradition," 61.
5. Quoted in William M. Halsey, *The Survival of American Innocence: Catholicism in an Era of Disillusionment, 1920–1940* (Notre Dame, IN: Univ. of Notre Dame Press, 1980), 140.
6. Quoted in Gannon, "Before and after Modernism," 358–59.
7. For the best summary of the influence of Thomism on American Catholic culture, see Halsey, *American Innocence*, 138–68.
8. For the best treatment of this, see James P. Gaffey, "The Changing of the Guard: The Rise of Cardinal O'Connell of Boston," *Catholic Historical Review* 59 (July, 1973): 225–244. See also Fogarty, *Vatican and the American Hierarchy*, 195–207. On Harkins's role in the Poels case and the charges brought against him in 1904, see pp. 109, 112, 114, 115 above.
9. SAB, Reilly to Dyer, Brighton, Feb. 15, 1909.
10. SAB, Hertzog to Dyer, Rome, Apr. 17, 1909.
11. SAB, Dyer to O'Connell, Boston, July 19, 1909 (draft).
12. SAB, Hertzog to [?], Rome, Nov. 23, 1909.
13. SAB, Hertzog to Dyer, Rome, Feb. 22, 1910.
14. *The Pilot* (Boston), Feb. 26, 1910, 4.
15. SAB, Bruneau to Dyer, Baltimore, Mar. 3, 1910.
16. AABo, O'Connell to Merry del Val, Boston, Feb. 24, 1910 (copy).
17. AAB, 107 D 2, Falconio to Gibbons, Washington, Mar. 8, 1910.
18. AAB 107 D 3, Gibbons to Falconio, Baltimore, Mar. 9, 1910 (copy).
19. AAB 107 D 5, Bruneau to Gibbons, Mar. 13, 1910.
20. AAB, 107 D 8, Gibbons to Merry del Val, Baltimore, Mar. 15, 1910 (copy). See also John Tracy Ellis, *The Life of James Cardinal Gibbons: Archbishop of Baltimore, 1834–1921* (Milwaukee: The Bruce Publishing Co., 1952), 2:475–76.
21. SAB, Vieban to Dyer, Brighton, May 9, 12, and 24, 1911. On the Sulpicians at Brighton, see Kauffman, *Tradition and Transformation*, 225–238.
22. AABo, O'Connell to Peterson, Boston, May 17, 1911.
23. *The Pilot* (Boston), Mar. 23, 1912, 1.
24. William Henry O'Connell, *Sermons and Addresses of His Eminence William Cardinal O'Connell, Archbishop of Boston* (Boston: The Pilot Publishing Co., 1922), 4:78–81. See also SAB, "Discourse with Cdl. O'Connell, Wash., 1920."
25. Fogarty, *Vatican and the American Hierarchy*, 204.
26. Gannon, "Before and after Modernism," 350.
27. For an extremely hagiographical biography of Drum, see Joseph Gorayeb, S.J., *The Life and Letters of Walter Drum, S.J.* (New York: America Press, 1928).
28. AWC, II A 10.1d(4), notes on Pentateuch.

29. See above, p. 123.
30. AWC, IIA.3b, "Retreat for Business Girls," July 2–6, 1915, New York.
31. Anon., "Father Walter M. Drum," *Woodstock Letters* 51 (1922): 125.
32. Interview with John J. Collins, S.J., Weston, MA, Mar. 18, 1983. Collins said he was shown a letter, implicating Drum, on the occasion of the funeral of Father William McClellan, S.J., at Woodstock, in May, 1951. The letter can no longer be found in AWC.
33. AWC, II A 10.7a(1).
34. C. Lattey, ed., *The New Testament, III, Pt. I: Epistles to the Thessalonians* (London: Longmans, Green and Co., 1913), vii.
35. AWC, II A 10a (3), Lattey to Drum, n.p. July 11, [1913]; Lattey, *Thessalonians*, 18n. See also 7n.
36. AWC, II A 10a (3), Lattey to Drum, n.p. Aug. 11, [1913] and Oct. 6 [1913].
37. Drum, quoted in Cuthbert Lattey, "Ecclesiastical Library Table: St. Paul and the Parousia," *American Ecclesiastical Review* 50 (March 1914): 349.
38. Ibid., 349–56.
39. AWC, II A 10a (3), Lattey to Drum, St. Bueno's, Oct. 5 [1914].
40. Walter Drum, S.J., "The Biblical Commission and the Parousia," *American Ecclesiastical Review* 53 (October 1915): 472–82.
41. AWC II A 10a (3), Lattey to Drum, St. Bueno's, June 15, 1916.
42. Emile Poulat, *Intégrisme*, 329–30.
43. Though both O'Connell and Farley had been in Rome earlier that summer for their *ad limina* visits, news of Sarajevo caused O'Connell to book passage back to Boston, while Farley fled to neutral Switzerland to await news about the pope's health. O'Connell was back in Boston less than two weeks when he received word of Pius X's death on August 20. He immediately booked passage on a ship back to Rome, only to have it diverted to New York to pick up Cardinal Gibbons. Irritated at the delay, as soon as the ship reached Naples, O'Connell rented a car to travel alone to Rome. The car broke down and he had to rejoin Gibbons, who was traveling by train. See Dorothy G. Wayman, *Cardinal O'Connell of Boston: A Biography of William Henry O'Connell, 1859–1944* (New York: Farrar, Straus, & Young, 1955), 172–76.
44. AANY, Corrigan to "dear Bishop," New York, June 21, 1892 (copy of form letter).
45. AAB 114 F 1, Ireland to Gibbons, St. Paul, Sept. 27, 1914. See also Fogarty, *Vatican and the American Hierarchy*, 206–7.
46. Aubert, *Church in the Industrial Age*, 471, 478–80.
47. Archives of the Archdiocese of Westminster, Merry del Val to Herbert Vaughan, Vatican, Apr. 2, 1896. Merry del Val was then secretary of the commission, under Mazzella's presidency, investigating Anglican orders. Gasparri was a member of the commission.
48. Poulat, *Intégrisme*, 330.
49. Benedict XV, *Ad Beatissimi Apostolorum*, in Claudia Carlen, I.H.M., ed., *The Papal Encyclicals* (Wilmington, NC: A Consortium Book, 1981), 3:148.
50. Poulat, *Intégrisme*, 600–602.
51. Burtchaell, *Biblical Inspiration*, 232–33.
52. Benedict XV, *Spiritus Paraclitus*, in Gaul and Louis (ed.), *Study of Scripture*, 51–52. Cf. Vatican II, *Dei Verbum*, no. 11 in Flannery, *Vatican Council II*, 756–57.
53. Benedict XV, *Spiritus Paraclitus*, in *Study of Scripture*, 52, 53–54.
54. Ibid., 54–55, 67.
55. ACUA, Hyvernat Papers.

56. AAS, 15 (1923), 616, Merry del Val to superior general of the Society of St. Sulpice, Dec. 22, 1923.

57. Ibid., 617. On this episode see Jean Levie, S.J., *The Bible, Word of God in Words of Men*, trans. S. H. Treman (New York: P. J. Kenedy & Sons, 1961), 124.

58. Wansbrough, *Père Lagrange*, 154.

59. E. Vogt, "John J. O'Rourke, S.J.," *Biblica* 39 (1958): 397–99, translated in *Woodstock Letters* 88 (1959): 415–17.

60. C. C. Martindale, S.J., "How to Read St. John's Gospel," *The Catholic World* 109 (August 1919): 622–36 and *The Catholic World* 110 (October 1919): 65–81.

61. Wansbrough, *Père Lagrange*, 146, 246.

62. AWC, II A, 10a(4) Heuser to Drum, Overbrook, PA, Dec. 11, 1919.

63. Ibid., Heuser to Drum, Overbrook, PA, Dec. 19, 1919.

64. Ibid., Burke to Drum, New York, Dec. 20, 1919.

65. Ibid., Burke to Drum, New York, Jan. 5, 1920.

66. AWC., II A10.7a (4), Ledochowski to Rockwell, Rome, Mar. 19, 1920 (copy).

67. Ibid., Heuser to Drum, Overbrook, PA, Oct. 7, 1920.

68. Walter Drum, S.J. "Ecclesiastical Library Table: Recent Bible Studies," *American Ecclesiastical Review* 62 (April 1920): 479.

69. Anon., "Father Walter M. Drum," *Woodstock Letters* 51 (1922), 128.

70. Aside from a newspaper account of his conversion to Catholicism, there are no McClellan papers in AWC.

71. See pp. 116–118 above.

72. ACUA, Minutes of Trustees Meetings, Apr. 26, 1911, 191–92.

73. Ibid., Oct. 12, 1911, Doc. A: Grannan to Gibbons, Rome, July 6, 1911 (copy).

74. Ibid., 196.

75. Charles P. Grannan, *A General Introduction to the Bible* (St. Louis: B. Herder Book Co., 1921).

76. ACUA, Office of Vice Rector, Biblical Institute, Cöln memo, Mar. 18, 1913, 5.

77. ACUA, Minutes of Trustees Meetings, Apr. 2, 1913, 208–9.

78. AAS, 27 (1924), 180–82.

79. ACUA, Vice Rector's Papers, Shahan and Curley to Bisleti, Washington, June 11, 1924 (copy).

80. ACUA, Vice Rector's Papers, Bisleti to Curley, Rome, July 31, 1924 (copy).

81. ACUA, Vice Rector's Papers, Curley to Schumacher, Baltimore, Nov. 10, 1924 (copy).

82. Robert J. North, S.J., "The American Scripture Century," *American Ecclesiastical Review* 150 (May 1964): 328–29.

83. SAB, RG 12, Box 9, Arbez, "Notes on Genesis."

84. SAB, RG 12 Box 10, "New Testament lecture notes."

85. SAB, RG 12 "Notes on Isaias."

86. Interview with Msgr. Erwin J. Becker, Santa Rosa, CA., Aug. 10, 1983. Becker had Arbez as a professor at Menlo Park.

87. Lawrence J. Shehan, *A Blessing of Years: The Memoirs of Lawrence Cardinal Shehan* (Notre Dame, IN: Univ. of Notre Dame Press, 1982), 45–46, 56.

88. This information was provided to the author by Rev. Robert F. McNamara, professor emeritus of Church History at St. Bernard's on Feb. 9, 1984.

89. Robert J. Miller and Robert F. McNamara, "Edward J. Byrne: Biblical Scholar," *The Sheaf* 10 (1963): 19–26.

90. Interview with Bishop Dougherty, South Orange, NJ, Mar. 15, 1983.

91. For some of the most outrageous passages, see Michael J. Gruenthaner, "The World of the Old Testament and Its Historicity," in *European Civilization: Its*

Origin and Development, ed. Edward Eyre (Oxford: Oxford Univ. Press, 1934), 1:512–13, 536–37, 580–81, 660–61.

92. *Times Literary Supplement,* December 13, 1934, 897.
93. For providing me with this information, I am grateful to Joseph A. Fitzmyer, S.J. The Library of Congress has the original 1934 edition with Gruenthaner's chapter. The Woodstock Theological Center Library has the reprint with the original table of contents, but without the chapter.
94. Robert North, S.J., "A Frontier Jerome: Gruenthaner," *American Ecclesiastical Review* 148 (May–June 1963): 399–401.
95. Francis X. Peirce, S.J., "Ecclesiastical Library Table: Again the Synoptic Problem," *American Ecclesiastical Review* 100 (January 1939), 81, 74.

CHAPTER 10

1. Pope, *English Versions* 482–83, 489–91, 498. Pope also says that the American bishops in 1935 urged that the Spencer edition be published, but there is no evidence of this in the minutes of the bishops' meetings.
2. SAB, Arbez, Minutes, Jan. 18, 1936. In addition to Arbez, Newton, Butin, and Callan, the following were also present: J. A. McHugh, O.P., of Maryknoll Seminary, C. J. Costello, O.M.I., of the Oblate Scholasticate, Washington DC, A. H. Dirksen, C.PP.S, of St. Charles Seminary, Carthagena, Ohio, Edward Donze, S.M., of the Marist Seminary, Washington D.C., M. Kennedy, O.F.M., of Holy Name College, Washington DC, J. L. Lilly, C.M., of St. Thomas Seminary, Denver, W. S. Reilly, S.S., of St. Mary's Seminary, Baltimore, J. E. Steinmueller of the Seminary of the Immaculate Conception, Huntington, NY, and F. Walsh, O.S.B., Secretary of the Confraternity of Christian Doctrine. Five others were not present but indicated their willingness to participate in the work: E. A. Cerny, S.S., of St. Mary's Seminary, Baltimore, W. A. Down, S.J., of St. Mary's Seminary, Mundelein, IL, L. P. Foley, C.M., of Kenrick Seminary, Webster Grove, MO, M. J. Gruenthaner, S.J., of St. Mary's College, Kansas, and M. Hofer of the Josephinum College, Worthington, OH.
3. ADKC, 116, Callan to O'Hara, Hawthorne, NY, Feb. 8, 1936.
4. AAS, 26 (1934), 315.
5. See ADKC, Box 39, File 350, Newton Memorandum: "Some Considerations Relating to the Present Response," Feb. 13, 1943; SAB, Arbez, "Principles Governing the Revision of the New Testament," Jan. 18, 1936.
6. ACBA, Breen to Newton, Milwaukee, Aug. 28, 1936.
7. SAB, Arbez, Minutes of meeting, Oct. 3, 1936.
8. SAB, Arbez, Informal meeting of editorial board, St. Louis, Oct. 9, 1937.
9. SAB, Newton to Arbez, Cleveland, Oct. 24, 1937.
10. SAB, Newton to Arbez, Feb. 19, 1938.
11. SAB, Newton to Arbez, April 6, 1938; Arbez, "Introduction" (draft).
12. ADKC, 348, Newton to O'Hara, Rome, June 11, 1938, and 350, Newton, "Some Considerations Relating to the Attached Response," n.d.. but after Aug., 1943. In this document, Newton listed the people with whom he had spoken in Rome in 1938.
13. ADKC, 348, Newton to O'Hara, Rome, July 1, 1938.
14. ADKC, 348, Newton, "England and the Revision," n.d.
15. ADKC, 349, Newton to O'Hara, Washington, Jan. 28, 1939.
16. ADKC, 349, Newton to O'Hara, Washington, Feb. 14, 1939.

17. ADKC, 108, Newton, "Some Considerations Relating to the Attached Response," n.d. but a note attached states that it was sent to O'Hara in a letter of Feb. 13, 1943 [sic].
18. ADKC, 348, Newton, "Revision of the Challoner-Rheims NT," n.d.
19. SAB, Newton to Arbez, Cleveland, Aug. 26, 1938.
20. Thomas J. Kennedy, "A Much-Debated Text in St. John's Gospel," Homiletic and Pastoral Review 39 (August 1939): 1164, 1175.
21. ADKC, 349, Newton to O'Hara, Kent, Ohio, July 24, 1939.
22. ADKC, 116, O'Hara to Callan, Kansas City, July 31, 1939.
23. Edward Cerny, S.S., "Problems of Bible Revision," Catholic Biblical Quarterly, 1 (1939): 363-68.
24. The New Testament of Our Lord and Savior Jesus Christ, translated from the Latin Vulgate: A Revision of the Challoner-Rheims Version, Edited by Catholic Scholars under the Patronage of the Episcopal Committee of the Confraternity of Christian Doctrine (Paterson, NJ: St. Anthony Guild Press, 1941), 3, 610.
25. Tisserant and Vosté to O'Hara, Rome, Mar. 6, 1941, in ibid.
26. ADKC, 350, Newton to O'Hara, Cleveland, Feb. 1, 1944.
27. Edward J. Byrne, "Presidential Address," Catholic Biblical Quarterly, 4 (January 1942): 7-8.
28. ADKC, 117, Callan to O'Hara, Hawthorne, NY, Dec. 8, 1941.
29. ADKC, 117, O'Hara to Callan, Kansas City, Dec. 12, 1941.
30. ADKC, 117, Tisserant to O'Hara, Rome April 17, 1942.
31. ADKC, 117, O'Hara to Tisserant, n.p., n.d. (draft).
32. ADKC, 117, O'Hara to McNicholas, Kansas City, May 15, 1942.
33. ADKC, 117, McNicholas to O'Hara, Cincinnati, May 16, 1942.
34. Ibid.
35. ADKC, 117, Newton to O'Hara, Cleveland, May 17, 1942.
36. Ibid.
37. ADKC, 117, O'Hara to McNicholas, Kansas City, May 21, 1942 (copy); O'Hara to Cicognani, Kansas City, May 21, 1942 (copy).
38. ADKC, 117, O'Hara to McNicholas, Washington, June 10, 1942 (copy).
39. ADKC, 117, Episcopal Committee of the CCD to Tisserant, n.d., n.p. (draft).
40. ADKC, 117, Cicognani to O'Hara, Washington, June 29, 1942. Cicognani cites the date of the bishops' letter as June 27, but in the letters of both Tisserant and Vosté, cited below, the date was given as June 23. There is no dated copy of the original.
41. ADKC, 117, Tisserant to O'Hara, Rome, Oct. 14, 1942 (copy).
42. ADKC, 117, Vosté to Callan, Rome, Oct. 14, 1942 (translation).
43. The New Testament, Confraternity edition, 701. The protests are in ADKC, 350, Willard Johnson to O'Hara, New York, Mar. 24, 1943 and David Robinson to O'Hara, Portland, OR, Apr. 3, 1943. Robinson also complained of the note to Rom 2:22 which said: "Although the Jew pretended to hold idols in abomination, and to regard even the least contact with them as defiling, he would not hesitate to steal idols from pagan temples, if he saw a chance to profit by doing so." See Confraternity edition, 406.
44. ADKC, 350, Newton to O'Hara, Cleveland, Apr. 5, 1943.
45. ADKC, 350, Newton to O'Hara, Cleveland, Apr. 24, 1943.
46. AAS, 35 (1943), 270-71.
47. Pius XII, Divino Afflante Spiritu, no. 21 in Gaul and Louis (eds.) Rome and the Study of Scripture, 92.
48. Amator Evangelii, "Communications from Our Readers," Homiletic and Pastoral Review 44 (March, 1944): 449.
49. Ibid., 451.

50. Lilly to editors, *Homiletic and Pastoral Review* 44 (May 1944): 615–16.
51. Amator Evangelii, "Communications from Our Readers," ibid. (May 1944), 616–19.
52. Michael J. Gruenthaner, S.J., "An Unfounded Charge of Heresy," *American Ecclesiastical Review* 110 (June 1944): 415.
53. ADKC, 117, O'Hara to Gruenthaner, Kansas City, June 27, 1944 (copy); and O'Hara to Lilly, Kansas City, June 27, 1944 (copy).
54. Amator Evangelii, "A Defense That Fails," *Homiletic and Pastoral Review* 44 (August 1944): 807–12.
55. "Meeting of the Catholic Biblical Association," *Catholic Biblical Quarterly* 4 (January 1941): 182.
56. ADKC, 108, Newton, "Some considerations relating to the attached response." A note attached states that Newton sent it to O'Hara with a letter of "Feb. 13/43" [*sic*].
57. ADKC, 280, O'Hara to McNicholas, Kansas City, Feb. 21, 1944 (copy).
58. ADKC, 280, O'Hara to Cicognani, Kansas City, Feb. 21, 1944 (copy).
59. ADKC, 280, Arbez to O'Hara, Washington, Feb. 24, 1944 (copy).
60. ADKC, 350, O'Hara to Newton, Kansas City, Mar. 1, 1944.
61. ADKC, 350, O'Hara, to Newton, Kansas City, Apr. 24, 1944.
62. ADKC, 290, Cicognani to O'Hara, Washington, Aug. 18, 1944.

CHAPTER 11

1. ACBA, "Plan for the Organization of a Scriptural Section of the Confraternity of Christian Doctrine," and "The Catholic Biblical Association of America, Minutes of Organization Meeting, New York, Oct. 3d [1936].
2. ACBA, Minutes of the Meeting of the Officers, Apr. 11, 1937.
3. ACBA, "The Catholic Biblical Association of America: Constitution."
4. ACBA, Bylaws.
5. ACBA, Meeting of Officers, Apr. 11, 1937.
6. Romain Butin, S.M., "Some Evidence of Revision of the Hebrew Text of the Pentateuch in Ancient Times" (paper delivered at First General Meeting, St. Louis, MO, Oct. 9–10, 1937), in *Proceedings of the Catholic Biblical Association of America*. (St. Meinrad, IN: Abbey Press), 16.
7. Ibid.
8. Ibid., 27–28.
9. *Supplement to Catholic Biblical Quarterly* 1 (1939): 8–12, 17–29. Prior to the meeting, the association had also circularized the hierarchy for support. "Patrons," who contributed $250 or more to the association, were Cardinal William O'Connell of Boston, Cardinal Patrick Hayes of New York, Bishop Thomas E. Molloy of Brooklyn, and O'Hara. "Life Members," who contributed $100 or more, were Archbishop John J. Mitty of San Francisco, Bishop Alexander McGavick of La Crosse, and Bishop Joseph Schrembs of Cleveland. "Associate members" were described in the constitution as those "persons or groups . . . who in some way promote the work of the Association." The bishops so designated were John H. Albers of Lansing, Joseph H. Conroy of Ogdensburg, Gerald P. O'Hara of Savannah, and Joseph E. Ritter of Indianapolis.
10. Pius X, *Pascendi Dominici Gregis*, in Claudia Carlen, I.H.M., *The Papal Encyclicals*, 3:75.
11. ACBA, Results of the Deliberations of the Executive Board of the Catholic Biblical Association, Apr. 24, 1938.
12. ACBA, Frey to Newton, Vatican, Apr. 11, 1938.
13. ADKC, 348, Newton, "Report on Reception of Bibl. Assoc. in Rome and

England." For Dyson's review of the proceedings, see *Biblica* 20 (1939): 106–7, and *Verbum Domini* 18 (1938): 256*.

14. ADKC, 348, Newton, "Report on Reception of Bibl. Assoc. . . ." See also 349, Newton to O'Hara, Cambridge, Aug. 6, 1938.

15. ADKC, 349, O'Hara to Newton, Great Falls, Aug. 23, 1938 (copy).

16. *Catholic Biblical Quarterly* 1 (January 1939): 9–14.

17. Charles Callan, O.P., "The Synoptic Problem," *Catholic Biblical Quarterly* 1 (January 1939): 55–63.

18. Wendell S. Reilly, S.S., "The Origin of St. Matthew's Gospel," *Catholic Biblical Quarterly* 2 (October 1940): 320.

19. *Catholic Biblical Quarterly* 3 (January 1941): 84.

20. *Catholic Biblical Quarterly* 4 (April 1942): 179–80.

21. Wendell S. Reilly, "The Literary Relations of the First Three Gospels," *A Commentary on the New Testament*, prepared by the Catholic Biblical Association under the patronage of the Episcopal Committee of the Confraternity of Christian Doctrine (n.p.: William H. Sadlier, 1942), 20.

22. Ibid., 21, 23, 24.

23. Mark Kennedy, "The Holy Gospel of Jesus Christ according to St. Matthew," in *ibid.*, 27–28.

24. Edward Cerny, S.S., "The Epistle to the Hebrews," in *ibid.*, 589–90.

25. *The New Testament*, Confraternity edition, 684n.

26. Albert Meyer, "The First Epistle of St. John," in *Commentary on the New Testament*, 645.

27. DS, 3681–3682. On the background to the Johannine Comma, see Raymond E. Brown, S.S., *The Epistles of John*, vol. 30 of *The Anchor Bible* (Garden City, NY: Doubleday & Co., 1982), 775–86, esp. 780–81.

28. John J. Collins, S.J., "The Epistle to the Philippians," in *Commentary on the New Testament*, 550.

29. Leo P. Foley, C.M., "The Pastoral Epistles," in *ibid.*, p. 570.

30. Joseph C. Nuesse to author, Washington, Oct. 7, 1985.

31. ACUA, Corrigan to Pizzardo, Washington, Mar. 13, 1942 (copy). For providing me with this and other information, I am grateful to Dr. C. Joseph Nuesse of the Catholic University.

32. W. F. Albright, *Bulletin of the American Schools of Oriental Research* 134 (April 1954): 4.

33. William H. McClellan, S.J., "Monotheism and the Historical Process," *Theological Studies* 3 (February 1942): 109–36.

34. Edward Cerny, S.S., "Bethel (Beitin)", *Catholic Biblical Quarterly*, 4 (1942): 68; "Lithostrotos," *ibid.*, 258; and "Jerusalem: Palace of Herod the Great," *ibid.*, 258.

35. Michael Gruenthaner, S.J., "Editorial Comments," *Catholic Biblical Quarterly* 5 (January 1943): 3.

36. Alexa Suelzer, S.P., "Modern Old Testament Criticism," in *The Jerome Biblical Commentary*, 603.

37. Richard F. Smith, S.J., "Inspiration and Inerrancy," *The Jerome Biblical Commentary*, 508.

38. Interviews with Monsignor Matthew Stapleton, Mar. 16, 1983 and Bishop John J. Dougherty, Mar. 9, 1983.

39. Anthony J. Cotter, S.J., "The Antecedents of the Encyclical *Providentissimus Deus*," *Catholic Biblical Quarterly*, 5 (April 1943): 117.

40. Ibid., 124.

41. Richard T. Murphy, O.P., "The Teachings of the Encyclical *Providentissimus Deus*," *Catholic Biblical Quarterly* 5 (April 1943): 132.
42. Ibid., 134–35, 138.
43. Stephen J. Hartdegen, O.F.M., "The Influence of the Encyclical *Providentissimus Deus* on Subsequent Scripture Study," *Catholic Biblical Quarterly* 5 (April 1943): 145–46, 150–55, 156–58.
44. Pius XII, *Divino Afflante Spiritu*, no. 21 in *Rome and the Study of Scripture*, 91–92.
45. Ibid., no. 23, p. 92.
46. Ibid., no. 31, p. 96.
47. Ibid., no. 33, pp. 96–97.
48. Ibid., no. 35, p. 97.
49. Ibid., no. 37, p. 98.
50. Ibid., no. 38, p. 99.
51. Ibid., nos. 46–47, pp. 101–2.
52. Pius XII noted that in "speaking of things of the physical order," the sacred writers "went by what sensibly appeared." Leo, Pius continued, stated that that "principle 'will apply especially to cognate sciences, and especially to history,' that is, by refuting, '*in a somewhat similar way the fallacies of the adversaries and defending the historical truth of Sacred Scripture from their attacks.*'" The italicized passage was taken from *Spiritus Paraclitus*—a fact that Pius acknowledged only in a footnote (see *Divino Afflante-Spiritu* no. 3, in *Rome and the Study of Scripture*, 82n.). In the original context, however, Benedict XV condemned any application of "sensible appearances" to history (see *Spiritus Paraclitus*, no. 2, in *ibid.* 53). Pius XII made other more jejune references in *Divino Afflante Spiritu* to the earlier encyclical in no. 9, p. 86n., and no. 33, p. 97n.
53. James Hennesey, S.J., "American Jesuit in Wartime Rome: The Diary of Vincent A. McCormick, S.J., 1942–1945," *Mid-America: An Historical Review* 56 (January 1974): 52–53.
54. ACBA, O'Hara to Murphy, Kansas City, Feb. 16, 1944.
55. ACBA, Albright to Cerny, Baltimore, Feb. 27, 1944; Cerny to Murphy, Baltimore, Feb. 29, 1944; Lilly to Albright, Washington, Mar. 11, 1944 (copy).
56. ACBA, Cerny to Lilly, Baltimore, July 10, 1944.
57. William F. Albright, "The Old Testament and Canaanite Language and Literature," *Catholic Biblical Quarterly* 7 (January 1945): 5–31.
58. "General Meeting, 1944," *Catholic Biblical Quarterly* 7 (January 1945): 102–4.
59. ACBA, Albright to Lilly, Baltimore, Aug. 28, 1944.
60. "General Meeting," *Catholic Biblical Quarterly* 9 (January 1947): 7. See also Francis S. Rossiter, "Forty Years Less One: An Historical Sketch of the C.B.A. (1936–1975)," *Catholic Biblical Quarterly* Supplement 39 (1977), 12.
61. ACBA, meetings, Lilly to Hartman, Perryville, MO, Dec. 17, 1948.
62. Rossiter, "Historical Sketch of the C.B.A.," 12.
63. Interview with Matthew Stapleton, Mar. 16, 1983.
64. ACUA, Skehan Papers, Albright to Skehan, Baltimore, Sept. 13, 1947.
65. ACUA, Skehan Papers, Albright to Skehan, Baltimore, Oct. 4, 1947.
66. Rossiter, "Historical Sketch of the C.B.A.," 5.
67. ACBA, Bea to Cicognani, Rome, May 23, 1945 (copy); Cicognani to Lilly, Washington, July 4, 1945.
68. ACBA, O'Hara to Lilly, Kansas City, Jan. 13, 1945.
69. ACBA, McClellan to Lilly, Woodstock, MD, Mar. 27, 1945.
70. ACBA, Lilly to McClellan, Washington, Apr. 7, 1945 (copy).
71. "General Meeting," *Catholic Biblical Quarterly* 8 (January 1946): 114–16.

72. Tisserant to members of CBA, Rome, June 9, 1946, in *Catholic Biblical Quarterly* 9 (January 1947): 1-2. For Vosté's address, see 3.
73. Ibid., 26-32. See Rossiter, "Historical Sketch of the C.B.A.," 10.
74. Ibid., 5, 6, 33-47.
75. *Catholic Biblical Quarterly* 9 (January 1948): 88-91.
76. ACBA, meetings, O'Hara to Lilly, Kansas City, July 29, 1948.
77. ACBA, meetings, Kleist to Lilly, St. Louis, Aug. 5, 1948.
78. "General Meeting," *Catholic Biblical Quarterly* 11 (January 1949): 7.
79. ADKC, 115, Kleist to O'Hara, St. Louis, Oct. 1, 1948.
80. ADKC, 115, O'Hara to Val Roche, Kansas City, May 6, 1949 (copy).
81. ADKC, 115, Reinert to O'Hara, St. Louis, May 27, 1949; O'Hara to Reinert, Kansas City, June 23, 1949 (copy).
82. "General meeting," *Catholic Biblical Quarterly* 11 (January 1949): 4.
83. DS, 3862-3864.
84. "General Meeting," *Catholic Biblical Quarterly* 12 (January 1950): 1. Interview with John L. McKenzie, Aug. 3, 1983.
85. ADKC, 350, O'Hara to Newton, Kansas City, May 31, 1945 (copy); Newton to O'Hara, Cleveland, June 3, 1945.
86. William L. Newton, "Four Current Versions Reviewed," *The Priest* 3 (June 1947): 427-28.
87. Interview with John J. Collins, S.J., Mar. 18, 1983 and with Matthew Stapleton, Mar. 16, 1983.
88. *Catholic Biblical Quarterly* 5 (January 1943), 3.
89. Robert North, S.J., "A Frontier Jerome: Gruenthaner," *American Ecclesiastical Review* 148 (June 1963), 408. Interview with John L. McKenzie, Aug. 3, 1983.
90. Interview with Msgr. Francis Rossiter, Mar. 14, 1983; ACPPS, Siegman to Oberhauser, Washington, Jan. 31, 1951.
91. ACBA, meetings, Lilly to Hartman, Perryville, MO, Apr. 24, 1949; "Annual Meeting," *Catholic Biblical Quarterly* 13 (January 1951): 1.
92. The membership roll for 1947-1948 lists Meyer as an associate member, but the other rolls list him as an active member; cf. *Supplement to the Catholic Biblical Quarterly* 10 (1948): 13 and *ibid.*, 12 (January 1950): 12.
93. Ibid., 10 (January 1948): 12-14.

CHAPTER 12

1. ACPPS, Siegman to Oberhauser, Washington, Feb. 3, 1951.
2. ACPPS, Siegman to Oberhauser, Washington, May 5, 1951.
3. ACPPS, Siegman to Oberhauser, Washington, Oct. 1, 1951.
4. ACPPS, Siegman to Oberhauser, Washington, Nov. 28, 1951 and Jan. 28, 1952.
5. ACPPS, Siegman to Oberhauser, Washington, Mar. 31, 1952.
6. See DS, 3886.
7. DS, 3897.
8. Jean Levie, S.J., pointed out the significance that the encyclical had not stated that "it is apparent how an opinion of this kind can in no way be reconciled." The encyclical's formula placed the adverb "in no way (nequaquam)" before "apparent," and thus left the way open for further theological development and reflection on how such a scientific opinion could be reconciled with the doctrine of original sin. See Jean Levie, S.J., "L'Encyclique 'Humani Generis,'" *Nouvelle Revue Theologique* 72 (September–October 1950): 789.
9. DS, 3898.
10. DS, 3887.

11. Augustin Bea, S.J., "L'Encyclica 'Humani Generis' e gli studi biblici," *Civiltà cattolica anno* 101, 4 (September 11 1950): 417-18.
12. DS, 3889.
13. See above, pp 240 and 375 n.52.
14. Aubert, *Church in a Secularised Society*, 622.
15. ACPPS, Siegman to Oberhauser, Washington, Jan. 28, 1952.
16. "General Meeting," *Catholic Biblical Quarterly*, 14 (January 1952): 63-67; ACBA, meetings, McKenzie to Hartman, West Baden Springs, IN, May 19, 1952.
17. "General Meeting," *Catholic Biblical Quarterly* 14 (October 1952): 350.
18. "General Meeting," *Catholic Biblical Quarterly*, 14 (October 1952): 352-53.
19. John L. McKenzie, "The Hebrew Attitude towards Mythological Polytheism," *Catholic Biblical Quarterly*, 14 (October 1952): 323-35. R. A. F. MacKenzie changed the title of his published article to "Before Abraham was . . .," *Catholic Biblical Quarterly*, 15 (April 1953): 131-40.
20. McKenzie, "Hebrew Attitude," 353.
21. "Constitution," *Supplement to the Catholic Biblical Quarterly* 16 (1954): 5.
22. Rossiter, "Historical Sketch of the C.B.A.," 3. See DS, 3887: ". . . Sacred Scripture must be expounded according to the mind of the Church, which has been constituted by Christ the Lord as the guardian and interpreter of the entire deposit of divinely revealed truth."
23. North, "American Scripture Century," 337.
24. "General Meeting," *Catholic Biblical Quarterly*, 15 (October 1953): 462-63. See A. Robert and A. Feuillet, *Introduction to the Old Testament*, translated from the second French edition by Patrick W. Skehan, et al. (New York: Desclee Co., 1968), 444.
25. See Millar Burrows, *The Dead Sea Scrolls* (New York: The Viking Press, 1955), 3-53.
26. "General Meeting," *Catholic Biblical Quarterly*, 15 (October 1953): 462-65.
27. *The Holy Bible, Translated from the Original Languages with Critical Use of All the Ancient Sources by Members of the Catholic Biblical Association of America, Sponsored by the Episcopal Committee of the Confraternity of Christian Doctrine* (Paterson, NJ: St. Anthony Guild Press, 1952), 1, iii-v, 8.
28. ACBA, Brown to Hartman, Washington, Aug. 3, 1952 [*sic*].
29. ACBA, Peirce to Hartman, Woodstock, Nov. 16, 1953.
30. Francis X. Peirce, S.J., "Mary Alone is the Woman of Genesis 3.15," *Catholic Biblical Quarterly*, 2 (1940): 245-52; "The Protoevangelium," *Catholic Biblical Quarterly*, 13 (July 1951): 239-52.
31. John L. McKenzie, *The Two-Edged Sword: An Interpretation of the Old Testament* (Milwaukee: The Bruce Publishing Co., 1956), 104.
32. Interview with John L. McKenzie, Aug. 3, 1983; Stanley to author, Toronto, Sept. 8, 1986.
33. On Murray, see Donald E. Pelotte, S.S.S., *John Courtney Murray: Theologian in Conflict* (New York: Paulist Press, 1976), 3-73. For Murray's relationship with the Americanist tradition, see 141-85. See also my *Vatican and the American Hierarchy*, 349-53, 368-81.
34. "General Meeting . . . , 1954," *Catholic Biblical Quarterly*, 16 (October 1954): 445. See John L. McKenzie, "American Catholic Biblical Scholarship 1955-1980," in John J. Collins and John Dominic Crossan, eds., *The Biblical Heritage in Modern Catholic Scholarship* (Wilmington, DE: Michael Glazier, 1986), 215.
35. "General Meeting," *Catholic Biblical Quarterly*, 16 (October 1954): 444-48.
36. "General Meeting," 17 (October 1955): 575-82.
37. Edward F. Siegman, C.PP.S., "The Decrees of the Pontifical Commission: A Recent Clarification," *Catholic Biblical Quarterly*, 18 (1956): 24. The phrase

"with complete freedom," in a reactionary move, is omitted from the text in *Rome and the Study of Scripture*, 175.

38. Ibid.

39. Ibid., 23.

40. Ibid., 26.

41. Ibid., 26–29.

42. R. A. F. MacKenzie, S.J., to author, Toronto, Feb. 2, 1987. As rector of the Biblical Institute, MacKenzie found copies of these letters among the papers of Father Vaccari. For Steinmueller's charge, see Joseph A. Fitzmyer, S.J., *A Christological Catechism: New Testament Answers* (New York: Paulist Press, 1982), 100n.

43. "General Meeting," *Catholic Biblical Quarterly*, 19 (January 1957): 94–96.

44. ACPPS, Siegman to Oberhauser, Washington, Feb. 28, 1957.

45. Ibid.

46. Ibid.

47. ACBA, meetings, MacKenzie to Hartman, Toronto, Apr. 29, 1957.

48. R. A. F. MacKenzie, S.J., "Some Problems in the Field of Inspiration," *Catholic Biblical Quarterly*, 20 (January 1958): 7, 8.

49. "General Meeting . . . , 1957," *Catholic Biblical Quarterly*, 19 (October 1957): 485–87.

50. "General Meeting . . . , 1958," *Catholic Biblical Quarterly*, 20 (October 1958): 499–501.

51. David M. Stanley, "Balaam's Ass, or a Problem in New Testament Hermeneutics," *Catholic Biblical Quarterly*, 20 (January 1958): 50, 51, 51–52.

52. Ibid., 52

53. Ibid., 54, 55.

54. Siegman to Stanley, Washington, Mar. 2, 1958. I am grateful to Father David M. Stanley, S.J., for providing me with copies of this and the following documents.

55. Siegman, "Editor's Comments" ms., copy given by Stanley.

56. Siegman to Stanley, Washington, Mar. 25, 1958.

57. Siegman to Stanley, Washington, Apr. 15, 1958, with enclosure.

58. ACBA, Hartdegen and Hartman to Episcopal Committee of the CCD, Washington, Nov. 13, 1957 (copy).

59. Ibid.

60. ACBA, Hartman to Brady, Washington, Nov. 13, 1957 (copy).

61. ACBA, Brady to Hartdegen and Hartman, Manchester, Mar. 7, 1958 (copy).

62. Ibid.

63. ACBA, Hartman to members of the executive board of the CBA, Washington, Mar. 27, 1958. Pointing out that Brady's letter was postmarked only on Mar. 14, Hartman sent a copy of the letter, together with copies of his and Hartdegen's earlier correspondence with Brady and the episcopal committee.

64. ACBA, Executive Committee of the CBA to Brady, Washington, Apr. 5, 1958 (first draft).

65. ACBA, Executive Committee of the CBA to Brady, Washington, May 25, 1958.

66. Ibid.

67. Ibid.

68. ACBA, Hartman, Skehan, and Hartdegen to Brady, Washington, May 25, 1958 (copy).

69. ACBA, Bourke to Murphy, Washington, July 27, 1959.

70. ACPPS, Siegman to Oberhauser, Washington, Feb. 28, 1957.

71. "General Meeting . . . , 1959," *Catholic Biblical Quarterly*, 21 (October 1959): 496–99.

72. Myles M. Bourke, "The Literary Genus of Mt. 1–2," *Catholic Biblical Quarterly*, 22 (October 1960): 160–75.
73. "General Meeting . . . , 1959," *Catholic Biblical Quarterly*, 21 (October 1959): 496–500. Charles F. Kraft, secretary of the SBL, had reported the SBL's resolution to Hartman and said that the suggestion came as a result of an article by John L. McKenzie in *The Journal of Biblical Literature*, the society's journal. See ACBA, Kraft to Hartman, Evanston, IL, Mar. 20, 1959 and Hartman to Kraft, Washington, Apr. 21, 1959 (copy).
74. AANY, Spellman Diary, Aug. 13, 1932.
75. ACBA, Vawter to Murphy, Denver, May 11, 1959.
76. ACBA, Siegman to Murphy, Rome, May 2, 1959.
77. ACBA, Siegman to Hartman, Rome, Nov. 16, 1958.

CHAPTER 13

1. Francis J. Connell, C.Ss.R., "Answers to Questions," *American Ecclesiastical Review* 140 (January 1959): 36.
2. Joseph C. Fenton, "The Case for Traditional Apologetics," *American Ecclesiastical Review* 141 (July 1959): 407, 408, 409.
3. Ibid., 409, 411.
4. Ibid., 413–14.
5. ACPPS, Siegman, memorandum, n.d.
6. ACPPS, Siegman to Byrne, Washington, Feb. 27, 1960.
7. ACPPS, Siegman to Byrne, St. Aloysius [June 21], 1960.
8. McEleney, memorandum, Apr. 14, 1960. I am grateful to Neil J. McEleney, C.S.P., for providing me with copies of this and of his letter to Spellman cited below. For providing other details on the meeting I am grateful to Monsignor Myles Bourke; Bourke to author, New York, Feb. 22, 1987.
9. McEleney to Spellman, Washington, Apr. 13, 1960 (copy). See n. 8 above.
10. McEleney, memo. See n. 8 above.
11. Interview with Myles Bourke, Mar. 9, 1983.
12. Joseph C. Fenton, "The Priest and the Ascetical Cultivation of the Faith," *American Ecclesiastical Review* 142 (March 1960): 193, 194–195.
13. Ibid., 196, 197, 197–198.
14. Gerald T. Kennedy, O.M.I., "Scripture Revisited: Second Look at the Matter," *American Ecclesiastical Review* 145 (July 1961): 7, 8.
15. Ibid., 9.
16. John L. Murphy, "The Teaching of Schleiermacher, Part II," *American Ecclesiastical Review* 145 (July 1961): 28–29, 29, 30.
17. Ibid., 30, 31.
18. Archbishop Egidio Vagnozzi, "Thoughts on the Catholic Intellectual," *American Ecclesiastical Review* 145 (August 1961): 74, 75.
19. Ibid., 75.
20. ACBA, Ernest Vogt, S.J., "Pro-Memoria sugli attachi contro il Pontificio Istituto Biblico," 3–5.
21. Antonino Romeo, "L'Enciclica 'Divino Afflante Spiritu' e le 'opiniones novae,' *Divinitas* 4 (December 1960): 387–456, Reference to Bourke is on 443.
22. Francis McCool to Bourke, Rome, May 22, 1962. The issue became all the more important on the eve of the council. The Biblical Institute was then seeking to gain support from Spellman and other prelates against the attacks on its orthodoxy. Bourke warned Francis McCool that, if Vogt and the institute clearly intended him as the "particular case," they would anger Spellman who

would then not offer his support. For providing me with a copy of the letter cited above and other information, I am grateful to Monsignor Bourke.

23. ACBA, Ernest Vogt, S.J., "Pro-Memoria," 5–6.
24. ACBA, Pizzardo to Bea, Feb. 3, 1961, mimeograph copy distributed to the CBA.
25. "Pontificium Institutum Biblicum et recens libellus R.mi D.ni A. Romeo," *Verbum Domini* 39 (fasci. 1961): 3–17.
26. ACBA, Murphy to Vogt, Washington, Mar. 13, 1961.
27. ACBA, Vogt to Murphy, Rome, Mar. 25, 1961.
28. Ibid.
29. [Murphy], "The Close of a Controversy," *Catholic Biblical Quarterly,* 23 (May 1961): 269.
30. *Catholic Biblical Quarterly,* 23 (October 1961): 465.
31. Archbishop Egidio Vagnozzi, "The States of Perfection and the Theological Virtues," *American Ecclesiastical Review* 145 (November 1961): 292.
32. ACBA, Whealon to Hartman, Cleveland, n.d.
33. Whealon to author, Hartford, May 17, 1983.
34. Interview with Archbishop Whealon, July 18, 1983.
35. ACSSP, Siegman to Byrne, Washington, July 13, 1961.
36. Ibid. Filas's article had appeared in *The Priest* for December, 1960, and Siegman's rejoinder had appeared in the issue for May, 1961. Vagnozzi had praised Filas for his "intelligent, sensible and measured evaluation of some contemporary Scriptural studies, which, as you justly saw, have created 'confusion and doubt in the presence of what appears to be exegetical anarchy.' " See ACPPS, Vagnozzi to Filas, Washington, Apr. 21, 1961 (copy), enclosed in Filas to Siegman, Chicago, Apr. 17, 1961.
37. ACPPS, Siegman to Byrne, Washington, July 13, 1961.
38. "General Meeting . . . , 1961," *Catholic Biblical Quarterly,* 23 (October 1961): 465, 466.
39. ACBA, Krumholtz to Murphy, Cincinnati, Sept. 14, 1961.
40. ACBA, "Summaries of the Papers [for 1961 meeting]."
41. *Catholic Biblical Quarterly,* 23 (October 1961): 465–68.
42. ACBA, "Paraphrased Record of the Discussion at the Business Session of the Twenty-Fourth General Meeting of the Catholic Biblical Association of America, Thursday, August 31, 1961," 1–5.
43. ACBA, Meetings, 1961, Skehan to Hartman, Washington, Aug. 23, 1961.
44. ACBA, Skehan submission to executive board meeting of CBA in Cincinnati, 1961 (Aug).
45. ACBA, "Paraphrased Record," 6
46. Ibid., 7–8.
47. Ibid., 8–9.
48. Ibid., 9–10. The original signed version is also in ACBA.
49. ACBA, press release, "Meeting of the Catholic Biblical Association"; Walter Abbott, S.J., to Roland Murphy, O.Carm., New York, Sept. 3, 1961.
50. ACBA, Murphy to members of the editorial board, Washington, Sept. 25, 1961; Murphy to O'Boyle, Washington, Sept. 20, 1961 (copy), with O'Boyle's final wording attached.
51. *Catholic Biblical Quarterly,* 23 (October 1961): 470.
52. ACBA, *Catholic Universe Bulletin,* Sept. 8, 1961; Whealon to author, Hartford, Aug. 9, 1983.
53. ACBA, Murphy to Vawter, Washington, Oct. 3, 1961, copy sent to Hartman.

54. Ibid.
55. Connell to "Your Excellency," Washington, Nov. 7, 1961, copy provided by Archbishop John F. Whealon.
56. ACBA, Fenton and Murphy to "Your Excellency," Washington, Nov. 7, 1961.
57. Ibid.
58. ACBA, Vawter to Murphy, Denver, Nov. 6, 1961.
59. ACBA, Roland E. Murphy, O.Carm., Joseph A. Fitzmyer, S.J., Thomas Barrosse, C.S.C., Patrick W. Skehan, John L. McKenzie, S.J., Bruce Vawter, C.M., Eugene H. Maly, Louis F. Hartman, C.SS.R., Joseph E. Fallon, O.P., to "Your Excellency," Nov. 30, 1961 (copy).
60. Ibid.
61. Ibid.
62. Ibid.
63. Vagnozzi to Whealon, Washington, Dec. 7, 1961. For this and the following letter, I am grateful to Archbishop Whealon.
64. Whealon to Vagnozzi, Cleveland, Dec. 18, 1961 (copy).
65. Ibid.
66. Ibid.
67. For the Pauline Congress, see *Biblica* 42 (1961): 492–95.

CHAPTER 14

1. See Fogarty, *Vatican and the American Hierarchy*, 195–207.
2. ACPPS, Siegman, memorandum, n.d.
3. ACPPS, Siegman to Byrne, Carthagena, OH, Feb. 5, 1962.
4. ACPPS, Memorandum concerning the Reverend Edward F. Siegman, C.PP.S., S.T.D., S.S.L., attached to McDonald to O'Boyle, Washington, June 25, 1962 (photocopy).
5. ACBA, Siegman to Murphy, Carthagena, OH, Mar. 27, 1962.
6. Ibid.
7. ACPPS, McDonald to Byrne, Washington, Apr. 18, 1962 (printed copy).
8. ACPPS, Byrne to McDonald, Dayton, May 1, 1962 (printed copy).
9. ACPPS, McDonald to Byrne, Washington, May 2, 1962 (printed copy).
10. ACBA, Byrne to McDonald, Dayton, May 3, 1962 (printed copy).
11. ACPPS, Siegman to McDonald, n.p., May 8, 1962 (printed copy); Siegman's own copy is in ACPPS.
12. ACPPS.
13. ACPPS.
14. ACPPS, Siegman, memorandum, n.d.
15. Ibid.
16. ACPPS, Siegman to Schmitz, n.p., May 30, 1962 (copy).
17. ACPPS, Byrne to O'Boyle, Dayton, June 16, 1962 (copy).
18. ACPPS, McDonald to O'Boyle, Washington, June 25, 1962 (photocopy).
19. ACPPS, O'Boyle to Byrne, Washington, June 26, 1962.
20. ACPPS, Siegman to Byrne, Carthagena, OH, July 2, 1962.
21. ACPPS, Siegman, memorandum.
22. "General Meeting . . . , 1962," *Catholic Biblical Quarterly*, 24 (October 1962): 424.
23. ACPPS, Siegman to Byrne, New Haven, Jan. 7, 1964.
24. *Homiletic and Pastoral Review* 62 (October 1961), quoted in William S. Schneirla, "Roma locuta . . . ?," *St. Vladimir's Seminary Quarterly* 6 (no. 2 1962): 84.
25. Ibid., 84–85.

26. Ernesto Cardinal Ruffini, "Literary Genres and Working Hypotheses in Recent Biblical Studies," *American Ecclesiastical Review* 145 (December 1961): 362–65.
27. ACBA, John L. McKenzie, "A Study in Parallels," ms.; McKenzie to Murphy, Chicago, Jan. 4 1961 [*sic*].
28. Gerald T. Kennedy, O.M.I., "The Holy Office *Monitum* and the Teaching of Scripture," *American Ecclesiastical Review* 145 (September 1961): 145–51.
29. Interview with William Moran, Mar. 17, 1983.
30. W. L. Moran, S.J., "Father Kennedy's Exegesis of the Holy Office *Monitum,*" *American Ecclesiastical Review* 146 (March 1962): 179.
31. Gerald T. Kennedy, O.M.I., "A Reply to Father Moran," *American Ecclesiastical Review* 146 (March 1962): 181.
32. Quoted in *ibid.*, 182.
33. Ibid., 183, 190.
34. Joseph Clifford Fenton, "Father Moran's Prediction," *American Ecclesiastical Review* 146 (March 1962): 192–201.
35. Patrick W. Skehan, "Why leave out *Judith?,*" *Catholic Biblical Quarterly,* 24 (April 1962): 147, 154.
36. ACBA, Thomas Barrosse, C.S.C., Joseph A. Fitzmyer, S.J., Roland E. Murphy, O.Carm., "Catholic Biblical Studies in the U.S.A." (galley).
37. Ibid.
38. Ibid.
39. ACBA, Fitzmyer to Murphy, Woodstock, April 25, 1962.
40. Schneirla, "Roma locuta . . . ?," 79–92.
41. "General Meeting . . . , 1962," *Catholic Biblical Quarterly,* 24 (October 1962): 421. Murphy's paper was not published in the *Catholic Biblical Quarterly,* but he had written an earlier article on the same topic, see John L. Murphy, "Unwritten Traditions at Trent," *American Ecclesiastical Review* 146 (1962): 233–63.
42. "General Meeting . . . , 1962," 422.
43. Ibid., 423–24. *Supplement to the Catholic Biblical Quarterly* 30 (1968): 5, 9–10.
44. "General Meeting . . . , 1962," 423–25.
45. Pelotte, *John Courtney Murray,* 77.
46. Vincent A. Yzermans, *American Participation in the Second Vatican Council* (New York: Sheed and Ward, 1967), 95.
47. Jedin, *Council of Trent,* 2:81–89.
48. Joseph Ratzinger, "Dogmatic Constitution on Divine Revelation: Origin and Background," in Herbert Vorgrimler, ed., *Commentary on the Documents of Vatican II* (New York: Herder and Herder, 1969), 3:159–60.
49. Xavier Rynne, *Vatican Council II* (New York: Farrar Straus Giroux, 1968), 35–36, 37. An English copy of Spadafora's pamphlet is in ACBA.
50. Joseph A. Fitzmyer, "A Recent Roman Scriptural Controversy," *Theological Studies* 22 (September 1961): 426–44. For providing me with information about the distribution of his article, I am grateful to Joseph Fitzmyer.
51. *Acta Synodalia Sacrosancti Concilii Oecumenici Vaticani II,* (Vatican: Typis Polyglottis Vaticanis, 1971), I, Part III, 48–51.
52. In Yzermans, *American Participation,* 105, 106, 108.
53. Ibid., 109.
54. For providing me with information on this episode, I am grateful to Archbishop Whealon; Whealon to author, Hartford, Jan. 23, 1987. See also Yzermans, 104.
55. Rynne, *Vatican Council II,* 90.
56. Interview with William Moran, Mar. 17, 1983.

57. ACBA, "Recommendations . . . ," approved by Committee on Theology, Nov. 23, 1962.
58. ACBA, Whealon to Hartman, Cleveland, Dec. 15, 1962.
59. ACBA, Hartman to Whealon, Washington, Dec. 21, 1962 (copy).
60. ACBA, Whealon to Hartman, Cleveland, Dec. 29, 1962 and Jan. 31, 1963.
61. Fogarty, *Vatican and the American Hierarchy*, 391.
62. ACBA, MacKenzie to Murphy, Toronto, May 5, 1963.
63. ACBA, MacKenzie to Murphy, Toronto, May 11, 1963. On the changing composition of the Biblical Commission, see Fitzmyer, *Christological Catechism*, 102.
64. MacKenzie to author, Toronto, Aug. 14, 1983.
65. ACBA, McCool to Murphy, New York, Sept. 15, 1963.
66. ACBA, MacKenzie, review of Steinmueller, attached to MacKenzie to Murphy, Toronto, May 5, 1963.
67. ACBA, Arthur to Francis Rossiter, Washington, Oct. 7, 1963 (copy).
68. ACBA, Hartman to Ahern, Washington, Sept. 4, 1963 (copy).
69. Cushing to Eugene Maly, Brighton, Sept. 25, 1962, introduction to *Catholic Biblical Quarterly* 25 (January 1962).
70. ACBA Meyer to Murphy, Chicago, Apr. 18, 1963.
71. ACBA, Murphy to Meyer, Washington, Apr. 28, 1963 (copy), with draft attached.
72. ACBA, Meyer to CBA, Chicago, May 3, 1963; in frontispiece of *Catholic Biblical Quarterly*, 25 (July 1963).
73. "Report of the Twenty-Sixth General Meeting," *Catholic Biblical Quarterly*, 25 (October 1963): 432, 434.
74. ACBA, Hartman to Lyonnet and to Zerwick, Washington, Sept. 4, 1963 (copies).
75. ACBA, MacKenzie to Hartman, Rome, Sept. 9, 1963.
76. ACBA, Zerwick to Hartman, Rome, Sept. 14, 1963.
77. MacKenzie to author, Toronto, Aug. 14, 1984.
78. Fogarty, *Vatican and the American Hierarchy*, 392–93.
79. Pelotte, *John Courtney Murray*, 87–88.
80. "Discourse of Cardinal Ottaviani," Mar. 2, 1953, in Fogarty, *Vatican and the American Hierarchy*, 371.

CHAPTER 15

1. Fitzmyer, *Christological Catechism*, 109n.
2. Ibid., 134, 135, 136.
3. Ibid., 137. For a commentary on the instruction, see 97–130. See also Joseph A. Fitzmyer, S.J., "The Biblical Commission's Instruction on the Historical Truth of the Gospels," *Theological Studies* 25 (September 1964): 386–408, which includes an earlier version of the same commentary with the instruction appended.
4. ACBA, Whealon to Hartman, Cleveland, Aug. 19, 1964. See also Whealon to Hartman, Cleveland, Aug. 12, 1964 and Hartman to Whealon, Washington, Aug. 15, 1964 (copy).
5. ACBA, McKenzie to Hartman, Chicago, Jan. 6, 1964.
6. ACBA, Hartman to McKenzie, Washington, Jan. 8, 1964.
7. "Twenty-Seventh General Meeting," *Catholic Biblical Quarterly*, 26 (October 1964): 468. The address, "Authority and Power in the New Testament," was published in the same issue, 413–22.
8. "Meeting," Ibid., 468.

9. "Meeting," Ibid., 469–70, 473.
10. In Yzermans, *American Participation*, 100.
11. Interview with Myles Bourke, Mar. 9, 1983.
12. Msgr. Francis J. Weber to author, Los Angeles, Mar. 9, 1987. Msgr. Weber, the archivist of the Archdiocese of Los Angeles, interviewed Cardinal Timothy Manning on this point.
13. In Yzermans, *American Participation*, 111.
14. Ibid., 112.
15. Ibid., 114.
16. Ibid., 115–16.
17. Fitzmyer, *Christological Catechism*, 102.
18. "Report of the Twenty-Eighth General Meeting . . . ," *Catholic Biblical Quarterly*, 27 (October 1965): 407–9.
19. Fogarty, *Vatican and the American Hierarchy*, 398–99.
20. In Yzermans, *American Participation*, 103–4.
21. Ibid., 103.
22. See *Dei Verbum*, no. 2, in Flannery, *Vatican Council II*, 750–51.
23. Ibid., no. 4, 751–52.
24. Ibid., no. 10, 755–56.
25. Ratzinger, "Dogmatic Constitution," in Vorgrimler, *Commentary on the Documents*, 3:184.
26. *Del Verbum* no. 12, in Flannery, *Vatican Council II*, 757.
27. Ibid., no. 13, 758.
28. Ibid., no. 19, 761.
29. Ibid., no. 22, 763.
30. *Dignitatis Humanae Personae*, in *ibid*, no. 10, 806–7. The biblical reference here is to Eph 1:5. In speaking of revelation as God's self-communication, as seen above, *Dei Verbum* referred to Eph 1:9.
31. Raymond E. Brown, S.S., Joseph A. Fitzmyer, S.J., and Roland E. Murphy, O.Carm., eds., "Editors' Preface," in *The Jerome Biblical Commentary*, xviii.
32. *Jerome Biblical Commentary*, 3–4, 270–71.
33. "General Meeting," *Catholic Biblical Quarterly*, 22 (October 1960): 433.
34. "General Meeting," *Catholic Biblical Quarterly*, 26 (October 1964): 470.
35. *The Catholic Review* (Baltimore), April 9, 1965.
36. ACBA, Fuller to Hartman, London, Sept. 23, 1957.
37. ACBA, Hartman to Fuller, Washington, Oct. 3, 1957 (copy).
38. Brown et al., *The Jerome Biblical Commentary*, 587.
39. Interview with Raymond Brown, Mar. 9, 1983.
40. "How to Read Your Bible," in *The New American Bible, Translated from the Original Languages with Critical Use of All the Ancient Sources by Members of the Catholic Biblical Association of America, sponsored by the Bishops' Committee of the Confraternity of Christian Doctrine* (New York: Catholic Book Publishing Co., 1970), [21].
41. Ibid., 1, 249.
42. Fitzmyer, *Christological Catechism*, 103.
43. Raymond E. Brown, S.S., *Biblical Exegesis and Church Doctrine* (New York: Paulist Press, 1985), 59–60.

Bibliography

I. SOURCES:

A. ARCHIVES:

Archives of the Archdiocese of Baltimore, 320 Cathedral Street, Baltimore, MD 21201.
Archives of the Archdiocese of Boston, 2121 Commonwealth Avenue, Brighton, MA 02135.
Archives of the Archdiocese of New York, St. Joseph's Seminary, Dunwoodie, NY 10704.
Archives of the Archdiocese of St. Paul, St. Paul Seminary, 2200 Grand Avenue, St. Paul, MN 55101.
Archives of the Catholic Biblical Association, The Catholic University of America, Washington, DC 20064.
Archives of the Catholic University of America, Mullen Memorial Library, the Catholic University of America, Washington, DC 20064.
Archives of the Diocese of Kansas City. The Catholic University of America, Washington, DC 20064. Microfilm.
Archives of the Diocese of Richmond, 811 Cathedral Place, Richmond, VA 23220.
Archives of the Sacred Congregation de Propaganda Fide, Piazza di Spagna 48, Rome 00187, Italy.
Archives of the Society of the Precious Blood, St. Charles Seminary, Carthagena, OH 45822.
Archives of Union Theological Seminary, 3041 Broadway at Reinhold Niebuhr Place, New York, NY 10027.
Archives of Woodstock College, Lauinger Library, Georgetown University, Washington, DC 20057.
Archivio Segreto Vaticano, Vatican City State.
Sulpician Archives, Catonsville, MD 21228.

B. PRINTED SOURCES:

Acta et Decreta Concilii Plenarii Baltimorensis Tertii in Ecclesia Metropolitana Baltimorensi habiti a die IX. Novembris usque ad diem VII. Decembris A.D. MDCCCLXXXIV. Baltimore: John Murphy, 1884.
Acta et Decreta Sacrorum Conciliorum Recentiorum: Collectio Lacensis. 7 vols. Freiburg im Br.: Herder, 1875.
Acta Synodalia Sacrosancti Concilii Oecumenici Vaticani II. Vatican: Typis Polyglottis Vaticanis, 1971.

Carlen, Claudia, I.H.M., ed. *The Papal Encyclicals.* 5 vols. Wilmington, NC: A Consortium Book, 1981.

Collectanea S. Congregationis de Propaganda Fide seu Decreta Instructiones Rescripta pro Apostolicis Missionibus. Rome: Typographia Polyglotta S.C.de Propaganda Fide, 1907.

Compte rendu du quatrième congrès scientifique international des Catholiques, tenu à Fribourg (Suisse) du 16 au 20 aot 1897. Fribourg: Imprimerie et librairie de l'oeuvre de Saint Paul, 1898.

Denzinger-Schönmetzer, eds. *Enchiridion Symbolorum Definitionum et Declarationum de rebus fidei et morum.* 36th ed. Freiburg: Herder, 1976.

Dyer, E. R., S. S. *Letters on the New York Seminary Secession.* Baltimore, 1906.

Ellis, John Tracy, ed. *Documents of American Catholic History.* 2 vols. Chicago: Henry Renery Co., 1967.

Epistolae Praepositorum Generalium ad Superiores Societatis. Rome: Typist Polyglottis Vaticanis, 1911.

Flannery, Austin, O.P., ed. *Vatican Council II: The Conciliar and Post Conciliar Documents.* Collegeville, MN: The Liturgical Press, 1975.

Hanley, Thomas O., S.J., ed. *The John Carroll Papers.* 3 vols. University of Notre Dame Press, 1976.

Kenrick, Francis Patrick. *Theologia Dogmatica.* 4 vols. 2d ed. Baltimore: John Murphy & Co., 1858.

Kenrick-Frenaye Correspondence: Letters Chiefly of Francis, The Patrick Kenrick and Marc Anthony Frenaye: 1830–1862. Trans. by Frederick E. Tourscher. Philadelphia: Philadelphia Archives, 1920.

Kenrick, Peter Richard. *Concio Petri Ricardi Kenrick Archiepis copi S. Ludovici . . . in Concilio Vaticano Habenda at non Habita.* Naples: Typis Fratrum de Angelis, 1870.

Lagrange, M.-J., O.P. *Père Lagrange: Personal Reflections and Memoirs.* Trans. by Rev. Henry Wansbrough. New York: Paulist Press, 1985.

Loisy, Alfred. *Mémoires pour servir à l'histoire religieuse de notre temp.* 3 vols. Paris: E. Nourry, 1931.

Newman, John Henry, *Letters and Diaries.* London: T. Nelson, 1961–.

Nolan, Hugh J., ed. *Pastoral Letters of the American Hierarchy, 1792–1970.* Huntington, IN: Our Sunday Visitor, 1970.

O'Connell, William H. *Sermons and Addresses of His Eminence William Cardinal O'Connell, Archbishop of Boston.* 4 vols. Boston: The Pilot Publishing Company, 1922.

Plus X. "Pascendi Dominici Gregis." In *American Catholic Quarterly Review* 32 (1907): 705–732.

Poels, Henry A. "A Vindication of My Honor." In *Annua Nuntia Lovaniensia,* edited with an introduction by Frans Neirynck, 225. 1982.

Rome and the Study of Scripture. St. Meinrad's, Ind., 1962.

Shehan, Lawrence. *A Blessing of Years: The Memoirs of Lawrence Cardinal Shehan.* Notre Dame, IN: University of Notre Dame Press, 1982.

Smith, H. Shelton, Robert T. Handy, and Lefferts A. Loescher, eds. *American Christianity: An Historical Interpretation with Representative Documents.* 2 vols. New York: Charles Scribner's Sons, 1963.

C. Bibles: Translations and Versions:

Kenrick, Francis Patrick. *The Acts of the Apostles, the Epistles of St. Paul, the Catholic Epistles, and the Apocalypse.* New York: Edward Dunigan and Brother, 1851.

———. *The Book of Job, and the Prophets.* Baltimore: Kelly, Hedian & Piet, 1859.

———. *The Four Gospels, translated from the Latin Vulgate, and diligently compared with the Greek Text, Being a Revision of the Rhemish Translation.* New York: Edward Dunigan and Brother, 1849.

———. *The Historical Books of the Old Testament.* Baltimore: Kelly, Hedian & Piet, 1860.

———. *The New Testament.* Baltimore: Kelly, Hedian & Piet, 1862.

———. *The Pentateuch.* Baltimore: Kelly, Hedian & Piet, 1860.

———. *The Psalms, Books of Wisdom, and the Canticle of Canticles.* Baltimore: Lucas Brothers, 1857.

Lattey, C., ed. *The New Testament, III, Pt. I: Epistles to the Thessalonians.* London: Longmans, Green and Co., 1913.

The Holy Bible, Translated from the Original Languages with Critical Use of All the Ancient Sources by Members of the Catholic Biblical Association of America, Sponsored by the Episcopal Committee of the Confraternity of Christian Doctrine. Paterson, NJ: St. Anthony Guild Press, 1952.

The New American Bible, Translated from the Original Language with Critical Use of All the Ancient Sources by Members of the Catholic Biblical Association of America, sponsored by the Bishops' Committee of the Confraternity of Christian Doctrine. New York: Catholic Book Publishing Co., 1970.

The New Testament of Our Lord and Savior Jesus Christ, translated from the Latin Vulgate: A Revision of the Challoner-Rheims Version. Edited by Catholic Scholars under the Patronage of the Episcopal Committee of the Confraternity of Christian Doctrine. Paterson, NJ: St. Anthony Guild Press, 1941.

D. Newspapers:

The Catholic Review (Baltimore), April 9, 1965.
The Pilot (Boston), March 23, 1912.
Times Literary Supplement, December 13, 1934.

II. SECONDARY WORKS:

A. Books:

Abell, Aaron I. *American Catholicism and Social Action: A Search for Social Justice.* Notre Dame: University of Notre Dame Press, 1963.

Ahern, Patrick H. *The Catholic University of America, 1887–1896: The Rectorship of John J. Keane.* Washington: The Catholic University of America Press, 1948.

————. *The Life of John J. Keane, Educator and Archbishop, 1839–1918.* Milwaukee: The Bruce Publishing Co., 1955.

Albright, William Foxwell. *From the Stone Age to Christianity: Monotheism and the Historical Process.* 2d ed. Baltimore: The Johns Hopkins Press, 1957.

Aubert, Roger. *Le pontificat de Pie IX (1846–1878).* Vol. 21, *Historie de L'eglise depuis les origines jusqu'a nos jours.* Paris: Bloud & Gay, 1952.

————. *The Church in a Secularised Society.* Vol. 5, *The Christian Centuries.* New York: Paulist Press, 1978.

————. *The Church in the Industrial Age.* Vol. 9, Hubert Jedin and John Dolan eds. *History of the Church.* New York: Crossroad, 1981.

Barmann, Lawrence F. *Baron Friedrich von Hügel and the Modernist Crisis in England.* Cambridge: Cambridge University Press, 1972.

Barry, Colman J., O.S.B. *The Catholic University of America: The Rectorship of Denis J. O'Connell.* Washington: The Catholic University of America Press, 1950.

Benoit, Pierre, O.P. *Aspects of Biblical Inspiration.* Trans. by J. Murphy-O'Connor, O.P. and S.K. Ashe, O.P. Chicago: The Priory Press, 1965.

Billington, Ray Allen. *The Protestant Crusade: A Study of the Origins of American Nativism, 1800–1860.* Chicago: Quardrangle Books, 1964.

Briggs, Charles A., and Baron Friedrich von Hügel. *The Papal Commission and the Pentateuch.* London: Longmans, Green, and Co., 1906.

Brown, Raymond E., S.S. *Biblical Exegesis and Church Doctrine.* New York: Paulist Press, 1985.

————., Joseph A. Fitzmyer, S.J., and Roland E. Murphy, O.Carm. eds. *The Jerome Biblical Commentary.* Englewood Cliffs, NJ: Prentice-Hall, Inc., 1968.

Bruneau, Joseph, S.S. *Harmony of the Gospels.* New York: The Cathedral Library Association, 1898.

Burrows, Millar. *The Dead Sea Scrolls.* New York: The Viking Press, 1955.

Burtchaell, James Tunstead, C.S.C. *Catholic Theories of Biblical Inspiration since 1810: A Review and Critique.* Cambridge: Cambridge University Press, 1969.

Commentary on the New Testament, A Prepared by the Catholic Biblical Association under the patronage of the Episcopal Committee of the Confraternity of Christian Doctrine. William H. Sadlier, Inc., 1942.

Chinnici, Joseph P., O.F.M. *The English Catholic Enlightenment: John Lingard and the Cisalpine Movement, 1780–1850.* Shepardstown, WV: The Patmos Press, 1980.

Congar, Yves, M. J., O.P. *Tradition and Traditions: An Historical and a Theological Essay.* New York: Macmillan Company, 1966.

Cross, Robert. *The Emergence of Liberal Catholicism in America.* Cambridge, Mass.: Harvard University Press, 1958.

Daly, Gabriel, O.S.A. *Transcendence and Immanence: A Study in Catholic Modernism and Integralism.* Oxford: Clarendon Press, 1980.

Delattre, A. J., S.J. *Un Catholicisme Américain.* Namur A. Godenne, 1898.
———. *Autour de la question biblique.* Liége: H. Dessain, 1904.
———. *Le Criterium a l'usage de la nouvelle exégèse biblique: résponse au R.P.M.-J. Lagrange, O.P.* Liége: H. Dessain, 1907.

DeVito, Michael J. *Principles of Ecclesial Reform according to the "New York Review."* New York: United States Catholic Historical Society, 1977.

di Bartolo, Salvatore. *I Criteri Teologici: La Storia dei Dommi e La Libertà delle Affermazioni.* Torino: Tipografia S. Giuseppe, 1888.

Finegan, Jack. *Light from the Ancient Past.* Princeton: Princeton University Press, 1959.

Fitzmyer, Joseph A., S.J. *A Christological Catechism: New Testament Answers.* New York: Paulist Press, 1982.

Fogarty, Gerald P., S.J. *The Vatican and the Americanist Crisis: Denis J. O'Connell, American Agent in Rome, 1885–1903.* Rome: Universita Gregoriana Editrice, 1974.

———. *The Vatican and the American Hierarchy from 1870 to 1965.* Stuttgart: Anton Hiersemann, Verlag, 1982.

Gaffey, James P. *Citizen of No Mean City: Archbishop Patrick Riordan of San Francisco (1841–1914).* Washington: A Consortium Book, 1976.

Gigot, Francis E., S.S. *General Introduction to the Study of the Holy Scriptures.* New York: Benzinger Brothers, 1900.

———. *Special Introduction to the Study of the Old Testament: Part I. The Historical Books.* New York: Benzinger Brothers, 1901.

———. *Special Introduction to the Study of the Old Testament: Part II. Didactic Books and Prophetical Writings.* New York: Benzinger Brothers, 1906.

Gorayeb, Joseph, S.J. *The Life and Letters of Walter Drum, S.J.* New York: America Press, 1928.

Grannan, Charles P. *A General Introduction to the Bible.* 4 vols. St. Louis: B. Herder Book Co., 1921.

Halsey, William M. *The Survival of American Innocence: Catholicism in an Era of Disillusionment, 1920–1940.* Notre Dame, IN: University of Notre Dame Press, 1980.

Hogan, John B. *Clerical Studies.* Boston, Mailer, Callahan & Co., 1898.

Houtin, Albert. *La question biblique chez les catholiques de France au XXe siecle.* Paris: Alphonse Picard et Fils, 1906.

Jedin, Hubert. *A History of the Council of Trent,* trans. by Dom Ernest Graf, O.S.B. St. Louis: B. Herder Book, Co., 1961.

Levie, Jean, S.J. *The Bible, Word of God in Words of Men.* Trans. by S. H. Treman. New York: P. J. Kenedy & Sons, 1961.

Maas, Anthony J., S.J. *Christ in Type and Prophecy.* 2 vols. New York: Benzinger Brothers, 1893.

———. *The Gospel according to Saint Matthew with an Explanatory and Critical Commentary.* St. Louis: B. Herder Book, Co., 1898.

———. *The Life of Jesus Christ according to the Gospel History.* 12th impression. St. Louis: B. Herder Book Co., 1947.

390 / BIBLIOGRAPHY

Marshall, John P. "Francis Patrick Kenrick, 1851–1863: The Baltimore Years." Ph.D. diss., The Catholic University of America, 1965.

McCool, Gerald A., S.J. *Catholic Theology in the Nineteenth Century: The Quest for a Unitary Method.* New York: The Seabury Press, 1977.

McKenzie, John L. *The Two-Edged Sword: An Introduction of the Old Testament.* Milwaukee: The Bruce Publishing Co., 1956.

Nolan, Hugh J. *The Most Reverend Francis Patrick Kenrick: Third Bishop of Philadelphia: 1830–1851.* Philadelphia: American Catholic Historical Society, 1948.

Noone, Bernard. "A Critical Analysis of the American Catholic Response to Higher Criticism as Reflected in Selected Catholic Periodicals—1870–1908." Ph.D. diss., Drew University, 1976.

Pelotte, Donald E., S.S.S. *John Courtney Murray: Theologian in Conflict.* New York: Paulist Press.

Pope, Hugh, O.P. *English Versions of the Bible.* St. Louis: B. Herder Book Co., 1952.

Poulat, Emile. *Intégrisme et Catholicisme intégral: un réseau secret international antimoderniste: La Sapinière (1909–1921).* Tournai: Casterman, 1969.

Ranchetti, Michele. *The Catholic Modernists: A Study of the Religious Reform Movement, 1864–1907.* London: Oxford University Press, 1969.

Ratzinger, Joseph Cardinal, with Vittorio Messori. *The Ratzinger Report.* Trans. by Salvator Attanasio and Graham Harrison. San Francisco: Ignatius Press, 1985.

Robert, A., and A. Feuillet. *Introduction to the Old Testament.* Trans. from the second French edition by Patrick W. Skehan, et al. New York: Desclee Co., 1968.

Rynne, Xavier. *Vatican Council II.* New York: Farrar, Straus and Giroux, 1968.

Schultenover, David G. S.J. *George Tyrrell: In Search of Catholicism.* Shepherdstown: The Patmos Press, 1981.

Turvasi, Francesco. *Giovanni Genocchi e la controversia modernista.* Vol. 20, *Uomini e Dottrine.* Rome: Edizioni di Storia e Letteratura, 1974.

Vidler, Alec R. *A Variety of Catholic Modernists.* New York: Cambridge University Press, 1970.

Vigouroux, Fulcran. *Les livres saints et la critique rationaliste: histoire et réfutation des objections des incrédules contre les saintes écritures.* 5 vols. Paris: A. Roger & F. Chernoviz, 1890.

Wayman, Dorothy G. *Cardinal O'Connell of Boston: A Biography of William Henry O'Connell, 1859–1944.* New York: Farrar, Straus, and Young, Inc., 1955.

Weber, Ralph E. *Notre Dame's John Zahm: American Catholic Apologist and Educator.* Notre Dame: University of Notre Dame Press, 1961.

Yzermans, Vincent A. *American Participation in the Second Vatican Council.* New York: Sheed and Ward, 1967.

B. ARTICLES AND CONTRIBUTIONS TO BOOKS:

Albright, W. F. "In Memoriam Roger T. O'Callaghan." *Bulletin of the American Schools of Oriental Re-search* 134 (April 1954): 4.

———. "The Old Testament and Canaanite Language and Literature." *CBQ* 7 (January 1945): 5–31.

Amator Evangelii. "Communications from Our Readers." *Homiletic and Pastoral Review* 44 (March 1944): 449–51.

———. "Communications from Our Readers." *Homiletic and Pastoral Review* 44 (May 1944): 616–19.

———. "A Defense that Fails." *Homiletic and Pastoral Review* 44 (August 1944): 807–12.

Anon. "Two of Woodstock's Founders." *Woodstock Letters* 29 (1900): 296–315.

———. "Father Walter M Drum." *Woodstock Letters* 51 (1922): 122–30.

Bea, Augustin S.J. "L'Encyclica 'Humani Generis' e gli studi biblici." *Civiltà cattolica* anno. 101, no. 4 (1950): 417–30.

Blehl, Vincent F., S.J. "Newman's Delation: Some Hitherto Unpublished Letters." *The Dublin Review* no. 486 (Winter 1960–1961): 298–302.

Bourke, Myles M. "The Literary Genus of Mt. 1–2." *CBQ* 22 (1960): 160–75.

Briggs, Charles A. "Modernism Mediating the Coming Catholicism." *North American Review* 189 (June 1909): 877–89.

———. "The Great Obstacle in the Way of a Reunion of Christendom." *North American Review* 186 (September 1907): 72–82.

———. "The Encyclical against Modernism." *North American Review* 187 (February 1908): 199–212.

———. "The Real and the Ideal in the Papacy." *North American Review* 184 (February 15, 1907): 347–63.

Brown, Raymond E., S.S. "Liberals, Ultraconservatives and the Misinterpretation of Catholic Biblical Exegesis." *Cross Currents* (Fall 1984): 311–28.

Brownson, Orestes. "Literary Notices and Criticisms." *Brownson's Quarterly Review* 2d New York ser. 4 (October 1859): 541–44.

———. "Literary Notices and Criticisms." *Brownson's Quarterly Review* 3d New York ser. 1 (July 1860): 403–07.

———. "Literary Notices and Criticisms." *Brownson's Quarterly Review* n. s. 3 (July 1849): 409.

———. "New Versions and the Vulgate." *Brownson's Quarterly Review* 3 (October 1846): 473–87.

Bruneau, Joseph. "Biblical Criticism." *American Ecclesiastical Review* 19 (October 1898): 383–90.

———. "A Page of Contemporary History on Biblical Inspiration." *American Ecclesiastical Review* 14 (March 1896): 240–54.

———. "Biblical Research." *American Ecclesiastical Review* 18 (1898): 272–85.

Burghardt, Walter J., S.J. "The Catholic Concept of Tradition in the Light of Modern Theological Thought." *Proceedings of the Sixth Annual Convention of the Catholic Theological Society of America* (1951): 42–76.

Butin, Romain, S.M. "Some Evidence of Revision of the Hebrew Text of the Pentateuch in Ancient Times." *Proceedings of the Catholic Biblical Association of America: First General Meeting, St. Louis, Missouri (October 9-10, 1937): 16–28.*

Catholic Biblical Association. "General Meeting . . . , 1938." Catholic Biblical Quarterly 1 (1939): 75–79.

Catholic Biblical Association. "General Meeting . . . , 1939." *Catholic Biblical Quarterly* 2 (1940): 74–80.

Catholic Biblical Association. "General Meeting . . . , 1940." *Catholic Biblical Quarterly* 3 (1941): 81–87.

Catholic Biblical Association. "General Meeting . . . , 1941." *Catholic Biblical Quarterly* 4 (1941): 175–85.

Catholic Biblical Association. "General Meeting . . . , 1942." *Catholic Biblical Quarterly* 5 (1943): 90–95.

Catholic Biblical Association. "General Meeting . . . , 1944." *Catholic Biblical Quarterly* 7 (1945): 100–05.

Catholic Biblical Association. "General Meeting . . . , 1945." *Catholic Biblical Quarterly* 8 (1946): 114–20.

Catholic Biblical Association. "General Meeting . . . , 1946." *Catholic Biblical Quarterly* 9 (1947): 1–8.

Catholic Biblical Association. "General Meeting . . . , 1947." *Catholic Biblical Quarterly* 10 (1948): 87–92.

Catholic Biblical Association. "General Meeting . . . , 1948." *Catholic Biblical Quarterly* 11 (1949): 1–8.

Catholic Biblical Association. "General Meeting . . . , 1949." *Catholic Biblical Quarterly* 12 (1950): 1–6.

Catholic Biblical Association. "General Meeting . . . , 1950." *Catholic Biblical Quarterly* 13 (1951): 1–7.

Catholic Biblical Association. "General Meeting . . . , 1951." *Catholic Biblical Quarterly* 14 (1952): 63–67.

Catholic Biblical Association. "General Meeting . . . , 1952." *Catholic Biblical Quarterly* 14 (1952): 350–54.

Catholic Biblical Association. "General Meeting . . . , 1953." *Catholic Biblical Quarterly* 15 (1953): 462–66.

Catholic Biblical Association. "General Meeting . . . , 1954." *Catholic Biblical Quarterly* 16 (1954): 444–48.

Catholic Biblical Association. "General Meeting . . . , 1955." *Catholic Biblical Quarterly* 17 (1955): 575–82.

Catholic Biblical Association. "General Meeting . . . , 1956." *Catholic Biblical Quarterly* 19 (1957): 93–98.

Catholic Biblical Association. "General Meeting . . . , 1957." *Catholic Biblical Quarterly* 19 (1957): 485–87.

Catholic Biblical Association. "General Meeting . . . , 1958." *Catholic Biblical Quarterly* 20 (1958): 499–506.

Catholic Biblical Association. "General Meeting . . . , 1959." *Catholic Biblical Quarterly* 21 (1959): 496–502.

Catholic Biblical Association. "General Meeting . . . , 1960." *Catholic Biblical Quarterly* 22 (1960): 430–35.

Catholic Biblical Association. "General Meeting . . . , 1961." *Catholic Biblical Quarterly* 23 (1961): 465–72.

Catholic Biblical Association. "General Meeting . . . , 1962." *Catholic Biblical Quarterly* 24 (1962): 420–29.

Catholic Biblical Association. "General Meeting . . . , 1963." *Catholic Biblical Quarterly* 25 (1963): 430–37.

Catholic Biblical Association. "General Meeting . . . , 1964." *Catholic Biblical Quarterly* 26 (1964): 468–74.

Catholic Biblical Association. "General Meeting . . . , 1965." *Catholic Biblical Quarterly* 27 (1965): 407–14.

Catholic Biblical Association. "General Meeting . . . , 1966." *Catholic Biblical Quarterly* 28 (1966): 478–83.

Cerny, Edward, S.S. "Bethel (Beitin)." *Catholic Biblical Quarterly* 4 (1942): 68–71.

———. "Jerusalem: Palace of Herod the Great." *Catholic Biblical Quarterly* 4 (1942): 258–61.

———. "Lithostrotos." *Catholic Biblical Quarterly* 4 (1942): 259–60.

———. "Problems of Bible Revision." *Catholic Biblical Quarterly* 1 (1939): 363–68.

Connell, Francis J., C.SS.R. "Answers to Questions." *American Ecclesiastical Review* 140 (January 1959): 34–38.

Conroy, James, S.J. "The Pope and the Scriptures." *American Catholic Quarterly Review* 19 (April 1894): 412–32.

Cotter, Anthony J., S.J. "The Antecedents of the Encyclical Providentissimus Deus." *Catholic Biblical Quarterly* 5 (April 1943): 117–24.

Drum, Walter, S.J. "Ecclesiastical Library Table: Recent Bible Studies." *American Ecclesiastical Review* 62 (April 1920): 479–87.

———. "The Biblical Commission and the Parousia." *American Ecclesiastical Review* 53 (1915): 472–82.

Fenton, Joseph C. "The Priest and the Ascetical Cultivation of the Faith." *American Ecclesiastical Review* 142 (March 1960): 189–98.

———. "The Case for Traditional Apologetics." *American Ecclesiastical Review* 141 (July 1959): 407–16.

———. "Father Moran's Prediction." *American Ecclesiastical Review* 146 (March 1962): 192–201.

Fitzmyer, Joseph A. "A Recent Roman Scriptural Controversy." *Theological Studies* 22 (September 1961): 426–44.

———. "The Biblical Commission's Instruction on the Historical Truth of the Gospels." *Theological Studies* 25 (September 1964): 386–408.

Fogarty, Gerald P. S.J. "Quest for a Catholic Vernacular Bible in America." Nathan O. Hatch and Mark A. Noll eds. *The Bible in America: Essays in Cultural History.* New York: Oxford University Press, 1982.

Gaffey, James P. "The Changing of the Guard: The Rise of Cardinal O'Connell of Boston." *Catholic Historical Review* 59 (April 1973): 257–70.

Gannon, Michael V. "Before and after Modernism: The Intellectual Isolation of the American Priest." John Tracy Ellis ed. *The Catholic Priest in the United States Historical Investigations.* Collegeville, MN: St. John's University Press, 1971.

Grannan, Charles A. "A Program of Scripture Studies." *Catholic University Bulletin* 1 (January 1895): 39–52.

———. "Higher Criticism and the Bible." *American Catholic Quarterly Review* 19 (July 1894): 563–81.

———. "The Human Element in Scripture." *The Catholic University Bulletin* 4 (July 1898): 174–81.

———. "Two-fold Authorship of Scripture." *The Catholic University Bulletin* 3 (April 1897): 132–59.

Gruenthaner, Michael J., S.J. "An Unfounded Charger of Heresy." *American Ecclesiastical Review* 110 (June 1944): 407–15.

———. "The World of the Old Testament and Its Historicity." *European Civilization: Its Origin and Development* 7 vols. Oxford: Oxford University Press, 1934, I, 501–965.

———. "Editorial Comments." *Catholic Biblical Quarterly* 5 (January 1943): 3.

Hartdegen, Stephen J., O.F.M. "The Influence of the Encyclical Providentissimus Deus on Subsequent Scripture Study." *Catholic Biblical Quarterly* 5 (April 1943): 145–58.

Hennesey, James, S.J. "American Jesuit in Wartime Rome: The Diary of Vincent A. McCormick, S.J., 1942–1945." *Mid-America: An Historical Review* 56 (January 1974): 32–55.

Heuser, Hermann J. "The books of the Abbe Loisy on the Index." *American Ecclesiastical Review* 30 (February 1904): 175–76.

———. "Father A. J. Maas, S.J.—An appreciation." *Woodstock Letters* 58 (1929): 417–23.

Ireland, John. "Is the Papacy an Obstacle to the Reunion of Christendom?" *North American Review* 184 (April 5, 1907): 694–709.

———. "The Pontificate of Pius X." *North American Review* 184 (February 1, 1907): 233–45.

Kennedy, Gerald T., O.M.I. "The Holy Office Monitum and the Teaching of Scripture." *American Ecclesiastical Review* 145 (September 1961): 145–51.

———. "A Reply to Father Moran." *American Ecclesiastical Review* 146 (March 1962): 181–91.

———. "Scripture Revisited: Second Look at the Matter." *American Ecclesiastical Review* 145 (July 1961): 1–14.

Kennedy, Thomas J. "A Much-Debated Text in St. John's Gospel." *Homiletic and Pastoral Review* 39 (August 1939): 1164–75.

Lagrange, M. J. "Miscellaneous: On the Pentateuch." *The Catholic University Bulletin* 4 (January 1898): 115–22.

Lattey, Cuthbert. "Ecclesiastical Library Table: St. Paul and the Parousia." *American Ecclesiastical Review* 50 (March 1914): 349–56.
Levie, Jean S.J. "L'Encyclique 'Humani Generis.'" *Nouvelle Revue Theologique* 72 (September–October 1950): 785–93.
Loisy, Alfred. "The Scriptural Account of the Disciples of Emmaeus." *American Ecclesiastical Review* 14 (May 1896): 446–57.
———. "Gethsemane." *American Ecclesiastical Review* 18 (March 1898): 225–33.
———. "The Transfiguration of Our Lord." *American Ecclesiastical Review* 17 (August 1898): 169–78.
———. "Vobiscum Sum." *American Ecclesiastical Review* 16 (May 1897): 495–503.
Maas, Anthony J. "Ecclesiastical Library Table: Recent Bible Study." *American Ecclesiastical Review* 32 (June 1905): 647–55.
———. "A Negative View of the Encyclical 'Providentissimus Deus.'" *American Catholic Quarterly Review* 20 (January 1895): 162–75.
———. "Adam's Rib—Allegory or History." *American Ecclesiastical Review* 9 (August 1893): 88–102.
———. "Biblical Criticism," *Messenger of the Sacred Heart* 35 (March 1900): 239–46, (June 1900): 512–22, (July 1900): 627–33.
———. "Criticisms and Notes." *American Ecclesiastical Review* 35 (October 1906): 435–36.
———. "Divisive Criticism." *Messenger of the Sacred Heart* 35 (February 1900): 116–26.
———. "Ecclesiastical Library Table: Recent Study." *American Ecclesiastical Review* 31 (October 1904): 395–403.
———. "Professor Briggs on the Theological Crisis." *American Ecclesiastical Review* 5 (September 1891): 198–211.
———. "Recent Phases in Bible Study." *American Catholic Quarterly Review* 22 (October 1897): 832–50.
———. "The Synoptic Problem." *American Ecclesiastical Review* 13 (September 1895): 171–73.
———. "Ecclesiastical Library Table: Recent Bible Study." *American Ecclesiastical Review* 36 (March 1907): 55–71.
———. "Ecclesiastical Library Table: Sacred Scripture." *American Ecclesiastical Review* 26 (February 1902): 218–24.
———. "Higher Biblical Criticism." *Messenger of the Sacred Heart* 35 (January 1900): 51–59.
MacKenzie, R.A.F. "Before Abraham was . . . ," *Catholic Biblical Quarterly* 15 (April 1953): 131–40.
———. "Some Problems in the Field of Inspiration." *Catholic Biblical Quarterly* 20 (January 1958): 1–8.
Martindale, C. C., S.J. "How to Read St. John's Gospel." *The Catholic World* 109 (July 1919): 459–74 (August 1919): 622–36, and 110 (October 1919): 65–81.
McClellan, William H. S.J. "Monotheism and the Historical Process." *Theological Studies* 3 (February 1942): 109–36.

McKenzie, John L. "American Catholic Biblical Scholarship 1955–1980." John J. Collins and John Dominic Crossman eds. *The Biblical Heritage in Modern Catholic Scholarship.* Wilmington, DE: Michael Glazier, 1986, p. 215.

———. "The Hebrew Attitude towards Mythological Polytheism." *Catholic Biblical Quarterly* 14 (October 1952): 323–35.

———. "Authority and Power in the New Testament." *Catholic Biblical Quarterly* 26 (October 1964): 413–22.

McNally, Robert E., S.J. "The Council of Trent and Vernacular Bibles." *Theological Studies* 27 (February 1966): 204–27.

Miller, Robert J., and McNamara, Robert F. "Edward J. Byrne: Biblical Scholar." *The Sheaf* 10 (1963): 19–26.

Mivart, St. George. "The Continuity of Catholicism." *The Nineteenth Century* 7 (January 1900): 56–72.

Moran, W. L., S.J. "Father Kennedy's Exegesis of the Holy Office Monitum." *American Ecclesiastical Review* 146 (March 1962): 174–80.

Murphy, John L. "The Teaching of Schleiermacher, Part II." *American Ecclesiastical Review* 145 (July 1961): 15–38.

———. "Unwritten Traditions at Trent." *American Ecclesiastical Review* 146 (April 1962): 233–63.

Murphy, Richard T., O.P. "The Teachings of the Encyclical Providentissimus Deus." *Catholic Biblical Quarterly* 5 (April 1943): 125–40.

Newton, William L. "Four Current Versions Reviewed." *The Priest* 3 (June 1947): 427–28.

Noone, Bernard, F.S.C. "American Catholic Periodicals and the Biblical Question, 1893–1908." *Records of the American Catholic Historical Society* 89 (1978): 85–108.

North, Robert J. "The American Scripture Century." *American Ecclesiastical Review* 150 (May 1964): 314–45.

———. "A Frontier Jerome: Gruenthaner, Part I." *American Ecclesiastical Review* 148 (May 1963): 289–302; "Part II." (June 1963): 398–411; "Part III." 149 (July 1963): 41–53.

Parsons, Wilfrid, S.J. "First American Editions of Catholic Bibles." *Historical Records and Studies* 27 (1937): 89–98.

Peirce, Francis X., S.J. "Mary Alone is the Woman of Genesis 3.15." *Catholic Biblical Quarterly* 2 (July 1940): 245–52.

———. "The Protoevangelium." *Catholic Biblical Quarterly* 13 (July 1951): 239–52.

———. "Ecclesiastical Library Table: Again that Synoptic Problem." *American Ecclesiastical Review* 100 (January 1939): 74–82.

Poels, Henry. "History and Inspiration." *The Catholic University Bulletin* 11 (January 1905): 22–64.

———. "History and Inspiration. II. The Fathers of the Church." *The Catholic University Bulletin* 11 (April 1905): 153–94.

———. "History and Inspiration. Saint Jerome." *Catholic University Bulletin* 12 (April 1906): 192–218.

Pontifical Biblical Institute. "Pontificium Institutum Biblicum et recens libellus R.mi D.ni A. Romeo." *Verbum Domini* 39 (1961): 3–17.

Ratzinger, Joseph. "Dogmatic Constitution on Divine Revelation: Origin and Background." Herbert Vorgrimler ed. *Commentary on the Documents of Vatican II*. New York: Herder and Herder, 1969, III, 155–66.

———. "The First Session." *Worship* 37 (August-September 1963): 529–35.

Reilly, Thomas a'K, O.P. "What Father Lagrange Says and Thinks." *American Ecclesiastical Review* 33 (October 1905): 422–30.

Romeo, Antonino. "L'Enciclica 'Divino Afflante Spiritu' e le "opiniones novae." *Divinitas* 4 (1960): 387–456.

Root, John D. "The Final Apostasy of St. George Jackson Mivart." *Catholic Historical Review* 71 (January 1985): 1–25.

Rossiter, Francis S. "Forty Years Less One: An Historical Sketch of the C.B.A. (1936–1975)." *Catholic Biblical Quarterly* Supplement 39 (1977): 1–14.

Ruffini, Ernesto Cardinal. "Literary Genres and Working Hypotheses in Recent Biblical Studies." *American Ecclesiastical Review* 145 (December 1961): 362–65.

Schneirla, William S. "Roma locuta . . . ?" *St. Vladimir's Seminary Quarterly* 6 no. 2 (1962): 79–92.

Schroeder, Joseph. "Theological Minimizing and its latest Defender." *American Ecclesiastical Review* 4 (February 1891): 115–32 (March 1891): 161–78, and (April 1891): 286–305.

Siegman, Edward F., C.PP.S. "The Decrees of the Pontifical Commission: A Recent Clarification." *Catholic Biblical Quarterly* 18 (January 1956): 23–29.

Skehan, Patrick W. "Why leave out Judith?" *Catholic Biblical Quarterly* 24 (April 1962): 147–54.

Stanley, David M. "Balaam's Ass, or a Problem in New Testament Hermeneutics." *Catholic Biblical Quarterly* 20 (January 1958): 50–56.

Storch, Neil T. "The Church and Modern Society: John Ireland and the Modernist Controversy." *Church History* 54 (September 1985): 353–65.

Vagnozzi, Archbishop Egidio. "Thoughts on the Catholic Intellectual." *American Ecclesiastical Review* 145 (August 1961): 73–79.

Vincent, L. H. "Le Père Lagrange." *Revue Biblique* 47 (1938): 321–54.

Vogt, E. "John J. O'Rourke, S.J.," *Biblica* 39 (1958): 397–99, translated in *Woodstock Letters* 88 (1959): 415–17.

von Hügel, Friedrich. "The Historical Method and the Documents of the Hexateuch." *Catholic University Bulletin* 4 (April 1898): 198–226.

Wiseman, Nicholas. "Miracles of the New Testament." *The Dublin Review* 27 (December 1849): 291–345.

———. "The Parables of the New Testament." *The Dublin Review* 27 (September 1849): 181–227.

Index

Aberle, 46
Action Francaise, 172
active virtues, 58, 65
Acton, John Emerich Edward
    Dalberg, First Baron Acton
    (1834–1902), 29, 30
Adam and Eve, 248, 252, 264. *See*
    also Polygenism
Ad beatissimi Apostolorum (1914),
    119, 185. *See also* Benedict
    XV
Aeterni Patris (1878), 34. *See also*
    Leo XIII
Ahern, Barnabas (1915–), 261,
    298, 304; Vatican II, 322,
    324, 327, 328, 340
Ahr, George W., Bishop of
    Trenton (1904–), 297
Aiken, Charles, 112
Akkadian, 13
Albers, John H., Bishop of
    Lansing (1891–1965), 373
Albright, William Foxwell, 234,
    235, 274, 279; Catholic
    Biblical Association, 241–43,
    245; *From The Stone Age to*
    Christianity, 234
Alfred, King, 149
Alfrink, Cardinal Bernard,
    Archibishop of Utrecht, 340
Allen, George, 28
Alonso–Schökel, Luis, S.J., 292,
    321
Alter, Karl J., Archbishop of
    Cincinnati (1885–1977), 298
"Amator Evangelii," 217–19,
    221, 232, 241, 275
Amelli, A., 360n.15
America, 182, 328

American Catholic Quarterly Review,
    48
American College, Rome. *See*
    North American College
American Ecclesiastical Review:
    biblical scholars, attacks on,
    281–84, 287–91; Catholic
    Biblical Association,
    resolution of, 299–310;
    editors. *See* Heuser, Herman;
    Fenton, Joseph C.; Scripture,
    articles on. *See* Bruneau,
    Joseph; Connell, Francis J.;
    Maas, Anthony J.; Murphy,
    John L.; and Peirce, Francis
    X.
American hierarchy, theology
    committee, 325
Americanism, xvi, 90, 121, 140,
    155, 157, 163, 281, 344;
    condemnation, 65–71,
    75–80, 134–35, 171, 173;
    effect in the U.S., 115, 118,
    174, 189; John Courtney
    Murray, 259–60; movement,
    57–60
American Revised Version, 207
American School of Oriental
    Research, 194, 268
Amos, 145
Anglicans, 47
Annales de philosophie chrétienne,
    121
Anti-Modernism, 158, 167, 169,
    170, 253, 288. *See also*
    Integrism
Antonianum, 262
Antoniutti, Ildebrando, 340
Apocalypse, 182, 183, 216